RESCUED BY

PERSONAL COMPUTERS

Kris Jamsa, Ph.D., MBA

JAMSA
P · R · E · S · S
...a computer user's best friend®

Published by
Jamsa Press
3301 Allen Parkway
Houston, TX 77019
U.S.A.

http://www.jamsa.com

For information about the translation or distribution of any Jamsa Press book, please write to Jamsa Press at the address listed above.

Rescued by Personal Computers

Printed in the United States of America.
98765432

ISBN 1-884133-54-1

Performance Manager Kong Cheung	*Technical Advisor* Phil Schmauder	*Proofer* Jeanne K. Smith
Copy Editor Rosemary Pasco	*Cover Photograph* O'Gara/Bissell	*Technical Editor* Phil Schmauder
Composition New Vision Media	*Illustrator* Colin Hayes	*Cover Design* Debbie Jamsa
Indexer Kong Cheung		

Jamsa Press is an imprint of Gulf Publishing Company:

Gulf Publishing Company
Book Division
P.O. Box 2608
Houston, TX 77252-2608
U.S.A.

http://www.gulfpub.com

Contents

continued on the following page

continued on the following page

Lesson 1

Entering the PC Age

Welcome to *Rescued by Personal Computers*. If you are just getting started with a PC, or if you have been working with a PC for a while but still do not feel confident in your skills, relax. This book's lessons are going to walk you step-by-step through all aspects of computing. Each lesson is short and focused, and should take only about 15 minutes of your time. So, if you can spend 15 or 30 minutes per night with this book, in one month's time you will have mastered a wide range of PC skills. Each of this book's lessons will teach you the day-to-day PC operations you must know, such as how to name your files, how to use file folders to organize your documents on disk, how to surf the World Wide Web, or how to send and receive electronic mail. As you master key concepts, you will also learn the ins-and-outs of your PC hardware, how to install programs on your system, as well as the meaning of terms such as megabytes, megahertz, and RAM.

As you make your way through this book's lessons, you will learn and try the latest state-of-the-art software programs, such as video conferencing and voice recognition. You will also learn how to use your PC's microphone and speakers to talk with other users across the Net for free, just as if you were talking on the phone! This lesson's goal is simply to introduce you to many of the concepts you will learn in the lessons that follow. Do not let any of this book's lessons intimidate you. You will find each lesson's discussion very easy to follow and, in some cases, even quite fun.

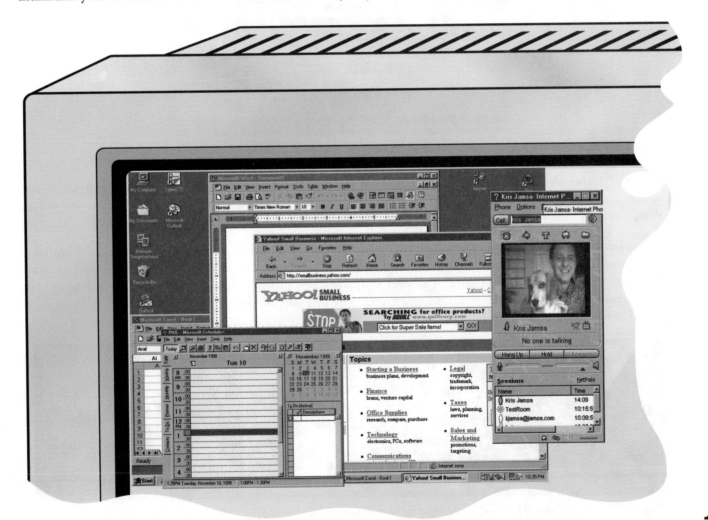

MASTERING WINDOWS

This book begins by teaching you how to set up and start your PC. You will learn about standard devices such as your keyboard, printer, and mouse and how you connect those devices to ports on your PC. As you learn how to use each device, you willl also learn the meaning of key terms such as megabytes, RAM, reboot, and megahertz. In fact, by the end of this book's lessons, you will be able to hold your own in a conversation about computers with just about anyone.

Next, you will "power on" your PC which, in turn, will start Windows. As you will learn, Windows is the first program your PC runs each time it starts. From within Windows, you will run your other programs, such as your word processor, spreadsheet, electronic-mail software, or your Web browser. Windows is so named, because each time you run a program, Windows displays that program's output within a framed region on your screen, called, a window. Figure 1.1 shows several programs running within Windows.

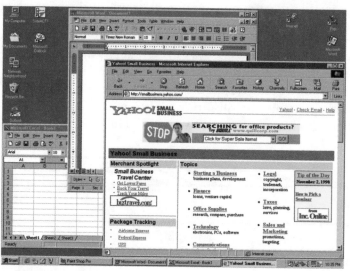

Figure 1.1 *Running programs within Windows.*

Several of this book's early lessons will teach you how to run programs, move or size a program's window on your screen, switch from one program to another, and how to end a program when you are done with it. Because you will use Windows each time you use your PC, it is essential that you feel confident with these key operations.

As you learn to master Windows, you will get to take some breaks along the way to have some fun. You will learn how to customize your screen appearance (which users call your Desktop). You may, for example, choose one of the Desktop's designs shown in Figure 1.2. And, after you learn to "point-and-click," "double-click," and how to "drag your mouse," you will download voice recognition software that you can use to direct Windows to perform specific operations by talking into your PC's microphone!

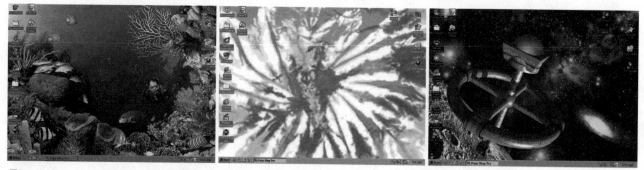

Figure 1.2 *Customizing the Windows Desktop to match your current mood.*

MANAGING YOUR FILES AND DISKS

Whether you use your PC to run a word processor, spreadsheet program, a Web browser, or even just for electronic-mail, you will eventually have to store information within a file on your disk. Unfortunately, most users are never taught a few simple steps that will put them in control of their files. Fortunately, this book's lessons present the file and disk operations you must know. You will learn how to manage the information that you store within files on your disk, by learning how to name, copy, move, delete, print, and rename your files. You will also learn how to organize your files by grouping them into related file folders. Also, you will learn how to clean up your disk by deleting files you no longer need. If you should happen to delete the wrong file, you will also learn how to recover that file from the Windows Recycle Bin.

By the time you finish this book's lessons, you will have mastered a special program called the Windows Explorer, within which you can manage the files you store on disk. Figure 1.3 shows the Windows Explorer, which lists your PC's disk drives, the file folders on each drive, as well as the files you have stored within each folder. As you will learn, the Explorer is very easy to use, and by using it, you can gain control of your files, and even find files that you may have previously misplaced on your disk.

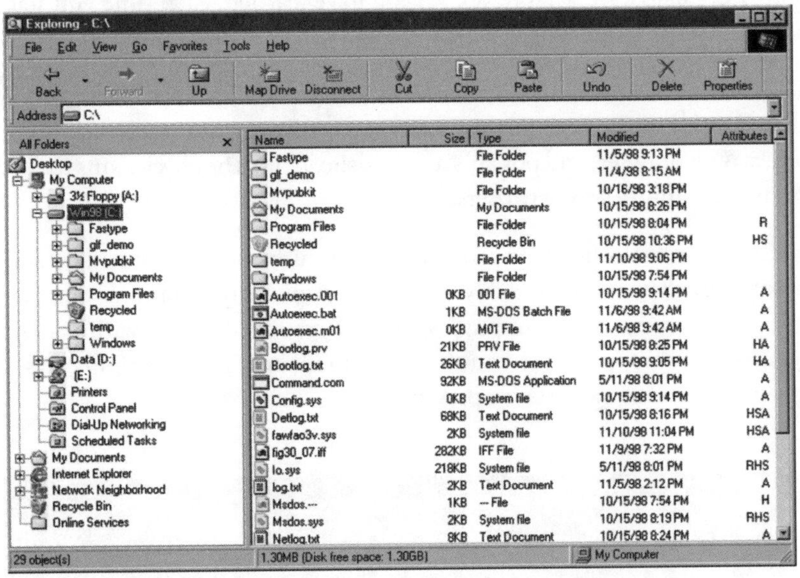

Figure 1.3 *Using the Windows Explorer to manage your disks, folders, and files.*

MASTERING YOUR PC'S HARDWARE

On a day-to-day basis, most users make extensive use of their PC, keyboard, monitor, printer, mouse, modem, and disk drives. This book's lessons examine each of these devices in detail. You will learn ways you can improve your keyboard's responsiveness, make your mouse pointer easier to see on your screen, reduce eye strain by fine-tuning your monitor settings, or reduce sore necks, hands, and wrists. You will also learn a few simple cleaning secrets you can use to maintain your hardware devices.

Then, you will examine other hardware devices such as PC-based video cameras, CD-ROMs and CD-ROM burners, Zip drives, and multimedia devices. You will also learn why installing more random-access memory (RAM) within your PC is one of the fastest and most cost-effective ways to improve your PC's performance.

If you travel with a notebook PC, this book's lessons will examine hardware devices that may make it easier for you to exchange files between your computers. In addition, you will learn about the latest palmtop PCs and even a cellular phone that opens up to display a keyboard and monitor, with which you can send and receive e-mail or surf the Web. Figure 1.4 shows just a few of the hardware devices you will explore throughout this book's lessons.

Figure 1.4 *This book examines a variety of hardware devices.*

UNDERSTANDING KEY SOFTWARE

Put simply, software (computer programs) is a file that contains a list of instructions that your PC executes. In other words, software tells your PC's hardware what to do. As you have learned, each time you start your system, your PC runs Windows, a special software program within which you can run your other programs, such as your word processor or Web browser.

To perform their PC-based tasks, most users only use a few software programs each day—typically a word processor, electronic-mail program, a Web browser, and possibly a spreadsheet. This book's lessons first examine these programs, introducing each program's capabilities to new users.

Then, this book introduces several other key programs most users should consider, such as a PC-based time management program, software that lets you quickly create and display presentations, database programs you can use to track key information, and even the latest computer games. If you use your PC within an office, this book will also examine several key business-software packages you should immediately put to use. Figures 1.5 through 1.8 present a few of the software programs this book's lessons present.

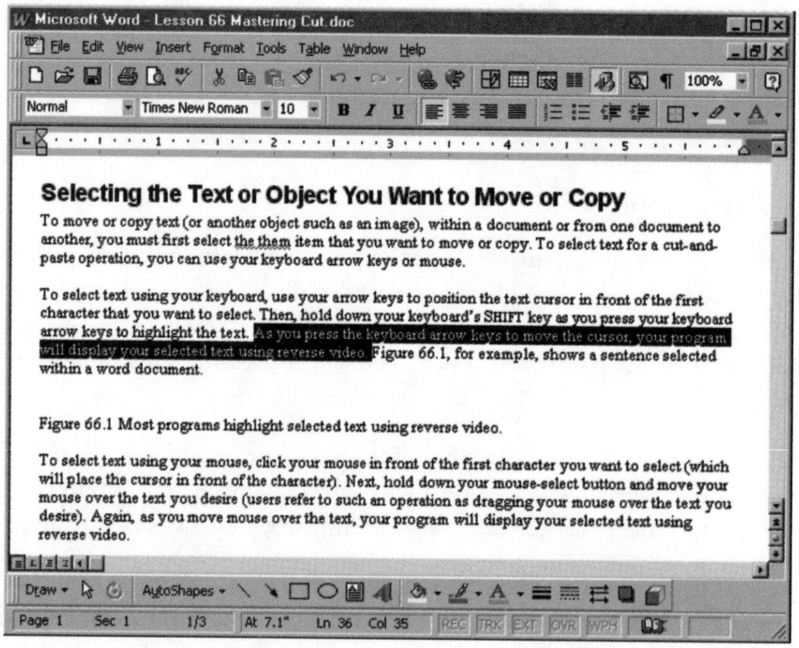

Figure 1.5 *Learning to master a word processor.*

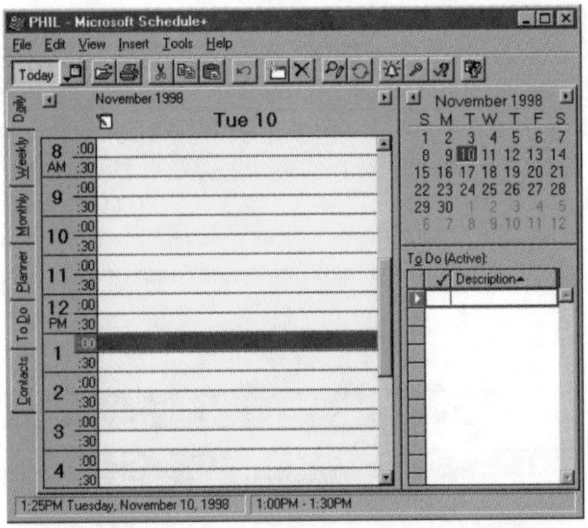

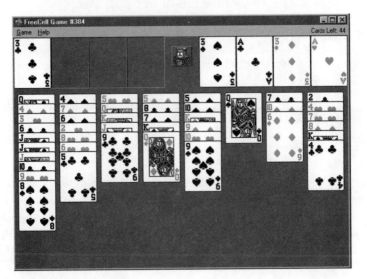

Figure 1.6 Using time-management software to get the most from your day.

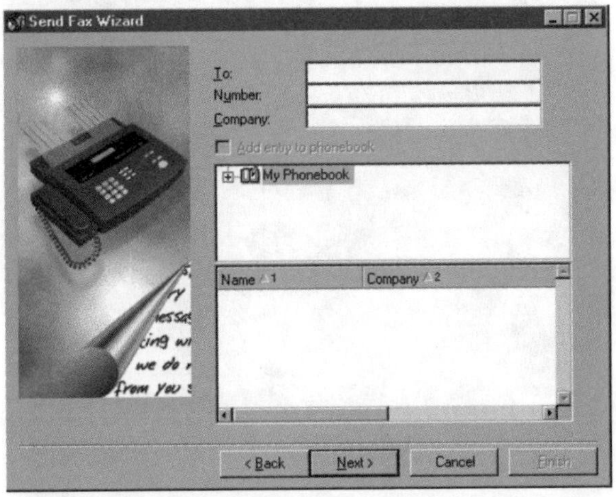

Figure 1.7 Using fax software to send and receive faxes from your PC.

Figure 1.8 Taking a break with PC-based games.

MASTERING MULTIMEDIA

Multimedia is the use of text, pictures, audio (sounds), and video to present information in a more meaningful way. Most PCs sold today fully support multimedia. In this book's lessons, you will first learn how to use multimedia programs, that Microsoft bundles with Windows, to play audio CDs in your PC, to record your own sounds, and to play back other media, such as a MIDI-based music file. Then, when you later travel out on the Internet and World Wide Web, you will learn how to play back music files as well as video files from sites across the Web, as shown in Figure 1.9. You will also learn how to use your PC to receive Internet-based radio broadcasts of the latest news, sports, business reports, and even classical music.

Figure 1.9 *Playing a multimedia video file from a site on the World Wide Web.*

MASTERING THE INTERNET

Each day, tens of millions of users connect to the Internet and World Wide Web to send and receive electronic mail or to browse any one of the millions of Web sites. If you have not yet "surfed the Web," relax. This book will first introduce you to the Internet and the World Wide Web and will then get you connected. You will learn how to use the Web's two most important applications: electronic-mail and Web browsing. After that, you will learn how to locate information on the Web using a search engine, how to shop on-line, and even how to encrypt your e-mail messages to protect them from hackers.

After that, the real fun begins! You will learn how to chat with users by exchanging typed messages which the members of your chat group immediately see, as well as how to use your PC's speaker and microphone to talk with users across the Internet for free! Finally, as shown in Figure 1.10, you will learn how to use an inexpensive PC-based video camera to send and receive video with other users across the Internet. Best of all, you will learn that, in most cases, you can run these programs using your existing PC and modem.

Figure 1.10 *Exchanging video with another user across the Web.*

WHAT YOU MUST KNOW

Every lesson in this book ends with a summary section that reviews the lesson's key concepts that you should know before you continue with the next lesson. In Lesson 2, "The Windows-Based PC versus the Mac Debate," you will examine several differences between the PC and Mac and issues you should consider if you are still shopping for a PC. Before you continue with Lesson 2, however, make sure you have learned the following key concepts:

✓ This book's lessons will examine the key PC concepts you must know to use your PC effectively.

✓ If you are new to PCs, don't worry, each lesson assumes that you have no prior experience with the topic.

✓ Each lesson should take 15 to 20 minutes of your time. Ideally, you will read the lessons in order, but if you want to skip around, reading the lessons out of order, you can. Make sure, however, that you eventually read each lesson's contents as many lessons present key PC skills you must know.

✓ Don't be afraid to experiment. As you read about a specific software program, spend a few moments, and take the software for a "test drive."

Lesson 2

The Windows-Based PC versus the Mac Debate

For many years, Mac and Windows users debated fiercely over whether the Mac or the PC was the system of choice. Then, for about two years, Apple essentially fell out of the marketplace—leaving only the most dedicated users to support the Mac's cause. Recently, however, with Apple's release of the iMac, the debate has started again, with users asking which system is better, faster, or which system the user should buy.

This lesson examines several key Mac versus PC issues. By the time you finish this lesson, you will understand the following key concepts:

• Since the first Apple and IBM PC, users have debated whether the Apple or PC-based system was the better system.

- Mac and PCs run different operating systems. The Mac runs software called System 8 and the PC runs Windows. The operating system is the first program that computers run after they start. Within the operating system, you will run other programs, such as your word processor or Web browser.

- In general, Mac and Windows-based PCs run the same set of programs. You can, for example, run Word, Excel, as well as a browser on a Mac or a PC. You cannot, however, run the same program; you must have a Mac-based version and a Windows-based version of the software (that is because the Mac and PC use different processors).

- For years most schools used only Apple computers. Today, however, many schools are switching to low-priced Windows-based PCs.

- To exchange files between a Mac and a PC, both systems should be running similar software (such as Word or Photoshop). Then, you can e-mail the document from one system to another, or, you can put the file on a floppy or Zip disk. (The Mac can normally read PC-based disks. The PC, however, may need additional software to read a Mac disk.)

COMPARING MAC AND PC SOFTWARE

A few years ago, Mac users would easily win the "which system is easier to use?" argument. PCs were difficult to configure, MS-DOS-based PC software was cumbersome, and adding new hardware to the PC was nearly impossible for most users. Today, however, with MS-DOS out of the picture and with new plug-and-play hardware cards readily available, the PC has become much easier to use. In addition, most Mac and Windows-based software programs have merged capabilities, making the programs very similar on both systems. In fact, if you consider a user's core programs, such as their word processing software, Web browser, spreadsheet software, or even graphics arts programs such as Photoshop and Illustrator, the Windows and Mac software programs are almost identical. In general, there will be times when a specific Mac program exceeds its Windows-based counterpart, just as there will be times when the Windows-based program is superior. The good news is, however, that if you know how to use a program on the Mac, you can normally sit down and use the program under Windows, and vice versa. Whether you choose a Mac or PC, you will find abundant software and hardware devices for either system. In fact, each of the software programs and hardware devices this book discusses are readily available for the Mac. So, in almost all cases, either a Mac or a PC will meet your needs.

MY KIDS ARE USING A MAC AT SCHOOL, BUT I USE A PC AT WORK

A few years ago, Apple owned the school-PC market. Almost every child was learning to use a computer on some type of Apple PC. Today, however, inexpensive Windows-based programs have made considerable headway into the school market. And, with Apple's poor market performance over the past few years, schools are now looking for a stable PC source. Today, and in the future, your children may have an Apple or they may have a Windows-based PC at school. As discussed in the previous section, most popular Apple-based programs are now available under Windows. So, if your child is running programs on an Apple at school, you can probably find those same programs (or very similar programs) for a Windows-based PC. Also, keep in mind that it is not essential that your child have the same type of PC at home and at school. Most children can learn to start and run programs on either system quite quickly. In some cases, the child who uses a Mac at school and a PC at home may develop better long-term computer skills.

A few years ago, the high price of computers meant a family would probably have only one PC. If a parent used a PC at work, the family was probably going to have a PC at home. Today, the price of PCs is dropping so quickly that many families will become multi-PC households. It will not be uncommon for kids and parents each to have their own PCs (which, as you will learn in Lesson 62, "Child Proofing the Internet and World Wide Web," is a great way to control the software your child can and cannot run).

I Hear that the Mac Is Faster

In Lesson 10, "Programs (Software) Make Your PC Perform," you will learn that a program is a list of instructions your computer's central processing unit (CPU) executes. The Mac and PC use two completely different processing units. The PC uses a CPU from Intel (a Pentium), and the Mac uses a Motorola-based processor. That is why you normally cannot run the software you bought for your PC on the Mac and vice versa. (Some Macs run software that can convert Windows-based software into a Mac format—a slow process—and some Macs include an Intel-compatible processor that can run the PC-based programs.) Within the CPU is a small clock that ticks millions of times per second. When you hear that a user has a 200Mhz (pronounced 200 megahertz) processor, the clock within the user's CPU ticks 200-million times per second. Lesson 12, "Understanding the Myriad of PC Speeds and Sizes," discusses processor speeds in detail. Each time the CPU's clock ticks, the CPU can execute an instruction. Therefore, (in general), a CPU with a 200Mhz clock can execute 200-millon instructions per second.

When users state that the "Mac is faster," the users are referring to the Mac CPU's clock speed, which is faster than that of the Intel-based mass market PCs. However, you need to realize that most users use, at best, about 20% of their CPU's capabilities. The CPU's speed is not really a factor. Instead, if users are concerned with performance, they should look at the devices they use most often, such as their modem, printer, and disk drives. In most cases, the user will not find a difference in speed between the Mac and Windows-based devices. In general, both the Mac and the Windows-based PC are fast enough to meet most user's needs.

Exchanging Files between Macs and PCs

As you have learned, the Mac and PC normally run the same programs, such as Word, Excel, or Photoshop. If you need to exchange software with a user that is running a Mac, you can normally e-mail the file to the user or copy the file to a floppy disk or Zip disk. (Lesson 39, "Exchanging Files Using a Zip Disk," discusses Zip-disk operations in detail.) If you must exchange files with a Mac user, ask the user what file formats he or she can read. In most cases, if you store a document within a Word format on the PC and then give the file to a user with Word on the Mac, the user will be able to open your file. Likewise, if a Mac users gives you a Photoshop-based graphics file, you can normally open the image using Photoshop on your PC. As Mac and Windows-based software has grown closer, so too has the ability to exchange files between Mac and PC users.

What You Must Know

As long as there are graphic artists, and as long as Steve Jobs is at Apple, there will probably be a debate over whether the Mac or the PC is the machine of choice. In reality, however, the Mac and PC become more the same every day. In this lesson, you found that, in general, either a Mac or PC should meet your needs. You can create documents with both, surf the Web with both, and exchange e-mail with users around the globe, with both. In Lesson 3, "Setting Up Your Personal Computer," you will learn how to unbox and hook up your PC. Before you continue with Lesson 3, however, make sure that you have learned the following key concepts:

- ✓ The Mac and PC run a different operating system. The Mac runs software called System 8 and the PC runs Windows.

- ✓ Most Mac- and Windows-based programs are quite similar. You can, for example, run Word, Excel, as well as a browser on a Mac or a PC.

- ✓ A few years ago, schools only used Apple computers. Today, the low-priced PCs are stealing considerable market share within the education channel.

- ✓ If you use common software programs, such as Word or Photoshop, you should be able to exchange documents easily with a Mac user.

Lesson 3

Setting Up Your Personal Computer

Unlike a television or toaster that you can bring home, plug in, and have working in a matter of minutes, setting up your PC will take you a little more time and may require a little more patience. This lesson examines the steps you must perform to set up your PC, monitor, and printer. By following the steps this lesson presents, however, you will be amazed at just how easy your PC is to set up. By the time you finish this lesson, you will understand the following key concepts:

- Before you set up your PC, consider carefully the location at which you will place the PC. Your location needs adequate lighting, access to phone and power plugs, as well as working space.

- Your PC contains many sensitive electronic components which static electricity can damage. Do not set your PC or any of your hardware devices onto your carpet. Your carpet may contain static electricity.

- To protect your PC equipment, you should plug your PC devices into a surge suppresser. If you live in an area where loss of power is common, you may want to consider using an uninterruptable power supply.

- You connect devices, such as your monitor and printer, to ports that reside on the back of your system unit. Users describe ports and cables by gender (such as male or female). A port's gender specifies whether the port provides plugs (a male) or receptacles (a female). Users also describe ports and cables in terms the number of pins they support, such as 9-pin or 25-pin cable.

- To protect yourself and your PC, never connect a device to your PC while either the device or your PC is plugged in and powered on.

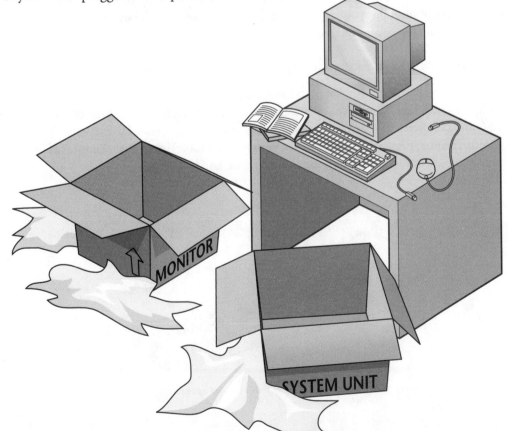

PICKING YOUR PC'S LOCATION

A key factor to your computer enjoyment that you must consider before you set up your PC is the location where you are going to place your system. The old adage "location, location, location," also applies to PCs. To start, you will want to place your PC in an area that is close to power and phone plugs, that is also well lit (but keep in mind that windows can create glare that reflects off your monitor), and an area that will provide you with ample room for your printer, a phone, papers, as well as a place for your files.

In Lesson 53, "Surfing Your Way to Information on the Web," you will learn how to use your PC to research topics across the Internet. With hundreds of millions of documents that discuss a wide range of topics, you will be surprised just how many documents you print, and must later file, on a regular basis. Likewise, in Lesson 51, "Using Electronic-Mail (E-mail) to Communicate Worldwide," you will learn how to exchange messages and other documents with users around the globe. Although each e-mail message you receive starts in an electronic form, many users have a habit of printing and filing key messages. So, as you move into the electronic age of computers, make sure that you provide plenty of space to file and store the paper documents that you will create. As you plan your PC's location, also think about installing a second phone line near your PC. By using the second phone line to connect your PC to the Internet, you will not tie up your voice line. Also, there will be times when you are connected to the Net that you will find it very convenient to have another user or a technical-support specialist on the phone to walk you through an operation.

UNPACKING YOUR PC

Before you open up your PC's boxes and spread your PC's parts about your room, take time to first organize the location where you plan to place your PC. Although taking the PC out of the box and setting it temporarily on your carpet may seem convenient, doing so will expose your PC's electronic components (the sensitive electronic circuit boards and chips) to static electricity. If possible, as you take items out of the box, move the item to its desired location, such as your desk or table. Also, within one of your PC's boxes, you should find a packing slip that details the hardware and software you should find as you set up your system. As you locate each item, place a check mark next to the item on the packing list. Later, you should put your packing slip in a safe location with your insurance files, just in case you must someday make an insurance claim on your PC.

STEP ONE: MAKE SURE YOU USE A SURGE SUPPRESSER

Although the PC's exterior consists of durable metal and hard plastic pieces, the PC's interior is made up of delicate electronic circuit boards and chips. One of the greatest dangers your PC faces is damage from excess current or voltage on the power line (surges of electricity). To protect your PC's electronics, plug your PC and your other hardware devices (such as your monitor, printer, external drives, and even your modem cable) into a surge suppresser. As shown in Figure 3.1, surge suppressers come in two primary types: as a wall plug and as a strip.

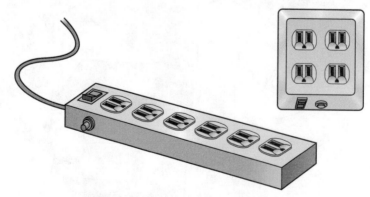

Figure 3.1 *Surge suppressers protect your hardware devices from power spikes.*

As you shop for surge suppressers, make sure that you purchase a suppresser and not just a power strip that does not offer any protection from electrical spikes. Also, make sure the suppresser that you choose has an Underwriter's Laboratory (UL) approval. If you live in an area that periodically loses power, due to either storms or blackouts, you should consider purchasing an uninterruptable power supply (UPS). In addition to providing surge protection, a UPS also works like a battery backup should you lose power. Normally, a UPS will provide you with 15 to 30 minutes of additional power, which should provide you with more than enough time to shut down your programs and save your data in the event of a power loss. As shown in Figure 3.2, an UPS is a small device that you plug into a wall outlet. Then, just as you would plug your devices into a surge suppresser, you plug your devices into the UPS.

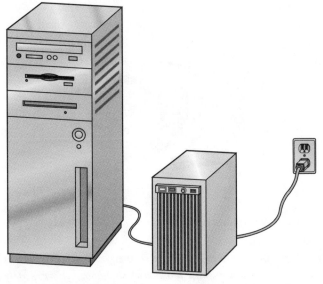

Figure 3.2 An uninterruptable power supply (UPS) provides you with 15 or minutes of power in the event of a power loss.

STEP TWO: SETTING UP YOUR SYSTEM UNIT

Regardless of whether you have a desktop or tower PC, the steps you will perform to set up your system are similar. As shown in Figure 3.3, if you examine the back of your system unit, you will find connectors to which you will attach your monitor, printer, keyboard, mouse, speakers, and microphone.

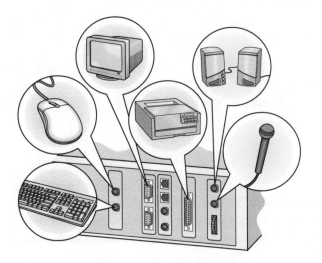

Figure 3.3 You connect devices to your system unit using ports specific to each device.

As you can see, most of the PC's connectors (ports) have a specific size and shape. By matching the ports to your device cables, you can normally identify which device you connect to which port. On the back of your system unit, you will also find a power plug to which you will connect your PC's power cord.

Do not plug in your PC at this time—you will plug in your PC last. As a rule, to reduce your chance of shock or damage to your hardware devices, never attach a device to your PC while your PC is plugged in and powered on. Users refer to ports and cables by gender: either male or female. A male port or cable has prong connectors, where as a female port or cable has receptacles into which you plug the male prongs. Figure 3.4 illustrates a male cable and female port. Users also describe port and cables by the number of pins they support, such as a 9-pin male cable or a 25-pin female port.

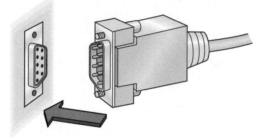

Figure 3.4 *A 9-pin male cable and a 9-pin female port.*

Note: *As you install your keyboard, mouse, monitor, and printer, there may be times when the location where you want to put a device does not match the length of cable you have to connect the device. Fortunately, most computer stores sell cable extensions for each of your common devices.*

ATTACHING YOUR KEYBOARD AND MOUSE

Depending on your mouse type (bus or serial mouse), you will connect your mouse to your PC using one of the connectors shown in Figure 3.4. If you have a serial mouse, locate the 9-pin serial port and attach your mouse to it. If, instead, you are using a bus mouse, take time to examine the ports closely on the back of your PC. One of the ports will have a keyboard label and one should have a label for a mouse.

ATTACHING YOUR MONITOR

To connect your monitor to your PC, locate the small port on the back of your system unit that matches the size and shape of your monitor cable. Be careful not to try to plug your monitor into the 9-pin serial port. Also, your monitor will have its own power cable. Do not plug your monitor in yet. You will plug in your system unit, monitor, and printer during your last step.

ATTACHING YOUR PRINTER

To connect your printer to your PC, you will attach a cable (called a parallel cable) between your printer and your PC. As shown in Figure 3.5, your printer cable has two distinct ends, one which you will attach to your PC and the other you will attach to your printer. Users describe the printer cable as having a 25-pin connector at one end and a Centronix connector at the other. Like your monitor, your printer has a power cable you will not yet plug in.

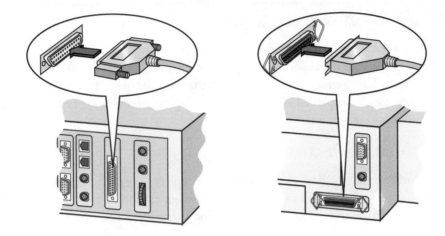

Figure 3.5 *Connecting your printer to your PC.*

ATTACHING YOUR MODEM

As you will learn in Lesson 48, "Understanding the Ins and Outs of PC Modems," your modem lets you connect to other remote computers as well as the Internet. Using your modem, you can browse the Web, send and receive e-mail messages, and even send and receive faxes. Depending on the number of phone lines you have available, the steps you must perform to use your modem may differ. If, for example, you will share a phone line between your modem and phone, you will connect your modem to the wall outlet, and then connect your phone to the modem, as shown in Figure 3.6.

Figure 3.6 *Sharing a phone line between a modem and a phone.*

If you examine the PC's modem port, you may find two phone-cable plugs. Normally, one of the plugs will have the label Line and the second the label Phone. Plug the cable that you connect to the wall outlet into the plug labeled Line and then plug your phone into the plug labeled Phone.

As you begin to surf for information on the Web, you will be amazed at how much time you actually spend online. Your friends and relatives may also be amazed and frustrated by how often, and for how long, your phone line is busy. So, in an ideal world, you will have one line for your phone and a second line for your modem—which will let you send and receive faxes or e-mail messages or surf the Web as you talk on the phone. If you are not sharing a line between your phone and modem, you can simply connect your phone's wall outlet to the plug labeled Line.

CONNECTING YOUR MULTIMEDIA SPEAKERS AND MICROPHONE

If your PC has multimedia speakers and a microphone, locate the corresponding sound-card ports on the back of your system unit. Again, the ports for your microphone and speakers will be similar in size and shape. Depending on your sound-card type, the ports may have a small label that specifies the port's purpose. If your sound-cards are not labeled, refer to the documentation that accompanied your PC. Depending on your speaker types, you may need to plug in your speakers, which you will do in just a few minutes.

STEP THREE: LAST MINUTE DETAILS

Before you plug in and power up your PC devices, you will want to look for any packing materials that the manufacturer may have left in your PC or printer. Often, a manufacturer will place cardboard inserts into your floppy-disk drive, and possibly your CD-ROM drive, to protect the drives during shipping. Take time now to look for such packing materials. Within your printer, you may also find packing materials, and, in some cases tape, that is holding various pieces in place. Normally, the installation instructions that accompany your printer will tell you where to look for such materials. Lastly, take time now to put your PC boxes in a safe location. Should you ever need to move your PC or send your PC for repair, your PC's original boxes will provide the best protection.

STEP FOUR: PLUGGING IN YOUR SYSTEM

Now that you have connected your PC's various devices to your system unit, you are now ready to plug in the devices. If you have not yet purchased a surge suppresser, you should consider stopping now and going to buy one. You are now ready to plug in your equipment. Plug in your printer, monitor, speakers, and PC system unit. The order in which you power on your devices does not matter. However, to avoid overloading a circuit, you should power your devices on one at a time.

WHAT YOU MUST KNOW

In this lesson, you learned how to set up your PC and its related devices. In Lesson 4, "Starting Your Personal Computer," you will learn what you should expect to see each time your system starts as well as steps you can perform to troubleshoot problems that may occur. Before you continue with Lesson 4, however, make sure you understand the following key concepts:

✓ As you set up your PC, do not set your PC or any of your hardware devices onto your carpet. Your carpet may contain static electricity that can damage your PC's sensitive electronics.

✓ One of the greatest threats to your PC is spikes of electricity that travel down the power lines. To protect your PC equipment, you should plug your PC devices into a surge suppresser.

✓ To connect devices to your system unit, you attach a device's cable to connectors on your system called ports. Users describe ports and cables by gender (such as male or female) that specify whether the port provides plugs or receptacles. Users also describe ports and cables in terms the number of pins they support, such as 9-pin or 25-pin cable.

✓ To avoid shock and to reduce the chance of damaging your PC's sensitive electronic equipment, never connect a device to your PC while either the device or your PC is plugged and powered on.

Lesson 4

Starting Your Personal Computer

After you put your PC together, as discussed in Lesson 3, "Setting Up Your Personal Computer," you are ready to start your system. For most users, starting a personal computer is as easy as simply turning on the PC's power. If you share a PC with other users, however, or if your PC is connected to a local-area network, the steps you must perform to start your system may differ. This lesson examines steps you must perform to start your PC, as well as steps you can perform to troubleshoot problems when your system fails to start. By the time you finish this lesson, you will understand the following key concepts:

- To start your PC, simply turn on your PC's power. Users refer to the process of turning on your PC as *powering on*.

- When you first power on your PC, your system will perform its built-in power on self test, during which it will examine its key internal components. If your system passes the power on self test, your system will then load the Windows operating system from your disk.

- If your PC is connected to a local-area network, or if you share your PC with another user, your system may display a dialog box that prompts you to type in your username and password. After you enter your username and password, Windows will display its Desktop, from which you can run other programs.

TURNING ON YOUR PC'S POWER

In most cases, to start a PC, you simply turn on the PC's power. When you "power on" your PC, you will hear your PC's internal fan start to whir. Inside its chassis, your PC will perform its power on self test (users refer to this power on self test as the *POST*). If your PC encounters errors during its self test, your monitor will display a message that briefly describes the error. In some cases, the error message may describe a problem that you can correct, such as a loose keyboard cable. In other cases, you may not understand the error message.

If you can correct the error (you might, for example, be able to plug in a loose keyboard cable), do so. In either case, turn off your PC's power, wait a few seconds, and then power your PC back on (users refer to the process of turning the PC off and then back on as *cycling the PC's power*). In some cases, restarting your PC in this way will solve the error. If, however, the problem persists, write down the error message and contact your PC manufacturer's technical support. If your PC successfully completes its power on self test, your monitor will display a count of the random-access memory that your PC contains, as shown in Figure 4.1.

Figure 4.1 *As the PC starts, it displays a count of the random access memory it contains.*

Next, your system will start the Windows operating system, which will display its Desktop, as shown in Figure 4.2. In Lesson 9, "Running Programs from within Windows," you will learn how to run programs, such as your word processor or Web browser, from the Windows Desktop.

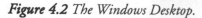

Figure 4.2 *The Windows Desktop.*

RESPONDING TO A USERNAME AND PASSWORD PROMPT

If you share a computer with another user, or if your PC is connected to a local-area network, Windows may display a dialog box, similar to that shown in Figure 4.3, that prompts you to type in a username and password.

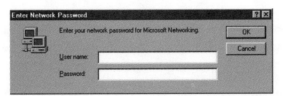

Figure 4.3 *The Enter Windows Password dialog box.*

If Windows displays this dialog box, type in the username your system administrator has assigned to you, press the Tab key, and then type in your password. Windows, in turn, will then display its Desktop.

PROTECT YOUR SYSTEM PASSWORD

If your PC is connected to a local-area network, and to access your system you must specify a username and password, do not let other users know your password. Should another user learn your password, that user could log on to the system as you and access your files. If you suspect that another user knows your password, you should change it immediately. Your system administrator can show you how.

Note: *Never disclose your password to someone who calls you on the phone and tells you that they need your password for system testing. Your system administrator has full access to your system without needing to know your password.*

TROUBLESHOOTING YOUR PC STARTUP

If your system fails to start when you turn on your PC's power, perform the following troubleshooting techniques:

- If, when you first power on your PC, you do not hear the PC's internal fan "whir," check to ensure your PC is plugged into a working outlet. You may want to plug a different device, such as a lamp, into the outlet to ensure the outlet is working. If your system is plugged into a surge suppresser, make sure the suppresser is working by trying it with another device. If your PC still fails to start, have a computer technician examine your PC's internal power supply.

- If your PC does not display its count of the amount of RAM your system contains, your PC is failing its power on self test. Try turning your PC off, waiting a few seconds, and then power your PC back on. If your PC still fails to start, you will need a computer technician to examine your system unit.

- If you hear your system fan, but nothing appears on your screen, make sure that your monitor is plugged into a working outlet and that your monitor cable is connected to your PC. In addition, make sure that the monitor's power cord is also connected securely to the monitor itself.

- If your PC displays a message similar to "Invalid System Setting" or "Invalid CMOS Setting," try cycling your PC's power (turn your PC off, wait a few seconds, and then power your PC on). If the error message remains, you will need a computer technician to examine your system.

- If your PC displays the message "Invalid System Disk," check to see if you have a floppy disk in your floppy drive. If you find a floppy disk in the drive, remove the disk and restart your system.

WHAT YOU MUST KNOW

In this lesson, you learned how to start your PC, which is normally as simple as turning on your PC's power. In Lesson 5, "Ending Programs and Shutting Down Your Personal Computer," you will learn how to end programs that are running and then how to shut down your PC. Before you continue with Lesson 5, however, make sure you understand the following key concepts:

✓ To start your PC, simply power on your system by turning on your PC's power.

✓ When you first power on your PC, your system will perform its built-in power on self test, during which it will examine its key internal components. If your system passes the power on self test, your system will then load the Windows operating system from your disk.

✓ If your system fails to start for any reason, you may be able to solve the problem by cycling your PC's power—in other words, by turning off your PC's power, waiting a few seconds, and then turning the power back on.

✓ If you share a PC with another user, or if your PC is part of a local-area network, Windows may display a dialog box after your system starts within which you must type in your username and password. Your system administrator will assign your username and password to you.

✓ Do not let other users know your system password. If you suspect another user knows your password, have your system administrator show you how to change your password.

✓ After your system starts (and after you log on to the system by typing your username and password), Windows will display its Desktop, which is your working area, while you run other programs.

Lesson 5

Ending Your Programs and Shutting Down Your System

In Lesson 4, "Starting Your Personal Computer," you learned how to turn on your PC and start Windows. Likewise, in Lesson 9, "Running Programs within Windows," you will learn how to run software programs. Because shutting down your PC is something you will probably do each day, this lesson first examines how to end programs and then how and when you should shut down your system. By the time you finish this lesson, you will understand the following key concepts:

- Before you turn off your PC's power, you must first end all programs you are currently running and then shut down Windows.

- To end a program, you can choose the program's File menu Exit option, click your mouse on the program's Close button, or you can use the program's Control menu.

- Never turn off your PC's power while programs are running. Should you do so, you run the risk of damaging files stored on your disk and losing the information the files contain.

- To shut down Windows, select the Start menu Shutdown option.

- To improve your system performance, you may want to get into the habit of restarting your system once a day.

- If you are using a notebook PC, your Start menu may contain a Suspend option that you can use to freeze your PC's current state, so you do not have to shut down and then later restart your system.

ENDING A PROGRAM

When you run a program within the Windows operating system, Windows will open a framed rectangular region on your screen, a window, within which it displays the program's output. When you later end the program, Windows will close the corresponding window. If you examine the menu bar that appears near the top of the program window, you will normally find a File menu, which, as shown in Figure 5.1, contains an Exit option that you can select to end the program's execution.

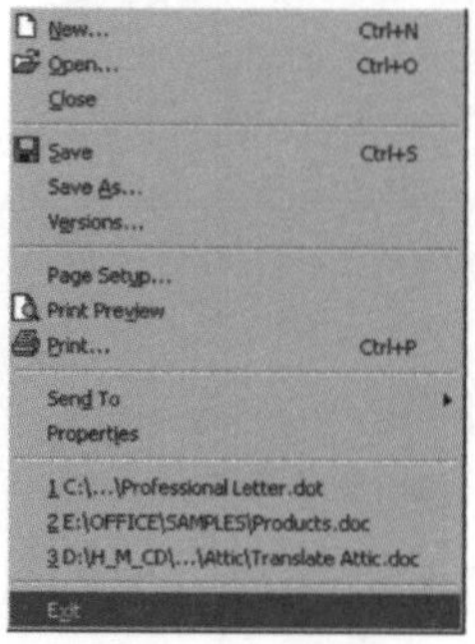

Figure 5.1 *Most programs provide a File menu Exit option that you can select to end the program.*

In addition to using the File menu Exit option to end a program, you can also end a program by clicking your mouse on the window's Close button. As shown in Figure 5.2, the Close button appears as an X at the right-hand side of the title bar, which Windows displays at the top of the program window.

Figure 5.2 *To end a program's execution, click your mouse on the title bar Close button.*

Finally, most program windows have a special Control menu which you can use to size, move, and close a window. As shown in Figure 5.3, the Control menu resides at the left-hand side of the title bar. To display the Control menu, click your mouse on the Control menu button.

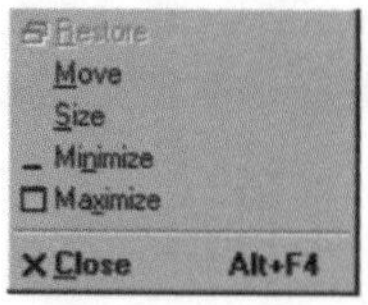

Figure 5.3 *Using the Control menu, you can size, move, and close a window.*

If you single-click your mouse on the Control menu, Windows will display the menu's options. If you double-click your mouse on the Control menu button, Windows will close the window, just as if you clicked your mouse on the Close button. Whether you choose to end a program using the File menu Exit option, by clicking your mouse on the Close button, or by using the Control menu, Windows will end the program and close the program's window.

SAVE YOUR DOCUMENTS BEFORE YOU END A PROGRAM

In Lesson 14, "Storing Information within Files," you will learn how to store and retrieve information with files. As you will learn, files let you store information from one computer session to another. For example, assume that you use your word processor to write and print a memo. If you want to keep an electronic copy of the memo (you might, for example, want to e-mail a copy of the memo to another user), you must store the memo within a file on your disk. If you do not save the memo to a file before you end the program, your word processor will discard your memo from memory and the memo's contents will be gone. As a rule, you must save your documents before you end a program, or you will lose the document's contents. Fortunately, before they end, most programs will prompt you to save your changes. For example, if you try to end Microsoft Word without saving a document's contents, Word will display a dialog box, similar to that shown in Figure 5.4, that asks you if you want to save the document to a file on disk.

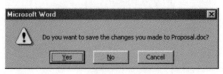

Figure 5.4 *Before it ends, Word will prompt you to save changes to documents you have yet to save to disk.*

In this case, if you select the Yes option, Word will display a Save As dialog box within which you can save the document's contents to a file on disk. If you instead select No, Word will discard your unsaved changes to the document. In Lesson 14, you will learn how to save a document's contents to a file using the Save As dialog box. Rather than relying on programs to prompt you to save your changes, however, you should instead use the File menu Save option to save your documents to files on disk before you end a program.

SHUTTING DOWN YOUR SYSTEM

Never turn off your computer while you have programs running. Should you turn off your PC's power with programs running, you run the risk of damaging the files that your programs (and Windows itself) have open. Instead, when you are done using your system, you should first end all your programs and then shut down Windows. After Windows shuts down, your monitor will display a message telling you it is Ok to turn off your PC's power. To shut down Windows, click your mouse on the Start button. Windows, in turn, will display the Start menu, as shown in Figure 5.5.

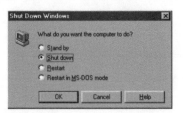

Figure 5.5 *The Windows Start menu.*

Within the Start menu, select the Shut Down option. Windows, in turn, will display the Shut Down Windows dialog box, as shown in Figure 5.6. To shut down your system, so you can turn off your PC's power, select the Shut down option and choose OK. If you want to "refresh" your system, as discussed next, select the Restart option and choose OK.

Figure 5.6 *The Windows Shutdown dialog box.*

Understanding a Notebook PC's Suspend Mode

If you are using a notebook PC, you may find that your Start menu contains a Suspend option. As you know, each time you turn on your PC's power, your system must first perform its power on self test and then load the Windows operating system from disk into memory. Then, as you run other programs, you must wait for Windows to load the programs from disk into memory as well. Later, when you shut down your system, you must first end each of your programs and then shut down Windows itself. All of these operations take time.

Because notebook PC users often carry their systems with them into meetings or on airline flights, hardware and software developers created the notebook PC's suspend mode to eliminate the user's need to continually shut down and later restart their system. When you select Suspend mode, your PC essentially freezes its current state and then reduces its power consumption. Later, to resume your work, you simply turn on your PC as you normally would. Because the PC did not shut down earlier, you don't have to wait for the time-consuming system restart process. In addition, if you had programs running when you suspended your PC, you can continue your work with those programs, right where you left off.

Refresh Your System by Restarting Daily

Users often debate as to when they should power off their PC. Some users will claim that continually powering the PC on and off is "hard" on the PC's internal components. A few years ago, that might have been the case. Today, however, it is OK to turn off the PC at the end of each day. In fact, turning off your PC's power at the end of the day will conserve energy. In the near future, PCs will shut themselves down after long periods of no use. Although software has become much more reliable in recent years, software programs still experience errors (programmers refer to such errors as *bugs*) that cause the programs to fail and to not give back resources to Windows (such as RAM) that other programs can use. When such errors occur, Windows may not get the resources back from the failed programs until the next time you restart your system. As a rule, you should restart your system once a day, normally the first thing in the morning. By "refreshing" your system in this way, you ensure that Windows starts the day with all its resources intact.

What You Must Know

In this lesson, you learned how to end programs within Windows and then how to shut down your PC. As you learned, you should never turn off your PC's power without first ending your programs and then using the Start menu Shutdown option to shut down Windows. In Lesson 6, "Understanding Your PC's Hardware," you will examine many common PC devices. Before you continue with Lesson 6, however, make sure you understand the following key concepts:

✓ Never turn off your PC's power without first ending your programs and shutting down Windows itself.

✓ Windows provides you with several ways to end a program. You can choose the File menu Exit option, click your mouse on the Close button, or you can use the program's Control menu.

✓ To shut down Windows, select the Start menu Shut Down option.

✓ Many users refresh the Windows environment once each day by shutting down and then restarting their PC.

Lesson 6

Getting Help Within Windows and Your Programs

Although the printed manuals that accompany Windows and Windows-based programs keep getting smaller and smaller, Windows and most Windows-based programs provide a lot of instructions within their on-line Help facilities (programs that display the Help text). Using a program's Help facility, you can look up key operations and concepts. The Help facility, in turn, will display information about a topic or the steps that you must perform to accomplish a task within a window on your screen. If you prefer to work from printed instructions, you can print the current Help topic.

Most users, however, never learn to use a program's on-line Help. In most cases, users can find answers to their questions or solutions to their problems within a program's on-line Help. This lesson briefly introduces the Windows Help facility; it is very much like the Help facility you will encounter within any Windows-based program. So, by learning to use Windows on-line Help, you will be ready to look up information within Word's on-line Help, Explorer's on-line Help, and even the Help facility within the Internet Explorer. If you have never used a program's on-line Help before, take time to learn how. You'll be surprised just how much information you can learn from within a program's on-line Help. By the time you finish this lesson, you will understand the following key concepts:

- To help you find answers to your questions and to help you perform specific tasks, Windows and most Windows-based programs provide a built-in Help facility.

- To start a program's on-line Help facility, you will use the Help menu which you will find within the program's menu bar. To Start the Windows Help facility, select the Start menu Help option.

- To help you perform specific operations and to troubleshoot specific problems, the Windows Help facility provides several Wizards (software programs) that will walk you step-by-step through the operations you must perform to accomplish a specific task.

- Within the Windows Help facility, you can look up information using a topic index, by performing a search for a specific topic, or by traversing topics presented in a table of contents format.

STARTING HELP

Within your application programs, such as your word processor, you will start the program's on-line Help facility using the program's Help menu. As shown in Figure 6.1, most programs place the Help menu as the right-most menu-bar entry.

File Edit View Insert Format Tools Table Window Help

Figure 6.1 You start a program's on-line Help facility using the program's Help menu.

To start the Windows Help facility, you select the Help option from the Start menu, as shown in Figure 6.2. Windows, in turn, will open the Windows Help window shown in Figure 6.3. Within the Windows Help Index sheet, you can use a topic index to locate the topic you desire.

Figure 6.2 To start the Windows on-line Help facility, select the Start menu Help option.

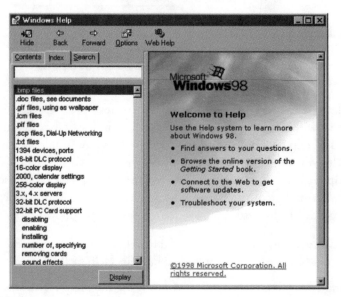

Figure 6.3 The Windows Help window.

USING HELP'S INDEX

Within the Windows Help Index sheet, you can look up Windows topics from an alphabetical list, much like you would use the index at the back of a book. Using your mouse, you can drag the scroll-bar slide that appears to the right of the topic list up or down to bring other topics into view. Or, you can press your keyboard's UP ARROW and DOWN ARROW keys to move through the list.

To drag the scroll-bar slide, aim your mouse pointer at the small box that appears within the scroll bar. Then, hold down your mouse-select button (normally the left button) and move the mouse pointer up and down the slider, without releasing your mouse button. As you move the slider, Windows Help will scroll additional topics into view.

If you are looking for a specific topic, such as modems, you can type your topic. As you type, Windows Help will move to the topic that most closely matches the letters you have typed. For example, when you type the letter M (for modems), Windows Help will display the first topic in the index that starts with the letter M.

When you then type the letter o, Windows Help will display the first topic that begins with the letters Mo, and so on. After you highlight the topic that you desire, click your mouse on the Display button. Windows Help, in turn, will display the topic's corresponding text within the window frame that appears to the right of the topic list. For example, if you display the topic Modems, Installing, Windows Help will display the text shown in Figure 6.4.

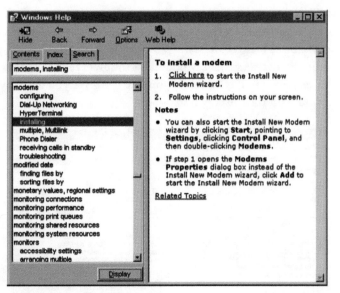

Figure 6.4 Displaying a topic's text within Windows Help.

PRINTING INFORMATION WITH HELP

If you prefer to read a topic's text from paper, as opposed to reading from within the topic-display window frame, right-click your mouse within the Windows Help topic-display frame. Windows Help, in turn, will display a pop-up menu similar to that shown in Figure 6.5. Within the pop-up menu, select the Print option to print the current topic.

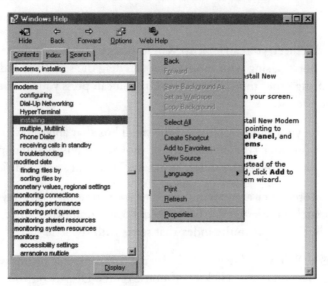

Figure 6.5 *Printing a topic's text within Windows Help.*

SEARCHING FOR A TOPIC WITHIN HELP

Normally, using the Windows Help Index sheet, you can find the topic you require. But, as is sometimes the case with a book, not every topic Windows Help discusses receives an index entry. If you cannot find a specific topic within the Index, click your mouse on the Windows Help Search tab. Windows Help, in turn, will display the Search sheet. Within the Search sheet, type in the topic you desire, such as Modems. Windows Help, in turn, will search its documents and display a list of matching topics, as shown in Figure 6.6. If you find the topic you desire within the topic list, highlight the topic and then click your mouse on the Display button.

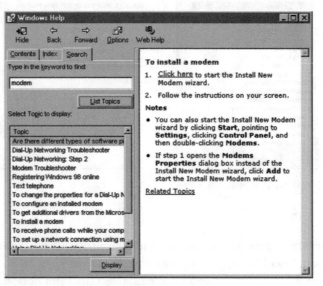

Figure 6.6 *Topics matching a search operation within Windows Help.*

USING HELP'S CONTENTS PAGE

To help users who are just learning a new program, most Help facilities provide a Contents page that works much like a book's table of contents. To display the Contents page within Windows Help, click your mouse on the Contents tab. Within the Contents sheet, click your mouse on the book icons to display topic lists, much like you would open the pages of a book. When you click a page icon within a topic list, Windows Help will display the topic's text, as shown in Figure 6.7.

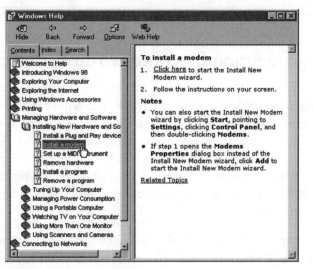

Figure 6.7 *The Windows Help Contents sheet presents information using a table of contents format.*

MOVING FROM ONE TOPIC TO ANOTHER

As you read information within a Help facility, there will be times when the topic text contains underlined text, which represents links to other topics. If you click your mouse on a link within a topic, Windows Help will immediately display the topic. As you read that topic's discussion, you may find links to other related topics. By clicking on topic links in this way, you can move quickly through related topics. After you read the information at a topic to which you have linked, you can click your mouse on the Back button that appears within the Windows Help toolbar to return to the previous topic.

UNDERSTANDING WINDOWS WIZARDS

To help you perform specific operations or troubleshoot specific problems, Windows Help provides some built-in Wizards (software programs) that will take you step-by-step through an operation. Most users will find the Wizards very helpful. If you experience a hardware problem, such as your printer won't print, you can use the Printer Troubleshooting Wizard to help you determine the problem. To list the Wizards available within Windows on-line Help, select the Search sheet an then search for **Wizards**.

WHAT YOU MUST KNOW

Each program you run within Windows will provide an on-line Help facility within which you can look up the steps you must perform to accomplish specific tasks within the program. Most programs provide tremendous amounts of information within their on-line Help. In this lesson, you learned how to use Windows on-line Help facility. Fortunately, the on-line Help you will encounter in other programs is very much the same. In Lesson 7, "Understanding Common Operations You Perform On a Window," you will learn how to move, size, minimize, and maximize windows that appear on your screen. Before you continue with Lesson 7, however, make sure you have learned the following key concepts:

✓ Windows and most Windows-based programs provide a built-in Help facility within which you can find step-by-step instructions for most operations. To start a program's on-line Help facility, you will use the Help menu which you will find within the program's menu bar.

✓ To Start the Windows Help facility, select the Start menu Help option.

✓ Within a Help facility, you can view information within a window on your screen, or you can print a copy of the information.

Lesson 7

Understanding Common Operations You Perform on a Window

As you have learned, each time you start your PC, your system first runs Windows. Within Windows, you can run your other programs, such as your word processor, spreadsheet, or Web browser. When you run a program, Windows will display the program's output within a framed region on your screen, called a window. Windows will display the output for each program that you run within a window on your screen. Depending on the programs you run, and possibly the number of programs you run at the same time, there may be times when you must move or size a window. In this lesson, you will learn how to perform common operations on windows. By the time you finish this lesson, you will understand the following key concepts:

- When you run a program, Windows will display the program's output within a framed window on your screen. If you run multiple programs at the same time, Windows will display each program's output within its own window.

- To move a window on your screen, use your mouse to drag the window's title bar to the screen location that you desire.

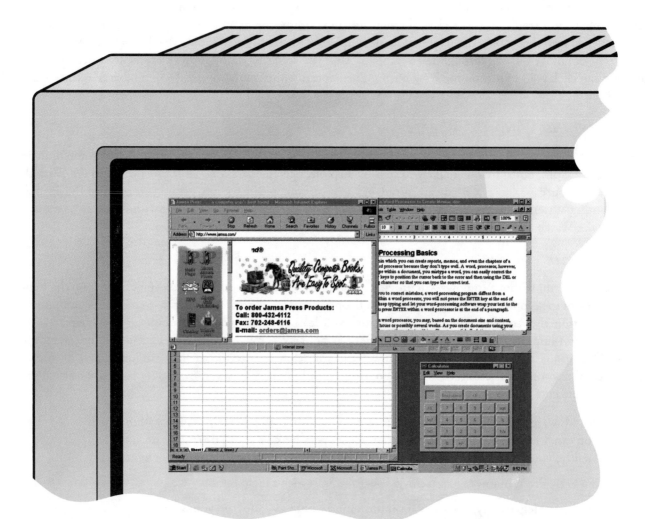

- To drag a window's title bar using your mouse, aim your mouse pointer at the title bar and then hold down your mouse-select button as you move your mouse. After the window is at the screen location you desire, release the mouse-select button.

- To size a window, use your mouse to drag the window's frame in or out to decrease or increase the window's size.

- As you work, there will be times when you will want to temporarily hide a program's window, without ending the program. In such cases, you can minimize the window into a Taskbar icon, by clicking your mouse on the window's Minimize button.

- To restore a minimized window to its previous size, click your window on the program's Taskbar button.

- Depending on a program's output, there will be many times when you will want to size a program's window so that the window fills your entire screen. To maximize a window's size in this way, click your mouse on the window's Maximize button. To restore a maximized window to its previous size, click your mouse on the window's Restore button.

MOVING ON A WINDOW ON YOUR SCREEN

Within Windows, you can run two or more programs at the same time. Windows, in turn, will display each program's output within a separate window on your screen. Figure 7.1, for example, shows Windows running four programs: the Microsoft Word word processor, the Excel spreadsheet, the Internet Explorer Web browser, and the Calculator accessory.

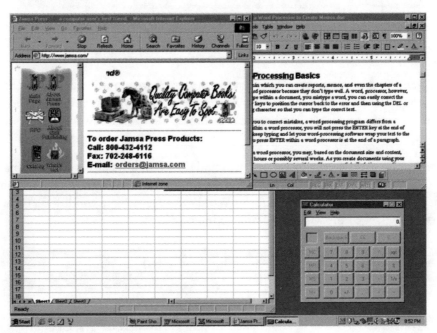

Figure 7.1 Running multiple programs within Windows.

When you run multiple programs within Windows, there may be times when you will want to move a program's window to a specific location on your screen. To move a window within Windows, you will use your mouse to drag the window to the location you desire. To start, aim your mouse pointer at the window's title bar that appears at the top of the window and that contains the program's name (the program's title). Next, hold down your mouse-select button (normally the left button) and move your mouse across your desk (do not release your mouse button as you move your mouse). Windows, in turn, will move the window to match your mouse movements. Users refer to moving objects using your mouse in this way as *dragging the object*. Figure 7.2 shows the same four programs previously shown, after the user has moved two of the programs to new locations on the screen.

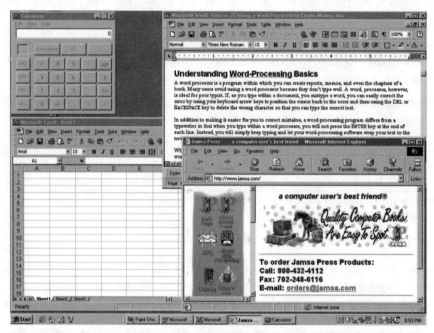

Figure 7.2 *To move a window, use your mouse to drag the window's title bar to the location that you desire.*

SIZING A WINDOW

When you run a program, Windows will open a window on the screen within which it displays the program's output. Normally, the program itself will tell Windows how big to make its window. Depending on the program's output or other items you are displaying on your screen, there may be times when you will want to increase or decrease the size of a program window.

If you examine a window on your screen closely, you will find that Windows places a thin frame around the outside of the window. To increase or decrease a window's size, you can use your mouse to drag the frame out or in, as your needs require. Figure 7.3, for example, shows Microsoft Word running within a window on the screen. In the second screen image, the user has dragged the window's frame to increase the window's size.

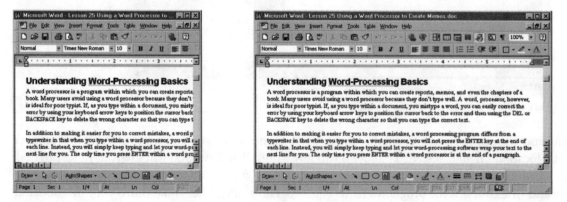

Figure 7.3 *To size a window, use your mouse to drag the frame that surrounds the window.*

When you size a window, you can drag the top or bottom frame to increase the window's height. Likewise, you can drag the left and right frames to increase the frame's width. If you want to increase a window's height and width at the same time, use your mouse to drag one of the window's corners. Occasionally, you will encounter a program, such as the Windows Calculator accessory, whose window's size you cannot change. Most programs, however, will let you size their windows as your needs require.

MINIMIZING A WINDOW TO A TASKBAR ICON

When you run multiple programs within Windows, there may be times when you will want to temporarily hide a window, without closing the window, which might require that you save and close a document that you plan to use again in the near future. In cases where you simply want to move a program's window out of the way, while letting the program continue to run, Windows lets you minimize the program's output into a Taskbar icon. Normally, Windows displays its Taskbar at the bottom of your screen, to the right of the Start button, as shown in Figure 7.4. As you can see within Figure 7.4, Windows displays a button on the Taskbar for each program that is currently running.

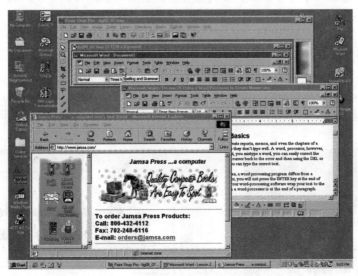

Figure 7.4 *Windows displays buttons within the Taskbar for each program you are currently running.*

When you want to hide a program's window, you can click your mouse on the program's Minimize button, which appears as a small dash in the button to the right of the program's title bar, as shown in Figure 7.5.

Figure 7.5 *To minimize (hide) a program's window, click your mouse on the window's Minimize button.*

In Figure 7.6, the user has three programs running (you can tell which programs are running by viewing the Taskbar buttons), but only one program's window is visible. That is because the user has minimized two of the windows.

When you minimize a program's window, the program continues to run. You simply don't see the program's output. When you are ready to work within the program again, you simply click your mouse on the program's Taskbar button. Windows, in turn, will restore the program's window to its previous size.

Figure 7.6 *Minimizing a window lets you hide the window's contents.*

MAXIMIZING A WINDOW TO FILL YOUR SCREEN DISPLAY

Depending on a program's output, there will be times when you will want to maximize the size of a program's window so you can view the program's output using your entire screen. Figure 7.7, for example, shows a program running within its normal window size and the same program running within a maximized window that fills the entire screen display.

Figure 7.7 *To display a window's output using your entire screen display, you must maximize the window.*

To maximize a window, click your mouse on the window's Maximize button that appears to the right of the window's title bar as a large box.

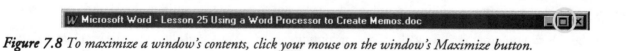

Figure 7.8 *To maximize a window's contents, click your mouse on the window's Maximize button.*

If you later want to restore the window to its previous size, click your mouse on the Restore button, that appears as two smaller boxes, as shown in Figure 7.9.

W Microsoft Word - Lesson 25 Using a Word Processor to Create Memos.doc

Figure 7.9 *To restore a window to its previous size, click your mouse on the window's Restore button.*

CLOSING A WINDOW

As you learned in Lesson 5, "Ending Your Programs and Shutting Down Your System," when you are done using a program, you should end the program, which will direct Windows to close the program's window. Lesson 5 discusses several ways you can close a window. The easiest, however, is simply to click your mouse on the window's Close button, which appears as a large X in a button to the right of the title bar, as shown in Figure 7.10.

W Microsoft Word - Lesson 25 Using a Word Processor to Create Memos.doc

Figure 7.10 *To close a program's window, which ends the program, click your mouse on the window's Close button.*

If you have opened a document within the program, such as a word-processing document or spreadsheet, your program will display a dialog box asking you if you want to save the changes you have made to your document before you exit the program which, in most cases, you will. If you direct the program to save your changes and you have not yet assigned a filename to your document, your program will display a Save As dialog box, within which you can specify the filename you desire. Lesson 14, "Storing Information within Files," discusses file operations in detail.

WHAT YOU MUST KNOW

Within Windows, each time you run a program, Windows displays the program's output on your screen within a framed, rectangular area called a window. Regardless of the program that you are running, you can perform several operations on the window, such as moving, sizing, minimizing, maximizing, and closing the window. In this lesson you learned to perform the operations that are common to all program windows. In Lesson 8, "Understanding Common Menu, Toolbar, and Dialog Box Operations," you will learn how to perform operations that are common to menus, toolbars, and dialog boxes within your programs. Before you continue with Lesson 8, however, make sure that you have learned the following key concepts:

✓ Windows will display each program's output within a framed window on your screen.

✓ If you run multiple programs at the same time, there may be times when one program's window covers another program. To move a window on your screen, use your mouse to drag the window's title bar to the screen location that you desire.

✓ Depending on a program's output, there may be times when you want to size the program's window as opposed to minimizing the window into a Taskbar icon or maximizing the window to full screen. To size a window, use your mouse to drag the window's frame in or out to decrease or increase the window's size.

✓ When you run multiple programs within Windows, there will be times when you may want to temporarily hide a program's window, without ending the program. In such cases, you can minimize the window into a Taskbar icon, by clicking your mouse on the window's Minimize button. When you are again ready to use the window's contents, you simply click your mouse on the program's Taskbar button to restore the window to its previous size.

✓ Depending on a program's output, there will be many times when you will want to size a program's window so that the window fills your entire screen. To maximize a window's size in this way, click your mouse on the window's Maximize button. If you later want to restore the window to its previous size, you can click your mouse on the window's Restore button.

Lesson 8

Understanding Common Menu, Toolbar, and Dialog Box Operations

To make your programs easier to use, most Windows-based programs make extensive use of menus, toolbars, and dialog boxes. In this lesson, you will learn techniques you can use within most programs to improve your productivity. By the time you finish this lesson, you will understand the following key concepts:

- Most Windows-based programs make extensive use of menus, toolbars, and dialog boxes to make the program easier to use.

- Take time to examine your program's menu options. The menu options control the operations the program can perform. By studying the options, you will gain considerable insight into the program's capabilities.

- Most Windows-based programs will display a menu bar near the top of their window. To select a specific menu, click your mouse on the menu name that appears in the menu bar or hold down your keyboard's ALT key and press the letter that appears underlined within the menu name.

- Within a menu or dialog box, there will be times when options or fields appear dimmed. Programs dim menu options and fields when you cannot currently perform the corresponding operation.

- When you type in a value into a dialog box text field, do not press your ENTER key unless you are done with your dialog-box entries. Most dialog boxes equate the ENTER key with the OK button. If you type text and then press ENTER, the dialog box will assume that you are done entering your date. Instead, after you type your text, press the TAB key to advance to the next field or click your mouse on the field you desire.

IMAGE TRAVERSING A PROGRAM'S MENU BAR

If you examine most of your program windows, you will find that just about every program you run provides a menu bar similar to that shown in Figure 8.1. Within the various menu bar menus, you will find options you can select that correspond to every operation the program will let you perform. To save your current document, for example, you will select the File menu Save option. To print your document, you will select the File menu Print option. To remove selected text from within your document, you will use the Edit menu Cut option, and so on. To better understand your program's capabilities, you should spend a few minutes with each of your programs, examining the program's menu options. Within your word-processing software, for example, you will find that the Insert menu lets you insert a picture into your document and from the Tools menu you can check your document's grammar or access a Thesaurus. By letting you perform operations using menu options, Windows-based programs become quite easy to use. As you examine your menu options within your various programs, you will find that options on several menus, such as the File and Edit menus, are quite similar from one program to the next.

| File Edit View Insert Format Tools Table Window Help |

Figure 8.1 *Programs provide menu bars that let you perform specific operations.*

To display a menu's options, click your mouse on the menu name, or, using your keyboard, hold down your keyboard's ALT key and press the keyboard key that corresponds to the letter that appears underlined within the menu name. For example, to display the File menu on the previous menu bar, you would press the ALT -F keyboard combination. (Users refer to such keyboard combinations as *hot keys*.) Likewise, to display the Edit menu options, you would press ALT - E. Your program, in turn, will display the menu's contents. Figure 8.2, for example, shows the File menu within the Microsoft Word word processor.

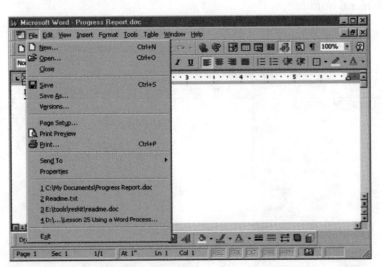

Figure 8.2 *Displaying the File menu within Microsoft Word.*

As you will learn in the next section, by examining menu options, you can better understand what operation your program will perform next.

UNDERSTANDING MENU OPTION TYPES

When you display a menu's contents within your programs, take a moment to examine the various menu options. Within the File menu shown in Figure 8.2, for example, you will find three dots (*ellipses*) to the right of some options. Likewise, you will see keyboard combinations to the right of other options. Windows displays the ellipses (…) next to a menu item to inform you that when you select that option, Windows will display a dialog box that prompts you for more information. If, for example, you select the File menu Save As option, Word will display the Save As dialog box that prompts you for the filename you want to use for your current document. Likewise, if you select the Print option, Windows will display the Print dialog box within which you can select a specific printer or type in the number of copies you want your program to print.

Many menus let you select an option from your keyboard by pressing a hot key combination. For example, within Word, if you press the CTRL+S keyboard combination, Word will save your document's contents, just as if you had selected the File menu Save option. Likewise, if you press the CTRL+P keyboard combination, Word will display the Print dialog box, just as if you had selected the File menu Print option.

By providing hot-key combinations for common operations, Windows-based programs let users who don't like to take their hands off the keyboard perform the operations quickly.

When you select a menu, there will be times when some menu options appear dimmed (light grey) while other options are black, as shown in Figure 8.3. Windows-based programs will dim menu options to indicate that you cannot currently select the option. For example, in Lesson 17, "Mastering Cut-and-Paste Operations," you will learn how to move text within a document using cut-and-paste operations.

To perform such an operation, you must first select the text that you want to move, and then select the Edit menu Cut option. Because you must select the text before you can use the menu option, the Edit menu will display the Cut option as dimmed, until you have selected text.

After you select the text, the Edit menu will enable the menu option, displaying the option using normal text. When an application displays a menu option as dimmed, the application is telling you that you must perform other steps first, before you can select the menu option.

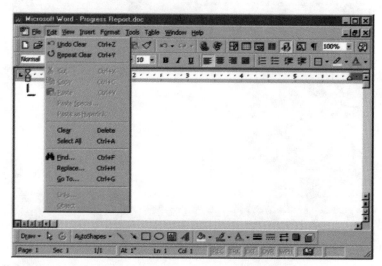

Figure 8.3 *Windows will display menu options you cannot select as dimmed.*

If you examine the Windows Start menu (which you can view by clicking your mouse on the Start button), you will find that several of the Start menu options have a right facing triangle. When you select such an option, Windows will cascade a submenu. For example, if you select the Start menu Programs option, Windows will display the Programs submenu. Likewise, as shown in Figure 8.4, if you select the Start menu Settings option, Windows will cascade the Settings submenu.

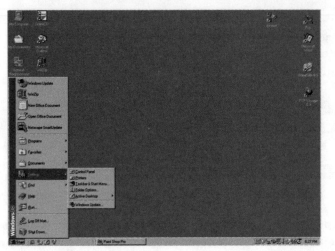

Figure 8.4 *Windows displays the right-facing triangle next to a menu option to indicate a cascading menu.*

Finally, as shown in Figure 8.5, there may be times when you encounter menu options with checkmarks beside them. Such menu options let you toggle a specific state on or off. If the option has a checkmark next to it, selecting the menu option will disable the corresponding state and will direct your program to turn off the checkmark's display. For example, in Figure 8.5, the checkmark next to the Ruler option tells you that Word is currently displaying a measurement ruler near the top of its window. If you select the Ruler option, Word will turn off the Ruler's display and will remove the checkmark. Later, you can select the Ruler option a second time to turn the ruler's display back on.

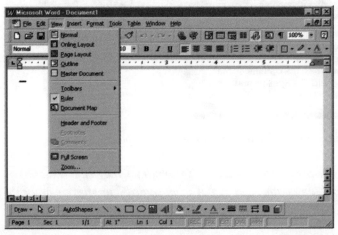

Figure 8.5 *Menu options with checkmarks beside them let you toggle a specific operation or state on or off.*

USING TOOLBAR BUTTONS

Although menu bars and hot keys make most operations easy to perform, most Windows-based applications try to give you one-button access to the operations you will perform most often, by placing icons within one or more toolbars that the program displays beneath its menu bar, as shown in Figure 8.6.

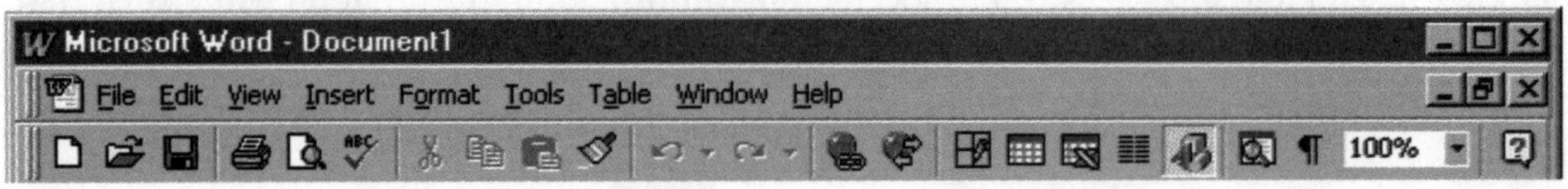

Figure 8.6 *Most Windows-based programs place toolbar buttons you can select to perform a specific operation within one mouse click.*

Again, within your programs, you should take time to learn each button's purpose. To help you learn what function a button performs, most programs will display a toolbar pop-up box that describes the button's purpose if you hold your mouse pointer over the button for a few seconds. Figure 8.7, for example shows a toolbar pop-up box describing the purpose of the ABC button within Word.

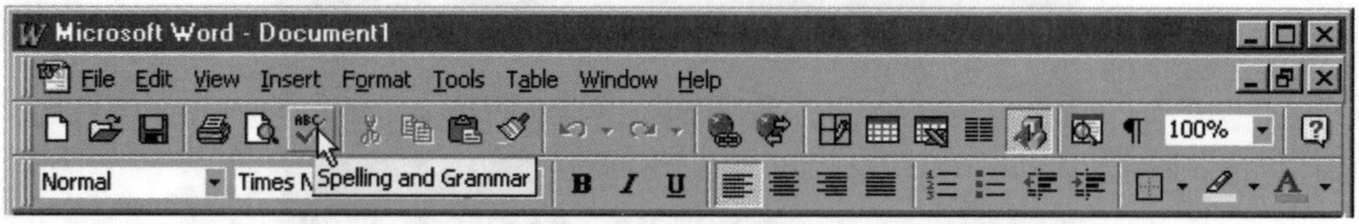

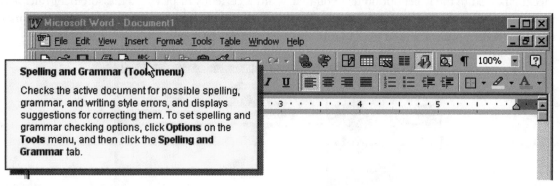

Figure 8.7 *To learn a toolbar button's task, hold your mouse pointer over the button for a few seconds.*

In addition to using toolbar pop-up box to determine a button's purpose, many programs provide a context-sensitive Help tool you can use to determine an object's purpose. Within the Word toolbar, shown in Figure 8.7, you will see a button that contains a large question mark—Word's context-sensitive Help button. If you click your mouse on the button, Word will change your mouse pointer into a question mark. Then, when you click your mouse on an object, such as a toolbar button, your program will display a pop-up box that defines the object's purpose. Figure 8.8, for example, shows the context-sensitive help that Word will display for the ABC toolbar button.

Figure 8.8 *Using context-sensitive help to determine an object's purpose.*

Note: *Many programs support several different toolbars, each of which you may want to use under different situations. For specifics on your program's toolbar, refer to the documentation that accompanied your program or use the program's on-line Help.*

TRAVERSING A DIALOG BOX

When you perform various operations within your programs, there will be times when your programs may need you to provide additional information before they can continue. For example, when you save a new word-processing document, your word-processing program must stop and ask you for the filename that you want to use.

Likewise, when you print your document's contents, you may want to tell your word-processing software that you only want to print a specific range of pages (say pages 5 though 10) and that you want to print three copies of those pages. When a Windows-based programs needs you to specify more information, the program will display a dialog box—so named, because you and the program are having an interactive dialogue. Figure 8.9, for example, shows the Print dialog box from within Microsoft Word.

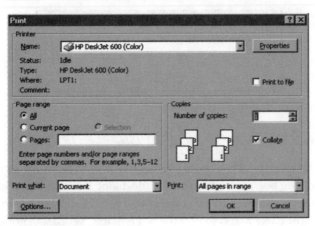

Figure 8.9 *The Print dialog box within Microsoft Word.*

Depending on the dialog box's purpose, the number and type of fields within the dialog box will differ. As you examine a dialog box, you may find that several fields have default values, meaning, if you don't change the field's value, your program will use the value shown. To assign a value to a field dialog box field, click your mouse on the field. In addition, by pressing your keyboard's TAB key, you can move from one field to the next. If you want to move back to a previous field, you can press the SHIFT-TAB keyboard combination. The following discussion examines different field types you may encounter within a dialog box. Also, if you examine the dialog-box fields closely, you will find that several fields support hot-key combinations. Within the Print dialog box, for example, you can press the ALT+C keyboard combination to select the Copies field or the ALT+G keyboard combination to select the Pages field.

As was the case with menus, depending on the operation you are performing, there may be times when fields within a dialog box apppear dimmed, to signify that you cannot select the field's value. After you make your selections within the dialog box, you can press ENTER or click your mouse on the OK button to put your values into effect. If you decide you don't want to perform the operation, you can click your mouse on the Cancel button or press your keyboard's ESC key.

TYPING TEXT WITHIN A TEXT FIELD

Many dialog boxes will provide text fields within which you can type specific text. For example, in the Print dialog box shown in Figure 8.9, you can click your mouse on the Pages field and type in the page numbers that you want Word to print. When you type text within a text field, do not press the ENTER key unless you are done using the dialog box. Within a dialog box, the ENTER key normally corresponds to the OK option. When you press ENTER, your program will assume you are done with the dialog box entries. After you type your text within a text field, press your keyboard's TAB key to advance to the next field or click your mouse on the field you desire.

SELECTING AN OPTION FROM WITHIN A PULL-DOWN LIST

Many dialog boxes will provide a list (or menu) of options you can select for a specific operation. Rather than clutter the dialog box with the entire list, the dialog box will use a pull-down list. If you examine the Print dialog box previously shown, you will find that the Printer Name field uses a pull-down list. If you click your mouse on the field's down-facing arrow, the dialog box will open the list, as shown in Figure 8.10. Within the list, you can then click your mouse on the item you desire. (You can also open a pull-down list using your keyboard by selecting the field and then pressing the CTRL-DOWN ARROW keyboard combination. If you decide not to change the current selection within the list, you can close the list by clicking your mouse outside of the list or by pressing the ESC key.

Figure 8.10 Opening a pull-down list within a dialog box.

USING A CHECKBOX WITHIN A DIALOG BOX TO ENABLE OR DISABLE AN OPTION

Many dialog boxes will use checkboxes to let you specify values for fields that require a yes-or-no or on-or-off response. For example, within the Print dialog box previously shown, the dialog box uses a checkbox to let you specify whether or not you want Word to collate your copies. In this case, if you place a checkmark within the checkbox, Word will collate the copies. If you remove the checkmark, so that the box is blank, Word will not collate the copies. Throughout this book's lessons, you will use checkboxes within dialog boxes to enable or disable specific operations.

USING A RADIO BUTTON TO SELECT A SPECIFIC OPTION

Depending on the operation you are performing, there may be times when you must select only one option from a list of options. In such cases, your dialog box will use radio buttons, so named because they behave much like the buttons on a car radio that let you select only one station at a time. The Print dialog box previously shown uses radio buttons to let you specify whether you want to print the entire document, the current page, your currently selected text, or a range of pages. Because the dialog box uses a radio button, you must choose only one option.

USING SPIN CONTROLS TO SPECIFY A VALUE

Many dialog boxes that require you to input numeric values take advantage of spin controls, upon which you can click your mouse to increase or decrease the field's current value. If you examine the Print dialog box, previously shown, you will find that the dialog box uses a spin control to let you specify the number of copies you want Word to print. By clicking your mouse on the spin control's up arrow, you direct the dialog box to increase the field's current value by one. Likewise, by clicking your mouse on the down arrow, you direct the control to decrement the value by one.

WHAT YOU MUST KNOW

As you run Windows-based programs, you will make extensive use of menus, toolbars, and dialog boxes. In this lesson, you learned operations you can use within most programs you will run. In Lesson 9, "Running Programs within Windows," you will learn different ways you can start programs within Windows. Before you continue with Lesson 9, however, make sure you have learned the following key concepts:

✓ To make their software easier to use, most Windows-based programs make extensive use of menus, toolbars, and dialog boxes.

✓ When you first run a program, you should take a few minutes to examine the program's various menu options. By studying the available options, you can learn quite a bit about the program's capabilities.

✓ To select a menu within a program, you can click your mouse on the menu name within the program's menu bar or hold down your keyboard's ALT key and press the letter that appears underlined within the menu name. To select a File menu, for example, you would press ALT -F.

✓ Within a menu or dialog box, there will be times when options or fields appear dimmed. Programs dim menu options and fields when you cannot currently perform the corresponding operation.

Lesson 9

Running Programs within Windows

In Lesson 4, "Starting Your Personal Computer," you learned that each time you turn on your PC, your system first runs the Windows operating system. Within Windows, you can run other programs, such as your word processor, Web browser, or even your e-mail software. As you have learned, Windows is so named, because each time you run a program, Windows opens a window, a rectangular region on your screen, within which Windows displays the program's output.

This lesson examines how you run programs within Windows. By the time you finish this lesson, you will understand the following key concepts:

- Each time you start your PC, your system starts the Windows operating system. Within Windows, you can run other programs, such as your word processor or e-mail software. Windows, in turn, will display the program's output within a framed rectangular region on your screen called a window.

- Within Windows, the easiest way to run a program is to select the program from the Start menu.

- Within Windows, you can end a program by clicking your mouse on the window's Close button (the X that appears to the right of the window's title bar). You can also end a program using the program's File or Control menu.

- If you have a program that you run on a regular basis, you may want to put a shortcut (an icon) to the program, upon which you can double-click your mouse to run the program.

- Windows lets you run multiple programs at the same time. However, only one program, which users call the active program, will respond to your keyboard and mouse operations. To select a program as the active program, click your mouse on the program's window or click your mouse on the program's Taskbar button.

WITHIN WINDOWS YOU CAN RUN A PROGRAM USING ONE OF SEVERAL TECHNIQUES

The primary reason that the Windows operating system exists is to help you run programs. As you will learn in this lesson, Windows provides you with several ways you can start (run) a program. If you are like most users, you will probably have two or three key programs that you will use on a regular basis. As you read through this lesson, pick the technique that you find easiest and then stick with it.

SELECTING A PROGRAM FROM THE WINDOWS START MENU

As you learned in Lesson 4, after Windows starts, it will display its Desktop, as shown in Figure 9.1. You can think of the Desktop as your work space within Windows. When you run programs, for example, Windows will open a window on your Desktop.

Figure 9.1 *The Windows Desktop is your working area within Windows.*

If you examine the Desktop closely, you will normally find a small Start button near the bottom left corner of your screen (although the button's location can differ). The easiest way to run programs within Windows is to first click your mouse on the Start menu button. Windows, in turn, will display the Start menu, as shown in Figure 9.2.

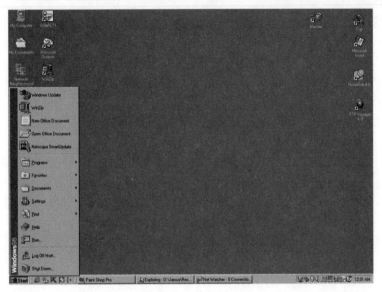

Figure 9.2 *The Windows Start menu.*

You can start most programs using the Start menu. In fact, you will find menu options for almost every program on your system by clicking your mouse on the Start menu Programs option. Windows, in turn, will display (users may call the process of displaying a secondary menu *cascading the menu*) the Programs submenu, as shown in Figure 9.3.

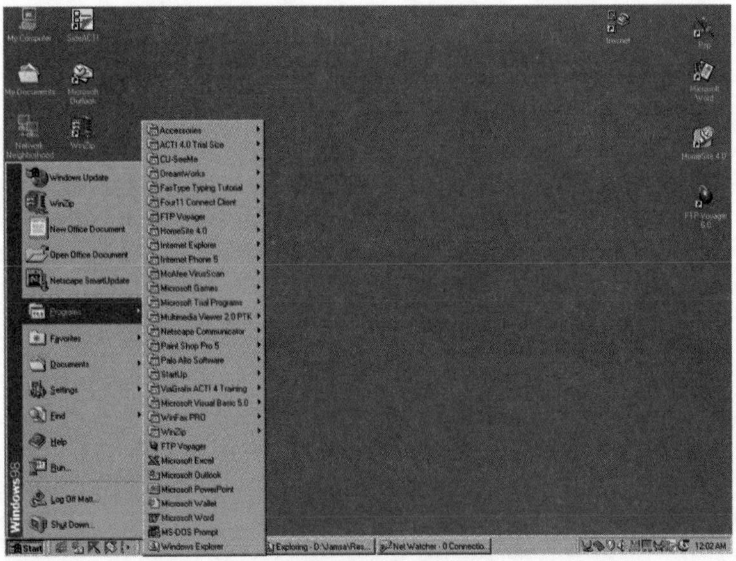

Figure 9.3 *Displaying program options within the Programs submenu.*

If the program you want to run appears within the Programs submenu, you can click your mouse on the program's menu option to run the program. Windows, in turn, will open a window on your desktop, within which it will display the program's output. In some cases, to locate your program, you may need to cascade additional submenus. For example, if you want to run the Internet Explorer Web browser, you should click your mouse on the Programs submenu Internet Explorer option. Windows, in turn, will cascade the Internet Explorer submenu, as shown in Figure 9.4, within which you can click your mouse on the Internet Explorer option to run the program.

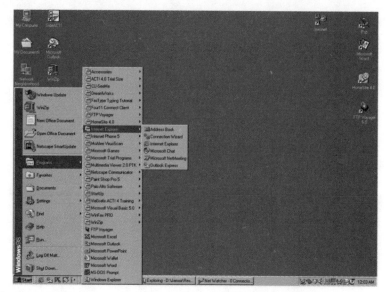

Figure 9.4 *Cascading the Internet Explorer submenu, within the Programs submenu.*

The first few times you view options within the Programs submenu can be intimidating. Fortunately, you probably only have a few programs that you run on a regular basis. Using the Start menu, you can start these programs quickly.

Depending on the number of programs installed on your system, your Programs submenu may have too many options for Windows to display on your screen at one time. If Windows is not displaying all the options on a menu, you can use your mouse pointer to scroll through the menu options. At the top and bottom of your menu, you may find an up-facing arrow and a down-facing arrow. By aiming your mouse pointer over one of the arrows, you can scroll through the menu options that are not currently in view.

TAKING THE START MENU FOR A TEST DRIVE

As you work with Windows, you will use the Start menu on a regular basis to run your programs. Take time now to examine the options on your Programs submenu. By examining the menu options, you can learn what software is installed on your system. Next, perform the following steps to run the Windows Calculator program, as shown in Figure 9.5.

Figure 9.5 *The Windows Calculator accessory program.*

1. Click your mouse on the Start button. Windows, in turn, will display the Start menu.

2. Within the Start menu, click your mouse on the Programs option. Windows, in turn, will cascade the Programs submenu.

3. Within the Programs submenu, click your mouse on the Accessories menu and choose Calculator. Windows will open a window on your screen, within which it will display the Calculator program's output.

To close the Calculator program's window, click your mouse on the window's Close button, the X that appears to the right of the window's title bar.

RUNNING A PROGRAM FROM WITHIN THE RUN DIALOG BOX

Most users will find that using the Start menu is the easiest way to run programs within Windows. Unfortunately, you can only use the Start menu to run programs that you have installed on your system. When you buy a new program, you must install the program onto your system, before you can run the program, by selecting it from an option on the Programs submenu. To install the program, you must run the program's installation program, which also does not reside on your system.

In cases when you must run a program that does not reside on your system (the only time most users must do so is when they install a new program), you can use the Start menu Run option, which directs Windows to display the Run dialog box, shown in Figure 9.6.

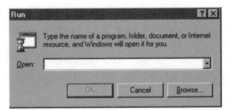

Figure 9.6 *The Run dialog box.*

Within the Run dialog box, you can run a program in one of two ways. First, if you know the program's name and location (disk drive and file folder), you type the information within the Open text field. As you will learn in Lesson 20, "Installing New Software on Your Personal Computer," most programs name their installation program *Setup.EXE*. If, for example, you insert a CD-ROM that contains an installation program into your CD-ROM drive, which for this example, we'll assume is drive E, you could run the Setup program by typing E:\Setup.EXE and pressing ENTER. Often, unfortunately, you may not know the name or location of the file you want to run. In such cases, you can click your mouse on the Run dialog box's Browse button, which will display a Browse dialog box within which you can look for the program file. In Lesson 16, "Using the Windows Explorer to Manage Your Files and Disks," you will learn how to use the Browse dialog box to search your disks for a specific file.

LAUNCHING A PROGRAM FROM A DESKTOP ICON

If you examine your Desktop, you will find several small icons, some of which may correspond to programs. To run a program using a Desktop icon, you simply double-click your mouse on the icon. For example, take time now to double-click your mouse on the Recycle Bin icon. Windows, in turn, will run the Recycle Bin program, opening a window within which it will display the program's output. In Lesson 18, "Recovering a Deleted File from the Windows Recycle Bin," you will learn how to use the Recycle Bin to recover a file whose contents you have inadvertently deleted. For now, simply close the Recycle Bin window by clicking your mouse on the window's Close button.

To make it easy to run the programs they frequently use, users will often put an icon on the Desktop that corresponds to a specific program. To run the program, the user simply double-clicks his or her mouse on the icon. Windows makes it very easy for you to place icons on your Desktop for the programs you frequently use. To start, select the Start menu Programs menu, as discussed in the previous section. Within the Programs submenu, locate the menu option for the program you desire. Then, aim your mouse pointer at the menu you open and hold down your mouse-select button (do not click your mouse on the option—hold the mouse button down). Next, while holding down your mouse-select button, move your mouse pointer to an unused location on your Desktop and then release your mouse-select button (users refer to such mouse operations as a drag-and-drop operation). Windows, in turn, will place an icon on your Desktop upon which you can double-click your mouse to start the program.

RUNNING A PROGRAM FROM WITHIN THE EXPLORER

In Lesson 16, "Using the Windows Explorer to Manage Your Files and Disks," you will learn how to locate files within the folders that reside on your disk. As you will learn, within the Explorer's files list, you can double-click your mouse on a file to open the file's contents. If, for example, you double-click your mouse on the word-processing document that you created within Microsoft Word, Windows will start Word and load your document for editing. Likewise, if you double-click your mouse on a file that contains an Excel spreadsheet, Windows will start Excel and load the spreadsheet. Likewise, if you double-click your mouse on a program file, Windows will run the corresponding program.

LAUNCHING A PROGRAM FROM THE TASKBAR

Each time you run a program, Windows places a button for the program onto the Taskbar. If you run two or more programs at the same time, you can use the Taskbar buttons to select the program within which you want to work. If you are using Windows 98, your Taskbar may contain program icons that are similar to those you will find on your Desktop. For example, Figure 9.7 shows the Quick Launch toolbar, from within which you can run the Internet Explorer Web browser or Outlook Express e-mail program.

Figure 9.7 *Windows 98 lets you run programs from toolbars on the Taskbar.*

Earlier in this lesson, you learned how to drag and drop a program from the Programs submenu onto the Windows Desktop. Using a drag-and-drop operation, you can (hold down your keyboard CTRL key) drag a program icon from the Programs submenu into a Taskbar toolbar. Later, you can click your mouse on the icon to run the program.

WINDOWS LETS YOU RUN MULTIPLE PROGRAMS AT THE SAME TIME

Within Windows, you can run two or more programs at the same time. When you run multiple programs at the same time, one of your programs is the current program that responds to your keyboard and mouse operations. You can determine the active program by examining each program's title bar. Windows will highlight the active program's title bar, while dimming the title bar of each inactive program. To switch from one program to another within Windows, simply click your mouse within the window of the program you desire. If the program's window is not visible, you can select the program by clicking your mouse on the program's Taskbar button. Within the Taskbar, Windows will highlight the active program by displaying the program's button, as depressed.

ENDING A PROGRAM

In this lesson, you learned several ways to start programs within Windows. As you might guess, Windows also provides several ways you can end a program. As you have done in this lesson, one of the easiest ways to end your program is to click your mouse on the window's Close button, the big X that appears to the right of the window's title bar. In addition, most programs will provide a File menu Exit option that you can use to end the program as well. In addition, most programs provide a special Control menu, as shown in Figure 9.8, within which you can select the Close option to end the program.

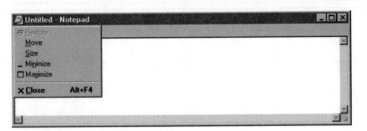

Figure 9.8 *Using a program's Control menu to end the program.*

In Lesson 14, "Storing Information within Files," you will learn that to store your work from one session with the computer to your next, you must store work within a file on disk. If you create or edit a document within a program, make sure you save your changes to a file on disk before you end the program.

WHAT YOU MUST KNOW

For your computer to be of use, you must use it to run programs, such as your word processor or Web browser. Each time your PC starts, your system runs the Windows operating system, a special program within which you will run your other programs. This lesson examined several ways you can start programs within Windows. In Lesson 10, "Programs (Software) Make Your PC Perform," you will learn more about programs, and how your PC actually runs them. Before you continue with Lesson 10, however, make sure that you have learned the following key concepts:

✓ Each time your PC starts, your system runs Windows, a special program within which you can run other programs.

✓ When you run a program, Windows will display the program's output within a framed rectangular region on your screen called a window.

✓ The easiest way to run a program within Windows is to select the program from a Start menu option.

✓ If a program is not installed on your system, you cannot run the program from the Windows Start menu. In such cases, you must run the program using either the Windows Explorer or the Run dialog box.

✓ To end a program within Windows, you can click your mouse on the window's Close button (the X that appears to the right of the window's title bar), or you can use the program's File menu or Control menu to close the program.

✓ If you have a program that you run on a regular basis, you may want to put a shortcut (an icon) to the program, upon which you can double-click your mouse to run the program.

✓ Windows provides a special program called the Explorer that you can use to manage your files and disk. Using the Explorer, you can display a list of the files on your disk. By double-clicking your mouse on a document file within the list, Windows will run the program that created the document and will load the document for editing. Likewise, if you double-click your mouse on a program file within the Explorer, Windows will run the corresponding program.

✓ If you run two or more programs at the same time, you can select the program within which you want to work by clicking your mouse on the program's window or by clicking your mouse on the program's Taskbar button.

Lesson 10

Programs (Software) Make Your PC Perform

In Lesson 6, "Understanding Your PC's Hardware," you learned that if you open your PC's system unit and look inside, you will find a myriad of circuit boards. Upon each circuit board you will find chips (integrated circuits) that house thousands (and, in some cases, millions) of electronic switches, called transistors. Despite the complexity of your PC's internal components, your PC's hardware is essentially powerless without software, the computer programs that direct the PC's operations. This lesson takes a close look at software and how it works. By the time you finish this lesson, you will understand the following key concepts:

- Within the PC, all operations occur based upon the presence or absence of electronic signals.

- Software, computer programs, coordinate the operations that the PC's hardware performs.

- A program is simply a list of instructions the PC's central processing unit (CPU) executes.

- Using a programming language, programmers define the instructions the CPU must perform to accomplish the program's task.

- Just as you can purchase word-processing or spreadsheet software, you can also purchase a programming language, such as Visual Basic, that you can use to create your own programs.

UNDERSTANDING THE "ONES AND ZEROS"

When users discuss computers and the operations that computers perform, you may occasionally hear expressions such as, "it's all ones and zeros" or "the process all comes down to ones and zeros." Within the computer, hardware devices such as the central processing unit (the CPU), memory, and even disks, work in terms of ones and zeros. Programmers refer to ones and zeros as binary digits (or *bits*). A binary digit is a number from the base two number system that can only have the value 0 or 1. In contrast, most people work in terms of the decimal (base ten) number system, whose digits can have a value from 0 through 9.

To understand why computers use the binary system, you must understand that everything that occurs within the PC happens because of the presence or absence of an electronic signal. In other words, if a wire contains a signal, a specific operation may occur. If the wire does not have a signal, the event will not occur. At any given time, the wire either has a signal or it does not—meaning, the wire is either on or off. To represent these two possible states, the PC uses the values 0 (for off) and 1 (for on). Assume, for example, that you design a new Beep processor—a chip that beeps when its wire contains a signal. When the wire is off (does not have a signal), your Beep processor is quiet. As shown in Figure 10.1, to generate a sound using your Beep processor, you would send a signal down the processor's wire. To stop the sound, you would simply stop the signal.

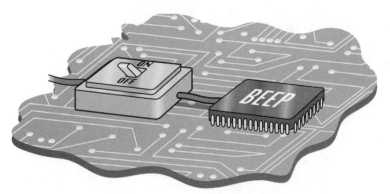

Figure 10.1 *Devices within a computer work based upon the presence or absence of electronic signals.*

Over time, you might enhance your Beep processor so that it supports four different sounds. To control these sounds, you could connect four different wires to the processor. Depending on which wire contains a signal, your processor would generate a different sound, as shown in Figure 10.2.

Figure 10.2 *Using four wires to control a chip's processing.*

Likewise, if you wanted your processor to generate eight different sounds, you could attach eight different wires to your chip. As you might guess, using the single-wire approach, you could quickly end up with many wires connected to your chip. If you wanted your chip to generate up to 64,000 sounds, you would need 64,000 wires—which would require a great deal of space. To reduce the number of wires they must attach to a chip, computer designers use logic within each chip that lets the chip determine the operation you desire based on the signals that come from combinations of wires. For example, assume your Beep chip generates four sounds. Rather than connecting four wires to your chip, you can connect two wires and include logic within your chip that determines which sound to play based on each wire's state. For example, if both wires are off, your chip would be quiet. If wire A is on and wire B is off, your chip might generate a soft noise. Likewise, if wire A is off and wire B is on, your chip might generate a loud noise. Finally, if both wire A and wire B are on, your chip might generate its loudest noise. Table 10.1 illustrates how your processor would use the signals on each wire to generate a sound.

Sound	Wire A	Wire B
No sound	No signal (0)	No signal (0)
Soft sound	Signal (1)	No signal (0)
Medium sound	No signal (0)	Signal (1)
Loud sound	Signal (1)	Signal (1)

Table 10.1 *Using two wires to represent four sounds.*

Next, assume that you want your Beep processor to generate eight different sounds. Rather than using eight wires, you can use three wires to represent the eight states, as shown in Table 10.2.

Sound	Wire A	Wire B	Wire C
1	0	0	0
2	0	0	1
3	0	1	0
4	0	1	1
5	1	0	0
6	1	0	1
7	1	1	0
8	1	1	1

Table 10.2 *Using three wires to represent eight states.*

In a similar way, to direct an Intel processor (your PC's CPU) to perform different operations, such as adding or subtracting numbers, the PC places different signals on the CPU's wires. During the 1940s and 50s, programmers would program computers by manually generating signals on specific wires within the computer by plugging cables into specific receptors. Today, programmers write software that controls which wires within the PC receive and do not receive such signals.

A PROGRAM IS A LIST OF INSTRUCTIONS THE CPU EXECUTES

Before a computer's electronic components can perform useful work, a program must tell the hardware the operation to perform. A program (software) is simply a list of instructions your PC's central processing unit (CPU) executes. Years ago (in the 1940s and 50s), programmers wrote their programs in terms of ones and zeros (in binary). To represent each operation the computer was to perform, the programmer used a specific set of ones and zeros. The sequence 0001, for example, might tell the CPU to add two numbers, whereas the sequence 0010 might tell the CPU to subtract the first number from the second.

For simple operations, such as programming a Beep processor, using the binary instructions was fairly easy. However, as the program's tasks increased in complexity, so too did the series of ones and zeros the programmer had to manage. Even a fairly simple program, that would generate a different sound every five seconds for a period of one hour, became very difficult to program using binary numbers. In fact, even a simple program's instructions could easily fill several printed pages with ones and zeros. If the programmer accidentally reversed two digits (put a one where a zero belonged), the program could fail. When a program did not work, the programmer had to dissect the series of ones and zeros, grouping them to form the program's specific instructions. Debugging (removing the errors from) programs in this way was a very time-consuming and often frustrating task.

PROGRAMMING LANGUAGES HELP PROGRAMMERS SPECIFY PROGRAM INSTRUCTIONS

To create a program, programmers must specify the instructions the CPU is to perform. To eliminate the programmer's error-prone need to work in terms of ones and zeros, programmers invented programming languages, such as Pascal, COBOL, FORTRAN, C/C++, Java, and BASIC. Using a programming language, programmers can express their program's instructions using statements that somewhat resemble English. (At least the programmers think the statements look English-like—users might disagree.)

Assume, for example, you want to create a program that displays a simple message on the computer screen, such as this book's name: "Rescued by Personal Computers." To create the program using ones and zeros, the programmer might easily fill a page of text. However, writing the same program using BASIC (the Beginner's All-purpose Symbolic Instruction Code), the programmer only needs to use one instruction, as shown here:

```
Print "Rescued by Personal Computers"
```

Likewise, using the C/C++ programming language, the program becomes:

```
void main(void)
{
   printf("Rescued by Personal Computers");
}
```

Using a programming language, programmers specify the program's instructions in a format they can write, read, and test much more easily than a combination of ones and zeros. Then, programmers use a special program called a compiler that converts the program statements into the ones and zeros the computer requires.

If you want to create your own programs, you must first select the language you want to use. Then, you must purchase the programming language from a computer store. You might start, for example, with the Visual Basic programming language. After you install the Visual Basic software on your PC, you can use Visual Basic to type in your program instructions. Then, you can direct Visual Basic to convert your instructions into the ones and zeros the computer understands. If your program works, you can then run the program or copy it to a disk that you give to another user. If your program has errors (bugs), you must determine the cause of the error, type in your correction, and then have Visual Basic generate a new series of ones and zeros that are based on your changes.

In Lesson 9, "Running Programs within Windows," you learned how to run programs using the Run dialog box, by selecting programs from the Start menu, and by double-clicking your mouse on a program file using the Windows Explorer. As it turns out, a program file (a file with the EXE extension) contains the ones and zeros that correspond to the instructions the PC is to perform, as shown in Figure 10.3.

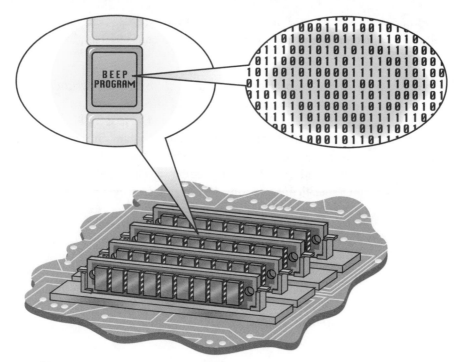

Figure 10.3 An executable program contains the ones and zeros a processor understands.

GAINING A BETTER PERSPECTIVE ON PROGRAMMING

As you have learned, programs consist of a list of instructions that tell the computer what to do. If the program displays a book's title on the screen, the program must specify the instructions the computer must perform to display the text. Likewise, if the program displays the current date and time on the screen, the program must contain instructions that tell the CPU to access the PC's built-in system clock to get the date and time, instructions that tell the CPU how to format the date and time for display and, finally, instructions that tell the CPU how to display the date and time.

Think, for a moment, about the program you most recently used. You may, for example, have used your Web browser to locate, display, and print information from a site on the World Wide Web. Before your program could perform such an operation, a programmer (or group of programmers) had to think about and create specific instructions for each operation.

Consider the Windows operating system that your PC runs each time your system starts. Windows consists of hundreds of small programs, each of which performs complex tasks. To create Windows, Microsoft employs several hundred programmers—each of whom may work on a specific piece of the Windows program code for years.

PROGRAMMING LANGUAGES USE A SPECIAL PROGRAM CALLED A COMPILER

When you purchase a programming language, such as Visual Basic, Java, or Visual C++, what you are really purchasing is a special program called the compiler. The compiler converts the programming statements that you will create using the programming language into the ones and zeros the PC understands. Each programming language requires its own compiler. Just as many different companies create and sell word processors, the same is true for programming languages. If you are interested in learning to program, turn to one of the Jamsa Press books that discusses a specific programming language, such as *Rescued by C++, Third Edition* or *Rescued by Visual Basic*.

WHAT YOU MUST KNOW

To perform useful work, your PC relies on software to tell its hardware which operations to perform. In short, software controls every task your PC performs. In this lesson, you learned that a program is simply a list of instructions the PC's central processing unit (CPU) performs. Although programmers write software using a programming language such as BASIC or C++, the computer only understands ones and zeros, which it uses to represent the presence or absence of electronic signals. In Lesson 11, you will learn how your PC uses its random-access memory (RAM). Before you continue with Lesson 11, however, make sure that you understand the following key concepts:

✓ Within the PC, computer chips use the binary values 1 and 0 to represent the presence or absence of an electronic signal.

✓ Software coordinates all of the operations a PC performs. Software is simply another name for computer programs.

✓ A program is simply a list of instructions the PC's central processing unit (CPU) performs to accomplish a specific task.

✓ Programmers use programming languages, such as Visual Basic, Java, or C++ to create programs.

✓ After a programmer defines the program statements using a programming language, the programmer runs a special program called a compiler that converts the program statements into the ones and zeros the PC understands.

Lesson 11

Understanding How Your PC Uses Its Memory (RAM)

Computers, like people, have both short-term and long-term memory. The computer's long-term memory consists of the files you store on disk. The computer's short-term memory, on the other hand, is your computer's fast electronic random-access memory, which users commonly refer to as RAM. The PC's short-term memory is so named because its contents are valid only while a specific program, such as Windows or Microsoft Word, is running. When you end a program, the PC discards the information the program has stored in RAM. Likewise, when you turn off your PC's power, your PC loses the contents of its short-term memory, which is why you store the information that you will need at a later time within a file on a disk (the computer's long-term memory). This lesson examines how your PC uses its random access (short-term) memory. By the time you finish this lesson, you will understand the following key concepts:

- Before your PC can run a program, the program must reside within your computer's random-access memory (RAM).

- When you run a program, Windows loads the program file from disk into RAM.

- If you run multiple programs at the same time, each program must reside in RAM.

- If you run more programs that Windows can fit in RAM at the same time, Windows uses a technique called virtual memory to combine space on your disk within space in RAM to give programs the illusion that your PC has more memory than it does.

- An easy and effective way to improve your system performance is to add more RAM.

PROGRAMS YOUR PC RUNS RESIDE WITHIN COMPUTER'S RANDOM-ACCESS MEMORY

As you learned in Lesson 9, "Programs (Software) Make Your PC Perform," a program consists of a list of instructions the PC's central processing unit (CPU) executes. When you install software on your computer (Lesson 20, "Installing New Software on Your PC," examines software installations in detail), the installation program places one or more executable program files (files with the EXE extension) that contain the program instructions onto your disk.

Before the CPU can run the corresponding program, the program's instructions must reside within the PC's random-access memory. Each time you run a program, Windows loads the program's instructions from the file on disk into RAM, as shown in Figure 11.1. When you end the program, Windows discards the program from RAM, releasing the memory for use by other programs.

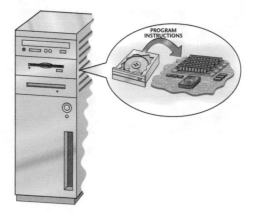

Figure 11.1 Before the CPU can execute a program, the program's instructions must reside within the PC's RAM.

WINDOWS SHARES YOUR PC'S RAM WITH TWO OR MORE PROGRAMS

As you have learned, each time you turn on your PC's power, your PC starts the Windows operating system. As it turns out, Windows, like all programs, must reside within your computer's memory before it can run. Later, when you use Windows to run other programs, Windows will load the second program file, its executable file, on disk into RAM, as shown in Figure 11.2.

Figure 11.2 Windows loads the programs you run from disk into RAM.

As you may know, within Windows, users can run two or more programs at the same time. For example, assume that you are running Microsoft Word, Excel, and the Internet Explorer at the same time, as shown in Figure 11.3.

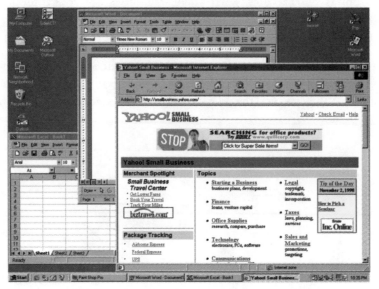

Figure 11.3 *Windows lets you run multiple programs at the same time.*

Within your PC's RAM, Windows will load each of the three programs into separate regions, as shown in Figure 11.4.

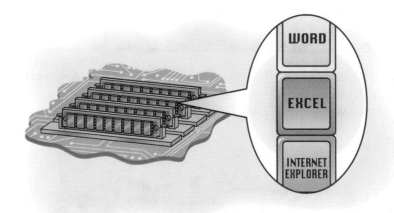

Figure 11.4 *When you run multiple programs, Windows loads each program into distinct areas in RAM.*

When RAM Becomes Full, Windows Swaps Programs between Memory and Disk

As you have just learned, when you run multiple programs within the Windows operating system, Windows loads each program into an unused region of RAM. Depending on the amount of RAM your PC contains, and the number and size of each program you run, Windows may eventually run out of locations in RAM into which it can load new programs.

When Windows cannot fit a program into memory, Windows frees up regions in RAM by moving your least recently used program from RAM into a special file on disk called the *swap file*. For example, assume, as shown in Figure 11.5, you are running Word, Excel, and the Internet Explorer and that you now want to run Microsoft Access, which Windows cannot fit into an unused area in RAM.

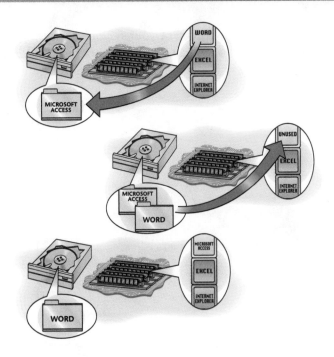

Figure 11.5 Windows cannot load Microsoft Access into an unused region in RAM.

To make room in RAM for Microsoft Access, Windows will move one program, in this case, Microsoft Word, into the swap file, as shown in Figure 11.6.

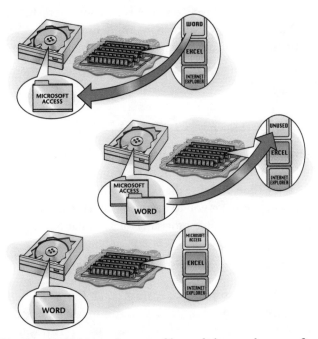

Figure 11.6 Windows moves files from RAM into the swap file on disk to make room for new programs.

Later, when you are ready to use Word (you click your mouse within Word's window on your screen), Windows must move Word back into memory. In this case, to make room for Word in RAM, Windows may move Excel into the swap file. Because the PC's hard disk is a mechanical device, the disk is much slower than the PC's high-speed electronic RAM. As a result, when Windows must swap programs between RAM and the swap file on disk, your system performance will slow down considerably. Often, you will be able to detect swapping by your system's sluggish performance and by the fact that you can hear the disk's activity. When you run a program, Windows not only loads the program's instructions into memory, but also the documents you open within the program, as shown in Figure 11.7.

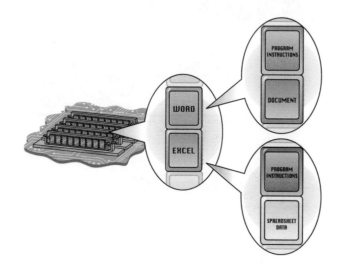

Figure 11.7 Windows loads a program's instructions and documents into RAM.

Understanding Virtual Memory

Before a program can run, the program must reside within your computer's RAM. If you run more programs than Windows can fit into RAM, Windows will exchange programs between RAM and a special swap file that resides on your disk. By combining space on your disk with space in your computer's electronic RAM, Windows creates the illusion that your PC has more physical memory than it actually does. Users refer to Windows use of memory as virtual memory.

Adding RAM Improves Your System's Performance

When users discuss ways to improve PC system performance, one of the first recommendations they will make is to add more RAM. By adding RAM, you reduce the amount of slow disk swapping that Windows must perform when you run multiple programs at the same time. Because the price of RAM has dropped significantly over the past year, adding RAM is an inexpensive and quick way for you to increase your system performance. At a minimum, your PC should contain 16MB of RAM. If you run multiple programs on a regular basis, you should install 32MB of RAM.

Understanding Cache Memory

As you have learned, before the CPU can run a program, the program's instructions and data must reside within the PC's random-access memory. When you shop for a PC, you may encounter the term cache memory. To improve the PC's performance, hardware designers often place a small but very fast memory between the CPU and RAM, as shown in Figure 11.8.

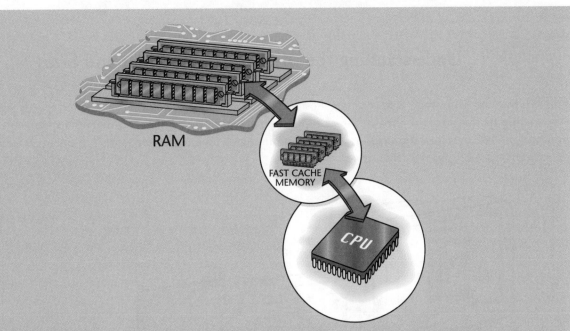

RAM

FAST CACHE MEMORY

CPU

Figure 11.8 Cache memory is a small, but very fast memory that resides between the CPU and RAM.

As the CPU executes the program, the PC loads frequently used instructions into the high-speed cache. Because the CPU can access the cache contents quickly, your system performance improves. Because the high-speed cache is expensive, most PCs have a minimal amount of cache, normally ranging from 128KB to 1MB. As you price PCs, you will find that PCs with more cache are proportionally more expensive than PCs that do not have cache.

WHAT YOU MUST KNOW

In this lesson, you learned how your PC uses its random-access memory, which users normally refer to as RAM. In Lesson 12, "Understanding the Myriad of PC Speeds and Sizes," you will learn how to tell the difference between bits and bytes as well as megabytes and megahertz. Before you continue with Lesson 12, however, make sure that you understand the following key concepts:

✓ When you run a program, Windows loads the program disk into your computer's random-access memory. Likewise, when you open a document from within the program, Windows must load the document from disk into RAM.

✓ Windows is a multitasking operating system that lets you run multiple programs at the same time. If you run multiple programs, Windows must load each program into memory.

✓ If Windows runs out of space in RAM, Windows will swap programs between RAM and a special file on your disk (a swap file), as needed.

✓ Because a disk drive is a mechanical device (a device with moving parts), the disk is much slower than your PC's electronic components. When Windows must swap programs between disk and RAM, your system performance will suffer. By adding RAM to your system, you may reduce the number of slow swap operations that Windows must perform and therefore increase your system performance.

Lesson 12

Understanding the Myriad of PC Speeds and Sizes

If there is one computer topic that confuses most PC users, it is the discussion of PC related speeds and sizes. If you browse computer magazines or the aisles of a computer store, you will encounter PCs that offer speeds such as a 466Mhz (pronounced 466 megahertz) processor, a 56Kbs (pronounced 56 kilobits per second) modem, as well as large MB (megabyte) and GB (gigabyte) disk drives.

This lesson examines common PC speeds and sizes. By the time you finish this lesson, you will understand the following key concepts:

- When discussing PC speeds and disk sizes, users often use the terms kilo, mega, and giga, such as kilobits, megahertz, and gigabytes. To better understand these terms, simply substitute the words, thousand, million, and billion.

- The PC represents the presence or absence of an electronic signal using a binary digit (a 1 or a 0). To manage information, the PC often groups binary digits (*bits*) into a sets of eight, forming a *byte*.

- Within the PC's central processing unit (CPU), there is a clock that coordinates the PC's operations. Each time the clock ticks, the CPU executes an instruction. The number of times the clock ticks per second determines the CPU's speed. A 266Mhz system, for example, has a clock that ticks 266 million times per second.

- If you surf the Web, your modem's speed can have a dramatic impact on the amount of time your system needs to download information, such as graphics from a Web site.

UNDERSTANDING KILO, MEGA, AND GIGA

Before you examine PC speeds and sizes, it is important that you understand three key prefixes: kilo, mega, and giga. In general, whenever you hear the term kilo, substitute the word thousand. Likewise, when you hear the term mega, substitute million, and for giga, substitute billion. In other words, if a user tells you that a file is "64 kilobytes" in size, you would know that the file contains roughly 64 thousand bytes. Likewise, a "300 megabyte" disk can store 300 million bytes of data. Whereas a "2 gigabyte" drive can store 2 billion bytes. Computer users often abbreviate the terms kilobyte, megabyte, and gigabyte using the letters KB, MB, and GB.

As it turns out, your use of the values one thousand, one million, and one billion for KB, MB, and GB are simply approximations. As shown in Table 12.1, 1KB is really 1,024 bytes. Likewise, 1MB is 1,048,576 bytes, and 1GB is 1,073,741,824 bytes. However, for most purposes, your approximations will meet your needs.

Term	Abbreviation	Approximation	Exact Value
Kilobytes	KB	One thousand	1,024
Megabytes	MB	One million	1,048,576
Gigabytes	GB	One billion	1,073,741,824

Table 12.1 Common abbreviations and values for kilobytes, megabytes, and gigabytes.

UNDERSTANDING BITS AND BYTES

Within a computer, all operations take place based on the presence or absence of electronic signals. At any given time, a wire either has an electric signal present (which the PC represents using the value 1) or the signal is absent (which the PC represents using the value 0). So, when computer users say that "the PC works in terms of ones and zeros," they are really saying that "the PC works in terms of electronic signals."

As you have learned, the PC uses the values 0 or 1 (which programmers refer to as binary digits because the digits can take on only two possible values, 0 or 1) to represent a signal's current state: off or on. The word *bit* is an abbreviation for binary digit. The value 0 is one binary digit, or one bit. The values 01 are two binary digits or two bits. Likewise, the values 010 correspond to three bits. To represent letters and numbers, the PC combines several bits of information into a set of eight bits, which users refer to as a *byte*, as shown in Figure 12.1.

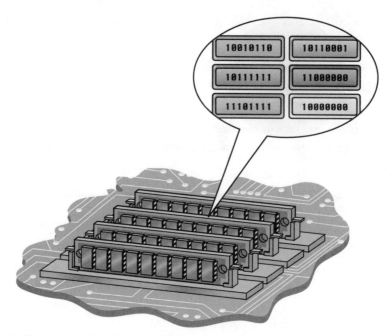

Figure 12.1 *To manage information, the PC groups binary digits into a collections of eight bits, called bytes.*

When you hear or read the term byte, you can often substitute the word *character*. For example, a 500-byte file, contains 500 characters of information. Likewise, a 1MB disk can store one-million characters of data. To help you better understand how much information today's disk drives can store, consider that one page of single-spaced text is about 4,000 characters (4,000 bytes or 4 kilobytes). A 2GB disk, for example, as shown in Figure 12.2, can store up to 500,000 pages of single-spaced text!

Figure 12.2 *A 2GB disk can store over 500,000 pages of single-spaced typed text.*

UNDERSTANDING YOUR PC'S PROCESSOR SPEED

When users discuss computers, they often describe the computer's processor (CPU) speed in terms of megahertz (which magazine ads abbreviate as MHz). One user's PC, for example, may have a 166MHz processor, while a user with a new system may have a 466MHz CPU. As you have learned, computer programs consist of lists of instructions the processor executes. The CPU's speed determines how fast the CPU can execute instructions.

Within the CPU, there is a small clock that coordinates the CPU's operations. In general, each time the clock ticks, the CPU performs a different operation. A 300MHz CPU, for example, can perform four times as many instructions per second as can a 75MHz processor.

As you learned in the previous section, computer users use the term mega as an abbreviation for one million. With respect to a processor's speed, the hertz in megahertz corresponds to clock ticks per second. The clock within a 75MHz CPU ticks 75-million times per second. Likewise, the clock within a 466MHz processor ticks 466-million times per second. With each clock tick, the CPU performs one instruction and, in some cases, two! (Some complex instructions, however, may require multiple clock ticks.)

UNDERSTANDING MODEM SPEEDS

In Lesson 53 "Surfing Your Way to Information on the World Wide Web," you will learn how to locate and download vast amounts of information from the Web using your PC modem. As you "surf" the Web for information, one of the biggest obstacles you will face is the speed at which your modem can send and receive information.

Users normally speak of modem speeds in terms of bits, as opposed to bytes, which makes a difference when you calculate how long it will take your modem to download a specific object. As you will recall, one byte consists of eight bits. A 28.8Kbs modem, for example, can send or receive around 28-thousand bits (binary digits) of data per second (or roughly 3,000 bytes). Likewise, a 56Kbs modem can send and receive about 56-thousand bits of data per second. To help you better appreciate the impact of modem speed on performance, Table 12.2 lists the times various modems will require to download 1MB file (about 8-million bits).

Modem	Time to Download a 1MB File
14.4Kbs	9 minutes 15 seconds
28.8Kbs	4 minutes 40 seconds
56Kbs	2 minutes 20 seconds

Table 12.2 *The time various modems require to download a 1MB file.*

Note: *Although it is not necessary a standard nomenclature, some users will use an uppercase B when referring to bytes (such as 1MB is one-megabyte) and a lowercase b when referring to bits (14.4Kbs is 14.4 kilobits).*

UNDERSTANDING DISK SPEEDS AND SIZES

To store information from one computer session to the next, you must place the information into a file that resides on a disk. As you have learned, disks differ by the amount of information they can store. Users express disk sizes in terms of bytes (characters) of information. Because today's disks can store so much information, users normally refer to a disk's storage capacity in terms of megabytes or gigabytes. A 1.44MB floppy disk, for example, can hold a little over 1.44-million bytes (because a megabyte is actually 1,048,576 bytes, a 1.44MB disk can actually store over 1,500,000 bytes). Likewise, a 500MB disk can store over 500-million bytes and a 2GB disk can store over 2-billion bytes.

In addition to understanding a disk's size, users should also pay attention to a disk's speed, which will control how fast the disk can access the information it stores and how fast the disk can record new information. Users typically refer to a disk's access speed, which may range from 8 to 20 milliseconds.

The smaller the disk's access speed, the faster the disk. In other words, a disk with a 10-millisecond access speed is faster than a disk whose access speed is 20-milliseconds. Depending on how often a user stores and retrieves information, the access speed of the user's disk can have a considerable impact on the user's overall system performance.

UNDERSTANDING MEMORY SIZE AND SPEEDS

Lesson 7, "Understanding How Your PC Uses Its Memory (RAM)," discusses how your PC uses memory to hold programs and data. When users discuss random-access memory, they normally talk in terms of megabytes. One system, for example, may have 32MB of RAM, while a second system uses 128MB. As a general rule, the more RAM your PC contains, the better your PC's performance. That is because Windows can store more programs and data (such as a word-processing document you are editing) in the computer's fast electronic memory, as opposed to continually moving items between RAM and your PC's slow mechanical disk drive.

Over the past few years, the price of memory has dropped dramatically. As a result, most newer PCs now ship with 32MB (or more) of RAM. In addition, most PCs can now hold several hundred megabytes of RAM. If you are concerned about speed, you can normally improve your system's performance by adding RAM.

UNDERSTANDING NETWORK SPEEDS

If your computer is connected to a local-area network and operations you perform across the network seem slow, you can ask your network administrator about your network speed. In the past, most networks used network cards and cables that supported 10-megabits per second (10Mbs). Today, most network cards support 100Mbs. In many offices, it is possible that some users have older network cards. If the operations you perform require large or frequent data transfers across the network, a faster network card may improve your performance.

WHAT YOU MUST KNOW

In this lesson, you learned several key terms that users often use to describe their processor's speed, a disk's storage capacity, or their modem type. In Lesson 13, "Storing Information on Disk," you will learn how your PC records and later reads the information that you store in files on your disk. Before you continue with Lesson 13, however, make sure that you understand the following key concepts:

✓ PC users often use the terms kilo, mega, and giga to describe PC speeds and sizes. In general, the term kilo stands for one thousand, mega for one million, and giga for one billion. A one megabyte file, for example, contains one million bytes.

✓ A PC's speed corresponds to the speed of its CPU's clock. Users use the term hertz to describe the number of times the CPU clock ticks per second. A 466 megahertz clock ticks 466 million times per second. Each time the clock ticks, the CPU executes an instruction.

✓ If you spend more than an hour a day connected to the Internet or the World Wide Web, you should upgrade your PC to the fastest modem type your phone lines will support.

Lesson 13

Storing Information on Disk

As you have learned, each time you shut down your PC, the contents of your PC's random-access memory (RAM) are lost. That is because RAM is electronic and requires a constant source of power if it is to retain its contents. Likewise, each time you end a program, Windows discards the information that the program had placed in RAM in order to make room for other programs. To keep information from one computer session to another, you must store the information within a file that your store on disk.

This lesson, examines disks and how they store information. By the time you finish this lesson, you will understand the following key concepts:

- Disks let you store information from one computer session to the next. To store information, a disk drive magnetizes the information onto the disk's surface.

- Always keep magnetic objects or electronic objects, such as your phone or TV set, that can generate a magnetic flux away from your disks.

- To record or read information, a disk drive uses an electronic device called a read/write head.

- Your PC's hard drive is a fast, non-removable drive that is normally capable of storing several hundred megabytes of data. Within your disk drive, the disk spins past the read/write head.

- To reduce your chances of a disk-head crash damaging your disk, never move your PC while it is powered on and your disks are spinning.

- A floppy drive lets you insert and remove low-capacity floppy disks, as your needs require. You should always store your floppy disks in a safe location when you are not using the disks.

- Each disk drive within your PC has a unique one-letter name. The A: drive normally corresponds to your floppy drive. Likewise, the C: drive is normally your hard disk. If you have a CD-ROM drive, the drive may be the D: or E: drive, depending on your system configuration. When you store a file on disk, you will use the drive name to select the drive onto you which you want to record your file's contents.

DISKS RECORD INFORMATION MAGNETICALLY

In Lesson 11, "Understanding How Your PC Uses Its Memory (RAM)," you learned each time you shut down your system, your PC loses the contents of its random-access memory (RAM). Because your PC's RAM stores information electronically, the PC's RAM must have a constant source of electricity. If you turn off your PC, its RAM loses its source of electricity and can no longer store information. If you had a PC that you never turned off, never restarted, that was guaranteed never to lose power due to a storm or blackout, and that had an unlimited amount of RAM, you would not need disks. However, because no such PC exists, users must store information on a disk.

Unlike your PC's RAM that stores information electronically, disks record information magnetically, much like you might record a television program on a VHS tape or a song on a cassette tape. Within a disk drive, there is a small device (called a read/write head) that can record (magnetize) or read information on the disk's surface. Within the drive, a disk spins rapidly past the read/write head each as shown in Figure 13.1. A floppy disk, for example, may spin past the read/write head at 300 revolutions per minute (RPMs), whereas a hard drive may spin at 3600 to 10,000RPMs.

Figure 13.1 *The disk drive contains a read/write head that records and reads information to and from a disk's magnetic surface.*

To better understand how the drive records information on your disk, examine a floppy disk. In the middle of the back of the floppy disk, you will find a small metal spindle opening. When you insert a floppy disk into a drive, the drive uses this spindle opening to spin the disk. The drive then opens the disk's metal shutter, as shown in Figure 13.2, to access the disk's surface. You can gently slide the shutter open to see the disk media. Do not, however, touch the surface—doing so may damage the disk and the information it contains.

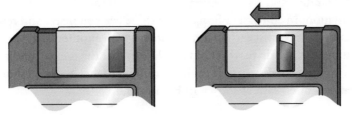

Figure 13.2 *The disk drive slides the metal shutter to reveal a floppy disk's media.*

Because disks magnetize information to their surface, the information does not require constant electricity, as does RAM. You must, however, keep your disks away from devices such as your phone, television, or even static electricity, that may result in a magnetic flux that changes the information recorded on the disk.

Note: *So that it can record and read information from the disk's surface the disk drive's read/write head must float very close to the disk's surface. As you have learned, within the drive, the disk spins past the head several thousand times per minute. If you bump your PC hard enough, you may cause the read/write head to touch the disk's surface (which users refer to as disk-head crash). Should your disk head touch your disk's surface, it will quite likely scrap your disk's surface destroying your disk and the information it contains. To reduce your chance of a disk-head crash, never move your PC while it is powered on and your disk is spinning within the drive.*

Do X-ray Machines Pose a Risk to Information Recorded on Disk?

Every day hundreds of thousands of travelers put their PCs through X-ray machines at airports and other facilities. The X-rays that the machine uses to examine your packages will not damage the information recorded on your disk drive. However, the motor that is driving the belt that moves packages through the machine may emit a magnetic flux that is strong enough to damage your disks. If you have key files on your disk that you have not yet backed up (Lesson 36, "Protecting Your Data Using Backup Files," discusses backups in detail), you can ask that the security personnel hand check your bag. In most cases, the security personnel may grumble that the X-ray machine won't harm your PC, and will then agree to hand check your bag.

Computers Use Removable Floppy Disks and High-Capacity Hard Disks

Within your PC, you will normally have at least two disk drives: a high-capacity fast hard drive and a floppy-disk drive that lets you insert and remove disks. Normally, you will not see your PC's hard drive, which resides within your PC's system unit. Instead, you may simply see the drive's front panel, as shown in Figure 13.3, that contains a small LED light that tells you when the disk is reading or recording information.

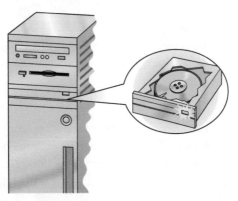

Figure 13.3 *Your PC's hard drive resides within your system unit.*

As you learned in Lesson 12, "Understanding the Myriad of PC Speeds and Sizes," most hard disks can store several hundred megabytes of information. In contrast, a floppy-disk drive lets you insert and remove small floppy disks, as your needs require. If, for example, you must exchange a document with another user, you can store the document on a floppy disk. To insert a floppy disk in a drive, you hold the disk so that the metal spindle holder faces down and the end of the disk with the shutter enters the disk first. If the disk contains a label, the label should be facing up and should be at the end of the disk that you insert last, as shown in Figure 13.4.

Figure 13.4 *Insert floppy disks into a drive with the shutter-end first and the disk's spindle holder facing down.*

To remove a floppy disk from a drive, you press the drive's eject button, which you will find near the drive opening, as shown in Figure 13.5. Never eject a drive while the disk's activation light is lit. The activation light tells you that your drive is reading from or writing to the disk. If you remove a floppy disk while your drive is recording information on the disk's surface, you may damage the disk and lose the information it contains.

Figure 13.5 *To remove a floppy disk from a disk drive, press the drive's eject button.*

LABELING YOUR FLOPPY DISK

If you use floppy disks to exchange files with other users, or keep a backup copy of a key file, your collection of floppy disks will grow quite quickly. To help you locate files that you store on your floppy disk, write down specifics about your files on a disk label that you attach to the floppy, as shown in Figure 13.6. When you create a disk label, be specific—the information you place on the label may help you locate a file quickly at a later time.

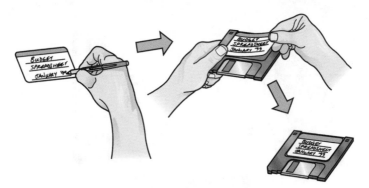

Figure 13.6 *Assign meaningful labels to your floppy disks that describe the disk's contents.*

STORE YOUR FLOPPY DISKS IN A SAFE LOCATION

As you have learned, floppy disks store information by magnetizing the data onto their surface. When you are not using your floppy disks, you should store them in a safe location, such as a floppy-disk storage container, as shown in Figure 13.7. As it turns out, many devices, such as your telephone or TV set, have the ability to generate a magnetic signal that can change the information stored on a disk. You must, therefore, keep your disks away from such devices. Many users have a bad habit of leaving floppy disks on their desk, close to their phone. Each time the phone rings, it may emit a magnetic flux capable of damaging the disk. Also, make sure that your disks do not get too hot or too cold—which might cause the disk surface to expand or contract—which, in turn, might change the information magnetized on the surface.

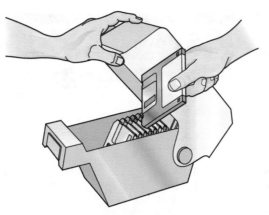

Figure 13.7 *Store your floppy disks in a safe location when your disks are not in use.*

WRITE-PROTECT YOUR FLOPPY DISKS WHOSE CONTENTS YOU DO NOT WANT TO CHANGE

Users often use floppy disks to exchange files with other users. If you are giving another user a floppy disk that contains key files, you may want to write-protect the floppy disk so that the user cannot inadvertently overwrite or delete the file's contents. The user can, however, copy the files from a write-protected floppy disk onto his or her system and then change the file's contents.

If you examine a floppy disk, you will find a small plastic slider in the top right corner of the disk. To store information on the disk, the slider must be down, closing the write-protect opening. As shown in Figure 13.8, to write-protect a floppy disk, you move the slider up, exposing the write-protect opening. When you insert a floppy disk into a disk drive, the drive will shine a light at the write-protect opening. If the light shines through the opening, the drive knows the disk is write-protected and the drive will not record information to or delete information from the disk.

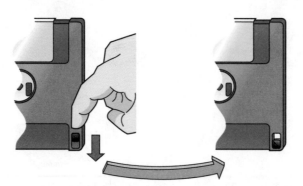

Figure 13.8 *To write-protect a floppy disk, move the write-protect slider up to expose the write-protect opening.*

UNDERSTANDING DISK DRIVE NAMES

To store and retrieve information to and from files on your disk, you use your disk drive's name to tell your software which disk you want to use. Each disk drive within your PC has a unique one-letter drive name. To specify the drive name within your programs, you type the drive letter followed by a colon (:). Your floppy disk drive, for example, is the A: drive. Likewise, your hard disk is the C: drive. If you have a second hard disk, it would be the D: drive. Your CD-ROM drive, for example, might then be the E: drive. In Lesson 16, "Using theWindows Explorer to Manage Your Files and Disks," you will use a special program called the Explorer to copy and move files from one disk to another and to delete files from your disk. The Explorer will display an icon for each of your disk drives, as shown in Figure 13.9.

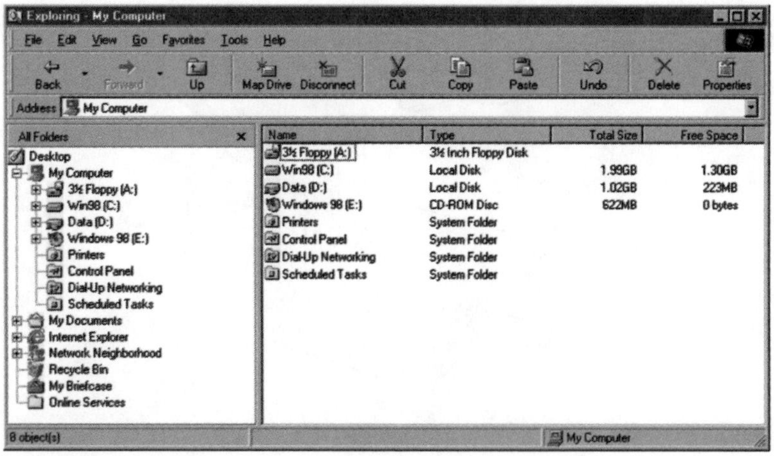

Figure 13.9 *The Explorer displays an icon for each of your PC's disk drives.*

Within the Explorer, you can click your mouse on the disk icon to display a list of the files and folders the disk contains.

UNDERSTANDING HOW DISKS STORE INFORMATION

As you have learned, to store information, your disk drive records data onto the disk's magnetic surface. To be able to store and retrieve information, your disk drive must record the information to specific locations on your disk, called *sectors*. To store a file's contents, you disk drive will record the file's contents within one or more 512-byte sectors (some disk drives use larger sectors). A disk sector, therefore, is simply a storage location on your disk.

To better understand how your disk stores information, picture your disk as containing thousands of circular tracks, as shown in Figure 13.10.

Figure 13.10 *A hard disk may contains thousands of storage tracks.*

Your disk drive divides each track into sectors, as shown in Figure 13.11. When the drive stores information, such as a file, the drive will record the information within one or more sectors.

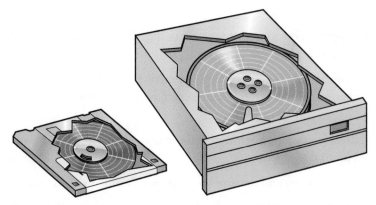

Figure 13.11 *A drive divides each storage track into small disk sectors, within which the drive will record data onto your disk's surface.*

When you store files on your disk, Windows uses a special table on your disk, called the file-allocation table, to keep track of each file's sectors.

UNDERSTANDING IDE AND SCSI DRIVES

If you shop for a hard disk, your salesperson may ask you if you want an IDE or SCSI drive. IDE is an abbreviation for Integrated Drive Electronics, which is a fancy way of saying the disk drive provides all the electronics it needs to record and retrieve information (as opposed to having to using a disk-controller card or chip within the PC to control the drive's operation). Normally, you will connect an IDE drive to your PC's motherboard (the PC's primary circuit board that houses your system's CPU and RAM). Depending on your motherboard, the number of IDE connectors you have may vary.

In contrast, SCSI is an abbreviation for Small Computer Systems Interface. Lesson 31, "Connecting Devices to Your Personal Computer," examines SCSI-based devices in detail. To connect a SCSI device to your PC, you must have a SCSI adapter card. For more information on adding or replacing a disk drive, turn to the book *Rescued by Upgrading Your PC, Third Edition*, Jamsa Press, 1999.

PREPARING A DISK FOR USE

When you purchase a hard disk or floppy disks, you may need to first *format* the disks for use under Windows before you can use the disks to store files. Installing and formatting a hard disk is a challenging process—one most users should leave to a hardware technician. As you will learn in Lesson 16, you can format floppy disks within the Windows Explorer. When you format a disk, Windows will examine each of the disk's sectors to make sure the sector is capable of storing information. If a sector is damaged, Windows will mark the sector as unusable within a special table, called the file-allocation table (or FAT), that Windows stores on disk. Each time you store a file on a disk, Windows uses the file-allocation table to determine which sectors are available for use. Likewise, when you use a file's contents, Windows use the file-allocation table to determine which sectors on the disk contain the file's data. If you are shopping for floppy disks, you can save time and effort by purchasing disks that are already formatted for use on an IBM PC.

WHAT YOU MUST KNOW

As you use your PC, you will store information within files on your disk. This lesson introduced disks and how they store information. In Lesson 14, "Storing Information within Files," you will learn how you store and retrieve information using files. Before you continue with Lesson 14, however, make sure you have learned the following key concepts:

- ✓ To store information from one computer session to the next, you must record the information within files that you store on a disk.

- ✓ Disk drives store information onto a disk by magnetizing the information to the disk's surface. Always keep magnetic objects or electronic objects that can generate a magnetic flux away from your disks.

- ✓ Your PC's hard drive is a fast, non-removable drive that is normally capable of storing several hundred megabytes of data.

- ✓ A floppy drive lets you insert and remove low-capacity floppy disks, as your needs required.

- ✓ Each disk drive within your PC has a unique one-letter name. The A: drive normally corresponds to your floppy drive. Likewise, the C: drive is normally your hard disk. If you have a CD-ROM drive, the drive may be the D: or E: drive, depending on your system configuration. When you store a file on disk, you will use the drive name to select the drive onto you which you want to record your file's contents.

- ✓ To reduce your chance of a disk-head crash damaging your disk, never move your PC while it is powered on and your disk heads are spinning.

Lesson 14

Storing Information within Files

In Lesson 13, "Storing Information on Disk," you learned that to store information, such as a word-processing document, from one session at your PC to the next, you must store the information within a file on your disk. In general, almost every program you run will require that you store information within a file on disk. You may, for example, store a spreadsheet document that contains your budget in a file, or you might store a database that contains your customer information within a file. Because file operations are so common, most programs will provide a File menu, whose options will let you create, save, and open files on your disk.

REPORT.DOC

BUDGET.XLS

JOE	555-6590
MARY	555-3343
JULIE	555-1919
BECKY	555-7657
COLIN	555-5452
FRANK	555-0034

PHONE LIST.MDR

This lesson introduces you to files and file operations. By the time you finish this lesson, you will understand the following key concepts:

- Each document you store on your disk will reside within its own file.

- When you store a document within a file, you must assign a name, that is not in use, to your file. Your filename should meaningfully describe the file's contents.

- Filenames consist of two parts, a basename that you specify, and a three-character extension that your application program assigns that describes your file's contents.

- Windows lets you use up to 255 characters (including spaces) within a filename.

- To save your document's contents and to assign a name to your document, you will use the File menu Save As option. After you assign your document a name, you can save changes you make to your document using the File menu Save option.

- To open a document that resides within a file on disk, you use your application's File menu Open option.

UNDERSTANDING HOW FILES RELATE TO YOUR DOCUMENTS

In Lesson 13, you learned that your disk drive records information on your disk by magnetizing the information within disk-storage locations called sectors. When you store a document, your program will place the document's contents into a file that your disk, in turn, will store within one or more sectors on your disk. For each file you create, Windows will keep track of which sectors your disk drive uses to store the file.

Eventually, depending on the size and number of files that you create, you may fill up your disk's available sectors. When your disk does not have enough space to store the information you are trying to save, Windows will display a dialog box telling you that your disk has insufficient space to store a file. At that time, you must move or delete files from your disk to free up disk space. In this lesson, you will learn how to delete files whose contents you no longer require.

NAMING YOUR FILES

As briefly discussed, you will store each document you create within its own file on disk. When you store a document within a file, you must assign a name to the file. When you choose a name for your file, choose a name that meaningfully describes the file's contents. Ideally, if another user were to see only your filename, the reader should be able to describe the file's contents. The following list, for example, illustrates some meaningful filenames:

1999 Sales and Marketing Budget.xls

Lesson 14 Rescued by Personal Computers.doc

Presentation to the Board of Directors.ppt

Customer Database.mdb

Personal Address Book.doc

As you can see, by simply reading these filenames, you have a reasonably good idea of the information each file contains.

Within Windows (and your Windows-based programs), your filenames can have up to 255 characters, which can include numbers, letters, and spaces. You cannot, however, use the following characters within your Windows-based filenames:

\ / | > < : * ? "

If you examine the previous filename list, you will find that each filename consists of two parts, which you separate using a period. The first part of the filename, the part that precedes the period, is the *basename*. The second part of the filename, the part that follows the period, is the *extension*. Normally, file extensions are three-characters long.

A file's extension tells you what type of information the file contains. A file with the *DOC* extension, for example, contains a word-processing document, that was probably created with Microsoft Word. A file with the *XLS* extension contains an Excel spreadsheet. Likewise, a file with the *PPT* extension contains a PowerPoint document. Normally, when you save a document within an application, you only need to specify the basename. The application, in turn, will assign the file's three-character extension. Table 14.1 defines several commonly used file extensions.

Extension	File Contents
AVI	A video file
BMP	Bitmap graphics file, such as a scanned photo
EXE	An executable program file
GIF	A low-resolution graphics image, which are common on the Web
HTML	A Web-based document that describes a Web page's content
ICO	An icon image
JPG	A high-resolution photo image
TXT	A text file
WAV	An audio file

Table 14.1 Several common file extensions.

SAVING A DOCUMENT'S CONTENTS TO A FILE ON DISK

Within most programs, you will save your current document's contents by selecting the File menu Save As option. Your program, in turn, will display the Save As dialog box, as shown in Figure 14.1.

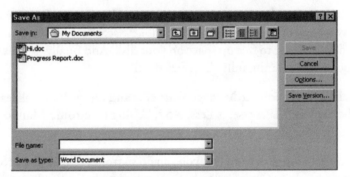

Figure 14.1 Saving a document to a file on disk using the Save As dialog box.

Within the Save As dialog box, type the filename you desire and then click your mouse on the Save button. Your program, in turn, will create a file on your disk, within which it will store your document's contents. Each time you make changes to your document's contents that you want to keep, you must save the changes to your document's file on disk. After you have assigned a name to your document, you will later save your document's contents by selecting the File menu Save option. The Save option differs from Save As in that when you select the Save option, your program will save your document's contents, without asking you to specify a filename. In other words, the first time you save your document to a file on disk, you will select the Save As option, so you can assign a name to document. After that, each time you save your file, you use the Save option.

Note: *In Lesson 15, you will learn how to better organize your documents by storing your files within specific folders on your disk. As you will learn in Lesson 15, you will use the Save As dialog box to specify the folder within which you want to store your file.*

OPENING AN EXISTING FILE

As you have learned, by storing your documents within a file, you can access the document's contents at a later time. Within most Windows-based programs, you will open your documents by selecting the File menu Open option. Your program, in turn, will display the Open dialog box, as shown in Figure 14.2. Within the Open dialog box, simply click your mouse on the file that you desire and then click your mouse on the Open button.

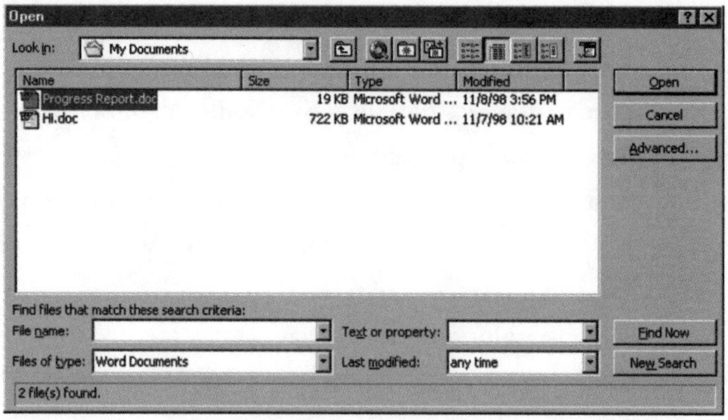

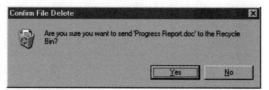

Figure 14.2 Opening a document's contents using the Open dialog box.

Note: *In Lesson 15, you will learn how to better organize your documents by storing your files within specific folders on your disk. As you will also learn in Lesson 15, when you store documents within specific folders, you must use the Open dialog box to specify the folder that contains the file you want to open.*

PERFORMING COMMON FILE OPERATIONS

As you have learned, you will store each document that you create within its own file on your disk. At work, there will be times when you must give a copy of a file to another user. Likewise, there will be times when you no longer need a file's contents, so you can delete the file to free up space on your disk. And finally, there will be times when the name that you assigned to a file no longer meaningfully describes the file's contents.

In Lesson 16, "Using the Windows Explorer to Manage Your Files and Disks," you will learn how to copy, delete, and rename files from within the Explorer. Likewise, is Lesson 52, "Using Electronic-Mail to Exchange Files with Other Users," you will learn how to send a file to another user within an e-mail message.

For now, however, if you must rename or delete a file, you can do so from within either a Save As or Open dialog box. As you have learned, within a Save As or Open dialog box, Windows will display the names of files that reside in the current folder. To delete a file, you click your mouse on the filename to select the file. Next, press your keyboard's DEL key. Windows, in turn, will display the Confirm File Delete dialog box, as shown in Figure 14.3, asking you to verify that you really want to delete the file. Within the dialog box, click your mouse on the Yes button. (Should you inadvertently delete the wrong file, you can undelete the file from the Recycle Bin, as discussed in Lesson 18, "Recovering a Deleted File from the Windows Recycle Bin.")

Figure 14.3 The Confirm File Delete dialog box.

To rename a file within a Save As or Open dialog box, right-click your mouse on the filename. Windows, in turn, will display a pop-up menu, as shown in Figure 14.4. Within the pop-up menu, click your mouse on the Rename option. Windows, in turn, will highlight the filename within an editing box. Using your keyboard arrow and BACKSPACE keys, edit the filename as you desire.

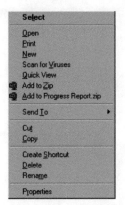

Figure 14.4 *Windows will display a pop-up menu when you right-click your mouse on a filename.*

An easy way to copy a document file onto a floppy disk that you can give to another user is simply to open the file within the application program you used to create the document, such as Word or Excel, and then use the File menu Save As option to save a copy of the file's contents to the floppy disk. To save a file to a floppy disk in drive A, for example, you would simply precede the filename that your program displays within the Save As dialog box with A:, as shown in Figure 14.5.

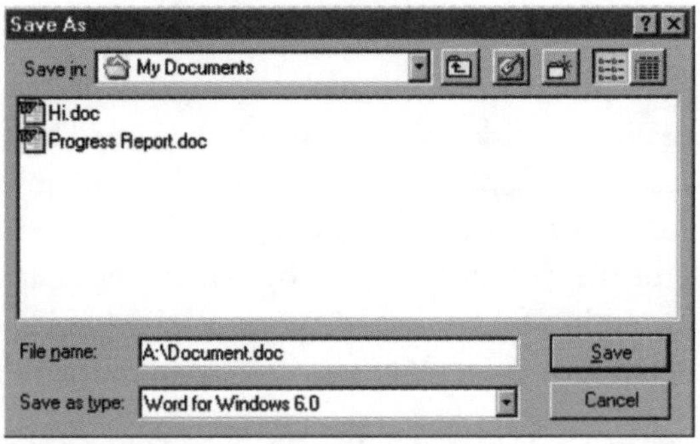

Figure 14.5 *Saving a copy a of document to a file on a floppy disk.*

UNDERSTANDING OTHER FILE ATTRIBUTES

As you have learned, each file on your disk must have a unique name. In addition to the filename, Windows also keeps track of the date and time you last changed your file's contents, the file's size, as well as several attribute values that control operations such as whether not you can change a file's contents. Because Windows uses your system's date and time to "time stamp" your most recent change to a file, you should keep your system date and time accurate. Over time, your disk may contain thousands of files. To locate a file that you created several months ago, you may have to use the file's date-and-time stamp.

Before you try to copy a file to a floppy disk, you may want to check whether or not the file will fit on the disk. In Lesson 16, you will learn how to use Windows Explorer to display the amount of free space a disk contains, as well as a file's size. To display a file's attributes, right-click your mouse on the file's name from within a file list (such as the file list Windows displays within the Save As and Open dialog boxes). Windows, in turn, will display a pop-up menu. Within the pop-up menu, select the Properties option. Windows will display a Properties dialog box, similar to that shown in Figure 14.6, within which you can view the file's size, date-and-time stamps, and file attributes.

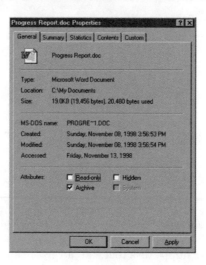

Figure 14.6 *Viewing a file's properties.*

For information on file attributes, such as the read-only and hidden attributes, turn to the book *1001 Windows 98 Tips*, Jamsa Press, 1998.

WHAT YOU MUST KNOW

When you use programs such as a word processor or spreadsheet program to create documents, you must then store the document's contents within a file on your disk. In this lesson, you learned how to use a program's File menu Save As and Save options to save your document to a file on disk. You also learned how to use the File menu Open option to open a document that resides within a file on disk. In Lesson 15, "Using Electronic Folders to Organize Your Files," you will learn how to better manage the files you store on disk by placing the related files into a file folder. You might, for example, place your business files within a folder named Work, your school files in a folder named School, and so on. Before you continue with Lesson 15, however, make sure you have learned the following key concepts:

- ✓ When you store a document on disk, you will store the document within its own file.

- ✓ When you store a document within a file on disk, you must assign a unique filename to your document. Within Windows, you can use up to 255 characters in your filenames, including space characters.

- ✓ When you assign a name to a file, choose a meaningful name that accurately describes the file's contents.

- ✓ Filenames consist of two parts, a basename that you specify, and a three-character extension that your application program assigns that describes your file's contents.

- ✓ To save your document's contents and to assign a name to your document, you will use the File menu Save As option. After you assign your document a name, you can save changes you make to your document using the File menu Save option.

- ✓ To open a document that resides within a file on disk, you use your application's File menu Open option.

- ✓ Each time you create or save a file, Windows records the current date and time to a file attribute. To keep your file's date-and-time stamps accurate, make sure your system date and time is correct.

Lesson 15

Using Electronic Folders to Organize Your Files

In Lesson 14, "Storing Information within Files," you learned that when you save a document's contents, you must store the document within a file on your disk. As you learned, when you store a document within a file, you should assign a meaningful name to the file that accurately describes the file's contents, which will help you locate the file on your disk at a later time. As you might guess, as the number of files you store on your disk increases, so too will your difficulty in finding a specific file.

In this lesson, you will learn how to create electronic file folders on your disk, within which you can group related files. You might, for example, create a folder named *Work* that contains your business documents. Likewise, you might create a folder named *Home* that contains your personal documents. If you are taking classes, you might create a folder named *School*, within which you place your class-related documents. This lesson examines the steps you must perform to create file folders on your disk and then to store files within the folders. By the time you finish this lesson, you will understand the following key concepts:

- To organize the files you store on your disk, you should create file folders, within which you group related files.

- To create a folder on your disk, click your mouse on the Create New Folder button that appears on the Save As dialog box toolbar. Windows will create a new folder within the current folder to which you can assign the folder name you desire.

- To save a document to a file on your disk, you use the Save As dialog box. Within the Save As dialog box, you can select the folder within which you want to store the file.

- Although your disk may contain many folders, Windows defines one folder as the current folder. Within the Save As and Open dialog boxes, Windows will display the current folder's list of files and subfolders.

- Within the current Save As and Open dialog boxes, you can change the current folder by double-clicking your mouse on a folder icon or by using the Up One Level toolbar button to move up one folder.

- To open a file that resides within a specific folder, you must open the folder from within the Open dialog box. Windows, in turn, will list the files and subfolders the folder contains.

- When you no longer need the files that a folder contains, you can delete the folder by clicking your mouse on the folder's icon and then pressing the DEL key. When you delete a folder, Windows, in one step, will delete all the files and subfolders the folder contains.

UNDERSTANDING THE CURRENT FOLDER

After you organize your files by creating folders on your disk, you may end up with dozens (if not more) of folders. Each folder, in turn, may contain files and subfolders. Although your disk may contain many folders, Windows only uses one folder as your *current folder*—the folder whose contents Windows will display within the Save As or Open dialog box.

Within the Save As or Open dialog box, you can select the folder you desire as the current folder. Windows, in turn, will display the folder's contents within the dialog box. If you use the Save As dialog box to create a file on your disk, Windows will create the file within the current folder. So, if you can't find a file that you previously saved on your disk, you probably stored the file in a folder that is different from your current folder. To locate the file, you must first open the folder within which you stored the file.

UNDERSTANDING THE MY DOCUMENTS FOLDER

When you install Windows on your system, the installation program creates a folder on your disk named *My Documents* within which you can store the documents you create. By default, many programs, when you select the File menu Save As option, will assume that you want to store your documents within the *My Documents* folder. Likewise, when you select the File menu Open option, the programs will assume you want to open a file that resides within the *My Documents* folder.

The *My Documents* folder is a good place for you to store your document files. However, to better organize your files, you should create subfolders within the *My Documents* folder. You might start by creating subfolders named *Work* and *Home*. Then, as you create files on your disk, you can store the files in the appropriate subfolder.

CREATING YOUR OWN FILE FOLDERS

To create a folder on your disk, you can use the Windows Explorer, discussed in Lesson 16, or you can create the folder from within the Save As dialog box. If you examine the Save As dialog box's toolbar, you will find a button whose icon of a file folder contains a star-like object near the folder's upper-right corner. As shown in Figure 15.1, this button is the Create New Folder button.

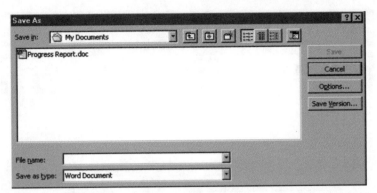

Figure 15.1 *The Save As dialog box provides a Create New Folder button you can use to create a subfolder.*

When you create a new folder, you first want to be in the folder within which you want to create a subfolder. For example, if you want to create a folder named Work within the *My Documents* folder, you must first select the *My Documents* folder as the current folder, and then use the Create New Folder button to create your folder. When you click your mouse on the Create New Folder button, Windows will create a new folder within the current folder, assigning the folder the name, *New Folder*. As shown in Figure 15.2, Windows will highlight the folder's name using reverse video, letting you type in the name you desire. In this case, you would type the folder name *Work*, and press ENTER. When you create a folder, make sure you assign a meaningful name to the folder that describes the folder's contents.

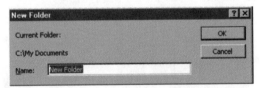

Figure 15.2 *Windows lets you assign a name to your newly created folder.*

Using the Save As dialog box's Create New Folder button, you can create folders within any folder on your disk.

STORING YOUR DOCUMENTS WITHIN A SPECIFIC FOLDER

In the previous section, you learned how to create your own folders. After you create a folder, you will want to store some of the documents that you create within that folder. To store a document within a specific folder, you must first open the folder (making it the current folder). If, for example, you just created a folder named *Work* within the *My Documents* folder, you can double-click your mouse on the *Work* folder to select it as the current folder. After you select the folder you desire, you simply save your document's contents to a file within the folder.

OPENING DOCUMENTS THAT RESIDE WITHIN A SPECIFIC FOLDER

In the previous section, you learned how to use the Save As dialog box to save your files within a specific file folder on your disk. When you later want to open the file's contents, you will select your program's File menu Open option, as discussed in Lesson 14. Your program, in turn, will display the Open dialog box, as shown in Figure 15.3.

Within the Open dialog box, Windows will display the list of files and subfolders that reside within the current folder. If you see the file you want to open within the current file list, simply double-click your mouse on the file to open it. If, instead, you see the folder icon for the folder within which the file resides, double-click your mouse on the folder icon. Windows, in turn, will make the folder the current folder and will display the folder's contents within the Open dialog box. If, however, you do not see the file or its folder within the Open dialog box, you may need to move to a different level within your folder list, as discussed next.

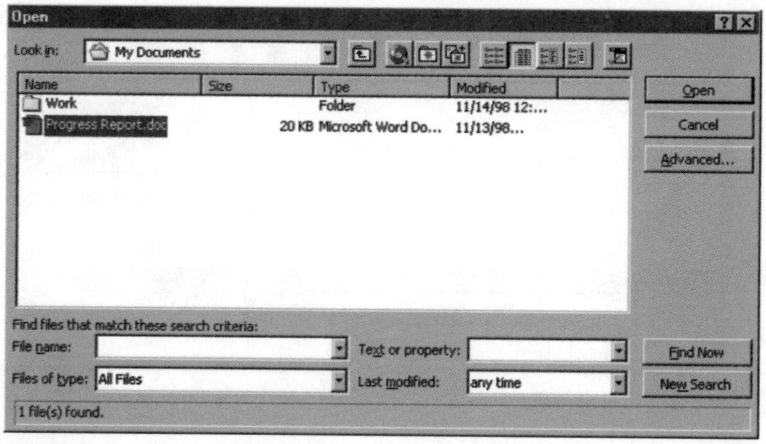

Figure 15.3 *The Open dialog box.*

MOVING UP ONE FOLDER LEVEL

When you use subfolders to organize the files a folder contains, you may end up with several levels of file folders. For example, assume that, within the *My Documents* folder, you are using a folder named *Home* to store your personal documents. Within the Home folder, you create folders named *Bills*, *Investments*, *Kids*, and *To Do*. To further organize each folder, you create the additional subfolders, as shown in Figure 15.4.

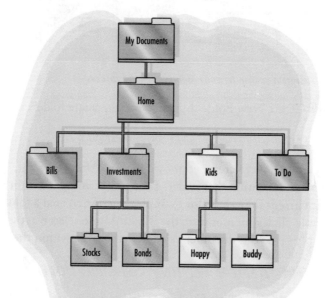

Figure 15.4 *Organizing your files using multiple levels of folders.*

Assume that your current folder is the *Bonds* subfolder and that you want to open a document within the *Kids* folder. Within the Open dialog box, you have two ways of moving to the *Kids* folder. First, you can move back up the folder list, one folder at a time, back to the *Home* folder. In this case, you would move first back up to the *Investment* folder and then up to the *Home* folder. If you examine the Open dialog box toolbar, you will see an folder icon that contains an up-pointing arrow, as shown in Figure 15.5.

Figure 15.5 *The icon with the up-pointing arrow directs Windows to move up one folder level.*

In this case, if you click your mouse on the Up One Level button, Windows will move you first into the *Investment* folder. If you click the Up One Level button again, Windows will move you into the *Home* folder. From within the *Home* folder, you can double-click your mouse on the *Kids* folder to display the files the folder contains. As you use file folders on your disk, you will make extensive use of the Up One Level folder to move from a subfolder back into a parent folder.

In addition to moving up your folder list one level at a time and moving back down the folder list to select the *Kids* folder, you can click open the Open dialog box's Look in pull-down list, as shown in Figure 15.6. Within the Look in pull-down list, you can click your mouse on the *Home* folder and then click your mouse on the *Kids* folder. Depending on your depth within a subfolder list, you may find it faster to use the Look in pull-down list to move directly to a folder than to move up the folder list one folder at a time.

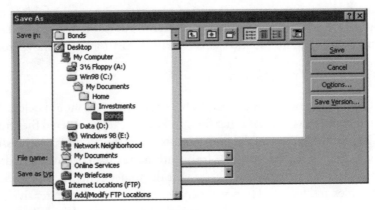

Figure 15.6 *Using the Look in pull-down list to select a folder.*

Understanding the Desktop Folder

Just as the Windows installation creates the *My Documents* folder, it also creates a special folder named the *Desktop* folder. Within the *Desktop* folder, Windows places icons for each item that appears on your *Desktop*, such as your program icons, the Recycle Bin icon, your Network Neighborhood icon, and so on. Using the Look in pull-down list or the Up One Level button, you can eventually display the Desktop folder's contents within a Save As or Open dialog box, as shown in Figure 15.7. The *Desktop* folder is the highest folder level on your system. After you are in the *Desktop* folder, you can no longer use the Up One Level button.

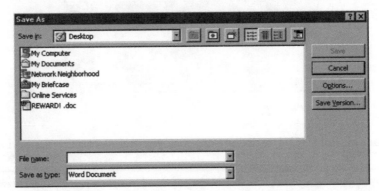

Figure 15.7 *Displaying the Desktop folder within a Save As dialog box.*

The *Desktop* folder is also home to a special folder named *My Computer*. Within the *My Computer* folder, Windows places icons for each of your disk drives, as shown in Figure 15.8.

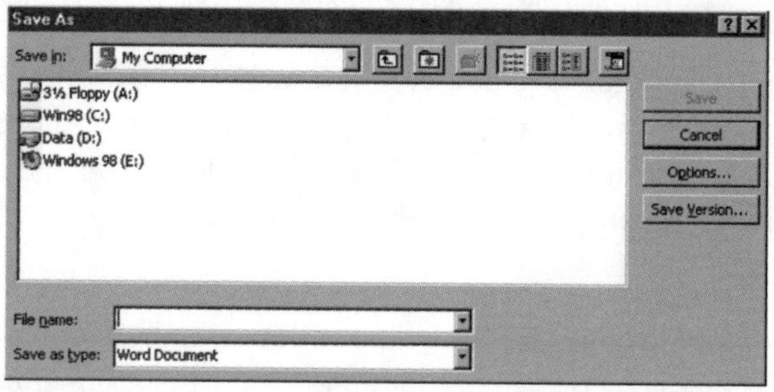

Figure 15.8 *The **My Computer** folder contains icons for each of your disk drives.*

If you want to save a file on a different disk, such as a floppy disk, you can first select the *My Computer* folder and then, within the *My Computer* folder, double-click your mouse on the disk drive you desire. Windows, in turn, will display a list of the folders the disk drive contains. To view the list of files within one of the folders, simply double-click your mouse on the folder. If you want to move back up one level, click your mouse on the Up One Level button. So, although your disks may contain hundreds of folders, Windows makes it quite easy for you to move from one folder to the next.

DELETING A FOLDER AFTER YOU NO LONGER NEED THE FILES THE FOLDER CONTAINS

In Lesson 14, you learned that when you no longer need a file's contents, you should delete the file from your disk to free up disk space that Windows can use to store other files. In Lesson 14, you deleted files from within the Open and Save As dialog boxes by clicking your mouse on the file's name to select the file and then pressing your keyboard's DEL key. In a similar way, you can delete a folder's contents from within the Open or Save As dialog box. When you delete a folder, however, you also delete every file and subfolder that the folder contains. In Lesson 16, you will learn how to use the Explorer to delete files and folders. However, because most users make extensive use of the Open and Save As dialog boxes to open and save documents, many users may choose to simply delete files and folders from within the dialog boxes, as opposed to running the Explorer. To delete a folder and its contents from within either the Save As or Open dialog box, perform these steps:

1. Make sure the folder does not contain any files or subfolders whose contents you may need now or in the future. When you delete a folder, you delete all the files and subfolders the folder contains.

2. Within the Save As or Open dialog box, click your mouse on the folder you want to delete and then press your keyboard's Del key. Windows, in turn, will display the Confirm Folder Delete dialog box, as shown in Figure 15.9.

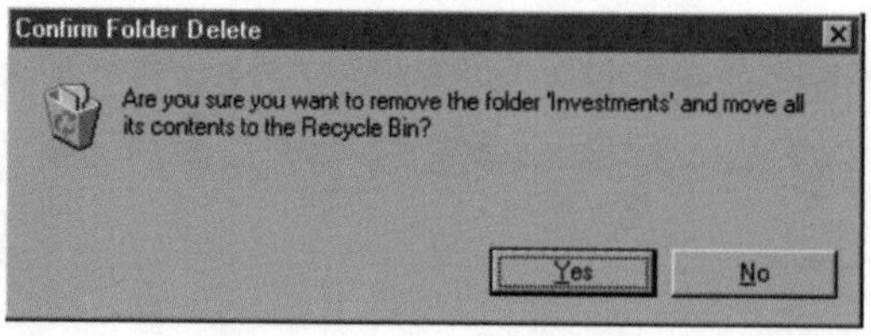

Figure 15.9 *The Confirm Folder Delete dialog box.*

3. Within the Confirm Folder Delete dialog box, click your mouse on the Yes option.

Note: *Should you inadvertently delete a folder whose contents you need, you may be able to recover the folder's contents from within the Windows Recycle Bin, as discussed in Lesson 18, "Recovering a Deleted File from the Windows Recycle Bin."*

WHAT YOU MUST KNOW

As the number of files you store on your disk grows, you must eventually organize your files by grouping related files into file folders, much like you would use a filing cabinet within an office to organize paper files. This lesson examined the steps you must perform to create your own folders and then the steps you must perform to store documents within the folders. In Lesson 16, "Using the Windows Explorer to Manage Your Files and Disks," you will learn to how to use a special program called the Explorer to copy, move, rename, and delete files and folders on your disk. Before you continue with Lesson 16, however, make sure you have learned the following key concepts:

✓ As the number of files you create on your disk grows, it will become more difficult for you to locate a specific file.

✓ To organize your files, you can create file folders on your disk within which you group related files.

✓ When you save a document to a file on disk using the Save As dialog box, you can select the folder within which you want to store the file.

✓ Although your disk may contain many folders, you must select one folder as the current folder. Within the Save As and Open dialog boxes, Windows will display the current folder's list of files and subfolders.

✓ Within the current Save As and Open dialog boxes, you can change the current folder by double-clicking your mouse on a folder icon or by using the Up One Level toolbar button to move up one folder.

Lesson 16

Using the Windows Explorer to Manage Your Files and Disk

In several of the previous lessons, you have learned how to store documents within files on your disk and then how to organize your files by grouping related files within file folders. In this lesson, you will learn how to use a special program called the Windows Explorer to delete, copy, rename, and move files and folders. One of the key elements that distinguishes a Windows "power user" from someone who simply uses Windows is the user's ability to manage files, folders, and disks within the Explorer.

This lesson will introduce you to key operations within the Explorer. By the time you finish this lesson, you will understand the following key concepts:

- Using the Windows Explorer, you can delete, copy, rename, and move files and folders on your disk. To start the Windows Explorer, select the Start menu Programs option. When Windows displays the Programs submenu, select the Windows Explorer option.

- The Windows Explorer window consists of two frames. Within the left-most frame, the Disks and Folders frame, the Explorer will display a list of your system's disk drives and the folders each drive contains. Within the right-most frame, the Explorer will display a list of the files and folders that reside in the current folder.

- To display a disk's or folder's contents within the Explorer, simply click your mouse on the disk's or folder's icon within the Disks and Folders frame.

- Within the Disks and Folders frame, the Explorer may precede a disk or file icon with a plus sign to indicate that the item has additional subfolders. If you click your mouse on the plus sign, the Explorer will expand its Disks and Folders display to list the subfolders.

- To delete a file or folder within the Explorer, click your mouse on the file or folder and then press the DEL key or click your mouse on the Delete button.

- To rename a file or folder within the Explorer, click your mouse on the file or folder and then press the F2 function key. The Explorer, in turn, will display an edit box within which you can type the name you desire.

- To move a file or folder within the Explorer, use your mouse to drag the file or folder's icon onto the folder to which you want to move the object. To copy a file or folder, simply hold down your keyboard CTRL key as you perform the drag-and-drop operation.

STARTING THE EXPLORER

To start the Windows Explorer, perform these steps:

1. Click your mouse on the Start menu Programs option. Windows, in turn, will display the Programs submenu.

2. Within the Programs submenu, click your mouse on the Windows Explorer option. Windows, in turn, will open the Explorer window, as shown in Figure 16.1.

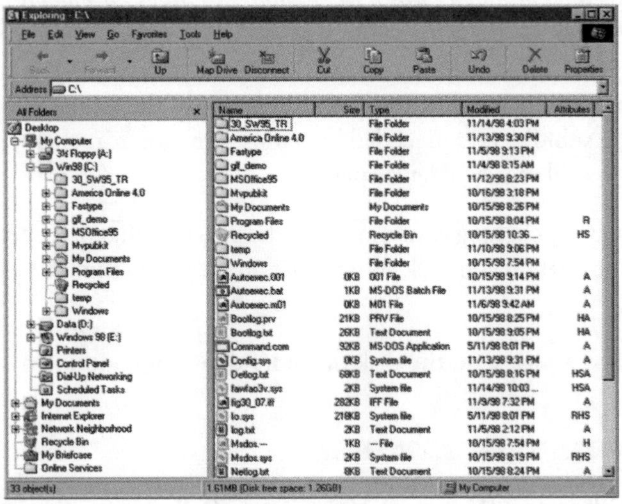

Figure 16.1 *The Windows Explorer.*

The Explorer window consists of two frames. Within the left-most frame, the Disks and Folders frame, the Explorer will display icons that correspond to your system's disks and the folders within your disks. Within the right-most frame, the Explorer will display a list of the files and folders that reside within the current folder (which you select by clicking your mouse on a folder or disk icon within the Disks and Folders frame). Take time now to click your mouse on the folders or disk icons, that appear within the Disks and Folders frame. Each time you select a new folder, the Explorer will list the folders contents within the right-most frame.

USING THE EXPLORER TO DISPLAY YOUR DISK'S FOLDERS AND FILES

As you just learned, to display a listing of a disk's or folder's contents within the Explorer, you simply click your mouse on the disk or folder icon that appears within the Explorer's Disks and Folders frame. If you examine the Disks and Folders frame closely, you will find that the Explorer precedes some of the disk and folder icons with a plus (+) or minus (-) sign. The plus sign preceding an object tells you that the Explorer can expand its display to list subfolders that reside within the object. For example, if you click your mouse on the plus sign that precedes the Windows folder, the Explorer will expand its Disks and Folders list to include a list of the subfolders that reside within the Windows folder, as shown in Figure 16.2.

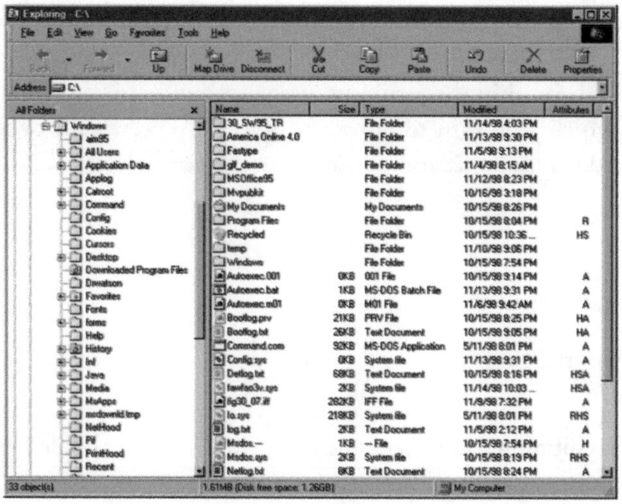

Figure 16.2 *Clicking your mouse on a plus sign within the Explorer's Disks and Folders frame directs the Explorer to expand its display of the disk or file to include a list of the subfolders that reside within the object.*

After you expand a folder's display, you can click your mouse on one of the folder's subfolders to display that folder's contents. Likewise, if one of the subfolders is preceded by a plus sign, you can click your mouse on that plus sign to direct the Explorer to expand that file's subfolder display.

After you expand a folder's display, by clicking your mouse on the plus sign that preceded the folder's icon, the Explorer will change the plus sign to a minus sign. If you click your mouse on the minus sign, the Explorer will collapse the folder's display, hiding its subfolders.

If a disk or file is not preceded by a plus sign, the disk or folder does not contain any subfolders.

RUNNING A PROGRAM WITHIN THE EXPLORER

As you learned in Lesson 10, "Programs (Software) Make Your PC Perform," the files with the *EXE* extension are program files that your PC can execute. Within the Explorer, you can run a program by double-clicking your mouse on the program file. For example, using the Explorer, display the files contained in the Windows folder. Then, within the Windows folder, locate the program file *Calc.exe*. When you double-click your mouse on the program file, Windows will run the Calculator accessory program, as shown in Figure 16.3. To close the Calculator program, simply click your mouse on the window's Close button.

Figure 16.3 *Running the Calculator accessory program from within the Explorer.*

In addition to letting you run programs by double-clicking your mouse on the *EXE* program file, you can also run programs, such as Word or Excel, by double-clicking your mouse on a document file. When you double-click your mouse on a document file from within the Explorer, Windows, in turn, will run the program that created the document and will load the document for use.

DELETING A FILE OR FOLDER WITHIN THE EXPLORER

As discussed in Lesson 14, to free up space on your disk, you should delete files whose contents you no longer need. Within the Explorer, to delete a file or folder, you simply click your mouse on the file or folder you want to delete and then press your keyboard DEL key or click your mouse on the Explorer's Delete button. Windows, in turn, will display a dialog box asking you to confirm that you want to delete the file or folder, as shown in Figure 16.4.

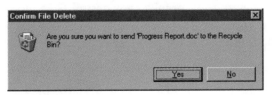

Figure 16.4 *The Confirm File Delete dialog box.*

To delete the file, click your mouse on the Yes button. If you decide you don't want to delete the file or folder, click your mouse on the No button.

When you delete a folder, Windows will delete all the files and subfolders the folder contains, in one step. Before you delete a folder, make sure you understand exactly which files and folders you are about to delete.

Should you inadvertently delete the wrong file or folder, you can likely recover the file or folder from within the Windows Recycle Bin, discussed in Lesson 18, "Recovering a Deleted File from the Windows Recycle Bin."

RENAMING A FILE OR FOLDER WITHIN THE EXPLORER

To rename a file or folder within the Explorer, right-click your mouse on the file or folder. Windows, in turn, will display a pop-up menu similar to that shown in Figure 16.5.

Within the pop-up menu, select the Rename option. The Explorer, in turn, will highlight the file or folder name in reverse video, displaying an edit box around the name, within which you can use your keyboard to type in the name you desire. After you type the new name, press ENTER or click your mouse outside of the edit box.

Note: *In addition to right-clicking on a file or folder and then using the pop-up menu to rename a file or folder, the Explorer lets you simply click your mouse on the file or folder and then press the F2 function key.*

Figure 16.5 *When you right-click your mouse on a file or folder within the Explorer, Windows will display a pop-up menu.*

COPYING OR MOVING A FILE OR FOLDER WITHIN THE EXPLORER

To move or copy a file or folder within the Explorer, you will normally perform a drag-and-drop operation that uses your mouse to drag a file or folder from its current location to a new folder (or disk). To perform a drag-and-drop operation, you aim your mouse pointer at the file or folder you desire. Then, hold down your mouse-select button as you move your mouse. Windows, in turn, will drag the file or folder as if it is attached to your mouse pointer. After you position the file or folder over the folder or disk within which you want to place it, simply release your mouse button.

When you drag and drop a file or folder to a folder on the same disk, the Explorer will move the file or folder to the new location. Likewise, if you drag and drop a file to a different disk, the Explorer will copy the file or folder. There may be times, however, when you want to copy a file or folder to the same disk. To perform a drag-and-drop copy operation, hold down your keyboard's CTRL keyboard before you start to drag the file or folder.

The best way to understand a drag-and-drop file operation is simply to do one. Insert a floppy disk into your floppy disk drive. Next, using the Explorer, open the Windows folder. Within the Windows folder, click your mouse on any file with the *TXT* extension, such as *Bootlog.txt* or *Detlog.txt*. Next, drag the file onto the floppy-disk drive icon that appears within the Explorer's Disks and Folders frame. When the Explorer highlights the floppy-disk icon, release your mouse-select button. The Explorer, in turn, will copy the file to the floppy disk.

SELECTING MULTIPLE FILES FOR AN OPERATION

In the previous sections, you have learned how to delete, copy, and move a file or folder. Often, when you perform these operations, you will want to use two or more files. To select multiple files for an Explorer operation, simply hold down your keyboard's CTRL key, as you click your mouse on each file. The Explorer, in turn, will highlight each file you select. Figure 16.6, for example, shows several selected files within an Explorer file list.

If the files you desire appear consecutively within the Explorer's file list, click your mouse on the first file, and then hold down your keyboard's SHIFT key and click on the last file in the list. The Explorer, in turn, will select each of the files that reside between the first and last file that you selected. After you select the files that you desire, you can perform delete, move, or copy operations.

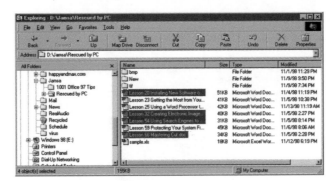

Figure 16.6 *Selecting multiple files for an Explorer operation.*

CREATING FILE FOLDERS WITHIN THE EXPLORER

In Lesson 15, you learned how to create file folders on your disk using the Save As dialog box. As you may have guessed, you can also use the Explorer to create folders on your disk. To create a folder within the Explorer, perform these steps:

1. Within the Explorer's Disks and Folders frame, click your mouse on the disk drive or folder within which you want to create the folder. The Explorer, in turn, will highlight the disk or folder, displaying a list of the files and folders it contains within the Explorer's right-most frame.

2. Select the Explorer's File menu and choose New. The Explorer will display the New submenu.

3. Within the New submenu, select the Folder option. The Explorer, in turn, will create a folder icon within its right-most frame, within which you can type the folder name that you desire.

4. Within the folder name edit box, type in your folder name and press ENTER.

FINDING A MISPLACED FILE

Despite the fact that you now know how to use the Windows Explorer to move through the file folders that reside on your disk, there may still be times when you misplace a file. Fortunately, Windows provides software that you can use to search your disk for a file. To search your disk for a file, perform these steps:

1. Click your mouse on the Start button. Windows, in turn, will display the Start menu.

2. Within the Start menu, click your mouse on the Find option. Windows will display the Find submenu, as shown in Figure 16.7.

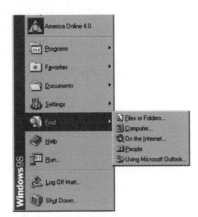

Figure 16.7 *The Find submenu.*

3.   Within the Find submenu, choose Files or Folders. Windows, in turn, will display the Find: All Files dialog box, as shown in Figure 16.8.

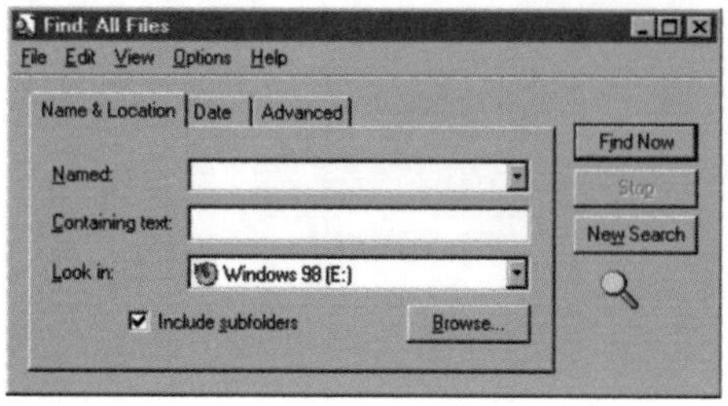

Figure 16.8 *The Find: All Files dialog box.*

Within the Find: All Files dialog box, click your mouse on the Named field and type in the filename for which you are searching and then click your mouse on the Find Now button. Windows, in turn, will examine the folders on your disk for the file. If Windows locates your file, Windows will display an entry for the file within the Find: All Files dialog box that tells you the folder within which the file is stored. Using the Explorer, you can move from its current location into the folder that you desire.

FORMATTING A FLOPPY DISK USING THE EXPLORER

In Lesson 13, "Storing Information on Disk," you learned that before you can use a new floppy disk, you must format the disk for use within Windows. To format a floppy disk within the Explorer, insert the new disk within your floppy drive. Next, right-click your mouse on the floppy-drive icon that appears within the Explorer's Disk and Folders frame. Windows, in turn, will display a small pop-up menu. Within the menu, select the Format option. The Explorer will display the Format dialog box, as shown in Figure 16.9, which you can use to format the floppy disk.

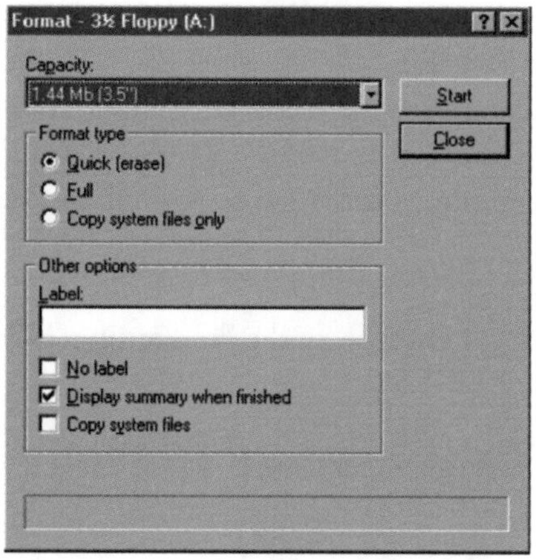

Figure 16.9 *Using the Format dialog box to format a floppy disk.*

VIEWING A FILE OR DISK'S PROPERTIES

As you perform different operations within Windows, there may be times when you need to know specifics about a file, such as when the file was created or last used. To display such information about a file, right-click your mouse on the file. Windows, in turn, will display a pop-up menu. Within the menu, select the Properties option. The Explorer, in turn, will display the File's Properties dialog box, as shown in Figure 16.10.

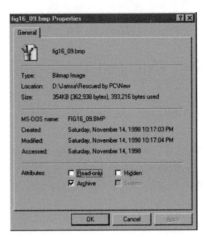

Figure 16.10 *Viewing specifics about a file within the Properties dialog box.*

In addition to displaying properties about a file or folder, the Explorer lets you display properties about a disk. As before, to display the disk's properties, right-click your mouse on the disk and then select the Properties option from within the Windows pop-up menu.

WHAT YOU MUST KNOW

As you use your PC on a daily basis, you will need to delete, rename, and copy files. In this lesson, you learned how to use the Windows Explorer to manage your files, folders, and disks. In Lesson 17, "Mastering Cut-and-Paste Operations," you will learn how to move or copy text and graphics from one location in a document or even from one program to another. Before you continue with Lesson 17, however, make sure you have learned the following key concepts:

✓ To start the Windows Explorer, select the Start menu Programs option. When Windows displays the Programs submenu, select the Windows Explorer option. Within the Explorer, you can delete, copy, rename, and move files.

✓ When you start the Explorer, its window will display two frames. Within the left-most frame, the Disks and Folders frame, the Explorer will display a list of your systems disk drives and the folders each drive contains. Within the right-most frame, the Explorer will display a list of the files and folders that reside in the current folder.

✓ Within the Explorer, you simply click your mouse on a disk or folder icon to display a disk's or folder's contents.

✓ To delete a file or folder within the Explorer, click your mouse on the file or folder and then press the DEL key or click your mouse on the Delete button.

✓ To rename a file or folder within the Explorer, right-click your mouse on the file or folder. Windows, in turn, will display a pop-up menu. Within the menu, choose Rename. The Explorer, in turn, will display an edit box within which you can type the name you desire.

✓ To move a file or folder within the Explorer, use your mouse to drag the file or folder's icon onto the folder to which you want to move the object. To copy a file or folder, simply hold down your keyboard CTRL key as you perform the drag-and-drop operation.

Lesson 17

Mastering Cut-and-Paste Operations

Throughout this book's lessons, you have examined a variety of software programs. As you use your programs, there will be times when you will want to move text or images from one location in your document to another or possibly from one program to another. In this lesson, you will learn that most programs make it quite easy for you to move and copy objects by performing cut-and-paste operations. Cut-and-paste operations are so named because they let you move objects within a document much as you would use scissors to cut text (or an image) from one piece of paper and then paste the object onto a second sheet of paper.

This lesson examines cut-and-paste operations in detail. By the time you finish this lesson, you will understand the following key concepts:

- Most Windows-based programs let you move or copy objects (such as text or images) from one location within a document to another or from one document to another, using cut-and-paste operations. Before you can perform a cut-and-paste operation, you must first select the item you want to move or copy.

- To select text within a document, you can use your keyboard or mouse. Most programs will highlight selected text using reverse video.

- To select text using your mouse, simply hold down your mouse-select button and drag the mouse pointer over the text you desire.

- To select text using your keyboard, hold down your keyboard's SHIFT key and use the arrow keys to highlight the text.

- To select an object such as a graphic image, click your mouse on the object.

- Most programs will highlight a selected object by placing sizing handles on the object's corners and sides.

SELECTING THE TEXT OR OBJECT YOU WANT TO MOVE OR COPY

To move or copy text (or another object, such as an image) within a document or from one document to another, you must first select the item that you want to move or copy. To select text for a cut-and-paste operation, you can use your keyboard arrow keys or mouse.

To select text using your keyboard, use your arrow keys to position the text cursor in front of the first character that you want to select. Then, hold down your keyboard's SHIFT key as you press your keyboard arrow keys to highlight the text. As you press the keyboard arrow keys to move the cursor, your program will display your selected text using reverse video. Figure 17.1, for example, shows a sentence selected within a word document.

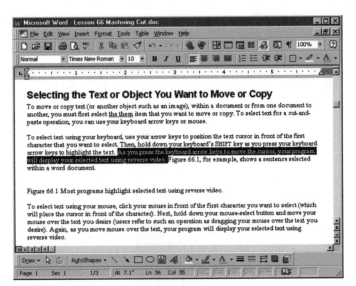

Figure 17.1 *Most programs highlight selected text using reverse video.*

To select text using your mouse, click your mouse in front of the first character you want to select (which will place the cursor in front of the character). Next, hold down your mouse-select button and move your mouse over the text you desire (users refer to such an operation as dragging your mouse over the text you desire). Again, as you move your mouse over the text, your program will display your selected text using reverse video.

If you decide to cancel your selection, simply release your keyboard's SHIFT key and press any of the arrow keys or click your mouse at any location within your document. Just as you can select text for a cut-and-paste operation, most programs will let you select graphics objects, such as a clipart illustration or photo. Normally, to select a graphics object, you simply click your mouse on the object. Your program, in turn, will normally display sizing handles on the corners and sides of the object to indicate the object's selection, as shown in Figure 17.2. (By dragging an object's sizing handles with your mouse, you can change the object's size.)

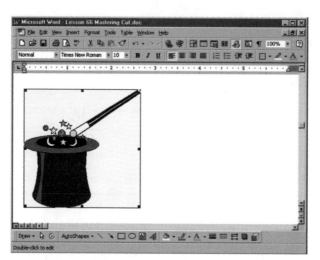

Figure 17.2 *Most programs display sizing handles on a selected object.*

UNDERSTANDING THE WINDOWS CLIPBOARD

Assume, for a moment, that you need to rearrange the paragraphs that appear on a printed page of text. To begin, you might use scissors to cut out the first paragraph, which you then temporarily place on your desk. Next, you might move the clipping from your desk so you could paste the clipping onto a new sheet of paper. In this case, your desk provides a temporary storage location while you look for a new sheet of paper and, possibly, your paste. When you move text or graphics from one location within a document to another, or from one program to another, you will use a temporary storage location called the Windows Clipboard. Although you will use the Clipboard on a regular basis to move and copy objects, you (unless you are a programmer or power user) will never actually see the Clipboard. Think of the Clipboard as a temporary storage location within Windows. The Clipboard can only hold one object at a time. Each time you place an object into the Clipboard, you overwrite the Clipboard's previous contents. Within programs such as Word and Excel, you will find an Edit menu similar to that shown in Figure 17.3.

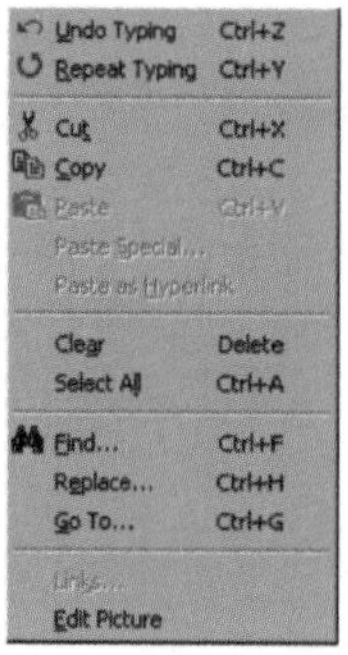

Figure 17.3 *An application's Edit menu.*

Within the Edit menu, you will normally find a Cut option and a Copy option. The Cut option will remove your selected text (or object) from your document and will place the object into the Clipboard. In contrast, the Copy option will place a copy of your selected object within the Clipboard. After you cut or copy an object to the clipboard, you are then ready to move the object to a new location in your document or into a new program. Assuming you are moving the object to a new location within the same document, you will use your keyboard arrow keys or mouse to position the cursor at the location where you want to place the document. Then, you will select the Edit menu Paste option to place a copy of the object at the current location (the original object will remain in the Clipboard). If you want to move the object into a different program, you will start the second program, open the document into which you want to place the object, position the cursor within the document to the location you desire, and then use the second program's Edit menu Paste option to copy the object from the Clipboard.

TRYING A CUT-AND-PASTE OPERATION

The best way to understand cut-and-paste operations is simply to try one. This example will use the Notepad accessory program that most Windows users will have on their system. If you have Word on your system, you can use it instead of Notepad. To start the Notepad accessory, perform these steps:

1. Click your mouse on the Start button. Windows, in turn, will display the Start menu.

2. Within the Start menu, click your mouse on the Programs menu Accessories option. Windows will display the Accessories submenu.

3. Within the Accessories submenu, click your mouse on Notepad. Windows will open a Notepad window. Within the Notepad window, type the following text:

   1. This is my most important point!
   3. This is my final point!
   2. This is my middle point!

As you can see, the text lists the points in the wrong order. To put the text in the correct order, you will use a cut-and-paste operation to move the middle line of text by performing these steps:

1. Within the Notepad window, use your keyboard arrow keys or your mouse to position the cursor at the start of the second line of text.

2. Hold down the Shift key and use your keyboard arrow keys to highlight the text or drag your mouse over the text.

3. Select the Edit menu Cut option. Notepad, in turn, will remove the text from your document, placing it into the Clipboard.

4. Use your keyboard arrow keys or the mouse to position the cursor after the last line of text.

5. Select the Edit menu Paste option to paste the text from the Clipboard into your document. Your text should now be in the correct order.

WHAT YOU MUST KNOW

As you create documents, you will often need to move or copy text. Within most Windows-based programs, you can perform cut-and-paste operations to move an object from one location within a document to another or from one program to another. In this lesson, you learned how to perform such cut-and-paste operations. In Lesson 18, "Recovering a Deleted File from the Windows Recycle Bin," you will learn how to recover a file or folder that you inadvertently deleted. Before you continue with Lesson 18, however, make sure you have learned the following key concepts:

✓ To move or copy an object within a Windows-based program, you must perform a cut-and-paste operation.

✓ To perform a cut-and-paste operation, you will select an object, use the Edit menu to Cut or Copy the object to the Windows Clipboard and then, later, use the Edit menu Paste object to copy the object from the Clipboard back into your document.

✓ To select text within a document, you can hold down your keyboard's SHIFT key and use the arrow keys to highlight the text you desire, or you can drag your mouse over the text. Most programs will highlight selected text using reverse video.

✓ To select an object such as a graphic image, click your mouse on the object. Most programs will highlight a selected object by placing sizing handles on the object's corners and sides.

Lesson 18

Recovering a Deleted File from the Windows Recycle Bin

In Lesson 17, "Using the Windows Explorer to Manage Your Files and Disks," you learned to use the Explorer to move, copy, rename, and delete files. Likewise, in Lesson 14, "Storing Information in Files," you learned that from within the Open and Save As dialog boxes, you can also rename and delete files. Every user, at some point, will delete a file whose contents they require. Fortunately, to help users recover files they recently deleted, Windows provides the Recycle Bin, a special folder from which you can remove a deleted file, much like you might pull a paper memo or report from your trash can.

This lesson examines the steps you must perform to recover a file from the Recycle Bin. By the time you finish this lesson, you will understand the following key concepts:

- Within Windows, when you delete a file, Windows does not actually remove the file from your disk, but rather, Windows moves the file into a special folder named the Recycle Bin.

- Using the Recycle Bin folder, you can undelete a file, restoring the file to its original folder location.

- To bypass the Recycle Bin when you delete a file, so Windows immediately removes the file from your disk, hold down the SHIFT key as you delete the file.

- The Recycle Bin does not hold an unlimited number of files. Eventually, when the Recycle Bin fills, the Recycle Bin will discard the files it has held the longest to make room for new files.

- When you are sure that you will no longer need a file's contents, you can remove the file from the Recycle Bin. In fact, if you do not need any of the files the Recycle Bin contains, you can flush the Bin's entire contents in one step.

UNDERSTANDING HOW THE RECYCLE BIN WORKS

As you learned in Lesson 14, to store information from one computer session to the next, you place the information within a file that your PC records onto a magnetic disk. When you no longer need a file's contents, you should delete the file from your disk. Unless you tell Windows to do otherwise, when you delete a file, Windows does not actually remove the file from your disk. Instead, Windows moves the file into a special folder, named the Recycle Bin. Think of the Recycle Bin as a temporary trash can. If you decide that you will never again need a file that the Recycle Bin contains, you can empty the Bin (users refer to the process of emptying the Recycle Bin as *flushing the Bin's contents*) to permanently remove the file from your disk, as shown in Figure 18.1. If you think of the Recycle Bin as a temporary trash can, think of emptying the Recycle Bin as dumping the trash can's contents into an incinerator. After you empty the Recycle Bin's contents, you can no longer recover your previously deleted files.

Figure 18.1 *When you remove a file from the Recycle Bin, Windows permanently removes the file from your disk.*

However, if you decide that you need the deleted file's contents, Windows will let you recover the file from the Recycle Bin. When you recover a file from the Recycle Bin, Windows will move the file from the Recycle Bin folder back to the file's original folder on your disk, as shown in Figure 18.2.

Figure 18.2 When you recover a file from the Recycle Bin, Windows will place the file back to its original location on your disk.

BYPASSING THE RECYCLE BIN WHEN YOU DELETE A FILE

If, when you delete a file, you are absolutely sure that you will not need the file's contents at a later time, you can direct Windows not to place the file into the Recycle Bin when you delete the file by holding down the SHIFT key when you press the DEL key or click your mouse on the Delete button. Normally, to delete a file, you will highlight the file within a dialog box or the Explorer's file list and then press the DEL key. Windows, in turn, will display a dialog box similar to that shown in Figure 18.3 that asks you if you want to move the file into the Recycle Bin. If you click your mouse on the Yes button, Windows will move the file. If you, instead, click your mouse on the No button, Windows will leave the file where it is.

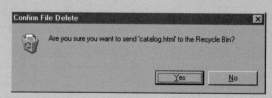

Figure 18.3 Windows prompt to move a selected file to the Recycle Bin.

If, however, you hold down the SHIFT key when you press the DEL key, Windows will display a dialog box similar to that shown in Figure 18.4 that asks you if you want to delete the file from your disk. By holding down the SHIFT key, you will direct Windows to bypass the Recycle Bin.

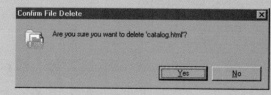

Figure 18.4 Bypassing the Recycle Bin when you delete a file.

RECOVERING A FILE FROM THE RECYCLE BIN

If you examine the Windows Desktop, you will find a small icon that corresponds to the Recycle Bin. Depending on whether or not the Recycle Bin is empty or has files you can undelete, Windows will display one of the icons shown in Figure 18.5.

Recycle Bin   Recycle Bin

Figure 18.5 Windows displays different Desktop icons for the Recycle Bin depending on whether the Recycle Bin contains files or is empty.

To view the Recycle Bin's contents, double-click your mouse on the Recycle Bin icon. Windows, in turn, will open a window, similar to that shown in Figure 18.6, that lists the files you can undelete (recover) from the Recycle Bin.

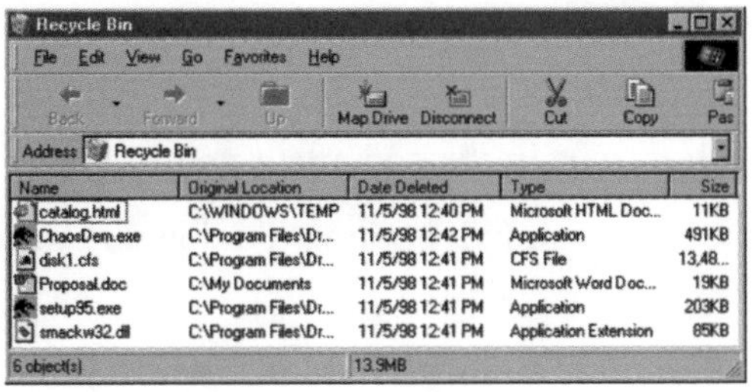

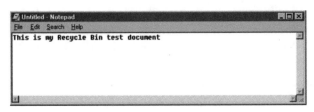

Figure 18.6 *The Recycle Bin folder lists files that you can undelete.*

To undelete a specific file or folder from the Recycle Bin's list, click your mouse on the file. The Recycle Bin, in turn, will highlight your selected file in reverse video. Next, select the Recycle Bin's File menu Restore option, as shown in Figure 18.7. The Recycle Bin, in turn, will move the file back to its original folder location.

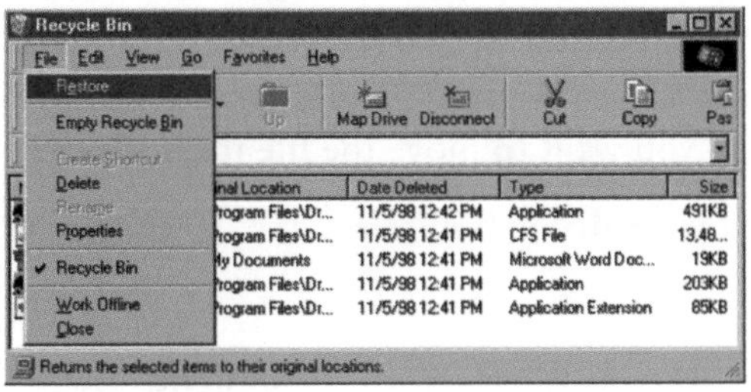

Figure 18.7 *To undelete a selected file, choose the Recycle Bin's File menu Restore option.*

If you want to undelete multiple files or folders from the Recycle Bin in one step, simply hold down your keyboard's CTRL key as you click your mouse on each file you desire. The Recycle Bin, in turn, will highlight each file you select using reverse video. After you select the files that you desire, choose the File menu Restore option to undelete the files.

TAKING THE RECYCLE BIN FOR A TEST DRIVE

One of the best ways to understand how the Recycle Bin works is simply to try it. To begin, you will need to create a file that you can delete. In this case, you will use the Windows Notepad accessory (a simple text editing program that all Windows users have) to create a file named *MyTest.Txt*. To create the file, perform these steps:

1. Click your mouse on the Start button. Windows, in turn, will display the Start menu.

2. Within the Start menu, click your mouse on the Programs option and then choose Accessories. Windows will display the Accessories submenu.

3. Within the Accessories submenu, click your mouse on the Notepad option. Windows, in turn, will start the Notepad program, opening a window on your screen, within which you can type the file's text.

4. Within the Notepad window, type the text: **This is my Recycle Bin test document** as shown in Figure 18.8.

Figure 18.8 *Typing a document's text within the Notepad accessory program.*

5. Within Notepad, select the File menu Save As option. Notepad, in turn, will display the Save As dialog box.

6. Within the Save As dialog box, type in the document name *MyTest.Txt* and choose Save.

7. Within Notepad, select the File menu Exit option. Windows, in turn, will close the Notepad window.

Next, to delete your document, you will use the Windows Explorer, which you examined in Lesson 17. To delete the *MyTest.Txt* document, perform these steps:

1. Click your mouse on the Start button. Windows will display the Start menu.

2. Within the Start menu, click your mouse on the Programs option and then choose Windows Explorer. Windows, in turn, will open an Explorer window.

3. Within the Explorer window, locate the file *MyTest.Txt* (which should reside in the My Documents folder). Click your mouse on the file's name and then press the DEL key or click your mouse on the Explorer's Delete button. Windows, in turn, will display the Confirm File Delete dialog box asking if you want to move the file to the Recycle Bin.

4. Within the Confirm File Delete dialog box, select Yes. The Explorer will move your file into the Recycle Bin.

Finally, to undelete your file from the Recycle Bin, perform these steps:

1. Double-click your mouse on the Desktop's Recycle Bin icon. Windows, in turn, will open the Recycle Bin.

2. Within the Recycle Bin's file list, click your mouse on the file *MyTest.Txt*. The Recycle Bin will highlight your file using reverse video.

3. Select the Recycle Bin's File menu and choose Restore. The Recycle Bin will move the file back to its original folder.

If you use the Explorer to examine the folder's contents, you will find the *MyTest.Txt* file. If you double-click your mouse on the filename, Windows will start the Notepad accessory program, loading the file so you can view its contents.

UNDERSTANDING WHY DELETING A FILE DOES NOT FREE UP SPACE ON YOUR DISK

As you have learned, when you no longer need a file's contents, you should delete the file from your disk so Windows can use the file's disk space to store other files. As you work, there may be times when you cannot perform a specific operation because you do not have enough disk space (your program will normally display a message such as "Insufficient Disk Space"). Before you will be able to perform the operation, you must free up space on your disk. To do so, you might delete several files whose contents you no longer need. However, when you try to perform the operation again, the program may still tell you that you do not have enough disk space.

Keep in mind that when you delete a file, you do not remove the file from your disk. Instead, you simply move the file to a different location—the Recycle Bin folder. To remove the file from your disk, you must remove the file from the Recycle Bin. To remove files from the Recycle Bin (and hence to remove the files from your disk), you have two choices. First, you can empty the Recycle Bin (flush its contents) by selecting the Recycle Bin's File menu and choosing the Empty Recycle Bin contents. Second, you can remove specific files from the Recycle Bin (while leaving others that you may later undelete), by selecting the file and then choosing the Recycle Bin's File menu and choosing Delete, or by clicking your mouse on the file and then pressing the DEL key. After you remove files from the Recycle Bin, Windows will remove the files from your disk, freeing up the file's disk space for other files to use.

THE RECYCLE BIN DOES NOT HAVE A FILE YOU PREVIOUSLY DELETED

If you realize that you have deleted a file whose contents you still need, stop what you are doing and undelete the file immediately. Otherwise, when you later open the Recycle Bin to recover the file, the file may not be there. In the previous section, you learned how to empty the Recycle Bin's contents and how to delete specific files. As it turns out, Windows reserves a fixed amount of space on your disk for the Recycle Bin. When the Recycle Bin becomes so full that it exceeds the amount of space Windows has allocated, the Recycle Bin discards the files that have been in the bin the longest. That is why, for example, a file that you deleted a few days ago may no longer be in the Recycle Bin. To make space for other files you deleted, the Recycle Bin may have discarded your file. To determine how much space your Recycle Bin has, and to optionally increase or decrease that space, right-click your mouse on the Desktop's Recycle Bin icon. Windows, in turn, will display a small pop-up menu. Within the menu, choose the Properties option. Windows will then display the Recycle Bin Properties dialog box, similar to that shown in Figure 18.9, that contains specifics about your Recycle Bin.

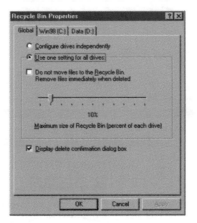

Figure 18.9 The Recycle Bin Properties dialog box.

WHAT YOU MUST KNOW

As you work, there will be times when you inadvertently delete one or more files. In this lesson, you learned how to use the Recycle Bin to undelete a file. In Lesson 19, "Cleaning Up Your Disk," you will learn how to free up disk space and how to clean up after programs that may not have deleted temporary files they created. Before you continue with Lesson 19, however, make sure that you understand the following key concepts:

✓ Unless you tell Windows to do otherwise, when you delete a file, Windows does not actually remove the file from your disk, but rather, Windows moves the file into a special folder named the Recycle Bin.

✓ By double-clicking your mouse on the Desktop's Recycle Bin icon, you can open the Recycle Bin folder from within which you can undelete a file, restoring the file to its original folder location.

✓ If you want Windows to bypass the Recycle Bin when you delete a file, hold down the SHIFT key as you delete the file.

✓ When the Recycle Bin becomes full, the Recycle Bin will discard the files it has held the longest to make room for new files.

✓ If you no longer need the files the Recycle Bin contains, you can flush (empty) the Recycle Bin's contents to free up the disk space the files consumed.

Lesson 19

Cleaning Up Your Disk

In Lesson 13, "Storing Information on Disk," you learned that to keep information from one computer session to the next, you must store the information within a file that your disk drive records onto a disk. When you no longer need a file's contents, you should delete the file from your disk, much like you would throw out a paper file that you no longer need. By deleting files from your disk, you free up the disk space the files consumed so that Windows can reuse the space to store other files.

In this lesson, you will learn several steps you can perform to remove unnecessary files from your disk. By the time you finish this lesson, you will understand the following key concepts:

- In general, you should take an hour each month to clean up the files you have created on disk, either by deleting files you no longer need from your disk or by moving files you may not need to a floppy disk.

- When you delete a file, Windows does not actually remove the file from your disk. Instead, Windows moves the file into the Recycle Bin folder. To actually remove a file from your disk, you must delete the file from the Recycle Bin or flush the Recycle Bin's contents.

- As they run, many Windows-based programs create temporary files that they store in the \Windows\Temp folder. Unfortunately, these programs do not always delete the files when they are done with them. You should examine the \Windows\Temp folder on a regular basis and discard any files the folder contains.

- If you are using Windows 98, you can use the Disk Cleanup Wizard to discard temporary files, flush the Recycle Bin, and to delete temporary files your browser may have downloaded from across the Web.

MANAGING YOUR OWN FILES

In Lesson 15, "Using Electronic Folders to Organize Your Files," you learned that you should use folders on your disk to manage the files that you create. In Lesson 17, "Using the Windows Explorer to Manage Your Files and Disks," you learned how to use the Windows Explorer to delete one or more files, when you no longer need the file's contents. If you think that you may need a file's contents at some point in the future, but you do not need the file now, you may want to move the file from your hard disk onto a floppy disk that you then store in a safe location. In general, you should clean up (delete or move unnecessary files from within) your own folders at least once a month.

FLUSHING THE WINDOWS RECYCLE BIN

In Lesson 18, "Recovering a Deleted File from within the Recycle Bin," you learned that when you delete a file, Windows does not actually erase the file's contents from your disk. Instead, Windows moves the file into a special folder called the Recycle Bin. If you later realize that you need the file's contents, you may be able to recover the file from the Recycle Bin—moving the file back to its original folder on your disk. Assume, however, that you need to free up disk space, so you delete a 20MB file named *CompanyInfo.DOC* from your disk . After you delete the file, however, you find that your disk does not have an additional 20MB of space. In fact, you find that your disk's free space has not increased at all!

The reason that deleting the file from your disk did not free up additional space is that Windows did not actually delete the 20MB file from your disk. Instead, Windows moved the file into the Recycle Bin. To recover the disk space, you must remove the file from the Recycle Bin. As you learned in Lesson 18, to empty the Recycle Bin, you have two choices. First, you can discard all the files in the bin, or second, you can remove a specific file. To empty the entire bin, perform these steps:

1. Within the Windows Desktop, double-click your mouse on the Recycle Bin icon. Windows, in turn, will open the Recycle Bin folder.

2. Within the Recycle Bin folder, select the File menu Empty Recycle Bin option. Windows will display a dialog box asking you to confirm that you want to discard the bin's contents. Click your mouse on the Yes option.

3. To close the Recycle Bin folder, click your mouse on the folder's Close button.

DETERMINING A DISK'S FREE SPACE

This lesson focuses on ways you can clean up a disk to free up space that Windows can use to store other files. To determine the amount of free space your disk currently contains, you can use the Windows Explorer to perform these steps:

1. Click your mouse on the Start button. Windows, in turn, will display the Start menu.

2. Within the Start menu, click your mouse on the Programs option. Windows will display the Programs submenu.

3. Within the Programs submenu, click your mouse on the Windows Explorer option. Windows will open an Explorer window.

4. Within the Explorer window, right-click your mouse on the disk drive whose free space you desire. Windows, in turn, will display a small pop-up menu.

5. Within the pop-up menu, click your mouse on the Properties option. Windows will display the Disk Properties dialog box, as shown in Figure 19.1.

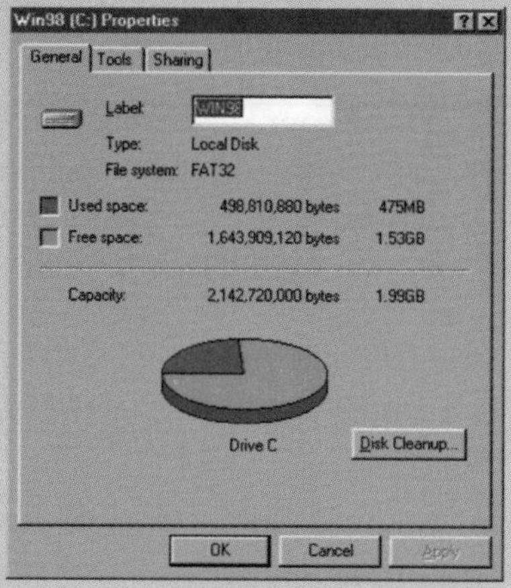

Figure 19.1 *The Disk Properties dialog box.*

6. Within the Disk Properties dialog box, you can see the disk's current free space. To close the dialog box, click your mouse on the OK button.

CLEANING UP THE TEMP FOLDER

As a program runs, there are many times when the program will create one or more temporary files. For example, in Lesson 21, "Getting the Most from Your Printer," you will learn that when you print a document, Windows normally (for performance reasons) does not send the document to your printer, but rather, Windows makes a copy of the document on your disk. Windows then uses the copy to print the document. Likewise, when you edit a document, many word processing programs will create a temporary backup copy of your file on disk. Normally, when such programs finish their processing, they discard the temporary file. Unfortunately, there are times when a program, for some reason, does not delete its temporary files. As a result, over time, what started out as temporary files, are now consuming considerable space on your disk.

As it turns out, most Windows-based programs create their temporary files within the *Windows**Temp* folder. You should get into the habit of cleaning out the *Windows**Temp* folder at least once a week, and more frequently, if you are low on disk space. To clean out the *Windows**Temp* folder, you will use the Windows Explorer to delete the files that the folder contains by performing these steps:

1. Click your mouse on the Start button. Windows, in turn, will display the Start menu.

2. Within the Start menu, click your mouse on the Programs option. Windows will display the Programs submenu.

3. Within the Programs submenu, click your mouse on the Windows Explorer option. Windows will open an Explorer window.

4. Within the Explorer window, select the Windows folder and then select the Temp subfolder. The Explorer, in turn, will display a list of the files the folder contains.

5. After you have selected the \Windows\Temp folder, click your mouse on the Explorer Edit menu and choose the Select All option. The Explorer, in turn, will highlight the folder's file list in reverse video. Next, click your mouse on the Delete button or press the DEL key. The Explorer will display a dialog box asking you to confirm that you want to move the files to the Recycle Bin. Select Yes.

6. To close the Explorer window, click your mouse on the window's Close button.

CLEANING UP YOUR DISK WITHIN WINDOWS 98

If you are using Windows 98, you can direct Windows to flush the Recycle Bin's contents, discard your temporary files, and even to delete files you have downloaded from across the Web, in one step, using the Disk Cleanup Wizard. To start the Disk Cleanup Wizard, perform these steps:

1. Click your mouse on the Start menu. Windows, in turn, will display the Start menu.

2. Within the Start menu, click your mouse on the Programs menu and choose Accessories. Windows will display the Accessories submenu.

3. Within the Accessories submenu, click your mouse on the System Tools option and choose Disk Cleanup. Windows, in turn, will display the Select Drive dialog box, as shown in Figure 19.2, that prompts you to select the drive you want to clean up.

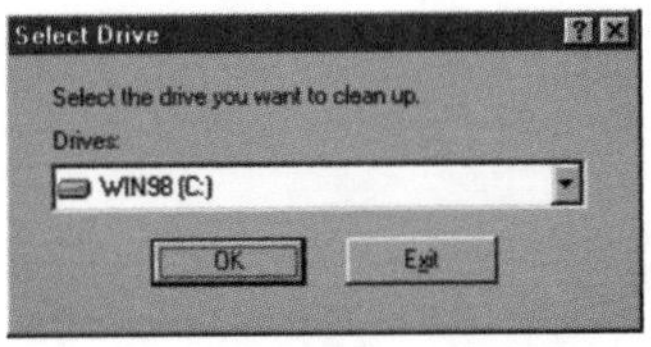

Figure 19.2 The Select Drive dialog box.

4. Within the Select Drive dialog box, use the pull-down list to select the drive you desire and then click your mouse on the OK button. Windows, in turn, will display the Disk Cleanup dialog box that lets you select the folders you want Windows to empty, as shown in Figure 19.3.

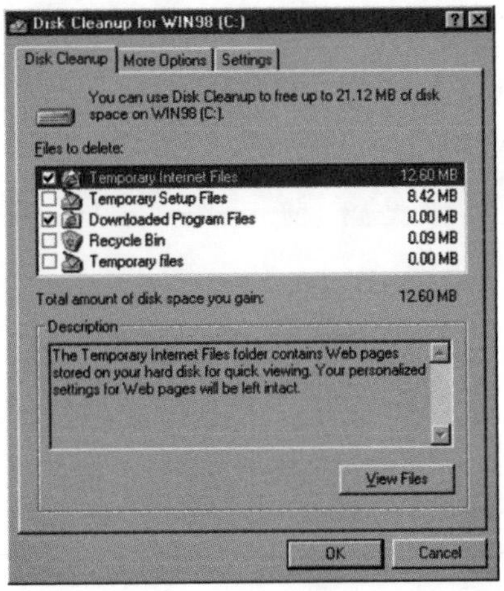

Figure 19.3 The Disk Cleanup dialog box.

5. Within the Disk Cleanup dialog box, place a checkmark next to each folder whose contents you want Windows to discard, and then click your mouse on the OK button. Windows, in turn, will display a dialog box asking you to confirm that you really want to delete the files. Select Yes.

Note: Within the Disk Cleanup dialog box Settings tab, you can select a checkbox that directs Windows to run the Disk Cleanup Wizard whenever your drive's disk space becomes low. For more information on the Disk Cleanup Wizard, refer to the book 1001 Windows 98 Tips, *Jamsa Press, 1998.*

UNDERSTANDING HOW INTERNET FILES CONSUME DISK SPACE

In Lesson 53, "Surfing Your Way to Information on the World Wide Web," you will learn that when you view a Web site's contents, your browser must download the site's text and graphics files to your PC in order to display them. As users "surf the Web" (move from one site to another), it is not uncommon for a user to return to a site he or she recently visited. Rather than forcing the user to wait once again for the files to download, most browsers store each site's files temporarily on your disk. Should you display a Web site's contents for a second time, your browser can retrieve the files quickly from your disk, as opposed to waiting for the files to download. As you might guess, over time your browser could build up a collection of such temporary files, which consume a considerable amount of disk space. Using the Disk Cleanup Wizard just discussed, you can quickly discard these temporary files. If you are not running Windows 98 (and thus do not have the Disk Cleanup Wizard), you can use the Windows Explorer to locate and delete your browser's temporary files.

In addition, using the Internet Properties dialog box, shown in Figure 19.4 (that you access by double-clicking your mouse on the Control Panel's Internet icon), you can delete the temporary Internet files and customize the settings that control how your browser manages such files.

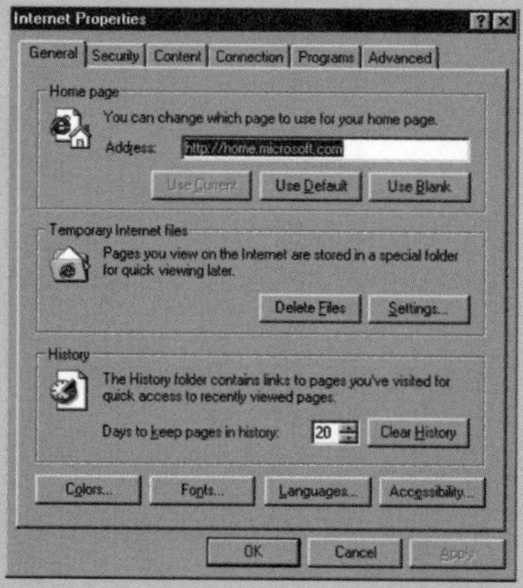

Figure 19.4 The Internet Properties dialog box.

DELETE UNNECESSARY E-MAIL MESSAGES

In Lesson 52, "Using Electronic-Mail to Communicate with Other Users," you will learn that when you receive electronic-mail messages from other users, your e-mail software will place the messages into your Inbox folder. Over time, the number of messages within your Inbox can become quite large and difficult to manage. Most e-mail programs, therefore let you organize your messages within other message folders. As rule, you will periodically want to clean out your e-mail folders by deleting messages you no longer require.

When you delete a message, your e-mail software normally does not remove the message from your disk, but rather, the e-mail software moves the message into a Deleted Messages folder (that works much like the Windows Recycle Bin, letting you later undelete the message should need the message's contents). If you are getting low on disk space, you should direct your e-mail software to discard the messages that your Deleted Messages folder contains. Depending on the e-mail software you are using, the steps you must perform to discard the Deleted Messages folder's contents will vary.

WHAT YOU MUST KNOW

Despite the size of your disk, over time you will eventually use up your disk's storage capacity. In this lesson, you learned several steps you should take on a regular basis to clean up the files on your disk. In Lesson 20 "Installing Software on Your Personal Computer," you will learn how to install new programs on your PC. Before you continue with Lesson 20, however, make sure that you understand the following key concepts:

✓ Just as you must periodically clean out the files in your desk, the same is true for the files that you store on your disk. Unless you have unlimited disk space available, you should take time each month to clean up your folders by deleting files you no longer need or moving files you may not need to floppy disks.

✓ Keep in mind that when you delete a file, Windows moves the file into the Recycle Bin. If you want to free up the disk space that the file consumed, you must delete the file from the Recycle Bin or flush the Recycle Bin's contents.

✓ Using the Windows Explorer, you should examine the \Windows\Temp folder on a regular basis and discard any files the folder contains.

✓ To help you manage your disks, Windows 98 provides the Disk Cleanup Wizard, software that will help you delete temporary files and to empty the Recycle Bin.

Lesson 20

Installing New Software on Your PC

As you learned in Lesson 10, "Programs (Software) Make Your PC Perform," software is the computer programs that direct your PC to perform a specific task. When you first unpack and set up your PC, you will find that your PC's manufacturer has installed several programs on your PC for you, such as Windows 98. In addition, you may find that your manufacturer has included CD-ROMs with your PC that contain computer games or other programs. Before you can use the programs that reside on the CD, you must install them onto your PC's hard disk.

If you are like most users, you will probably soon purchase other software such as Microsoft Office (which contains a word processor, spreadsheet) or other programs, such as an Internet browser. Before you can use your newly purchased software, you must install the software onto your PC.

This lesson examines the steps you must perform to install software onto your PC. By the time you finish this lesson, you will understand the following key concepts:

- To run a program, Windows must load the program from your disk into RAM. When you purchase a new program, you must install the program's files onto your hard disk.

- Installing software that you do not own on your system is software piracy. If you do not own a software program, do not install the program on your PC.

- Each program you purchase should provide an installation program that loads the program onto your hard disk.

- To make it easier for users to install software, most programs name their installation program *Setup.EXE*. You can run the *Setup.EXE* installation program using the Start menu Run option or by double-clicking your mouse on the program file within the Windows Explorer.

UNDERSTANDING THE INSTALLATION PROCESS

As you have learned, to run a program Windows loads the program file from disk into RAM. When you purchase new software, you must install the software from its CD-ROM (or floppy disk) onto your PC's hard disk. To install a program onto your hard disk, you will run a special installation program that resides on the installation CD-ROM. The installation program, which is normally named *Setup.EXE*, will copy files from the installation CD-ROM onto your hard drive.

To run a program's installation program, you will insert the program's CD-ROM into your CD-ROM drive. Depending on the software you are installing, the installation program may automatically start. In most cases, however, you must start the installation program yourself. To simplify software installations, most programs name their installation program *Setup.EXE*. To start the installation, you simply run the *Setup.EXE* program, either using the Start menu Run option or by double-clicking your program from within the Windows Explorer.

Depending on the software you are installing, you may need to restart your system before you can run your new software. As a rule, you should end your other programs before you start a software installation. That way, should you have to restart your system, you do not have to worry about the programs you are currently running.

INSTALL ONLY PROGRAMS THAT YOU OWN

When you purchase software, you will receive a CD-ROM or floppy disk with which you can install the software onto your PC. In the past, a user owning a software program would let a friend borrow and install the software on a different PC. Put simply, such actions constitute software piracy (stealing) and are against the law.

You should, therefore, install only software you own on your system. If you are interested in trying a program (before you buy the program), visit the Web site of the company that creates the software. Many companies provide trial versions of their software that you can download across the Web for free. Such trial software runs for a limited time period (such as 30 days), which should give you ample time try out a program.

As a rule, if you do not own the software, do not install the software.

Most Software Programs Name Their Installation Program Named Setup.EXE

To install new software on your PC, you will run an installation program that your software manufacturer normally includes on your program's CD-ROM. If you are installing your new software from floppy disks, one of the disks will normally have a label that says Setup Disk. If your floppy disks do not have a disk labeled Setup, the floppy labeled Disk 1 will normally contain the installation program. To start the software installation, insert the program's CD-ROM into your CD-ROM drive or insert the correct floppy disk into your floppy drive, as shown in Figure 20.1.

Next, you must run the installation program that will copy your new program's files from the CD-ROM or floppy disk onto your PC's hard disk. To make software installations consistent from one program to the next (which makes it easier for users to install software), most software manufacturers name their installation program *Setup.EXE*. To install Microsoft Office from a CD-ROM, for example, you would insert the CD-ROM and then locate and run the program *Setup.EXE* that resides on the CD.

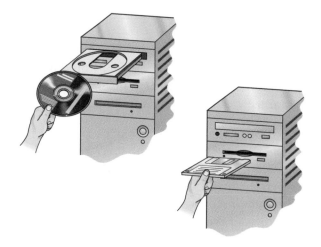

Figure 20.1 *To install a new software program onto your PC, insert the CD-ROM or installation floppy disk.*

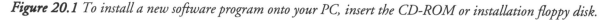

Likewise, to install Netscape Navigator (a popular Web browsing program), you would insert the Netscape CD-ROM into your drive and then locate and run the program named *Setup.EXE* that resides on the disk. Because most manufacturers name their installation program *Setup.EXE*, to load a program onto your hard disk, you will normally look for and run the *Setup.EXE* program on the CD-ROM that contains your new software. If you are installing a program from floppy disks, the disk labeled Setup Disk or Disk 1 will normally contain a program named *Setup.EXE* that you can run to install your software. In the next section, you will learn how to run the *Setup.EXE* program.

Two Ways to Run the Setup.EXE Program

If the *Setup.EXE* program does not automatically start when you insert you new program's CD-ROM into your CD-ROM drive, or if you are performing your software installation using one or more floppy disks, there are two ways you can run the *Setup.EXE* installation program: using the Start menu Run option or from within the Windows Explorer, discussed in Lesson 17, "Using the Windows Explorer to Manage Your Files." As you will learn, both ways are very easy.

Using the Start Menu Run Option to Run the Setup.EXE Program

As you have learned, Windows provides the Start menu to make it easy for your to run (start) your programs. To run the *Setup.EXE* installation program using the Start menu Run option, perform these steps:

1. Insert the CD-ROM or floppy disk that contains your new software into the corresponding disk drive.

2. Within Windows, click your mouse on the Start button, which normally appears at the bottom left-hand corner of your screen. Windows, in turn, will display the Start menu, as shown in Figure 20.2.

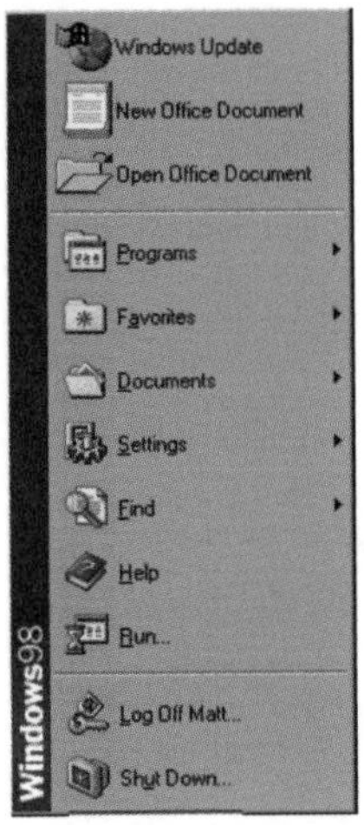

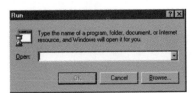

Figure 20.2 *The Windows Start menu.*

3. Within the Start menu, click your mouse on the Run option. Windows, in turn, will display the Run dialog box, as shown Figure 20.3.

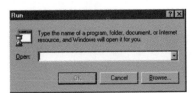

Figure 20.3 *The Run dialog box.*

4. Within the Run dialog box, type the command D:\SETUP, replacing the drive letter D with the drive letter that corresponds to your CD-ROM or floppy disk drive. For example, if your CD-ROM drive is drive E, you would type E:\SETUP. If you are installing the software from a floppy disk in drive A, you would type A:\SETUP. Next, click your mouse on the OK button. Windows 98, in turn, will start the *Setup.EXE* program, which will walk you through the program's installation.

USING THE WINDOWS EXPLORER TO RUN THE SETUP.EXE PROGRAM

As you learned in Lesson 17, the Windows Explorer is a special program that you can use to manage your files. Using the Explorer, you can list, move, copy, print, and delete files. In addition, by double-clicking your mouse on a program file, you can use the Explorer to start programs. To run the *Setup.EXE* installation program using the Explorer, perform these steps:

1. Within Windows, click your mouse on the Start button. Windows, in turn, will display the Start menu.

2. Within the Start menu, click your mouse on the Programs option. Windows, in turn, will display the Programs submenu, as shown in Figure 20.4.

Figure 20.4 *The Programs submenu.*

3. Within the Programs submenu, click your mouse on the Windows Explorer option. Windows, in turn, will start the Explorer program, as shown in Figure 20.5.

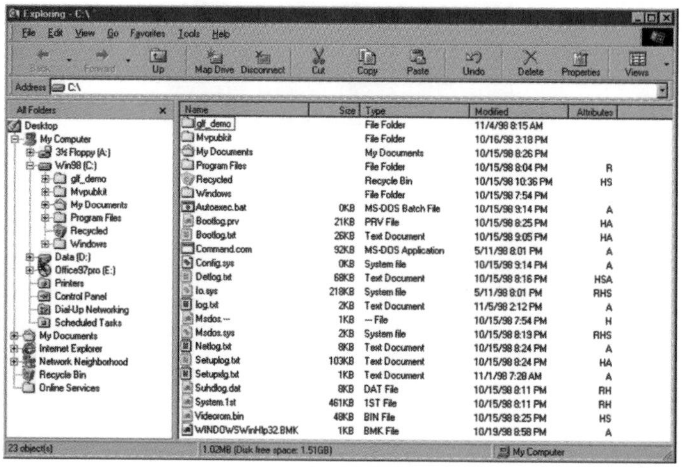

Figure 20.5 *The Windows Explorer.*

4. Within the Explorer's drives and folders frame (the left-most window frame), click your mouse on the drive that contains your new software (such as drive A, if you are installing the software from floppy disks, or drive D or E if you are installing the software from a CD-ROM drive). The Explorer, in turn, will list the disk's contents within its right-most frame.

5. Within the Explorer's content list (the right-most window frame), locate the file named *Setup.EXE* (you may only see the word Setup). Next, double-click your mouse on the file's icon. The Explorer, in turn, will start the Setup program, which will walk you through the program's installation.

RUNNING YOUR NEW SOFTWARE

In Lesson 9, "Running Programs within Windows," you learned how to run programs using the Start menu. After the installation completes, you will normally find a new entry within the Start menu Programs submenu that corresponds to your new program. To run your program, simply click your mouse on the program's menu option.

VIEWING A PROGRAM'S README FILE

When software manufacturers ship software, they normally finish their printed documentation before they finish the software itself. As a result, the software manufacturer often has key pieces of information that they do not include within the manual. To get the information to you, however, the software manufacturers often place a file on their CD-ROM named *Readme.Txt*, or something similar.

Using the Windows Explorer, discussed in Lesson 17, you should examine your new program's CD-ROM for such a file. If the file exists, double-click your mouse on the file's name. Windows, in turn, will open the Notepad accessory to display the file's contents. Within Notepad, you can scroll through the file's contents. Often, the information within the Readme file will not apply to you. However, if you have problems installing the software on your system, the Readme file is a good place to start looking for answers.

SOMETIMES YOU MUST REINSTALL SOFTWARE

Over time, you may find that one of your software programs that you have been using on a regular basis stops working or starts experiencing errors. Often, the easiest way for you to solve the problem is to simply reinstall the program. In other words, simply run the program's Setup program again, overwriting the existing program files on your disk.

REGISTERING YOUR SOFTWARE WITH THE SOFTWARE MANUFACTURER

When you purchase software, the box that contains your software will normally contain a registration form that you can return to the software manufacturer. Although the software manufacturer will use the registration form for marketing purposes, by submitting the form you may receive future software upgrades for free or newsletters from the company regarding ways to better use their products. In some cases, a company may not provide you with technical support for their product until they have received your registration form.

If your PC has a modem, many installation programs will let you register your software on-line. If you have a few minutes, take time to register. Software companies are interested in and will respond to your feedback. If you found the installation process difficult, let the company know that. If you like the manual, tell them.

WHAT YOU MUST KNOW

When you purchase new software, you must normally install the software on your PC's hard disk before you can run the program. To simplify software installations, most software manufacturers name their installation program *Setup.EXE*. In this lesson, you learned several ways to run the *Setup.EXE* program to install software on your PC. In Lesson 21, "Getting the Most from Your Printer," you will examine your printer, how Windows prints data to your printer, and more. Before you continue with Lesson 21, however, make sure that you understand the following key concepts:

✓ Before you can run a new program, you must install the program onto your hard disk.

✓ To load a program onto your hard disk, you must run the program's installation program.

✓ To simplify program installations, most programs call their installation program *Setup.EXE*. To run the *Setup.EXE* program, you can use the Start menu Run option or double-click on the program from within the Windows Explorer.

✓ Depending on the software you are installing, Windows may need to restart your system following the software installation. As a rule, before you start a software installation, you should end other programs that are currently running.

✓ After you complete your software installation, you should take a few moments to complete the program's registration card. Some companies may not provide you with technical support if you are not a registered user.

Lesson 21

Getting the Most from Your Printer

Although the local-area networks, the World Wide Web, and electronic-mail were supposed to produce a "paperless" office, it seems that most users generate more paper today than they did in the past. This lesson examines printers in detail. In addition, this lesson examines the Windows printing process and why Windows spools the jobs you print to disk. You will also learn how you can view the progress of your print jobs and how you can end a job that you have started to print.

By the time you finish this lesson, you will understand the following key concepts:

- Windows stores information about each printer connected to your system or available in the network within a special Printers folder. To display the Printers folder, select the Start menu Settings option and choose Printers.

- Like most of your hardware devices, Windows lets you customize various printer settings. To configure a printer's settings, right-click your mouse on the printer's icon within the Windows Printers folder and choose Properties.

- When you print a document within a Windows application, Windows does not immediately print the document. Instead, to improve your system performance, Windows spools the document to a file on disk. Then, Windows runs a program to oversee your document's printing.

- When you print documents using a Windows-based program, Windows will display a small printer icon on your Taskbar. If you double-click your mouse on the printer icon, you can display a dialog box that contains a list of the documents your printer is currently printing. In addition, from within the dialog box, you can cancel a specific job's printing or cancel all print jobs.

UNDERSTANDING PRINTER TYPES

Just as there are a variety of PC types, there are also various printer types, well suited to perform specific tasks. For general office correspondence, for example, an inexpensive ink-jet printer works very well. As you will learn in this lesson, most color printers use ink-jets. An ink-jet printer is so named because to print, the printer uses small plastic ink cartridge that uses jets to spray ink on to the page, as shown in Figure 21.1.

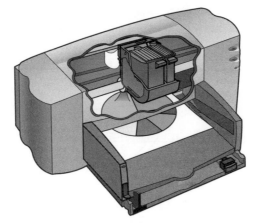

Figure 21.1 An ink-jet cartridge prints by spraying ink onto the page.

Ink-jet printers normally do not print text as sharply as a laser printer because there are limitations in how precisely the printer can spray ink. Tractor-feed printers are so named because they use a use a mechanical tractor-like device to move paper through the printer, as shown in Figure 21.2. Tractor-feed printers are normally low-resolution printers that are well-suited for printing large amounts of text quickly.

Figure 21.2 A tractor-feed printer uses tracks on the edge of the paper to move the paper through the printer.

Finally, laser printers are high-quality printers that are well-suited for text or graphics. Although the name laser printer leads many users to believe that the printer uses a laser to burn an image onto a page, that is not really the case. Instead, inside the printer is a print drum whose surface the laser places an electrical charge at specific locations so that ink attracks to the drum as the drum passes by the toner. Then, as the drum passes by the paper, it transfers the ink onto the page. Because the laser within the printer is very precise, the images the laser printer creates are quite sharp.

UNDERSTANDING DOT-MATRIX AND POSTSCRIPT PRINTERS

As you shop for printers, you may encounter the terms dot-matrix printer and Postscript printers. A dot-matrix printer creates the characters it prints by placing ink at specific dot locations within a grid (matrix). Figure 21.3, for example, shows how a dot-matrix printer might form the number 21.

Figure 21.3 *A dot-matrix printer fills in dot patterns to represent various characters.*

As you might guess, the greater the number of dots the printer uses to create a character, the sharper the character's image. Most tractor-feed and ink-jet printers use a limited number of dots to construct characters which is why the page you print using such a printer is not as sharp as that of a laser printer, which uses a greater number of dots.

In Lesson 10, "Programs (Software) Make Your PC Perform," you learned that programming languages let programmers specify instructions that tell the PC's processor how to perform a specific task. Postscript is a programming language for printers which, programs use to tell the printer how to print a specific page or object on a page. Not all printers support Postscript. In fact, if you shop for laser printers, you will find that printers that support Postscript cost several hundred dollars more than printers that don't. Graphic artists and publishers make extensive use of Postscript to print illustrations and photographs. If you only print text on your printer, you will not require Postscript capabilities.

USING A COLOR PRINTER

Over the past few years, high-quality color printers, like many PC devices, have become affordable. Today, color ink-jet printers are the most widely used color printers. In fact, you can buy a color ink-jet printer for a few hundred dollars. Such printers normally use a single ink cartridge that holds red, green, and blue ink (as discussed in Lesson 32, "Creating Electronic Images Using Scanners and Digital Cameras," computers mix the red, green, and blue colors to create various colors within the color spectrum), or the printer uses three separate cartridges (and, possibly, a fourth for black ink). When you use a color ink-jet printer, you should purchase special coated paper that you use for printing your color images. Standard printer paper will absorb too much ink and will look muddy. In contrast, the ink will not absorb into the coated paper and, instead, will dry on the paper's surface, creating a sharp image.

In addition to color ink-jet printers, there are color laser printers that use a red, green, and blue toner cartridge (or multiple toner cartridges) to create images. Color laser printers are still considerably more expensive than their ink-jet counterparts.

At the high-price end, you will find dye-sublimation printers that use a chemical process to create photo-quality images. Although the quality of a dye-sublimation printer is second to none, an inexpensive dye-sublimation printer costs several thousand dollars and, depending on the image size you need, a printer can cost $25,000 or more. In addition, each image you print using a dye-sublimation printer costs about two to three dollar in supplies.

REPLACING YOUR PRINTER'S TONER OR INK-JET CARTRIDGE

Eventually, and maybe sooner than you expect if you use your printer a lot, you will need to replace your printer's toner or ink-jet cartridge. When you purchase a new cartridge, you will find instructions that accompany the cartridge that walk you step by step through the cartridge-installation process. In general, however, you will perform the following steps:

1. If you are using a laser printer, turn off and unplug your printer. If you are using an ink-jet printer, your printer may have a button that you press that will slide the ink-jet cartridge into view.

2. Unbox your new cartridge. Save the box so you can place your old cartridge into it.

3. Open your printer cover and gently remove your old cartridge from your printer, as shown in Figure 21.4. Place the cartridge into the box that your new cartridge came in. Be careful not to spill toner as you move the laser cartridge. If you have an aerosol blower, you may want to clean out any paper or dust that has accumulated in your printer, as discussed in Lesson 38, "Preventative Maintenance You Can Perform to Increase Your PC's Longevity."

Figure 21.4 *Gently remove your toner or ink-jet cartridge.*

4. Most laser-printer cartridges have a small plastic seal that you should now remove. Likewise, most ink-jet cartridges have a small piece of tape covering the ink-jets, which you should now remove.

5. Gently insert the new cartridges into your printers and close your printer cover.

6. Plug in and power on your laser printer or put your ink-jet printer on-line. The ink-jet printer may have a Primer button that you can press to prepare the ink-jet cartridge for use.

UNDERSTANDING THE WINDOWS PRINTERS FOLDER

As you learned in Lesson 15, "Using Electronic Folders to Organize Your Files," Windows lets you group related files within a folder on your disk. In a similar way, Windows provides a special Printers folder, within which Windows places information about your local printer (or printers, if you have more than one), as well as the network printers you use. Figure 21.5 shows the Printers folder. Depending on the Printers attached to your system, the contents of your Printers folder may differ from that shown here.

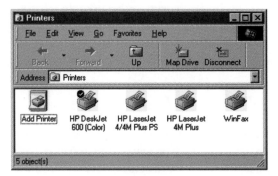

Figure 21.5 *Windows stores information about your printers within the Printers folder.*

To display the Printers folders, perform these steps:

1. Click your mouse on the Start button. Windows, in turn, will display the Start menu.

2. Within the Start menu, click your mouse on the Settings Option. Windows, in turn, will cascade the Settings submenu, as shown in Figure 21.6.

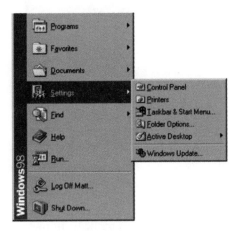

Figure 21.6 *The Settings submenu.*

3. Within the Settings submenu, click your mouse on the Printers icon. Windows, in turn, will open the Printers folder.

INSTALLING PRINTER SOFTWARE WITHIN WINDOWS

When you purchase a new printer, you will normally receive a Setup disk or CD-ROM that contains an installation program, similar to those discussed in Lesson 20, "Installing New Software on Your PC," that you can run to install the software on your system that Windows must have to communicate with your printer.

If your printer did not come with such a disk, you may be able to install software for your printer from the Windows CD-ROM by using the Windows Add Printer Wizard. To start the Add Printer Wizard, click your mouse on the Add Printer icon within the Printers folder, previously shown in Figure 21.5.

CUSTOMIZING YOUR PRINTER SETTINGS

In Lesson 45, you will learn that Windows lets you fine-tune many of your hardware device settings. Printers are no exception. Within the Printers folder, Windows will display an icon for each printer connected to your system. If you right-click your mouse on a printer icon, Windows will display a pop-up menu.

Within the menu, choose the Properties option. Windows, in turn, will display the printer's Properties dialog box. Depending on the printer's type and capabilities, the contents of the Properties dialog box will vary. Figure 21.7 illustrates a printer's Properties dialog box. Within the Properties dialog box, you can configure various printer settings.

In addition, you can print a test page to verify that the printer is working. (If you cannot print from within a specific application, such, as Microsoft Word, you can try printing a test page from within the Properties dialog box to determine if Windows can print to the printer, which will help you determine if the problem is your printer, Windows, or Word.)

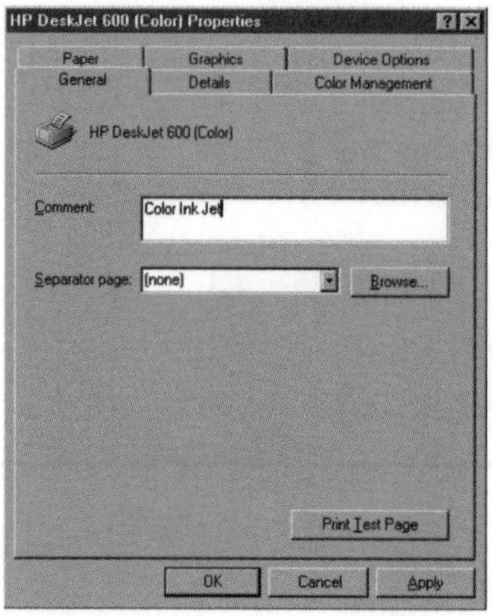

HP DeskJet 600 (Color) Properties

| Paper | Graphics | Device Options |
| General | Details | Color Management |

HP DeskJet 600 (Color)

Comment: Color Ink Jet

Separator page: (none)   Browse...

Print Test Page

OK   Cancel   Apply

Figure 21.7 *Using a Printer's properties dialog box, you can customize many printer settings.*

UNDERSTANDING WINDOWS PRINTING PROCESS

When you print a document within a Windows-based program, Windows normally does not send your document's contents directly to the printer. Instead, as shown in Figure 21.8, Windows copies the document's contents to a file on your disk called a *spool file*.

Windows Spool File

Figure 21.8 *When you print a document, Windows spools the document's contents to a file on your disk.*

Windows spools your print jobs to disk to improve your system performance and to let you continue to work as your document prints. Compared to your computer's fast electronic components, your printer is very slow (because the printer has slow moving mechanical parts). After Windows spools your document to disk, Windows runs a program whose only responsibility is to oversee your document's printing. If Windows did not spool your document, your application program would have to manage your document's printing, which means you would probably have to wait for the printing to complete before you could perform other operations within the program. Because Windows spools your printer output, you can perform other operations within your program or even end the program and start a different program while your output is printing.

CONTROLLING YOUR PRINT JOBS

When you print within a Windows-based program, Windows will normally display a small printer icon within its Taskbar, as shown in Figure 21.9.

Figure 21.9 As you print, Windows displays a small printer icon on the Taskbar.

If you double-click your mouse on the printer icon, Windows will open a printer window, similar to that shown in Figure 21.10, that shows you the jobs the printer is currently printing.

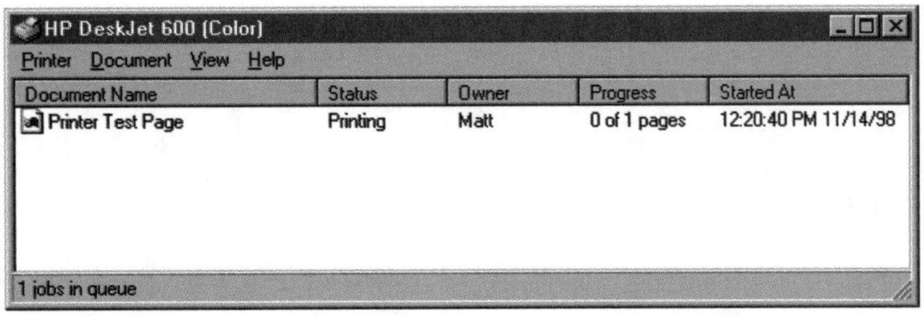

Figure 21.10 A printer window that lists the jobs a printer is currently printing.

Within the printer window, you can see what percentage of your current job has printed, as well as the jobs that will print next. If, for some reason, you want to end a job's printing, click your mouse on the job within the printer list and then select the Document menu Cancel Printing option. If the job you cancel is the current job, Windows will stop printing the job. If the job you cancel has not yet started to print, Windows will simply remove the job from the printer list. If you want to cancel all the jobs in the list, select the Printer menu Purge Print Documents option.

Note: When you cancel the current print job, Windows may have already sent several pages to your printer that you printer has stored in memory. To let you stop the pages from printing, your printer may provide a Reset or Cancel button. Or, you may simply need to cycle the printer's power.

WHAT YOU MUST KNOW

In this lesson, you examined various printer characteristics, ways you can configure your printer within Windows, as well as the how Windows spools your print jobs to disk, before it actually starts printing them. In Lesson 22, "Getting the Most from Your Keyboard and Mouse," you will examine keyboard and mouse operations and ways you can improve your keyboard and mouse responsiveness. Before you continue with Lesson 22, however, make sure you have learned the following key concepts:

- ✓ Windows uses a special folder called the Printers folder to store information about each printer connected to your system or available in the network.

- ✓ To display the Printers folder, select the Start menu Settings option and choose Printers.

- ✓ Within the Printers folder, right-click your mouse on a printer's icon and select Properties to display the Printer's Properties dialog box.

- ✓ Within a Printer's Properties dialog box, you can view or change the printer's current settings.

- ✓ To improve your system performance, Windows spools the documents that you print to a file on disk. Then, Windows runs a program to oversee your document's printing.

- ✓ When you print documents using a Windows-based program, Windows will display a small printer icon on your Taskbar. If you double-click your mouse on the printer icon, you can display a dialog box that contains a list of the documents your printer is currently printing. In addition, from within the dialog box, you can cancel a specific job's printing or cancel all print jobs.

Lesson 22

Getting the Most from Your Keyboard and Mouse

Throughout this book, you will examine many different hardware devices, such as printers, disk drives, and even PC-based video cameras.

This lesson examines two of the devices you will use most often: your keyboard and mouse. By the time you finish this lesson, you will understand the following key concepts:

- If you are just learning to type, you should consider purchasing a typing tutor program. Many typing tutor programs teach you to type using interactive video games.

- Most keyboards have three sections of keys: the standard typing keys, cursor movement keys, and the numeric keypad.

- To help users enter numbers quickly, keyboards provide a numeric keypad that functions much like a 10-key calculator. To select the numeric keypad's operation, you use the NumLock key.

- Within Windows, you will make extensive use of mouse operations, which users refer to as "point and click operations." To point your mouse, you simply aim the mouse pointer that appears on your screen at the object you desire. To move your mouse pointer across the screen, you simply move your mouse across your desk. To click your mouse, you simply press and release the mouse-select button (normally the left-mouse button)

- Many operations within Windows require that you double-click your mouse by pressing and releasing the mouse-select button two times in quick succession.

- If you work with a keyboard for several hours a day, you may find that your wrists become quite sore. To reduce stress on your wrists, you should consider purchasing a keyboard and mouse pad. You may also consider purchasing an ergonomic keyboard that positions your hands in a manner that reduces strain on your wrists.

- Depending on your preferences, you may want to speed up or slow down your keyboard and mouse responsiveness. Using the Keyboard and Mouse icons you will find within the Windows Control Panel, you can fine-tune your mouse and keyboard operations.

GETTING TO KNOW YOUR KEYBOARD

Many new users often put off using their PC because they simply are not good typists. As it turns out, however, there is a lot you can do with your PC without having to do that much typing. For example, in Lesson 53, "Surfing Your Way to Information on the World Wide Web," you will learn that when you "surf the Web," you can often move from one site to another with a simple click of your mouse. Over time, even if you just type a little, your typing is going to improve.

TAKE ADVANTAGE OF TYPING TUTOR SOFTWARE

When most people think about learning to type, they can quickly think of a list of ways they would much rather spend their time. Fortunately, there are several interactive typing tutors that will increase your typing skills in a matter of hours and that you will find are much like playing a video game. For example, Figure 22.1 shows the FasType typing tutor (a shareware program) that you can download from the Trendtech Web site at *www.trendtech.com*. (The file you download from Trendtech is a ZIP file, which you must unzip using Winzip before you can install the software. For more information on Winzip, refer to Lesson 56, "Compressing Files Using the Winzip Utility.") Most computer stores will sell several different typing tutor programs. You will find that the typing tutor software is inexpensive and a great investment of your time.

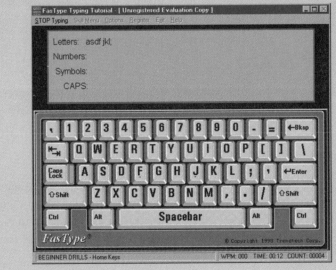

Figure 22.1 *Learning to type using the FasType typing tutor.*

UNDERSTANDING KEYBOARD TYPES

Today, most PCs ship with a standard keyboard that is flat in appearance. If you have typed with a typewriter in the past, you will find that the keyboard's keys match those of your typewriter. As you will learn in this lesson, the keyboard also includes special purpose function keys, arrow and cursor keys, as well as a small numeric keypad. As you talk with other users, you may hear the term "QWERTY" to describe the keyboard's key location.

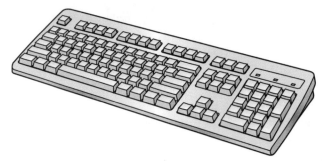

Figure 22.2 *The layout of a standard PC keyboard.*

RECOGNIZING QWERTY KEYBOARDS

If you examine your keyboard (or if you examine a typewriter), you will find that the top row of keys begin with the letters Q, W, E, R, T, Y. Although the "QWERTY" keyboard is the standard worldwide, it is possible that, in the future, the arrangement of keys on the keyboard may change. As it turns out, the arrangement of keys on the keyboard is not the most optimal in terms of improving typing speed. Instead, the original layout (the QWERTY layout) was chosen to support the moving hammers in old typewriters (the hammers, which moved to strike a ribbon of ink to transfer ink onto a page, would sometimes jam if a user typed too fast. The QWERTY key layout minimized such jamming).

In the future, you may find keyboards whose keys use a layout defined by August Dvorak in the 1930s. The Dvorak layout is optimal for fast typing. Its goal is to minimize finger movement by placing the most frequently used keys on the home row. Then, again, in the future we may eliminate keyboards altogether and simply talk to the PC.

USING YOUR KEYBOARD ARROW KEYS

Within programs such as your word processor or spreadsheet, you will often need to position the text cursor at a specific location within your document. For example, assume that you are typing an e-mail message and you have mistyped this book's title, as follows (omitting the word **by**):

Rescued Personal Computers

To insert the word **by** into the text, you must position the text cursor just after the word **Rescued**. To position the cursor, you have two choices. First, you can click your mouse at the location you desire. Second, you can use your keyboard arrow keys (which some users refer to as the cursor keys) to position the cursor. As shown in Figure 22.3, most keyboards provide two sets of arrow keys. The first set sits between your standard keys and the numeric keypad, and the second set resides on the numeric keypad itself.

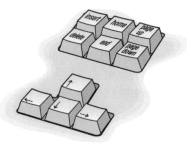

Figure 22.3 *The keyboard's arrow keys let you position the text cursor within a document.*

If you press the arrow keys that appear on the numeric keypad, and the cursor does not move (your program may, instead, display a series of numbers), you must press your keyboard's NumLock key, as discussed next.

USING NUMLOCK TO TOGGLE BETWEEN ARROW KEYS AND THE NUMERIC KEYPAD

In Lesson 26, "Automating Your Calculations Using Spreadsheet Software," you will learn how spreadsheets simplify many operations that bookkeepers and accountants use to perform using an adding machine (most bookkeepers refer to adding machines as 10-key calculators because the machine contains a key for each digit from 0 though 9). To help users enter numbers quickly using the PC's keyboard, most keyboards provide a numeric keypad that closely resembles the 10-key calculator, as shown in Figure 22.4.

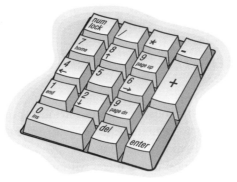

Figure 22.4 *The numeric keypad lets users type numbers quickly.*

On most keyboards, the numeric keypad can either work as numeric keys or as cursor movement keys. To control the numeric keypad's operation, you use the NumLock key. The NumLock key works as a toggle switch, meaning that each time you press the key, it changes the keypad's function. That is, if the keypad keys are currently working as cursor movement keys, pressing the NumLock key will direct your PC to change the keypad into a numeric keypad, or vice versa. Some keypads will illuminate a small LED light when the numeric keypad is selected. If you are using a notebook PC, you may find a numeric keypad printed lightly on your standard keys—possibly using a white or blue ink. Normally, your notebook's keyboard will have a special function key, that also appears in the same color, that you can press to enable the keys—much like you would use your keyboard's SHIFT key.

USING THE CAPSLOCK KEY TO TOGGLE BETWEEN UPPERCASE AND MIXED-CASE TEXT

As you run different programs, there may be times when you will want to type text using only uppercase letters. Rather than having to continually hold down the SHIFT key as you type, you can press your keyboard's CapsLock key. When the CapsLock key is active, each key you press will appear in uppercase. (If you want to type a lowercase letter, simply press the SHIFT key as you type.) Like the NumLock key, the CapsLock key works as a toggle. Each time you press the CapsLock key, you toggle CapsLock operations on or off. Some keypads will illuminate a small LED light when CapsLock operations are active.

UNDERSTANDING YOUR KEYBOARD FUNCTION KEYS

At the top of most keyboards, you will find a row of keys labeled F1 through F12. These keys, users call the keys function keys (and hence the letter F within each key's name), may direct your current program to perform a specific operation. One program, for example, might print your current document each time you press the F5 function key. A second program, however, may save your document to disk when you press the F5 key, while a third program may ignore the key entirely. The operation the function keys perform depends completely on your current program.

USING THE ESC KEY TO CANCEL AN OPERATION

As you run programs within Windows, you will encounter many different dialog boxes. For example, Figure 22.5 shows a Print dialog box that you can use to print the current document.

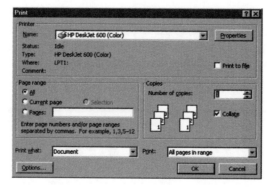

Figure 22.5 *A Print dialog box.*

Within the Print dialog box, you can click your mouse on the OK button to print the document, or you can click your mouse on Cancel, should you decide you do not want to print your document's contents. In most cases, you can also cancel a dialog box by simply pressing your keyboard's Esc key. So, if you are a fast typist and you do not like to take your hands off the keyboard, you can now cancel dialog boxes without having to click your mouse.

USING THE INS KEY TO INSERT OR OVERWRITE TEXT

Earlier in this lesson, you learned how to use the keyboard's arrow keys to position the text cursor. When you edit text within a document, there will be times when you will need to insert text and other times when you will want to type over existing text. To control such editing operations, you use your keyboard's INS key. (INS is an abbreviation for Insert.) Like several other keyboard keys, the INS key works as a toggle, that switches you between insert and overwrite mode. If, when you type text within an existing sentence, your new text overwrites existing text, and you wanted to insert the new text, simply press the INS key to select insert mode.

USING THE TAB KEY WITHIN A DIALOG BOX

When you create documents within a word processor, you will use the TAB key often to indent text. In addition, you will also use the TAB key within dialog boxes to move from one field in the dialog box to the next. For example, Figure 22.6 shows the Page Setup dialog box within Microsoft Word. As you can see from the highlight, the current dialog box field is the Top margin field. To move to the Bottom margin field, you can click your mouse on the field or you can simply press the TAB key. Each time you press the TAB key, Windows will move to the next field.

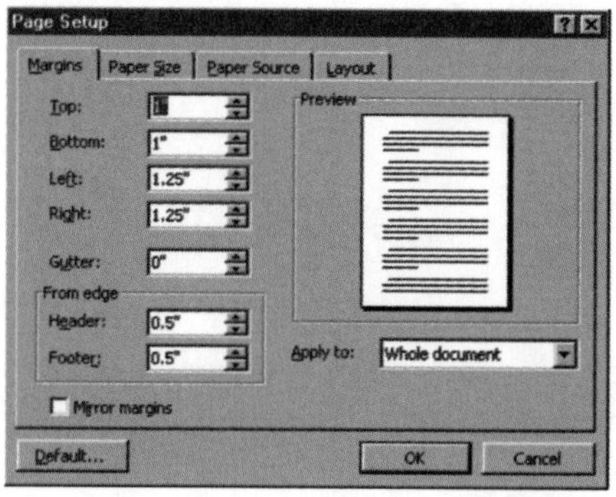

Figure 22.6 *The Page Setup dialog box.*

Just as there are times when you must move forward one field within a dialog box, there will also be times when you must move back one or more fields. To move back a field, you simply hold down your keyboard's SHIFT key as you press TAB.

CONTRASTING THE DEL AND BACKSPACE KEYS

As you edit text within a document, there will be times when you must delete one or more characters. To delete characters, you can use your keyboard's DEL or BACKSPACE keys. The difference between the two keys is the character that the key deletes. If you press the BACKSPACE key, for example, your program will delete the character to the left of the cursor. In contrast, if you press the DEL key, your program will delete the character to the right of the cursor.

UNDERSTANDING KEYBOARD COMBINATIONS

As you use your PC, some keyboard operations will require that you press two or more keys at the same time (which users refer to as a keyboard combination). For example, to switch between programs within Windows, you can hold down your keyboard's ALT key and then press TAB (which users will refer to as the ALT-TAB keyboard combination). Windows, in turn, will display a small box within the center of your screen, as shown in Figure 22.7, that contains icons for each of your active programs. By pressing the TAB key (while still holding down the ALT key), you can highlight the program to which you want to switch. When you release the ALT key, Windows will switch to your selected program.

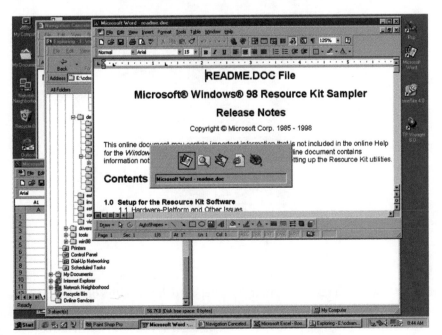

Figure 22.7 *Switching between programs by pressing the Alt-Tab keyboard combination.*

USING A NOTEBOOK PC'S SPECIAL PURPOSE KEYS

If there is a downside to using a notebook PC, it is that the notebook's keyboard is small, and therefore, somewhat difficult to use. To make the best use of a limited number of keys, many notebook PCs assign special keyboard combinations to specific operations. As briefly discussed earlier in this lesson, you may find that several keys on your keyboard contain numbers or symbols that appear in a different color. Normally, you find a special function key on your keyboard that appears in the same color as the special purpose keys that enables the keys' use. In other words, you use the special function key much like you would a SHIFT key, meaning, when you press the special function key, you enable the keyboard's special purpose keys. Using a special purpose key, for example, you might switch your notebook's video display from the notebook's screen to an external monitor (or projector) that you have connected to the notebook's video port.

IMPROVING YOUR KEYBOARD'S RESPONSIVENESS

As you type, there may be times when you want to repeat a specific character. To do so, you can simply hold down the character's keyboard key. After a brief delay, your PC will start repeating the character. Likewise, when you edit text, there may be times when you want to position the text cursor by holding down one of the arrow keys. Depending on your preferences, you may want to fine tune your keyboard's responsiveness, so that your keyboard either speeds up or slows down repeat-key operations.

To fine tune your keyboard settings, perform these steps:

1. Click your mouse on the Start button. Windows, in turn, will display the Start menu.

2. Within the Start menu, click your mouse on the Settings menu Control Panel option. Windows will open the Control Panel folder, discussed in Lesson 45, "Configuring Your System Settings."

3. Within the Control Panel folder, double-click your mouse on the Keyboard icon. Windows, in turn, will display the Keyboard Properties dialog box, as shown in Figure 22.8.

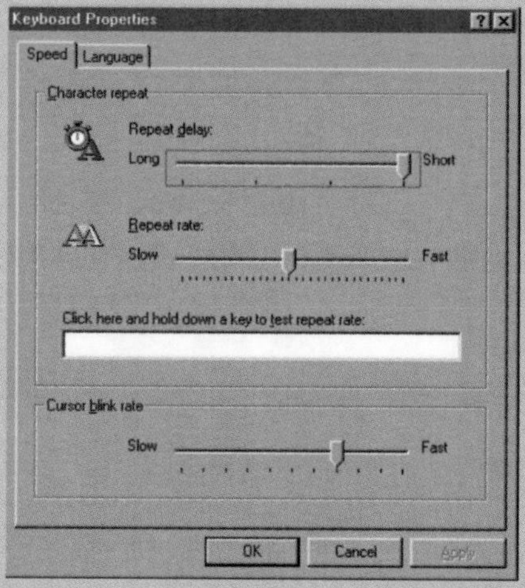

Figure 22.8 The Keyboard Properties dialog box.

4. Within the Keyboard Properties dialog box, use the Repeat delay slider and the Repeat rate to control your keyboard's responsiveness. The Repeat delay specifies how long you must hold down a key before Windows starts to repeat the key's character. The Repeat rate, in turn, specifies how fast Windows will then repeat the character as you hold down the key. Using your mouse, move the slider to the right or to the left to select the setting you desire. For fastest response, you want a short Repeat delay and a fast Repeat rate.

5. After you adjust the slider, click your mouse within the dialog box's test box and then hold down any key to watch how fast Windows repeats the key. After you select the delay and rate you desire, click your mouse on the OK button.

6. To close the Control Panel folder, click your mouse on the folder's Close button.

UNDERSTANDING MOUSE OPERATIONS

To make your computer easy to use, Windows lets you "point and click" your mouse on objects that appear on your computer screen. To use a mouse, you must point (aim) the mouse pointer that appears on your screen at specific objects, such as menus or icons. To move your mouse pointer across the screen, you simply move your mouse across your desk, as shown in Figure 22.9.

Figure 22.9 *To move your mouse pointer across your screen, you move your mouse across your desk.*

After you aim your mouse pointer at the object you desire (which may take a little practice if you are "mousing" for the first time), you must then click your mouse on the object. As shown in Figure 22.10, to click your mouse, you simply press and release the mouse-select button (which is normally the left-mouse button).

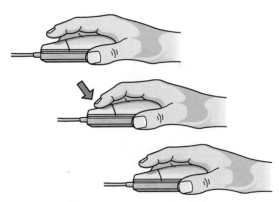

Figure 22.10 *To click your mouse, press and release the mouse-select button.*

Within Windows, there will be times when you must click one time on an object (such as a menu) and other times when you must double-click (such as on a program icon). To double-click your mouse, you simply press and release the mouse-select button twice in quick succession (you should hear your mouse make a "click" "click" sound). The first few times you double-click your mouse, you may not perform the operation fast enough for Windows to recognize the double-click operation. To double-click, you must click your mouse two times in less than a second.

As discussed, to click your mouse, you will normally use the left-mouse button (which users refer to as the mouse-select button). Within Windows, some operations will require that you right-click your mouse on an object. To perform a right-click operation, you simply aim your mouse pointer at the object that you desire and then press the right-mouse button. As you read books, magazines, and even the Windows on-line help, the instructions will tell you whether you should click, double-click, or right-click your mouse.

If you are using a notebook PC, your PC may use a small touch pad, as opposed to a mouse, as shown in Figure 22.11. To move the mouse pointer using the touch pad, you simply slide your finger across the pad's surface. Likewise, to click or double-click the mouse, you simply tap the pad once or twice using your finger.

Figure 22.11 *Many notebook PCs provide a touch pad that works in place of a mouse.*

Other notebook PCs may provide a small mouse control that appears near the center of your keyboard, as shown in Figure 22.12. The PC places the control on the keyboard to keep it close to your fingers as you type. In addition, the PC will place two mouse buttons near your thumbs—one for the left-mouse button and one for the right-mouse button—that you can again access without having to move your hands far from the keyboard.

Figure 22.12 *Using a keyboard-based mouse control to move the mouse cursor.*

Also, some notebook PCs will provide a built-in trackball, as shown in Figure 22.13, that you can move using your thumb to position the mouse pointer.

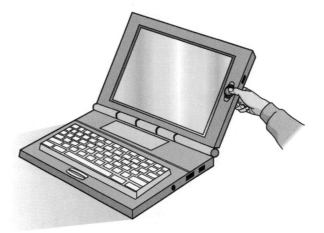

Figure 22.13 *Using a trackball to move the mouse pointer.*

Finally, if you do not like your notebook PC's mouse control or touch pad, you can always attach a small trackball to your notebook PC or connect a standard mouse to the notebook's serial port, as shown in Figure 22.14.

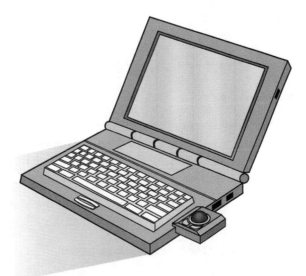

Figure 22.14 *Attaching a trackball or standard mouse to a notebook PC.*

UNDERSTANDING MOUSE DRAG OPERATIONS

Within Windows, there will be times when you must "drag" an object using your mouse. You might, for example, drag a file icon onto a folder to move the file. To perform a drag operation using your mouse, you aim your mouse pointer at the object and then hold down your mouse-select button (do not release the mouse button as you would for a click operation). Then, while holding down your mouse-select button, move your mouse across your desk. Windows, in turn, will drag the object you have selected. After you drag the object to the location you desire, simply release the mouse-select button.

IMPROVING YOUR MOUSE'S RESPONSIVENESS

Depending on your preferences, you can increase or decrease the speed at which your mouse pointer moves across the screen as you move your mouse across your desk. If, for example, you are just getting started, you may want to slow down your mouse to make the pointer easier to aim. In addition, if you have trouble double-clicking your mouse fast enough for Windows to recognize the double-click operation, you can fine-tune the amount of time Windows will wait for you to click your mouse the second time. To fine-tune your mouse settings, perform these steps:

1. Click your mouse on the Start button. Windows, in turn, will display the Start menu.

2. Within the Start menu, click your mouse on the Settings menu Control Panel option. Windows will open the Control Panel folder, as discussed in Lesson 45.

3. Within the Control Panel folder, double-click your mouse on the Mouse icon. Windows, in turn, will display the Mouse Properties dialog box, as shown in Figure 22.15.

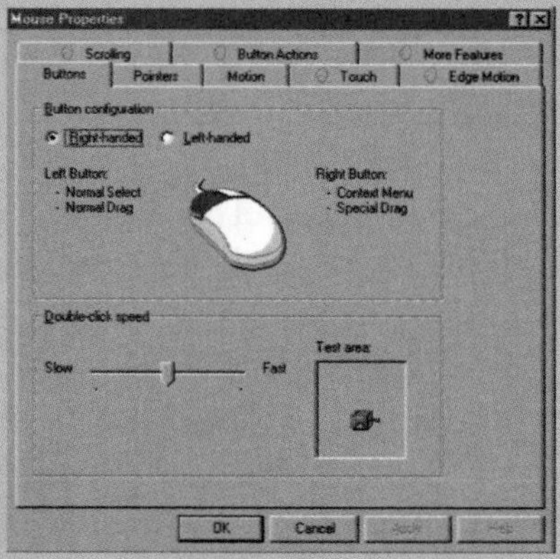

Figure 22.15 *The Mouse Properties dialog box.*

4. If you want to speed up or slow down the speed at which you double-click your mouse, use the Double-click speed slider to select the speed you desire. After you adjust the speed, double-click your mouse on the test button. If you double-click fast enough that Windows recognizes your double-click operation, Windows will pop the Jack out of the Jack in the box.

5. Within the Mouse Properties dialog box, click your mouse on the Motion tab. Windows, in turn, will display the Motion sheet, as shown in Figure 22.16.

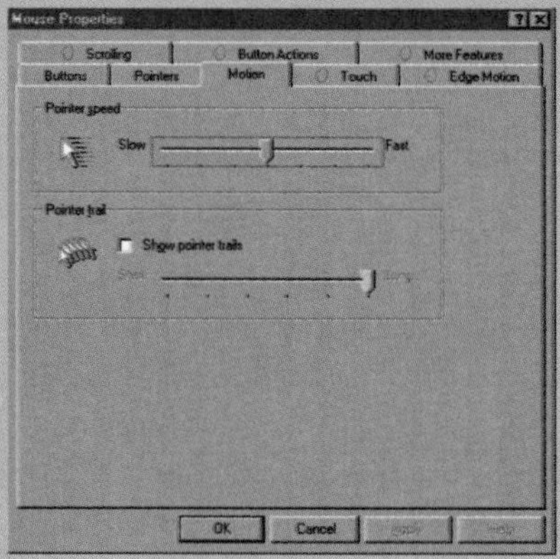

Figure 22.16 *The Mouse Properties dialog box Motion sheet.*

6. Within the Motion sheet, use the Pointer speed slider to fine tune how fast Windows moves your mouse pointer across your screen as you move the mouse across your desk.

7. After you select the settings you desire, click your mouse on the OK button.

8. To close the Control Panel folder, click your mouse on the folder's Close button.

Note: If you are left handed, you may want to reverse the operation of your mouse buttons, making the right-mouse button your mouse-select button. To reverse the mouse buttons, click your mouse on the Right-handed or Left-handed radio button that appears within the Mouse Properties dialog box.

REDUCING SORE WRISTS

If you spend considerable time using a keyboard or mouse, your wrists may become sore due to your repetitive typing or mouse operations. As shown in Figure 22.17, one way to reduce the strain on your wrists is to use a pad that elevates your wrist. You can find pads for your keyboard and mouse at most computer stores.

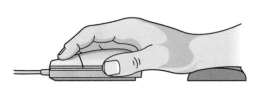 

Figure 22.17 *Using keyboard and mouse pads to relieve wrist strain.*

If you spend considerable time typing, you may want to purchase a keyboard similar to that shown in Figure 22.18, whose ergonomic design reduces strain on your wrists by better positioning your hands.

Figure 22.18 *Using an ergonomic keyboard to relieve wrist strain.*

USE MOUSE TRAILS TO MAKE YOUR MOUSE EASIER TO SEE

If you find that your mouse pointer is difficult to see on your screen, you can direct Windows to display mouse trails, which are a series of mouse pointers that chase your pointer across the screen, as shown in Figure 22.19.

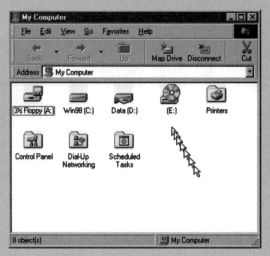

Figure 22.19 *Mouse trails make your mouse pointer easier to see.*

You can enable mouse trails by placing a checkmark within the Show pointer trails checkbox that appears within the Mouse Properties dialog box Motion sheet, previously shown in Figure 22.16.

WHAT YOU MUST KNOW

As you use your PC, the three devices you will use the most are your keyboard, mouse, and monitor. In this lesson, you examined various aspects of your keyboard and mouse. In Lesson 23, "Getting the Most from Your Monitor," you will examine key monitor operations. Before you continue with Lesson 23, however, make sure you understand the following key concepts:

✓ If you do not type or don't type well, you should purchase and use a typing tutor program.

✓ Keyboards consist of three parts: the standard typing keys, cursor movement keys, and the numeric keypad.

✓ The keys on a numeric keypad can function either as a 10-key calculator or as cursor-position arrow keys. To select the numeric keypad's operation, you use the NumLock key.

✓ Windows and Windows-based programs make extensive use of mouse operations. Within Windows, you will often have to click, double-click, or right-click your mouse. To click your mouse, you simply press and release the mouse-select button one time. To double-click your mouse, you must press and release the mouse-select button two times in quick succession. Finally, to right-click your mouse, you simply press and release your right-mouse button.

✓ To relieve stress from your wrists as you type or perform mouse operations, you should consider purchasing a keyboard pad and mouse pad. In addition, you may want to purchase an ergonomic keyboard whose shape positions your hands in a manner that reduces strain on your wrist.

✓ Using the Keyboard and Mouse icons you will find within the Windows Control Panel, you can fine-tune your mouse and keyboard operations.

Lesson 23

Getting the Most from Your Monitor

Throughout this book's lessons, you have examined specific PC hardware devices. In this lesson, you will examine the device you look at the most, the PC's monitor. As you will learn, there is a lot more to a monitor than simply images on the screen. In fact, if you have headaches or a stiff neck, your monitor may be an underlying cause. This lesson examine several simple steps you can perform to fine-tune your monitor use. By the time you finish this lesson, you will understand the following key concepts:

- If your monitor's brightness or contrast is not set correctly, you may strain your eyes, which in turn, may cause you to experience headaches. Most monitors provide controls that you can use to adjust its brightness and contrast.

- Your monitor's position can induce neck and shoulder pain. Ideally, you should place your monitor so that the top of the monitor is at or is slightly below your eye level.

- If your monitor consumes too much of your desk space, consider buying a flatscreen monitor.

- If your monitor is near a window, your monitor may reflect glare that strains your eyes. To reduce the glare, you can use an antiglare screen.

- Your monitor's resolution defines the number of picture elements (pixels) it can use to display an image. The higher your monitor's resolution, the sharper your image quality.

- When you shop for a monitor, you should consider the monitor's size, dot pitch, and vertical refresh rate.

FINE-TUNING YOUR MONITOR SETTINGS

If you spend several hours a day at your PC, you can eliminate considerable eye strain and possibly reduce your headache frequency by simply fine-tuning your monitor settings. To start, on most monitors, you will find a set of knobs that you can use to adjust your monitor's brightness, contrast, and alignment. Depending on your monitor's type, your monitor may contain knobs or buttons you can use to adjust the various settings. As shown in Figure 23.1, many monitors cover the knobs with a small plastic cover.

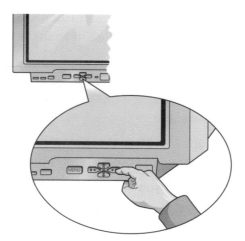

Figure 23.1 *Many monitors place their controls behind a small plastic cover.*

Take time now to adjust your monitor's brightness and contrast. If either your monitor's brightness or contrast is set poorly, your monitor can cause considerable eyestrain and headaches. Also, as shown in Figure 23.2, you can use your monitor's controls to adjust your screen's horizontal and vertical alignment. Ideally, nothing on your screen should be out of view. Depending on your monitor's type, you may be able to size the monitor's image to better fill your screen.

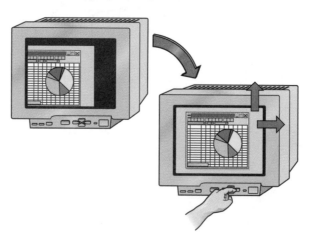

Figure 23.2 *Using the monitor's controls to align the screen's contents.*

POSITIONING YOUR MONITOR

If you work with a PC within your office, you many never have given much thought to your monitor's location. Likewise, if you were in a hurry to get your PC up and running, your monitor's current placement may not be ideal. Unfortunately, if you place your monitor too high or too low, you monitor may cause you to experience neck and shoulder pain. As shown in Figure 23.3, you should place your monitor so that the top of your monitor is even with or slightly below your eyes.

Figure 23.3 *By positioning your monitor correctly, you can reduce neck and shoulder strain.*

In addition, if you place your monitor next to a window, your monitor may reflect glare that causes you to experience eye strain which can lead to headaches. If you are unable to move your monitor away from the window, you can buy an antiglare screen that you attach to the front of your monitor, as shown in Figure 23.4.

Figure 23.4 *Using an antiglare screen, you may be able to reduce the amount of glare that your monitor reflects.*

TAKING ADVANTAGE OF FLATSCREEN MONITORS

Today, many users purchase a mini-tower PC that fits nicely under their desk. Unfortunately, most users then let their monitor consume much of their desk. If your desk space is at a premium, you may want to take advantage of a flatscreen monitor, similar to that shown in Figure 23.5. As you can see, the monitor requires much less space than a traditional monitor, freeing up additional desk space.

Figure 23.5 *Using a flatscreen monitor to consume less space on your desk.*

UNDERSTANDING YOUR MONITOR'S RESOLUTION

When you shop for a monitor, you will learn that your monitor's *resolution*, which corresponds to the number of picture elements (pixels) the monitor can use to display an image, is what influences the sharpness of a monitor's display. As shown in Figure 23.6, if you could look very closely at images on your screen, you could see the small picture elements that compose the image.

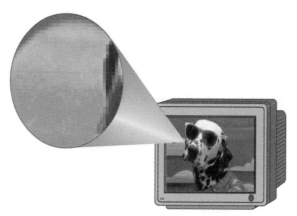

Figure 23.6 Each image on your screen consists of individual picture elements—pixels.

The more pixels, the higher the monitor's resolution and the sharper the image. Users describe a monitor's resolution in terms of pixels across the screen by pixels down the screen. As shown in Figure 23.7, common screen resolutions include 640x480, 800x600, 1024x768, 1280x1024, and 1600x1200.

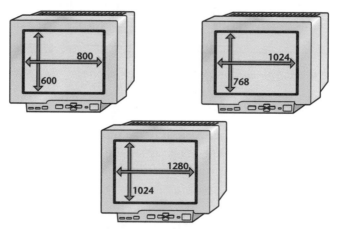

Figure 23.7 A monitor's resolution describes the number of pixels across the screen by the number of pixels down the screen.

As you shop for a monitor, make sure the monitor will support the screen resolutions you desire. Then, you must make sure that your video card (within your PC's system unit) supports the same resolutions. For more information on upgrading your monitor or video card, refer to the book *Rescued by Upgrading Your PC, Third Edition*, Jamsa Press, 1998.

UNDERSTANDING ACTIVE AND PASSIVE NOTEBOOK PC DISPLAYS

If you are shopping for a notebook PC, your salesperson may ask you if you want an active or passive display. In general, the terms active and passive describe the electronics the monitor provides, or does not provide, to enhance the screen display. An active display provides additional electronics that sharpen the display appearance. In contrast, a passive display does not.

Because an active display will provide a sharper image, it will also cost more. However, as you have learned in this lesson, having a high-quality monitor can reduce your eye strain. The only disadvantage of an active display occurs when you use your notebook PC to work while you travel. Because it provides a sharper image display, a person who is sitting next to you can read your notebook PC's screen contents, whereas, if you are using a less expensive, passive display, he or she cannot.

SHOPPING FOR A MONITOR

If you flip through the pages of a computer magazine, or spend a few minutes in the aisle of a computer store, you will find a variety of PC monitors, most of which look quite similar on the outside. To start, you should select a monitor whose size meets your needs. In general, monitor sizes range from 14 inches to 21 inches. As shown in Figure 23.8, you determine a monitor's size by measuring its diagonal.

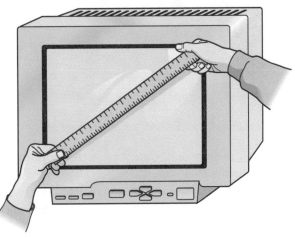

Figure 23.8 *A monitor's size corresponds to the length of the diagonal across the monitor's screen.*

As you shop, you will find that as monitors increase in size, they also increase in cost. However, if you spend considerable time in front of your PC, to reduce eyestrain you will want at least a 17-inch display. After you select the monitor's size, you must then consider the monitor's *dot pitch*. To display an image, your monitor illuminates red, green, and blue phosphors for each picture element (or pixel) on your screen. As shown in Figure 23.9, a monitor's dot pitch specifies the distance between two phosphors of the same color. By knowing the distance between successive colors, you know the distance between the monitor's picture elements and hence the monitor's sharpness. The smaller the dot pitch, such as 0.28mm, the sharper the monitor's image.

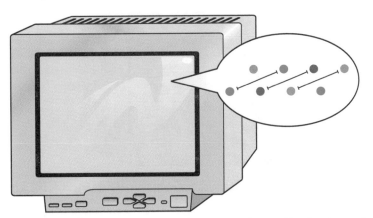

Figure 23.9 *A monitor's dot pitch influences the monitor's sharpness. The smaller the dot pitch, the sharper the image.*

After you find a monitor with the dot pitch you desire, you will want to know the monitor's vertical refresh rate. To illuminate the red, green, and blue phosphors, the monitor has an electron gun that it moves across and down your screen, as shown in Figure 23.10. The electron gun heats the phosphors, causing them to illuminate. For a monitor to display an image, the electron gun must continually refresh the phosphors.

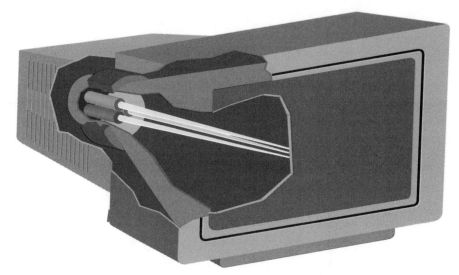

Figure 23.10 To display an image, the monitor uses an electron gun to heat red, green, and blue phosphors.

A monitor's vertical refresh rate tells you the length of time it takes the monitor's electron gun to move down your screen. If your monitor's refresh rate is too slow, the image will appear wavy, which may strain your eyes. Most monitors will refresh the screen 60 to 72 times per second. Your salesperson may tell you that the monitor's vertical refresh rate is 60Hz (60 hertz) or 72Hz. As you will recall from Lesson 12, "Understanding the Myriad of PC Speeds and Sizes," the letters Hz, pronounced hertz, correspond to cycles per seconds. A monitor whose refresh rate is 72Hz refreshes its screen 72 times per second.

When you ask about a monitor's refresh rate, ask what the monitor's refresh is for the monitor's highest resolution. Some monitors have satisfactory refresh rates at low resolutions, but not at higher resolutions. Also, make sure your monitor achieves its refresh rates using noninterlaced refresh operations. To improve their refresh rates, some less expensive monitors will only refresh every other line of pixels (called interlacing). Although such interlacing may let the monitor support higher resolutions, interlacing creates a wavy screen image that will strain your eyes. You want a noninterlaced monitor that refreshes every line, even at high resolutions. Figure 23.11 illustrates how an interlaced monitor skips rows of pixels as it refreshes the screen.

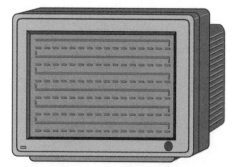

Figure 23.11 An interlaced monitor skips every other row of pixels as it refreshes the screen, which may cause an undesirable wavy screen appearance.

CONNECTING YOUR NOTEBOOK PC TO A STANDARD MONITOR

As you know, a notebook PC has its monitor built-in. If you use your notebook PC to give presentations, there may be times when you will need to display your notebook's screen contents on a different monitor. For example, you may want to show your presentation on a large screen that many users can see. On the back of most notebook PCs, you will find a monitor port to which you can connect a monitor, as shown in Figure 23.12. By pressing a special function key on your notebook PC's keyboard, you can toggle the notebook's display between its built-in monitor and the external monitor.

Figure 23.12 *Most notebook PCs let you connect a standard monitor.*

WHAT YOU MUST KNOW

If you spend several hours a day with your PC, your monitor may strain your eyes, neck, and shoulders. In this lesson, you learned several simple steps you can perform to fine-tune your monitor settings. In Lesson 24, "Customizing Your PC Desktop and Screen Saver," you will learn how to customize your Desktop background, colors, and screen-saver settings. Before you continue with Lesson 24, however, make sure you understand the following key concepts:

✓ If you examine your monitor, you should find controls you can use to adjust your monitor's brightness and contrast, which may reduce eye strain as you view your monitor.

✓ If you have been experiencing a sore neck or shoulder, examine your monitor's position. If your monitor is too high or too low, your monitor may induce neck and shoulder pain.

✓ If you work in an office with bright lights or many windows, you can reduce the glare your monitor reflects using an antiglare screen.

✓ Resolution defines the number of picture elements (pixels) a monitor uses to display an image. The higher a monitor's resolution, the sharper the monitor's image quality.

✓ When you shop for a monitor, you should consider the monitor's size, dot pitch, and vertical refresh rate.

Lesson 24

Customizing Your PC Desktop and Screen Saver

Within an office, workers often customize their work environment by placing family pictures, posters, or other items on their desk. In a similar way, Windows makes it easy for users to customize their PC Desktop by changing screen colors, assigning an image to the Desktop background, or by selecting unique settings for a screen saver.

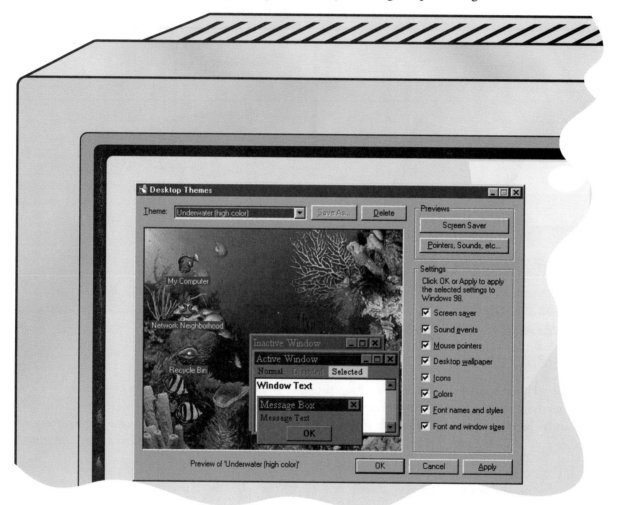

In this lesson, you will learn ways to customize the Windows Desktop. By the time you finish this lesson, you will understand the following key concepts:

- To make your PC "feel more like home," Windows lets you customize your Desktop by assigning a specific background image, selecting a color scheme, and by enabling a screen saver.

- To control the appearance of the Windows Desktop, you will use the Display Properties dialog box. To open the Display Properties dialog box, right-click your mouse on an unused area on the Desktop. Windows, in turn, will display a pop-up menu. Within the pop-up menu, choose Properties.

- A Windows wallpaper is an image that Windows displays on your Desktop. Windows provides several wallpaper images from which you can select or, if you have a photograph in an electronic format, you can display your own image on the Desktop.

- A screen saver is a special program Windows runs when your system has been inactive for a specific period of time. As it runs, the screen saver will display various images for the purpose of preventing any one image from remaining on your screen for too long (which could damage your monitor).

- Windows 98 provides a set of Desktop Themes that you can select to assign a background image, screen colors, animated icons, and a custom screen saver.

CHANGING YOUR DESKTOP SETTINGS

As you have learned, each time you start your system, Windows displays its Desktop, similar to that shown in Figure 24.1. The Desktop is so named because it provides your working area that you will use to run other programs.

Figure 24.1 *The Windows Desktop.*

To help you customize your Desktop, Windows lets you change the colors of common screen elements (such as menu bars, window title bars, and so on), change the Desktop's background image, or select and customize a screen saver. Figure 24.2, for example, shows several different Desktops.

Figure 24.2 *Windows lets you customize the Desktop's appearance.*

147

Depending on your version of Windows, the images that Windows provides which you can use to customize your Desktop may vary. This lesson will discuss the capabilities all users will have and then cover features provided with Windows 98. To begin, right-click your mouse (click your mouse's right button) on an unused area on your Desktop. Windows, in turn, will display a pop-up menu similar to that shown in Figure 24.3.

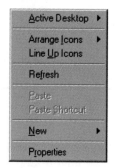

Figure 24.3 *Right-clicking your mouse on the Desktop directs Windows to display a pop-up menu.*

Within the pop-up menu, select the Properties option. Windows, in turn, will display the Display Properties dialog box, as shown in Figure 24.4.

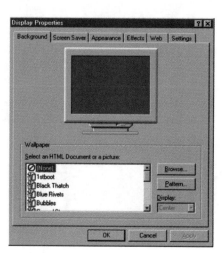

Figure 24.4 *The Display Properties dialog box.*

Within the Display Properties dialog box, you can select different tabs to customize different parts of your Desktop.

ASSIGNING A BACKGROUND PATTERN OR WALLPAPER

Within the Desktop Properties dialog box Background sheet, Windows lets you select a pattern or wallpaper image that Windows will display on the Desktop, behind your icons. A pattern is an image Windows creates (using a simple shape) to fill your entire Desktop area. To select a pattern, click your mouse on the pull-down Pattern list. Windows, in turn, will display the names of the available patterns. As you click your mouse on a pattern name within the list, Windows will preview the pattern within the small monitor that appears within the Display Properties dialog box. Figure 24.5 shows how Windows will preview several such patterns.

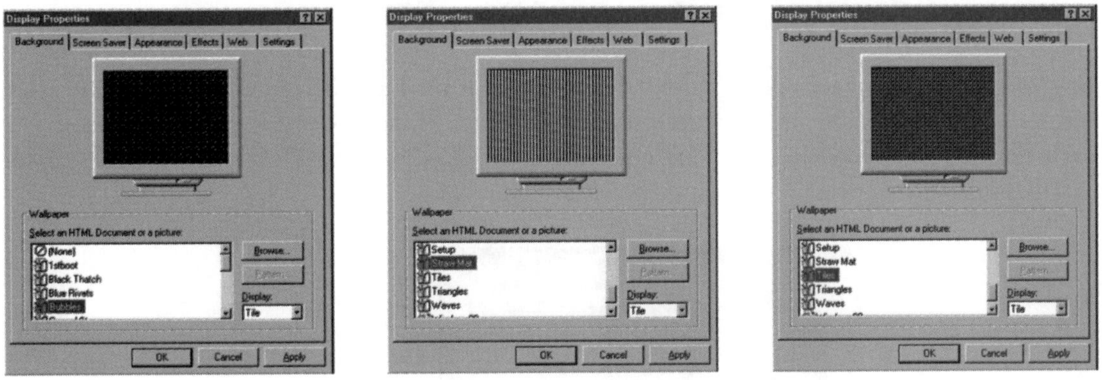

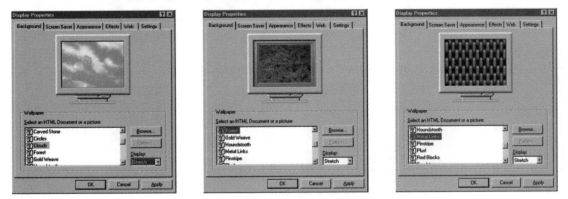

Figure 24.5 *Previewing background patterns within the Display Properties dialog box.*

If you find a pattern that you like, highlight the pattern's name within the list and then click your mouse on the OK button. Windows, in turn, will fill your Desktop with the pattern image. Should you later grow tired of the image, simply open the Display Properties dialog box again and select a new pattern.

Within the Display Properties dialog box Background sheet, you can also assign a wallpaper to the Desktop. A wallpaper is an image, such as a photo of your family, that resides in a BMP (bitmap) file. Within the dialog box's Wallpaper list, Windows provides several background images that you can use for Desktop wallpapers. In addition, if you click your mouse on the Browse button, Windows will open a dialog box that you can use to search your disk for other BMP files. In Lesson 32, "Creating Electronic Images Using Scanners and Digital Cameras," you will learn how to convert your photos into electronic image files. By selecting such an image file as your Wallpaper image, you can display a photograph of your family, your dog, or any other item you desire, on your Desktop.

As you highlight wallpaper names within the Wallpaper list, Windows will preview the wallpaper image within the small monitor that appears within the Display Properties dialog box. Again, if you find an image you desire, simply highlight the wallpaper name within the Wallpaper list and then click your mouse on the OK button. Figure 24.6 shows several Wallpaper images within the Display Properties dialog box preview monitor.

Figure 24.6 *Previewing wallpaper images within the Display Properties dialog box.*

Note: *If the background pattern or wallpaper image you select does not fill your screen, select the Tile button within the Display Properties dialog box to direct Windows to place multiple copies of the image on your screen (as if Windows were covering your screen background with small tiles).*

CUSTOMIZING YOUR DESKTOP COLORS

In addition to letting you specify the image that Windows displays as your Desktop background, Windows also lets you customize the colors it uses to display various screen objects, such as title bars, buttons, menus, and so on. To customize the colors of items on your Desktop, click your mouse on the Display Properties dialog box Appearance Tab. Windows, in turn, will display the Appearance sheet, as shown in Figure 24.7.

Figure 24.7 *The Display Properties dialog box Appearance tab.*

Within the Appearance sheet, you can assign specific colors to individual Desktop items. However, to help you coordinate your color selections, Windows predefines several color schemes that you can select as your own. Within the Appearance tab, click your mouse on the Schemes pull-down list. Windows, in turn, will display a list of its predefined color schemes. As you highlight a color scheme name, Windows will preview the scheme's colors with the screen objects that appear within the dialog box. Figure 24.8 shows three sample color schemes.

Figure 24.8 *Previewing color schemes within the Display Properties dialog box.*

If you find a color scheme that you like, highlight the scheme's name within the list and click your mouse on the OK button. As before, should you later grow tired of the color scheme, simply use the Display Properties dialog box to select a new scheme.

SELECTING A SCREEN SAVER

As you learned in Lesson 23, "Getting the Most from Your Monitor," to display an image, your monitor illuminates red, green, and blue phosphors. If you leave the same image on your screen for a long period of time (it would probably take several weeks), it is possible that you can damage your monitor so that the image appears permanently "burned into" your screen. In fact, even if youturn your monitor off, you will see a slight ghosting of the image.

To prevent such damage to a monitor, software developers created programs called screen savers, that will activate when you are not actively using your system and will then display a series of different images so that your monitor cannot "burn in" any one image. Later, when you resume your work (either type or move your mouse), the screen saver program will end and Windows will redisplay your previous screen contents.

Today, users normally run screen savers to hide the contents of their screen when they are not actively using their system. In this way, should another user enter your office, the screen saver may prevent the other user from viewing the documents you have open on your screen. Also, should you need to leave your desk, Windows lets you password protect most screen savers. When you password protect your screen saver, another user cannot turn off your screen saver (to read your screen contents) without first typing in a password that only you should know.

To assign a screen saver to your system, click your mouse on the Display Properties dialog box Screen Saver tab. Windows, in turn, will display the Screen Saver sheet, as shown in Figure 24.9.

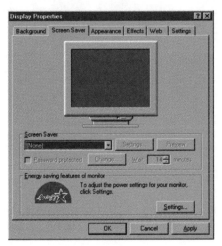

Figure 24.9 *The Display Properties dialog box Screen Saver sheet.*

Within the Screen Saver sheet, click your mouse on the pull-down Screen Saver list. To preview a screen saver, click your mouse on the screen saver name and then click your mouse on the Preview button. Windows, in turn, will activate the screen saver so you can see (and possibly hear) its presentation. If you move your mouse or press a key, Windows will stop the screen saver and returns you to the Screen Saver sheet.

After you select the screen saver you desire, you can use the Screen Saver sheet to specify the amount of inactive time Windows will wait before starting the screen saver and you can password protect your screen saver.

Note: *For more information on customizing screens savers, refer to the book **1001 Windows 98 Tips**, Jamsa Press, 1998.*

TAKING ADVANTAGE OF DESKTOP THEMES

If you are using Windows 98, you can select a Desktop Theme that not only specifies your Desktop background and colors, but also animates many of the icons on your Desktop. In addition, each Desktop theme customizes the sounds Windows plays for various system events. To select a Desktop theme, perform these steps:

1. Click your mouse on the Start button. Windows, in turn, will display the Start menu.

2. Within the Start menu, click your mouse on the Settings Option and then choose Control. Windows, in turn, will open the Control Panel folder, discussed in Lesson 45, "Configuring Your PC's System Settings."

3. Within the Control Panel, double-click your mouse on the Desktop Themes icon. Windows will display the Desktop Themes dialog box, as shown in Figure 24.10. If your Control Panel folder does not contain the Desktop Themes icon, see the following section which discusses installing the Desktop Themes from the Windows 98 CD-ROM.

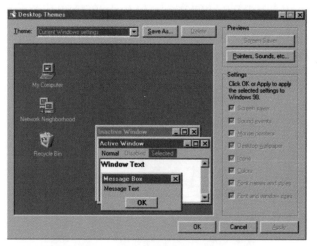

Figure 24.10 *The Desktop Themes dialog box.*

4. Within the Desktop Themes dialog box, click your mouse on the Themes pull-down list. As you click your mouse on a theme, Windows will preview the theme, as shown in Figure 24.11.

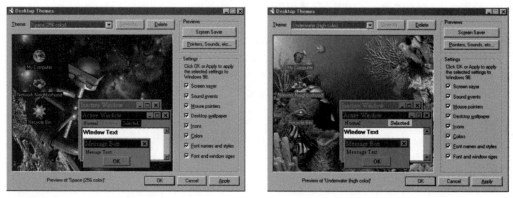

Figure 24.11 *Previewing Desktop Themes.*

5. After you select the Theme you desire, click your mouse on the OK button.

INSTALLING THE DESKTOP THEMES

If you are using Windows 98 and your Control Panel does not contain the Desktop Themes icon, you can install the Themes from the Windows 98 CD-ROM by performing these steps:

1. Click your mouse on the Start button. Windows, in turn, will display the Start menu.

2. Within the Start menu, click your mouse on the Settings option and choose Control Panel. Windows will open the Control Panel folder.

3. Within the Control Panel folder, double-click your mouse on the Add/Remove Programs icon. Windows will display the Add/Remove Programs dialog box.

4. Within the Add/Remove Programs dialog box, click your mouse on the Windows Setup tab. Windows, in turn, will display the Windows Setup sheet.

5. Within the Windows Setup sheet, place a checkmark next to the Desktop Themes component and then click your mouse on the OK button. Windows, in turn, may prompt you to insert the Windows CD-ROM as it installs the software.

UNDERSTANDING USER PROFILES

If you share a PC with another user, you probably find it frustrating if, each time you sit down at the PC, the other user has changed your Desktop's appearance. When two or more users share a PC, Windows lets the users each create a user profile, within which Windows stores the settings each user desires. Before each users starts working, the current user simply logs into the system by specifying a username and password. Windows, in turn, will then assign the current user's profile. For more information on user profiles, see your system administrator or refer to the book *1001 Windows 98 Tips*, Jamsa Press, 1998.

WHAT YOU MUST KNOW

Today, many users spend several hours a day at their PC. To help users feel comfortable with their systems, Windows lets users customize their Desktop settings. In this lesson, you learned how to assign a background image to the Desktop, change color schemes, activate a screen saver, and use the Windows 98 animated Desktop Themes. In Lesson 25, "Using a Word Processor to Create Memos, Letters, and Reports," you will learn how to perform essential word-processing operations. Before you continue with Lesson 25, however, make sure you understand the following key concepts:

✓ Within Windows, the Desktop is the your electronic work space. Windows lets you customize your Desktop using the Display Properties dialog box.

✓ To open the Display Properties dialog box, right-click your mouse on an unused location on the Desktop. Windows, in turn, will display a small pop-up menu. Within the pop-up menu, choose the Properties option.

✓ A screen saver is a program that Windows runs after your PC has been inactive for a specific interval of time. The screen saver displays random images on your screen.

✓ Windows 98 provides a set of Desktop Themes that provide a background image, color scheme, as well as animated icons and sounds.

Lesson 25

Using a Word Processor to Create Memos, Letters, and Reports

In the past, one of the primary reasons users bought PCs was to take advantage of word-processing software. Today, users make extensive use of electronic-mail software, a Web browser, and their word processor. This lesson examines Microsoft Word, the most widely used word processor in the world. If you are not using Word, don't worry, the concepts this lesson presents will apply to all word processors. In addition, this lesson will show you how to run the WordPad accessory program, a simple word processor that Microsoft bundles with Windows. As you will learn, word-processing software makes it easy for you to create, spell check, and print your documents. In addition, the word processor makes it easy for you edit to your document's contents.

By the time you finish this lesson, you will understand the following key concepts:

- Word-processing software, such as Microsoft Word, lets you can create letters, memos, and reports.
- If, as you are typing your document, you mistype a word, you can use your keyboard arrow, BACKSPACE, and DEL keys to easily correct the word.

- When you type documents using a word processor, you will normally not press the ENTER key at the end of each line of text. Instead, you will simply keep typing and let the software wrap the text for you. In general, the only time you press the ENTER key within a word processor is at the end of a paragraph or to manually set your spacing between objects.

- Before you print your document or save your document for the final time, you should use the word processor to spell check your document's contents..

- Within most word processors, you can save your document to a file on disk using the File menu Save option. Likewise, you can print your document's contents by selecting the File menu Print option. To open an existing document from a file on your disk, you will use the File menu Open option.

UNDERSTANDING WORD-PROCESSING BASICS

A word processor is a program within which you can create reports, memos, and even the chapters of a book. Many users avoid using a word processor because they don't type well. A word processor, however, is ideal for poor typists. If, as you type within a document, you mistype a word, you can easily correct the error by using your keyboard arrow keys to position the cursor back to the error and then using the DEL or BACKSPACE key to delete the wrong character so that you can type the correct text. In addition to making it easier for you to correct mistakes, a word-processing program differs from a typewriter in that when you type within a word processor, you will not press the ENTER key at the end of each line. Instead, you will simply keep typing and let your word-processing software wrap your text to the next line for you. The only time you press ENTER within a word processor is at the end of a paragraph.

When you create documents using a word processor, you may, based on the document size and content, work on your document for several hours or possibly several weeks. As you create documents using your word processor, you will store the document's contents within a file on your disk. Each time you edit your document, you must save your changes to the file on disk (which you can do by selecting the File menu Save option). If you exit your word-processing program without saving your changes to the file on disk, you will lose your changes and the document will contain its original contents. Word-processing programs make it easy for you to insert, delete, or edit text. In general, you simply use your mouse or keyboard arrow keys to position the text cursor within your document and then start typing (or deleting) the text you desire. After you make your changes to the document, you can save your document's new contents to the document file on disk. Figure 25.1 shows a document within the Microsoft Word word processor.

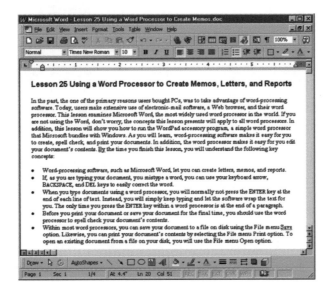

Figure 25.1 *Using Microsoft Word to edit a word-processing document.*

USING THE WORDPAD WORD PROCESSOR

If you do not have Microsoft Word installed on your system, you can use the WordPad accessory program that Microsoft bundles with Windows to create simple word-processing documents. Using WordPad, you can create, edit, format, print, and save word-processing documents. You cannot, however, spell check your document. To run the WordPad accessory program, perform these steps:

1. Click your mouse on the Start button. Windows, in turn, will display the Start menu.

2. Within the Start menu, click your mouse on the Programs menus. Windows will cascade the Programs submenu.

3. Within the Programs submenu, click your mouse on the Accessories option and then choose WordPad. Windows, in turn, will run the WordPad accessory.

For more information on using the WordPad word processor, refer to the book *1001 Windows 98 Tips*, Jamsa Press, 1998.

SPELL CHECKING YOUR DOCUMENT

Before you print or save your document's contents, you should use your word processor to check your document's spelling (which users refer to as *spell checking the document*). Within Word, you can spell check the current document by selecting the Tools menu Spelling option or by clicking your mouse on the toolbar's Spelling icon. Word, in turn, will examine the spelling of each word within your document. If Word encounters a word that may be misspelled (Word may simply not recognize a word you have used), Word will display the Spelling dialog box, as shown in Figure 25.2, within which it may offer replacement words. Within the Spelling and Grammar dialog box, you can direct Word to replace the word (or every occurrence of the word with a replacement word that either you or Word provides). If the word is spelled correctly, but Word does not recognize the word within the Spelling and Grammar dialog box, you can direct Word to add the word to its dictionary. As a rule, you should spell check your document before you print your document's contents or save your document to disk.

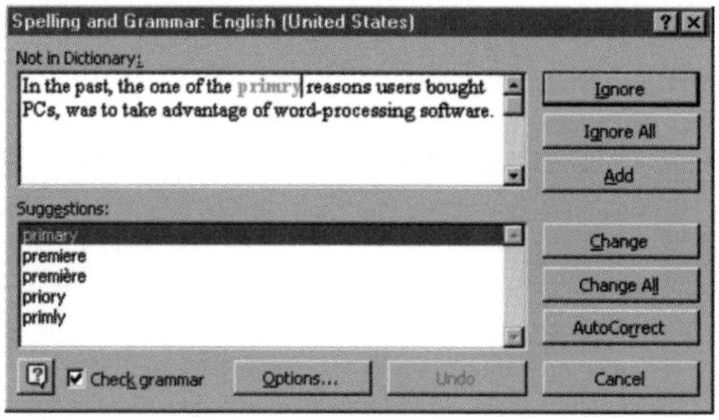

Figure 25.2 The Spelling and Grammar dialog box.

It's important that you understand that simply because the word processor's spell checker does report any errors, does not mean that your document is error free. A spell checker, for example, would consider both of the following sentences correct:

A very big bear just flew past my window.

A vary big bare jest flu passed my window.

Within both sentences the words are spelled correctly. However, the second sentence uses words that are not correct—the words are spelled correctly—they are just the wrong words.

SAVING YOUR DOCUMENT

Like most Windows-based programs, within Word, you save a document's contents using the File menu Save As option. When you select the Save As option, Word, in turn, will display the Save As dialog box, within which you can specify the folder and filename within which you want to save your document's contents. When you save your documents, assign a filename that meaningfully describes the document's contents. In addition, as discussed in Lesson 14, "Storing Information within Files," you may want to precede your filenames with the current year, month, and day, such as *99-01-23 Budget Proposal.Doc.* By preceding your filenames with the current date, you can control the order that Windows uses to display your filenames within the Explorer file list and within Open dialog boxes, which will help you locate your files at a later time. As you have learned, the first time that you save your document, you should use the File menu Save As option. Word, in turn, will display the Save As dialog box, within which you can select a folder and filename. After that, to save the file's contents, you can select the File menu Save option or click your mouse on the toolbar Disk icon. Word, in turn, will save your current changes to the existing document file.

OPENING AN EXISTING DOCUMENT

As you just learned, using the File menu Save As option, you can save your document's contents to a file on disk. When users work on large documents, it is not uncommon for users to work on the same document for several days, weeks, or months. To open an existing document, select the File menu Open option or click your mouse on the toolbar Open icon (which appears as an open yellow file folder). Word, in turn, will display the Open dialog box, within which you can locate and open the file you desire. To make it easy for you to open a document you have recently used, Word tracks your most recently used files within the File menu, as shown in Figure 25.3. To open a document that appears within the File menu's recently used file list, simply click your mouse on the file you desire. After you open a document's contents, you can use your word-processing software to edit the document's existing text.

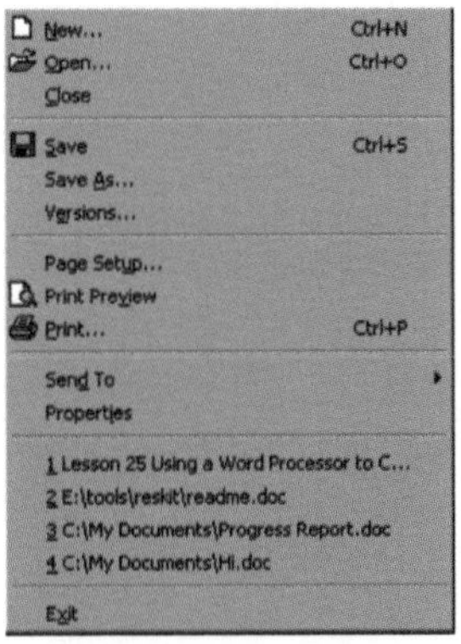

Figure 25.3 *Word tracks your recently used documents within the File menu.*

PRINTING YOUR DOCUMENT

After you create your document, you will quite likely want to print its contents. As is the case in most Windows-based programs, within Word you can print your current document by clicking your mouse on the toolbar's Printer icon or by selecting the File menu Print option. Before you print your document, however, you may want to first preview how Word will actually print its contents. To preview your printout, click your mouse on the toolbar's Print Preview icon (the icon that looks like a magnifying glass examining a printout) or select the File menu Print Preview option. Word, in turn, will preview your printout, as shown in Figure 25.4. Within the Print Preview window, you can zoom in on specific cells, adjust your document's current margins, and change your printer settings. Then, after you are satisfied with your document's format, you can click your mouse on the Print button to print your document's contents. Likewise, if you decide you don't want to print your document's contents, you can click your mouse on the Close button to return to Word's standard document view.

157

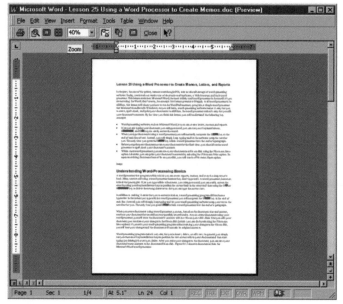

Figure 25.4 *Previewing a printout within Word.*

HIGHLIGHTING TEXT WITHIN YOUR DOCUMENT

Within your word processor, there will be times when you will want to highlight specific text, perhaps by changing the text's typeface or font size. Within Word, you can change your text's font using one of two techniques. To start, if you have already typed your text, you can select the text you want to highlight and then use the toolbar font list or font size controls to select the font or font size you desire.

To select text within Word, you can use your keyboard or mouse. To select text with your keyboard, use your keyboard arrow keys to position the text cursor in front of the first character in the text you desire. Next, hold down your keyboard's SHIFT key and press your keyboard arrow keys to move the text cursor over the characters. As you move the text cursor, Word will highlight your text using reverse video. If you have not yet typed your text, you can use the toolbar font and font size controls to select the font or font size you desire. Then, as you start typing, Word will use your newly selected font.

WHAT YOU MUST KNOW

As you work with your PC, you will make extensive use of a word processor to create letters, memos, reports, and other documents. In Lesson 26, "Automating Calculations Using Spreadsheet Software," you will learn how to use a spreadsheet program, such as Microsoft Excel, to automate many calculations you may currently perform by hand. Before you continue with Lesson 26, however, make sure you have learned the following key concepts:

- ✓ As you type, word-processing programs make it easy for you to correct errors. If you mistype a word, you can use your keyboard arrow keys, the BACKSPACE key, and DEL key to easily correct the word.

- ✓ Within a word processor, you will normally not press the ENTER key at the end of each line of text. Instead, you will simply keep typing and let the software wrap the text for you. Normally, the only time you press the ENTER key within a word processor is at the end of a paragraph or to manually force spacing between lines of text.

- ✓ After you type your text, you should use the word processor's spell check software to verify your word spellings.

Lesson 26

Automating Calculations Using Spreadsheet Software

Years ago, when the IBM PC first hit the market, the software program that fueled the PC's widespread use was a spreadsheet program named VisiCalc. Using VisiCalc, business people could automate many of the calculations they were performing by hand. By automating their calculations with a spreadsheet, business people could ask "what if" questions which they could quickly answer using their spreadsheet, such as "What would happen to our profit levels if we reduced our price per unit by $1?"

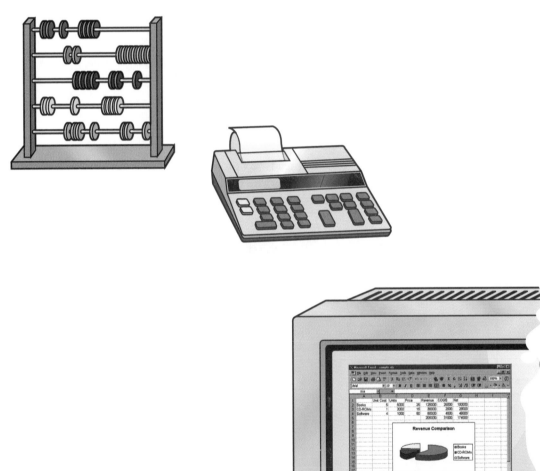

Today, Microsoft Excel is the most widely used spreadsheet program. This lesson examines basic spreadsheet operations that you can perform within Excel. By the time you finish this lesson, you will understand the following key concepts:

- Spreadsheets consist of a table of cells, each of which has a unique name.

- Spreadsheets name cells based on the cell's row and column position, such as A1 (column A, row 1) or B2 (column B, row 2). Within each cell, you can store a number, text, or a formula.

- To assign a value to a cell, click your mouse on the cell or use your keyboard arrow keys to highlight the cell. Then, type the cell's value. As you type, Excel will display the text you type within a formula bar that appears above the cell table.

- To change a cell's value, simply select the cell and type in the new value that you desire.

- Excel lets you perform "what if" operations which let you analyze how your results would change if you changed a specific value, such as your product's price. To perform "what if" operations, you will create one or more formulas within your spreadsheet.

- To perform calculations within a spreadsheet, you assign a formula to a cell. Within Excel, your formulas must start with an equal sign.

- To simplify common operations, such as adding up a row or column of values, Excel provides several built-in functions.

- When you use a function or when you chart data, you may need to specify a range of values, such as a column or row of numbers. To specify a range of values, use the name of the first cell in the range, followed by a colon (:), and then the last cell in the range, such as A1:A5.

Understanding Rows, Columns, and Cells

When you run a spreadsheet program such as Excel, the spreadsheet program will display an electronic spreadsheet that consists of thousands of cells, which the spreadsheet organizes into rows and columns, as shown in Figure 26.1. As you type in your data, you will store each of your numbers within a spreadsheet cell.

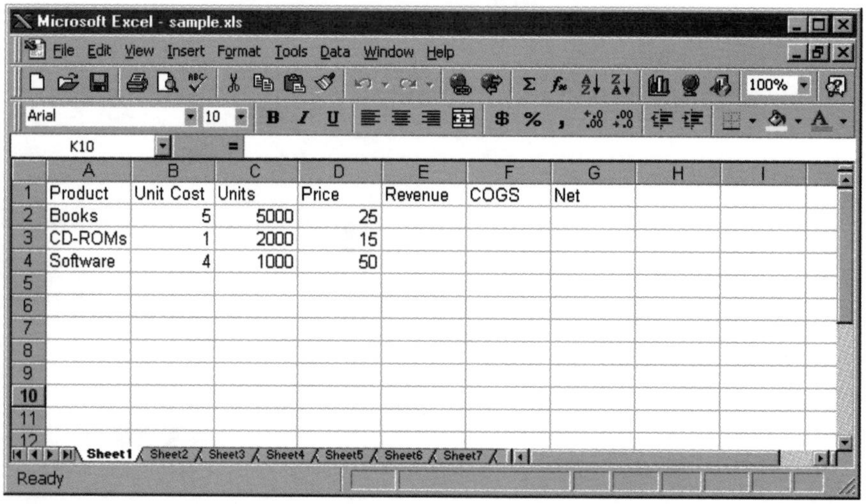

Figure 26.1 *Spreadsheets consist of rows and columns of cells within which you store your data.*

Each spreadsheet cell has a unique name that you can use to reference the cell's contents. As shown in Figure 26.2, spreadsheets use letters to identify each column and numbers for each row. The first cell, for example, is A1. If you move across the row to the right, the second and third cells, as shown in Figure 26.2, are B1 and C1. Likewise, if you move down the first column, the second and third cells are A2 and A3.

When you enter values within a spreadsheet, you must place each number within a unique cell. To select a cell, you simply click your mouse on the cell or use your keyboard's arrow keys to select the cell. Within a cell, you can type in a number, text (such as a label), or you can type an equation.

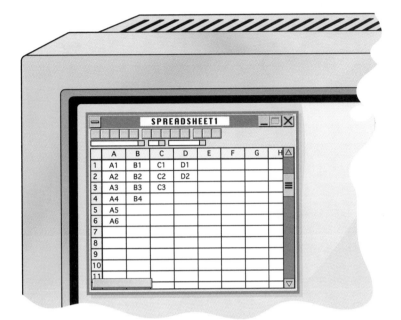

Figure 26.2 *Spreadsheets assign unique names to each cell.*

As you type a cell's value, your software will display the numbers or letters you type within a text field, called the formula bar, that appears above the spreadsheet cells, as shown in Figure 26.3.

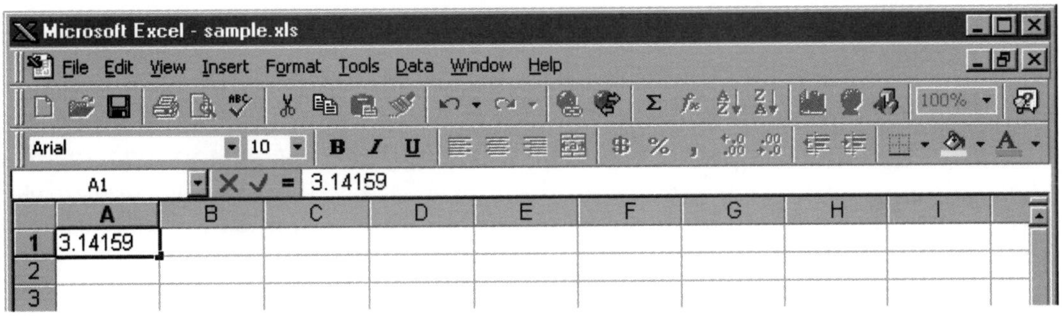

Figure 26.3 *As you type a cell's text, number, or formula, your spreadsheet software will display the values you type within the formula bar.*

After you type a value, you must press ENTER or the TAB key, or click your mouse on a different cell, before your spreadsheet software will assign your new value to the cell. If you must edit a cell's value, you select the cell (by clicking your mouse on the cell, for example), and then use your keyboard arrow keys to edit the value that appears within the formula bar. If you have Excel on your PC, start Excel now. To start Excel, click your mouse on the Start menu Programs options. Windows, in turn, will display the Programs submenu. Within the Programs submenu, click your mouse on the Microsoft Excel option (depending on how Excel was installed on your system, the Excel menu option may reside within a Microsoft Office submenu). Windows, in turn, will start Excel, which will display a blank spreadsheet. Within the spreadsheet, enter the values shown in Figure 26.4. To enter a value within a cell, simply click your mouse on the cell and then type the cell's corresponding values. As you enter the values, make sure that you use the same row and column for each value as shown in Figure 26.4. The spreadsheet will determine a company's revenues, costs (COGS stands for cost of goods sold—what each unit sold costs to make), and profits from three various products: Books, CD-ROMs, and Software.

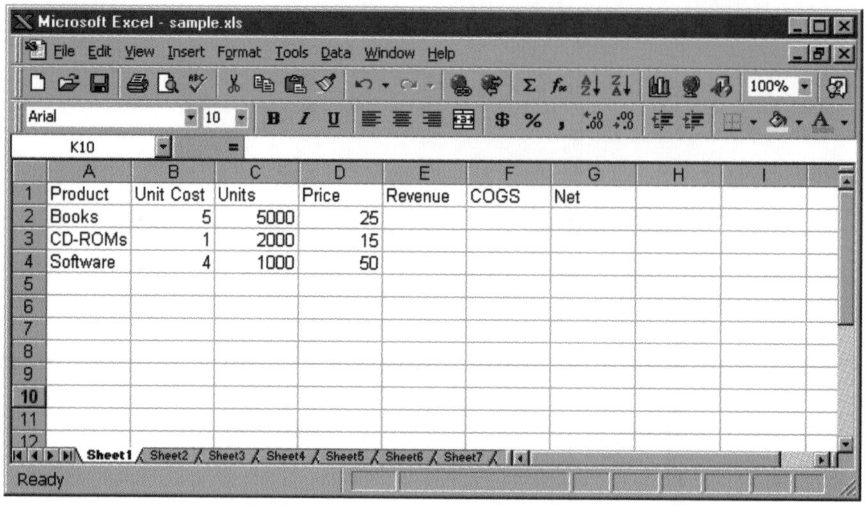

Figure 26.4 *Entering text and numeric values within an Excel spreadsheet.*

After you type in your values, you are ready to perform simple calculations using the values.

PERFORMING SIMPLE OPERATIONS

To perform calculations using a spreadsheet, you must assign a formula to a cell. A *formula* is simply an equation. For example, using the spreadsheet shown in Figure 26.4, assume that you want to calculate the company's revenue from the sale of books. To determine the revenue, you would use the equation Revenue = Price * Units. For example, if the company sold 1,000 books at $5 a book, the company's revenues would be $5,000.

When you create spreadsheets within Excel, you express your formulas in terms of cell names. To determine the book revenue, for example, you must multiple the book units (cell C2) times the book price (cell D2). In this case, you will assign the equation to the book revenue cell, which is cell E2. To assign a formula to a cell, select the cell and then type in an equal sign, followed by the equation. In this case, click your mouse on cell E2. Within the cell, type formula =C2*D2. After you type the formula, press ENTER or click your mouse a different cell. Excel, in turn, will display the result of your formula (which, in this case, should be 125,000 within the cell). If Excel did not display your result, but rather, displayed something such as C2*D2, you simply need to precede your equation with an equal sign. Using this technique, assign the formulas listed in Table 26 to the corresponding cells.

Cell	Formula
E3	=C3*D3
E4	=C4*D4
F2	=B2*C2
F3	=B3*C3
F4	=B4*C4
G2	=E2-F2
G3	=E3-F3
G4	=E4-F4

Table 26 *Formulas to assign to cells within the Excel spreadsheet.*

After you enter the formulas, your spreadsheet should appear as shown in Figure 26.5.

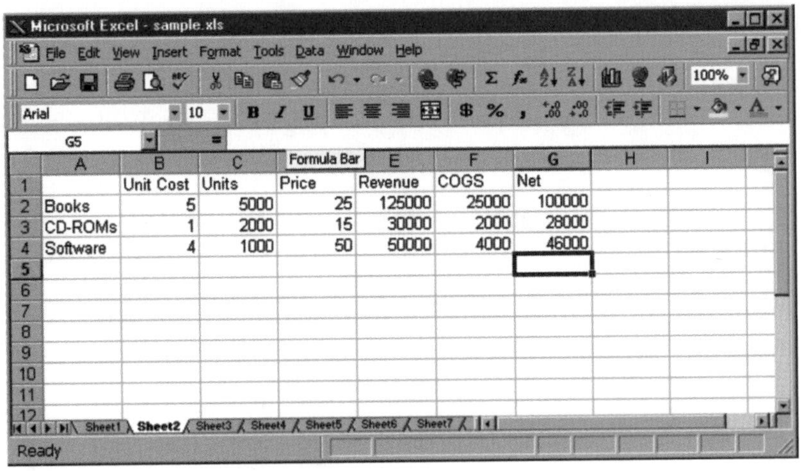

Figure 26.5 *Automating calculations using Excel formulas.*

PERFORMING "WHAT IF" OPERATIONS

As briefly discussed, the power of spreadsheet programs is the ability to perform "what if" operations. Using the current example, you might ask yourself, "What would our profits be if we increase our book price to $30?" To find out, you simply select the book price cell (D2) and type in the value 30. Your spreadsheet will automatically update any formulas on your spreadsheet that use cell D2. Likewise, you might ask, "What would be our profit if we could reduce our CD-ROM cost to $0.50?" To find out, you simply need to select the CD-ROM cost cell (B3) and type in the value 0.50. As your spreadsheets become more complex, your ability to perform such "what if" operations will become very valuable.

USING BUILT-IN FUNCTIONS

To help you perform common operations, Excel provides several built-in functions that you can use within your formulas. For example, in most spreadsheets, you will eventually add (sum) a row or column of values. For example, using the current example, assume that you want to know your total revenues. To add up the revenues column, you could use a formula, such as =E2+E3+E4. However, if you wanted to add up 100 numbers or 1,000 numbers, creating such a formula would be very time consuming. Instead, you can use the built-in *sum* function, within which you tell Excel the first and last values you want to sum. In this case, your formula becomes =sum(E2:E4). For now, assign the formula to cell E5. Then, assign the formula =sum(F2:F4) to cell F5 and the formula =sum(G2:G4) to cell G5. Your spreadsheet, in turn, will add up the columns, as shown in Figure 26.6.

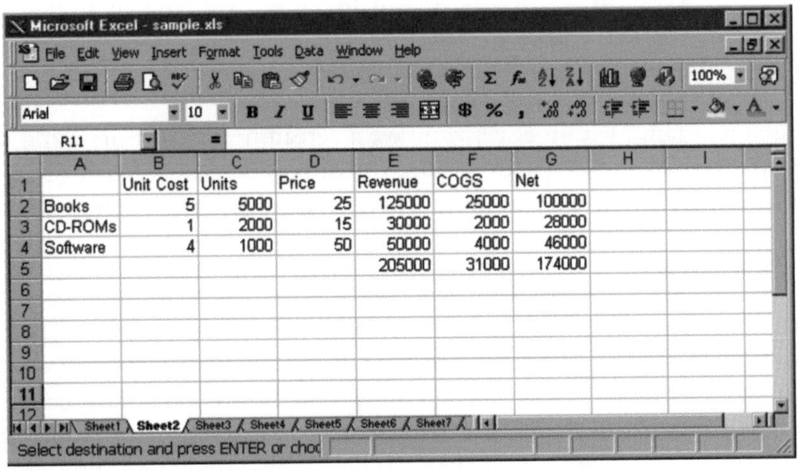

Figure 26.6 *Using the sum function to add a column of numbers.*

CHARTING SPREADSHEET DATA

Spreadsheets also make it very easy for you to chart your data. For example, assume, using the current example, you want to compare your book, CD-ROM, and software revenues using a pie chart. Within Excel, you can create a 3-D pie chart, similar to that shown in Figure 26.7, in a matter of mouse clicks.

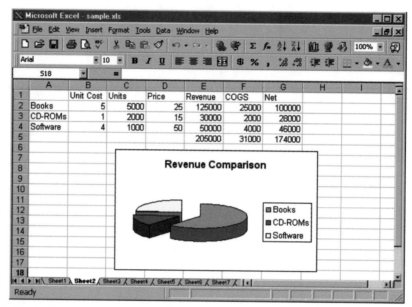

Figure 26.7 *Using a 3-D pie chart to present information.*

To create the 3-D pie chart, you would perform these steps:

1. Within Excel, click your mouse on the Insert menu Chart option. Excel, in turn, will start the Chart Wizard, which you first use to select the chart type you desire.

2. Next, you must specify the cell range you want to chart. In this case, you want to chart your revenues which appear in cells E2, F2, and G2. To specify the range, type E2:G2 and then click your mouse on the Next button. The Wizard, in turn, will then let you assign title and legend information to your chart.

3. Finally, the Chart Wizard will ask you select the location within your spreadsheet where you want to place your chart. After you make your final selection, Excel will display your chart.

SAVING YOUR SPREADSHEET TO DISK

Like most Windows-based programs, within Excel you save a spreadsheet's contents using the File menu Save As option. When you select the Save As option, Excel, in turn, will display the Save As dialog box, within which you can specify the folder and filename within which you want to save your spreadsheet's contents.

PRINTING YOUR SPREADSHEET'S CONTENTS

After you create your spreadsheet, you will quite likely want to print your spreadsheet's data or charts and graphs of the data. As is the case in most Windows-based programs, within Excel you can print your current document by clicking your mouse on the toolbar's Printer icon or by selecting the File menu Print option. Before you print your spreadsheet, however, you may want to first preview how Excel will actually print the spreadsheet's contents. To preview your printout, click your mouse on the toolbar's Print Preview icon (the icon that looks like a magnifying glass examining a printout) or select the File menu Print Preview option. Excel, in turn, will preview your printout, as shown in Figure 26.8.

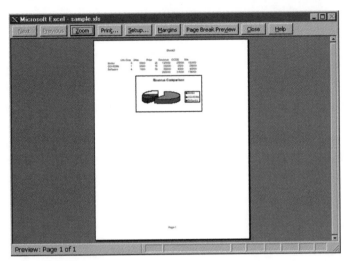

Figure 26.8 *Previewing a printout within Excel.*

Within the Print Preview window, you can zoom in on specific cells, adjust your document's current margins, and change your printer settings. Then, after you are satisfied with your document's format, you can click your mouse on the Print button to print your spreadsheet's contents. Likewise, if you decide you don't want to print your spreadsheet's contents, you can click your mouse on the Close button to return to Excel's standard spreadsheet view.

WHAT YOU MUST KNOW

If you work with numbers, either sales figures, expenses, inventories, and so on, you can save considerable time by automating your calculations using a spreadsheet. This lesson introduced the Microsoft Excel spreadsheet program. In Lesson 27, "Building Professional Quality Presentations in Minutes Using PowerPoint," you will learn how to use Microsoft PowerPoint to create slides and handout materials for a presentation. Before you continue with Lesson 27, however, make sure you have learned the following key concepts:

- ✓ Spreadsheets consist of a table of cells. Within each cell, you can store a number, text, or a formula. Each cell has a unique name.

- ✓ Spreadsheets assign cell names based on the cell's row and column position.

- ✓ To enter a value within a cell, simply click your mouse on the cell or use your keyboard arrow keys to highlight the cell. As you type the cell's value, Excel will display the text you type within a formula bar that appears above the cell table.

- ✓ To change a cell's value, simply select the cell and type in the new value that you desire.

- ✓ To perform calculations within a spreadsheet, you assign a formula to a cell. Within Excel, your formulas must start with an equal sign.

- ✓ To simplify common operations, such as adding up a row or column of values, Excel provides several built-in functions.

- ✓ When you use a function or when you chart data, you may need to specify a range of values, such as a column or row of numbers. To specify a range of values, use the name of the first cell in the range, followed by a colon (:), and then the last cell in the range, such as A1:A5.

Lesson 27

Building Professional Quality Presentations in Minutes, Using PowerPoint

With the advent of powerful word-processing and spreadsheet programs, employers and teachers now expect higher quality reports and financial summaries from their employees and students. In a similar way, audiences who attend presentations also expect presenters to have high-quality hand outs and visual aids. This lesson introduces PowerPoint, a presentation package that Microsoft bundles with its Office software suite. Using PowerPoint, you can quickly create high-quality presentations which you can print and hand out, display on a screen using a projector you connect to your PC, or print and hand out to your audience.

By the time you finish this lesson, you will have learned the following key concepts:

- To help you create professional quality presentations, Microsoft bundles the PowerPoint presentation software program within the Microsoft Office suite.

- Using PowerPoint's AutoContent Wizard, you can quickly build a presentation template, whose slides you can then edit to create your presentation.

- To edit a slide within PowerPoint, simply click your mouse on the slide's text and then type in the text that you desire.

- To move from one slide to the next in PowerPoint, you can press your keyboard's PGUP and PGDN keys or use your mouse to drag the scroll slider.

- If you are using your PC to show your presentation, you can display your slides in full-screen mode by selecting PowerPoint's View menu Slide Show option.

- PowerPoint uses many of the same menus and toolbar buttons as Microsoft Word and Excel. For example, to print your current slides, you can click your mouse on the toolbar Print icon. Likewise, to spell check your presentation, you can click your mouse on the toolbar Spelling icon.

- If you don't give presentations, you may still want to use PowerPoint to create memos and small reports, within which you use bulleted points to summarize a topic's key points.

GETTING STARTED WITH POWERPOINT

PowerPoint, like each of the programs within the Office Suite, is a very powerful program with numerous capabilities. Many publishers, in fact, have written complete books on PowerPoint. This lesson's goal, therefore, is simply to introduce you to PowerPoint and its capabilities. To start PowerPoint, click your mouse on the Start menu Programs option. Windows, in turn, will display the Programs submenu. Within the Programs submenu, click your mouse on the Microsoft PowerPoint option (depending on how PowerPoint was installed on your system, the PowerPoint menu option may reside within a Microsoft Office submenu). Windows, in turn, will start PowerPoint (which may display a Tip of the Day dialog box that you can close by clicking your mouse on the OK button) which will display the PowerPoint dialog box, as shown in Figure 27.1, within which you can direct PowerPoint to start the AutoContent Wizard, which will walk you through the steps of creating your first presentation, or to create a new blank presentation, or to open an existing presentation.

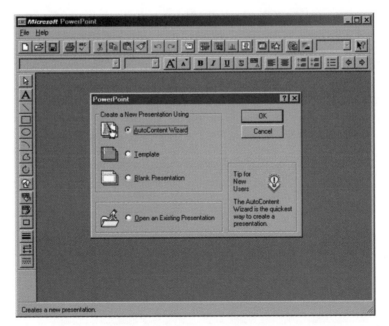

Figure 27.1 *Selecting the operation you want PowerPoint to perform within the PowerPoint dialog box.*

For now, select the AutoContent Wizard button and click your mouse on OK. PowerPoint, in turn, will start the AutoContent Wizard which will help you create a draft presentation whose content you can replace with your own text. To start, as shown in Figure 27.2, the AutoContent Wizard will first ask you to provide information about yourself and your presentation.

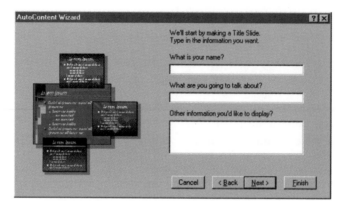

Figure 27.2 *The AutoContent Wizard's prompt for speaker and topic information.*

After you provide your name and presentation topic, click your mouse on the Next button. The AutoContent Wizard, in turn, will then display a dialog box, as shown in Figure 27.3, that asks you about your presentation type.

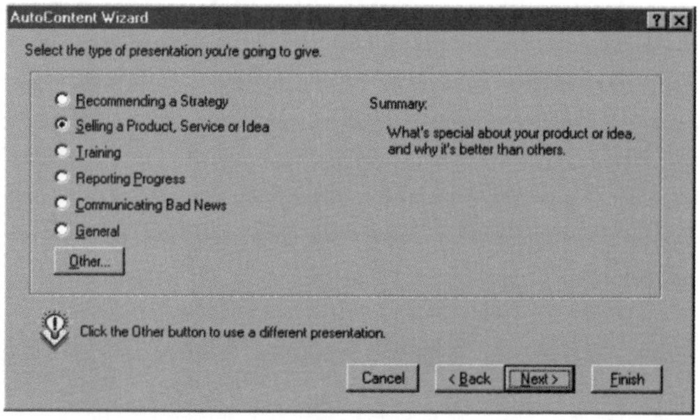

Figure 27.3 *The AutoContent Wizard's prompt for your presentation type.*

After you select the presentation type that best suits your needs, click your mouse on the Next button. The AutoContent Wizard, in turn, will display a dialog box, as shown in Figure 27.4, that asks you what type of presentation style you desire and for about how long you will be speaking.

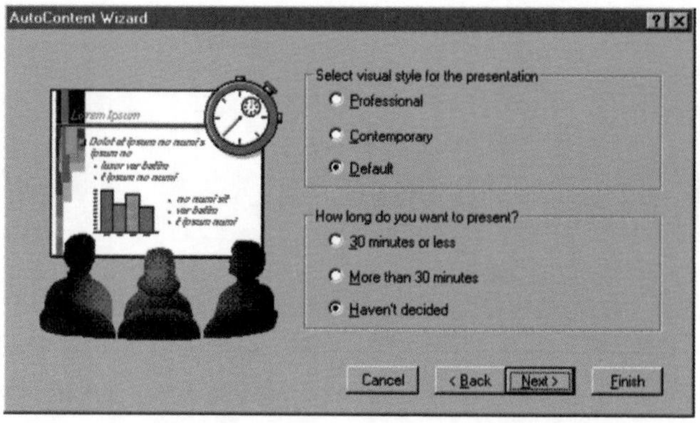

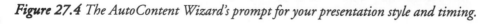

Figure 27.4 *The AutoContent Wizard's prompt for your presentation style and timing.*

After you specify how you want PowerPoint to style your presentation and your presentation length, click your mouse on the Next button. AutoContent Wizard, in turn, will display its final dialog box, as shown in Figure 27.5, that asks you how you will present your presentation and if you want to print hand outs.

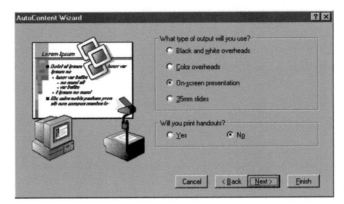

Figure 27.5 *The AutoContent Wizard's prompt for your presentation media and hand out requirements.*

After you select your presentation and specify whether or not you need hand outs, click your mouse on the Next button. The AutoContent Wizard will display a dialog box that tells you that you are done. Within the dialog box, click your mouse on the Finish button. Based on your previous selections, the AutoContent Wizard will create a sample presentation for you, whose slides you can edit to include your own text and charts. Figure 27.6, for example, shows the first six slides PowerPoint will create for you if you are creating a presentation to sell a product. To view a slide within PowerPoint, simply press your keyboard's PGUP and PGDN keys or use your mouse to drag the scroll-bar slider. After you display a slide's contents, you can click your mouse on the slide's text to edit the slide's contents. By editing the sample slides, you can have your presentation complete quickly.

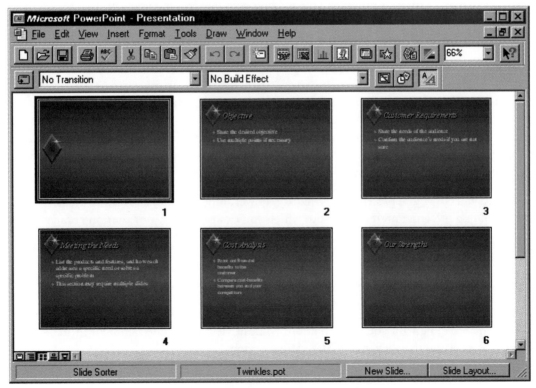

Figure 27.6 *Sample slides from an AutoContent Wizard presentation template.*

Note: After you create your slides, click your mouse on the PowerPoint toolbar Spelling button to spell check your presentation.

PREVIEWING YOUR PRESENTATION

After you edit your slides to include your text, you can preview your presentation by selecting the View menu Slide Show option. PowerPoint, in turn, will display the Slide Show dialog box, within which you can specify the slides you want to preview. PowerPoint will then fill your screen display with your opening slide. To move to the next slide, press the PGDN key or the spacebar, or click your mouse-select button. To return to the previous slide, press the PGUP key. To end the preview and to return to Slide view, within which you can edit your slide's contents, press the ESC key.

SAVING YOUR PRESENTATION

Like most Windows-based programs, within PowerPoint you save a spreadsheet's contents using the File menu Save As option. When you select the Save As option, PowerPoint, in turn, will display the Save As dialog box, within which you can specify the folder and filename within which you want to save your spreadsheet's contents.

PRINTING YOUR PRESENTATION

After you create your presentation, you will want to print copies for your files as well as copies you can hand out to your audience. As is the case in most Windows-based programs, within PowerPoint you can print your current document by clicking your mouse on the toolbar's Printer icon. If you want to print a specific slide or slides, you can do so selecting the File menu Print option. PowerPoint, in turn, will display the Print dialog box. Within the Print dialog box, you can specify which slides you want to print as well the format PowerPoint uses to print them. For example, if you are printing handouts of your slides, you may choose to place two or more slides on the same page.

USING A PC-BASED PRESENTATION

If you must give presentations on a regular basis, you should consider purchasing a portable projector system that you can attach to your PC's video port. Using the projector, you can show your PowerPoint presentations on a screen or even against a wall. This lesson introduced just a small portion of PowerPoint's capabilities. As it turns out, within a PowerPoint presentation, you can insert simple animations, special sound effects, and even video clips.

WHAT YOU MUST KNOW

In this lesson, you learned that PowerPoint helps you create professional quality presentations quickly. If you never have given presentations, you may want to keep PowerPoint in your toolset. By creating and printing memos or short reports using PowerPoint, you can create documents with a professional look and feel. In Lesson 28, "Storing and Retrieving Information Using Databases," you will learn the basics behind creating and using databases to store and retrieve information. Before you continue with Lesson 28, however, make sure you understand the following key concepts:

✓ To help you create you presentations quickly, PowerPoint provides an AutoContent Wizard that builds a presentation template into which you can type your presentation content.

✓ To edit a slide within PowerPoint, simply click your mouse on the slide's text and then type in the text that you desire.

✓ To move from one slide to the next in PowerPoint, you can press your keyboard's PGUP and PGDN keys or use your mouse to drag the scroll slider.

✓ After you are done with your presentation, you can view your slide's content in full-screen mode by selecting the View menu Slide Show option.

✓ Many users use PowerPoint to create memos and small reports, within which they use bulleted points to summarize a topic's key points.

Lesson 28

Storing and Retrieving Information Using Databases

In Lesson 14, "Storing Information within Files," you learned to store information on your disk, you must store the information within a file. In its simplest sense, a database is a file that contains information. If, for example, you type the names and phone numbers of all your friends into a file, you essentially have a database. If someone asked you for a specific person's phone number, you could open your file and scroll through its contents to find the phone number you desire. Likewise, if someone asked you to provide the names of all your friends that live in California, you could eventually provide that list as well.

This lesson examines database software, that makes it easy for you to store and later retrieve information. Although there are several popular database programs, this lesson will focus on Microsoft Access. By the time you finish this lesson, you will understand the following key concepts:

- A database is a collection of information. Within a database, each entry is a record. Each record, in turn, consists of one or more fields. Using database software, you can sort records based upon one or more fields.

- Microsoft Access stores databases using one or more tables. Within a table, the rows correspond to records and each column corresponds to fields within a record.

- A query is a database operation that extracts the records that meet a specific criteria. One query might request all people that live in California. A second query might request all entries of persons who have purchased a product in the past year.

- Database queries can become quite complex. You can query a database based upon multiple fields. You might, for example, want a list of entries of people that live in California, that are 50 years of age or older, and have bought two or more products in the past six months.

- Many word processors let you create custom letters by merging database fields into a word-processing document. Users refer to such operations as a mail merge.

Storing Information within a Record

Although one could view a word-processing document that contains names and phone numbers for a group of people as a database of contact information, you have learned that retrieving specific information from within the file could become difficult at best. By using a database program, such as Microsoft Access, you can better organize the information you store to provide greater flexibility of retrieval in the future. Within a database, each entry you store becomes a *record*. If your database contains five names and phone numbers, your database would have five records. Within a record, you divide information into fields. With regard to an address book database, you might divide your records into first name, last name, street address, city, state, zip, area code, and phone number. When you later enter your information within your database, you would enter the data based upon the fields you have defined. Later, you can use the database software to sort your information upon any of the fields. In addition, you can easily determine (based on the state field) which of your friends live in California.

An Access Database Stores Records within One or More Tables

Within the Microsoft Access database program, you store your information within one or more tables. Each row within a table corresponds to a record, and each column to a field. Figure 28.1, for example, shows how Access would represents your Address Book database (which you might simply call Friends).

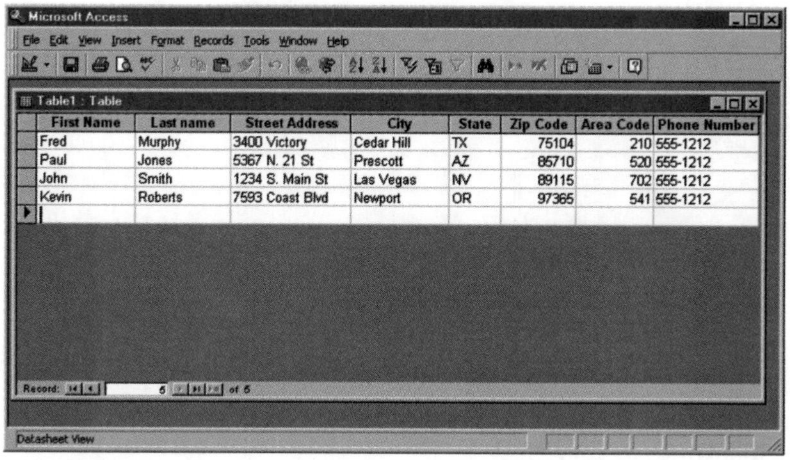

First Name	Last name	Street Address	City	State	Zip Code	Area Code	Phone Number
Fred	Murphy	3400 Victory	Cedar Hill	TX	75104	210	555-1212
Paul	Jones	5367 N. 21 St	Prescott	AZ	85710	520	555-1212
John	Smith	1234 S. Main St	Las Vegas	NV	89115	702	555-1212
Kevin	Roberts	7593 Coast Blvd	Newport	OR	97365	541	555-1212

Figure 28.1 *Access stores database records within a table.*

To create a table within Access, you must first define the table's fields—assigning each field and name and telling Access the type of value the field will store. After you create your table, you can simply type your data into the corresponding database fields. After you type in a field's value, you can press your keyboard arrow keys or the TAB key to advance the cursor to the next field. When you reach the last field within the record, you press the ENTER key to direct Access to create a new record.

Sorting and Querying Data within a Database

Across the Internet, several on-line booksellers advertise having over 1,000,000 different books for sale. Figure 28.2 shows a simple book database. In this case, the database lists only Jamsa Press books. Each record within the database corresponds to a specific book. The database divides each record into four fields: the Author, Title, Price, and ISBN.

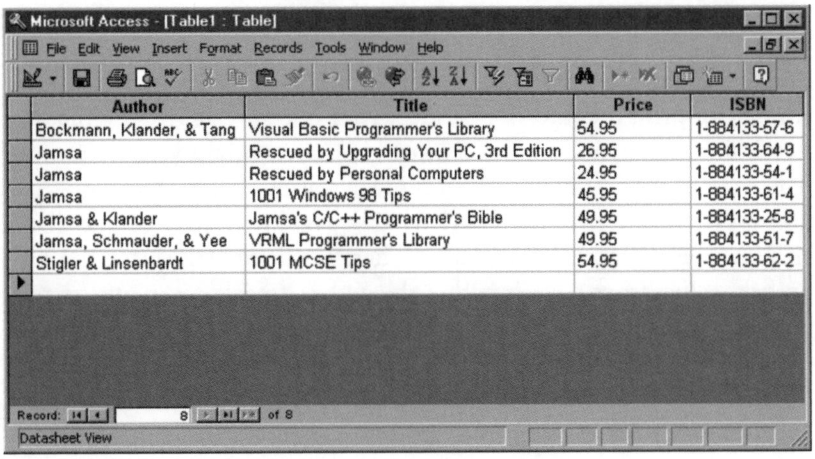

Author	Title	Price	ISBN
Bockmann, Klander, & Tang	Visual Basic Programmer's Library	54.95	1-884133-57-6
Jamsa	Rescued by Upgrading Your PC, 3rd Edition	26.95	1-884133-64-9
Jamsa	Rescued by Personal Computers	24.95	1-884133-54-1
Jamsa	1001 Windows 98 Tips	45.95	1-884133-61-4
Jamsa & Klander	Jamsa's C/C++ Programmer's Bible	49.95	1-884133-25-8
Jamsa, Schmauder, & Yee	VRML Programmer's Library	49.95	1-884133-51-7
Stigler & Linsenbardt	1001 MCSE Tips	54.95	1-884133-62-2

Figure 28.2 *A simple book database.*

Using Access, you can quickly sort the data in the database. For example, Figure 28.3 shows the books sorted by title and the book's sorted by price. To sort data within the database, you simply tell the database software the field upon which you want to sort the data. The database software, Access in this case, will take care of the rest, displaying sorted records, as shown in Figure 28.3.

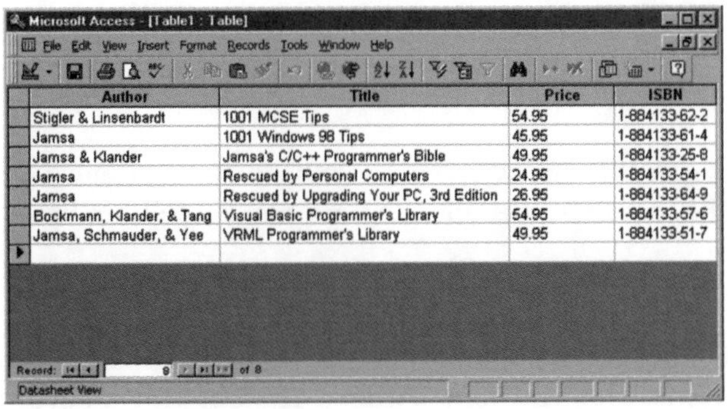

Author	Title	Price	ISBN
Stigler & Linsenbardt	1001 MCSE Tips	54.95	1-884133-62-2
Jamsa	1001 Windows 98 Tips	45.95	1-884133-61-4
Jamsa & Klander	Jamsa's C/C++ Programmer's Bible	49.95	1-884133-25-8
Jamsa	Rescued by Personal Computers	24.95	1-884133-54-1
Jamsa	Rescued by Upgrading Your PC, 3rd Edition	26.95	1-884133-64-9
Bockmann, Klander, & Tang	Visual Basic Programmer's Library	54.95	1-884133-57-6
Jamsa, Schmauder, & Yee	VRML Programmer's Library	49.95	1-884133-51-7

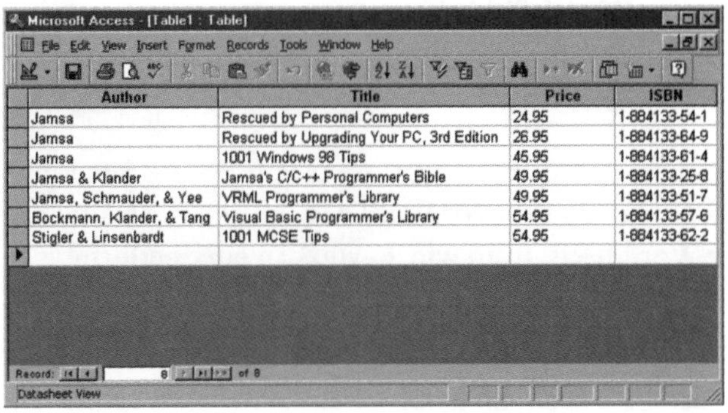

Author	Title	Price	ISBN
Jamsa	Rescued by Personal Computers	24.95	1-884133-54-1
Jamsa	Rescued by Upgrading Your PC, 3rd Edition	26.95	1-884133-64-9
Jamsa	1001 Windows 98 Tips	45.95	1-884133-61-4
Jamsa & Klander	Jamsa's C/C++ Programmer's Bible	49.95	1-884133-25-8
Jamsa, Schmauder, & Yee	VRML Programmer's Library	49.95	1-884133-51-7
Bockmann, Klander, & Tang	Visual Basic Programmer's Library	54.95	1-884133-57-6
Stigler & Linsenbardt	1001 MCSE Tips	54.95	1-884133-62-2

Figure 28.3 *Databases make it very easy for you to sort data.*

Using a database program, you can store information based on two or more fields. Within a book database, for example, you might direct the database software to sort the data first by author, and then by title. In that way, when you view an author's books, the database software would display the books in alphabetical order.

Using a Database Query to Select Specific Records

When you use a database, there will be times when you want to extract specific information from within the database. In the case of the book database, you might want to list books written by a specific author, or, you might want to list books priced at $39.95 or less. To extract information from a database, you must define a *query*. In general, a query is simply your request criteria.

Within Access, when you query a database, Access will create a new table that contains the matching information. When you create a query, you can select specific fields from the database. You might, for example, request that your query return only the name and phone number of your friends that live in California. Or, you may want the query to return the name, area code, and phone number.

Depending on your query's criteria and the records in your database, your query might return no matching records, all the records in the database, or some number of records in between.

UNDERSTANDING MAIL-MERGE OPERATIONS

In the previous examples, the database operations have simply displayed the table's contents. For many applications, you may simply want to view or print the records that meet your query's criteria. At other times, however, you may want to use your result within a different program. For example, you might want to create a custom letter within Microsoft Word that you want to send to all your friends in California. Using Word and Access, you can perform a *mail-merge operation* that lets you place the result of a database query into a custom letter. Briefly, to perform a mail-merge operation within Word, you first create your letter. Then, you specify the locations within the letter when you want Word to merge in field values from records within the query. Your letter might start, for example, something like this, where the items within the left and right brackets correspond to fields within your database:

> <First Name> <Last Name>
> <Address>
> <City>, <State> <Zip>
>
> Dear <First Name>,

When you later perform the mail-merge operation, Word will extract each field, one record at a time and, build the corresponding custom letter, which might begin as follows:

> John Doe
> 1232 Main Street
> Sugar Land, Texas 77479
>
> Dear John,

For more information on performing a mail-merge operation within Word, refer to your documentation that accompanied Word or Word's on-line Help. If you don't have Microsoft Access, you can store your data within Excel or Word itself, from which, you can later perform your merge.

WHAT YOU MUST KNOW

A database program is software that helps you store and later retrieve information. Within a database program, you organize your data into distinct records. Each record, in turn, consists of fields that define the specific values, such as a person's name, age, phone number, and so on. Using your database software, you can sort your data based on a specific field or, using a query, you can select records from your database that meet specific criteria, such as all customers who have purchased a product in the last three months. In this lesson, you briefly examined the Microsoft Access database software. In Lesson 29, "Organizing Your Life Using a Software-Based Personal Information Manager," you will learn how scheduling and time-management software can help you make the best use of your time. Before you continue with Lesson 29, however, make sure you understand the following key concepts:

- ✓ A database is a collection of information. The true power of a database is not its storage capabilities, but rather, its retrieval capabilities.

- ✓ When you create a database, you define the fields that make up a record. To create a book database, for example, your fields might include the Author, Title, Publisher, Price, and ISBN. Microsoft Access stores databases using one or more tables. Within a table, the rows correspond to records and each column corresponds to fields within a record.

- ✓ Using database software, you can sort records based upon one or more fields.

- ✓ To retrieve specific information from within a database, users define queries. In general, a query extracts the records from the database that meet a specific criteria.

Lesson 29

Organizing Your Life Using a Software-Based Personal Information Manager

In today's hectic times, most of us have too much to do and too little time to do it. To help better organize our time, many of us carry calendars or scheduling notebooks. If you have decided to keep your PC with you at all times, you can take advantage of time-management software that will track your appointments and, if you would like, remind you of your appointments at specific intervals. If you work in an office where multiperson meetings are common, you probably know how difficult it can be to schedule a meeting at a time that fits each attendee's schedule, and to reserve an available office within which you can hold the meeting. As you will learn in this lesson, if your office has a local-area network and users in your office update their schedules on a regular basis, you can use scheduling software to automatically determine the first time the attendees are available to meet. The scheduling software will then send each attendee notification of the meeting, wait for each attendee's confirmation, and then even reserve a meeting room.

This lesson examines time-management software using Schedule+, a program Microsoft bundles with various office programs, such as Outlook Express. By the time you finish this lesson, you will understand the following key concepts:

- To make the best use of your time, you should consider using time-management software to track your appointments and your "To Do" lists.

- Using time-management software, you simply type in each of your appointments. You can then either track your appointments using your PC or print out a hard copy of your schedule that you can insert into your hand-held binder.

- To ensure that you do not miss key appointments, most time-management programs let you assign alarms to key appointments. The software will then display a reminder an hour, day, or a week before the appointment time.

- Within an office, you can use schedule-management software that runs on your local-area network to coordinate meeting times and places with other users. To schedule a meeting, you simply specify the meeting's attendees. The schedule-management software, in turn, will then check each user's schedule to determine when each attendee is available to meet.

- Most time-management programs also let you track your key contacts, giving you all the information you need about your appointments in one place.

UNDERSTANDING SCHEDULE-MANAGEMENT SOFTWARE

If you examine the software within a computer store, you will find there are numerous time-management and schedule-management programs. Although each program's capabilities may differ, most will let you perform the following activities:

- Enter and prioritize items within a "To Do" list
- Track daily appointments
- Remind you of upcoming appointments
- View and print your appointments for a specific day, week, month, or year
- Automate your contact database, tracking names, phone numbers, and addresses

If you work in a office that has a local-area network, you will want scheduling software that lets users across the network interact with one another's schedules to coordinate meetings. The following sections examine how you perform several schedule-management activities using the Schedule+ software.

MANAGING YOUR DAILY SCHEDULE

Time-management software exists to help you organize your day and make the most efficient use of your time. To start, you will use time-management software to schedule your day. Figure 29.1, for example, shows a daily planner within Schedule+. Most time-management programs will divide your day into half-hour increments. Depending on your needs, you can normally configure your software to display more (such as every 15 minutes) or less (such as every hour) time intervals. In addition, many time-management programs let you schedule appointments at a specific time, such as a 12:20 flight.

To enter an appointment, you simply click your mouse on the appointment time and type in specifics about the appointment. Normally, when you schedule appointments, you have information such as the person's phone or fax number in front of you. You may find it convenient to include such information at the end of your appointment text so you can use it to contact the individual should you need to change the appointment at a later time. After you complete your appointment list, you can print a hard copy of your appointments.

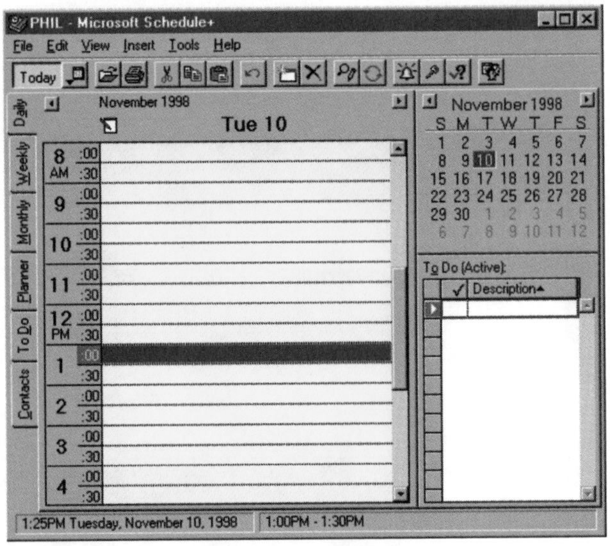

Figure 29.1 *Using time-management software to schedule your day.*

Many time-management programs let you customize your printout. You might, for example, print your week's or month's appointments on one page, or you might print your daily appointments in a format that fits into your hand-held daily planner.

VIEWING PAST, CURRENT, AND FUTURE APPOINTMENTS

After you enter your appointments, your time-management software will keep your appointments within a database on your disk—which gives you a permanent record of each appointment's date and time. If you must, for example, check when you last met with a specific customer, you use the time-management software to search your past appointments. Many employees, for example, find that printing a list of their past appointments provides a very convenient way to show their boss just how busy (and productive) they have been. In addition to letting you view your daily appointments on the screen, most time-management programs will let you view the current week's or current month's appointments. Figure 29.2, for example, shows a week of appointments within Schedule+. Likewise, Figure 29.3 shows the current month's appointments.

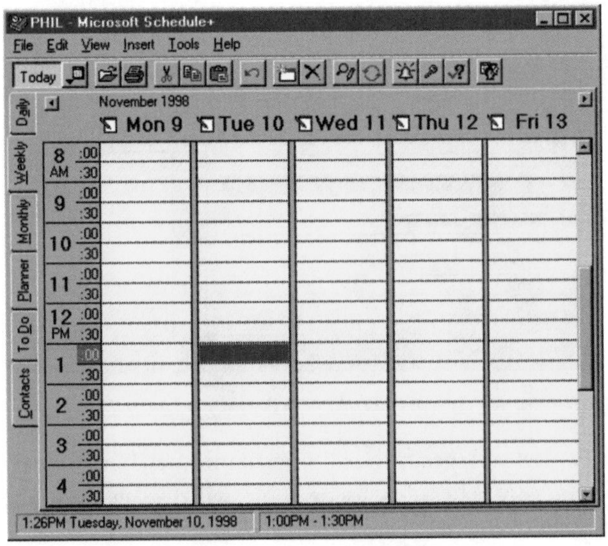

Figure 29.2 *Displaying the current week's appointments within Schedule+.*

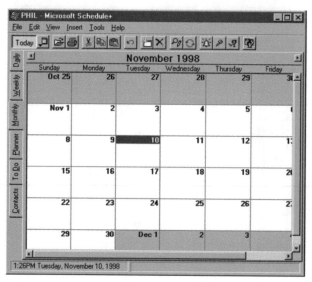

Figure 29.3 *Displaying the current month's appointments within Schedule+.*

ASSIGNING ALARMS (REMINDERS) TO KEY APPOINTMENTS

One of the biggest benefits of using a software-based time-management program, rather than tracking your schedule on paper, is that you can use the software to remind you of key appointments. For example, assume that you have a 12:30 meeting with your company's CEO.

After you record the appointment in your schedule, you can use your program to assign a reminder to the appointment. As shown in Figure 29.4, for example, Schedule+ will display a small bell next to the appointment within your schedule to indicate that you have set a reminder.

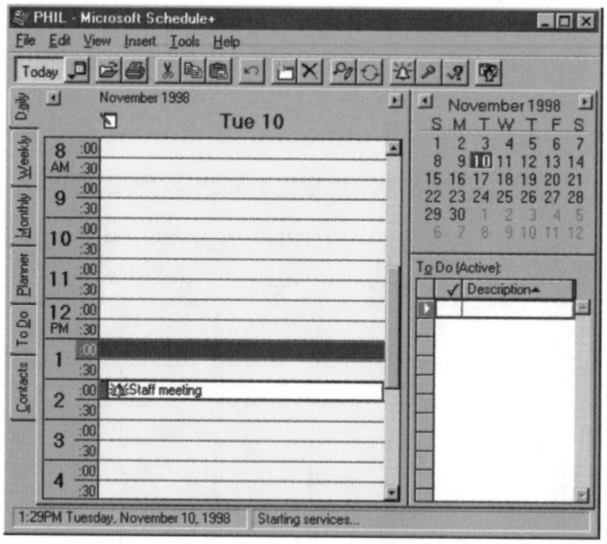

Figure 29.4 *Time-management software lets you set reminders for key appointments.*

Most time-management programs will let you specify the number of minutes, hours, days, or weeks before the appointment that you want your software to remind you. Schedule+, for example, will display a reminder similar to that shown in Figure 29.5. Within the Schedule+ Reminder dialog box, you can reschedule the reminder as your needs require.

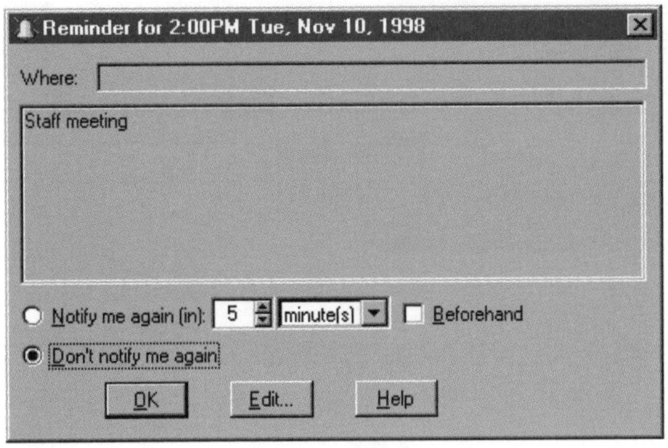

Figure 29.5 *Using time-management software to remind you of key appointments.*

USING THE SCHEDULE+ "TO DO" LIST

In addition to helping you track your appointments, most time-management programs also let you track tasks that you must accomplish. Figure 29.6, for example, shows a "To Do" list within Schedule+.

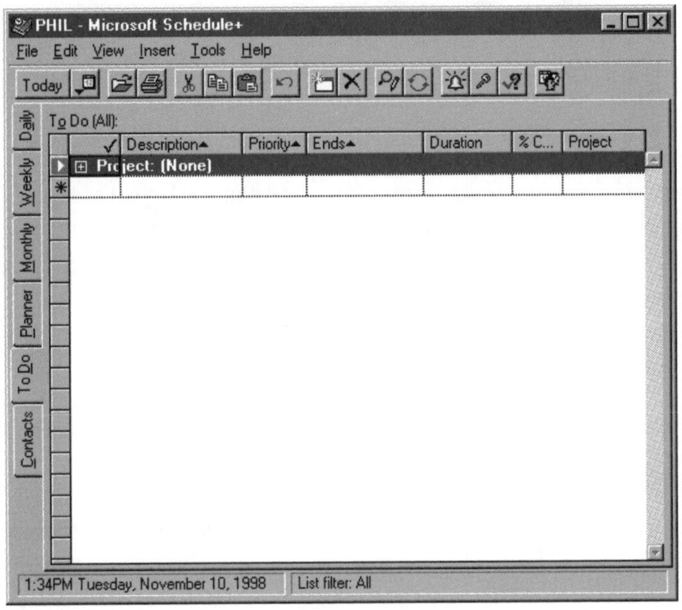

Figure 29.6 *Most time-management programs let you track the things you must do.*

To help you better organize your tasks, Schedule+ lets you group tasks by projects. Within each project, Schedule+ lets you group subtasks, to which you can assign a priority and a start date. As your tasks become due, Schedule+ will display the tasks on your appointment schedule.

TRACKING KEY CONTACTS

As briefly discussed, most time-management programs will let you track your key contacts, which essentially makes your PC an electronic Rolodex. Figure 29.7, for example, shows the Schedule+ contact list. Within the list, Schedule+ lets you look up, add, or update information about each contact.

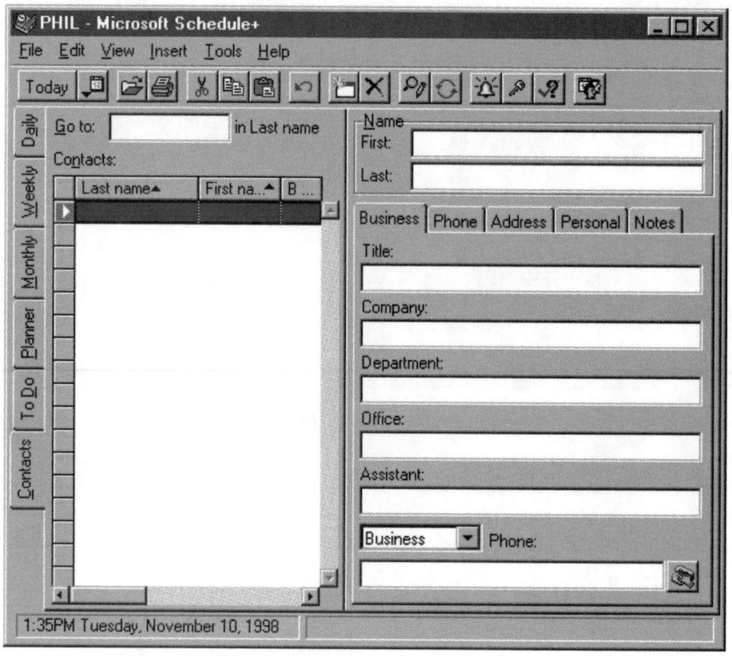

Figure 29.7 *Using Schedule+ to manage your contact database.*

WHAT YOU MUST KNOW

Ideally, your PC should make you more productive. Unfortunately, the PC also provides you with many new ways to consume time (such as surfing the Web or exchanging e-mail messages). If you are looking for ways to improve your productivity, you should consider using time-management software. This lesson examined the Schedule+ software that Microsoft bundles with programs such as Office and Outlook Express. Using Schedule+, you can manage your appointments, your tasks, as well as your contact list. In Lesson 30, "Maximizing Your Business Using PC Software," you will examine other programs that may make your working hours more productive. Before you continue with Lesson 30, however, make sure you understand the following key concepts:

✓ Time-management software exists to help you make the best use of time.

✓ Using time-management software, you can track your appointments, tasks, and contact lists.

✓ Most time-management programs let you assign alarms to key appointments that will remind you of the appointment an hour, day, or a week before the appointment time.

✓ If you work in an office that uses a local-area network, you can use schedule-management software to coordinate meeting times and places with other users.

✓ If you prefer to carry a hand-held schedule notebook, most time-management programs will let you print copies of your appointments in a format that you can then insert into your notebook.

Lesson 30

Maximizing Your Business Using PC Software

If you have a small business or if you are thinking about starting one, there are several software programs that you should place high on your priority list. Hopefully, over time, your business will outgrow the software that this lesson presents. Until that time, the programs this lesson discusses may help you leverage your time and your staff. This lesson examines several key business software programs. By the time you finish this lesson, you will understand the following key concepts:

- Using business software, you can best leverage your time, money, and staff.

- Businesses need software to manage their books, billing and receipts, employees and payroll, and much more.

- Across the Web, you will find sites that offer key business programs. At these sites, you can often download demo programs and find many business tips.

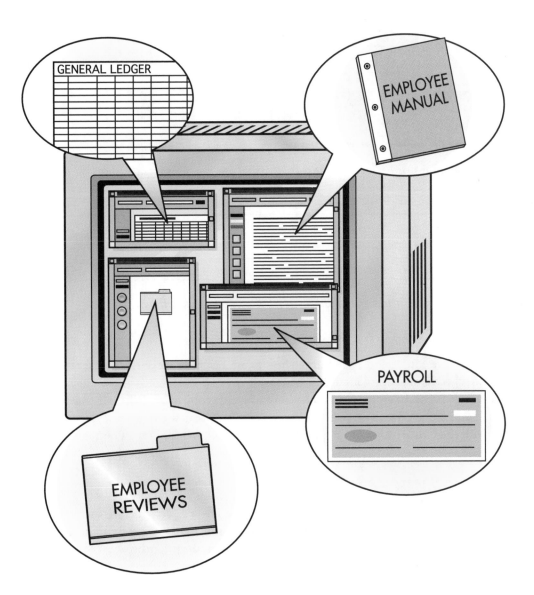

Start Your Business with a Good Business Plan

Probably the most important factor to having a successful business (even more important than having a strong product or a great idea) is a solid business plan. As it turns out, no matter what type of business you are planning, your business will share many characteristics common to all businesses. You must, for example, plan for financing, personnel, sales and marketing, your break-even budgets, inventory management, and so on.

Most business planning software programs will walk you through the key planning aspects and will then produce a printed report that you can use to guide your business operations and even to present to potential investors. Table 30.1 lists several sites that you can visit to learn more about specific business planning software. A few of the sites offer sample programs that you can and should download. Figure 30.1, for example, shows several screen images from the demo version of Business Plan Pro that you can download from across the Web.

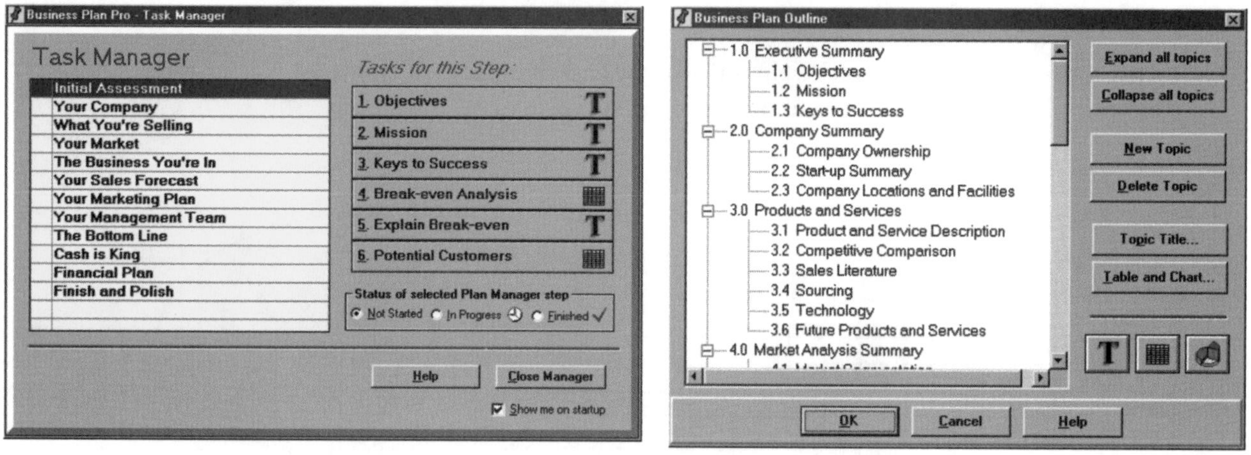

Figure 30.1 *Images from Business Plan Pro, a software program you can use to create your business plan.*

Business Software	Web Site
Business Plan Pro	www.palo-alto.com
BizPlan Builder	www.jian.com
PlanMaker	www.planmaker.com

Table 30.1 *Web sites you can visit to learn about specific business planning software.*

Microsoft Office Provides Key Software

In several of this book's previous lessons, you learned how to use a word processor, spreadsheet program, presentation software, as well as a schedule-management utility. Microsoft Office provides each of these key programs. Today, most users are familiar with Microsoft Word and Excel—both of which come with Office. If you are purchasing software for your staff, make sure Office is high on your list. As you need to hire new employees, you will find many applicants who are familiar with the Office programs. Figure 30.2 shows Excel, Word, PowerPoint, and Schedule+ running on a user's computer.

Employee Review Software

If you have employees, you will eventually need to give employee reviews. To structure such reviews, you should take advantage of employee review software. Such software will walk you through common review criteria and suggest appropriate wording that should reduce the possibility of an employee suing you in the future because of his or her review.

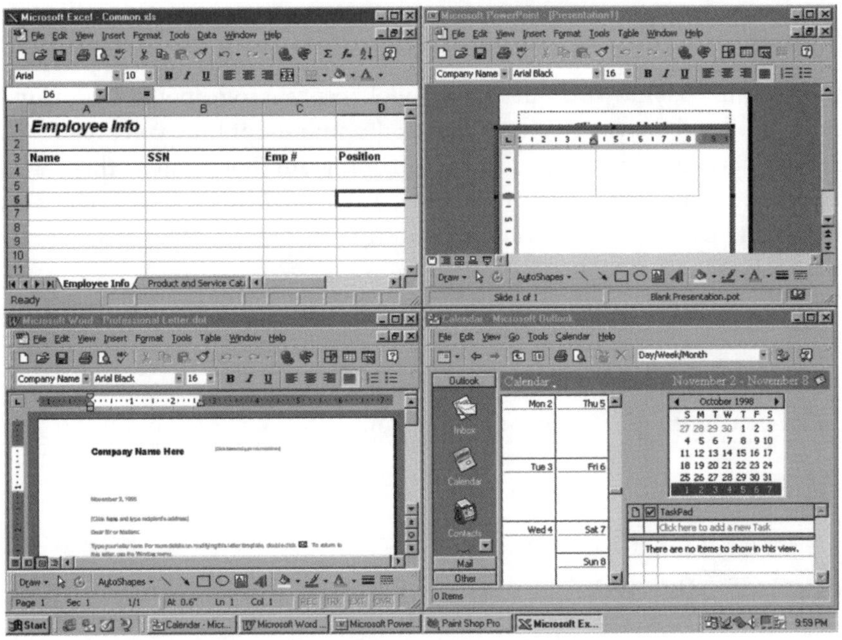

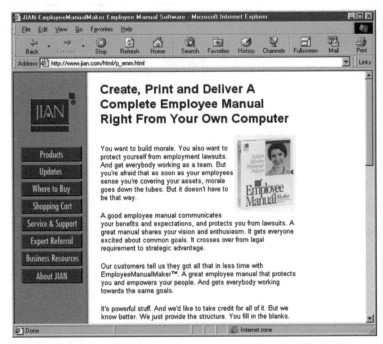

Figure 30.2 *Running programs from the Microsoft Office suite.*

If you have employees or plan to have employees in the future, your employees must know your company's rules and regulations as well as its policies and benefits. The best way to present such information to your employees is to use an employee manual. If you require that your employees sign that they have received and read your manual, an employee will have a much harder time in the future trying to prove that he or she was unaware of a specific policy. Fortunately, there are several software programs that can help you put together an employee manual quickly. Figure 30.3, for example, shows the Jian Web site where you can learn about the Jian Employee Manual Maker.

Figure 30.3 *Information about the Jian Employee Manual Maker at the Jian Web site at www.jian.com.*

ACCOUNTING AND PAYROLL PROGRAMS ARE ESSENTIAL

To some extent, every successful business owner becomes a bookkeeper at some point. Unfortunately, as your business grows, your bookkeeping tasks will increase. To help reduce the amount of time you spend balancing the books and calculating payroll expense, you must have a good accounting program. Fortunately, there are several very good and relatively inexpensive accounting programs readily available. Table 30.2 lists several Web sites you can visit to learn more about general ledger and payroll programs and, possibly, to download demo programs.

Software Program	Web Address
QuickBooks	www.quickbooks.com
AccPac Plus	www.accpac.com
Peachtree Office Accounting	www.peachtree.com

Table 30.2 *Web sites that feature accounting software.*

PROJECT MANAGEMENT SOFTWARE

If your business develops new products, you will need a way to manage the various stages of your product's development. You might, for example, use a Pert or Gantt chart to identify your program's key stages. To better manage such projects, you should take advantage of project management software, such as Microsoft Project, as shown in Figure 30.4.

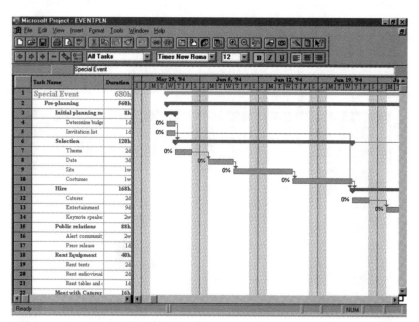

Figure 30.4 *Tracking project stages using Microsoft Project.*

SALES MANAGEMENT SOFTWARE

If your business has customers, you will want to develop a database that contains customer information, to-do lists, follow-up appointments, as well as call tracking. Using sales management software, you can help your sales staff make the best use of their time. In addition, you can use the software to generate reports that monitor each salesperson's effectiveness. Across the Web, you will find several sales management programs, the most widely used of which is Act!, as shown in Figure 30.5.

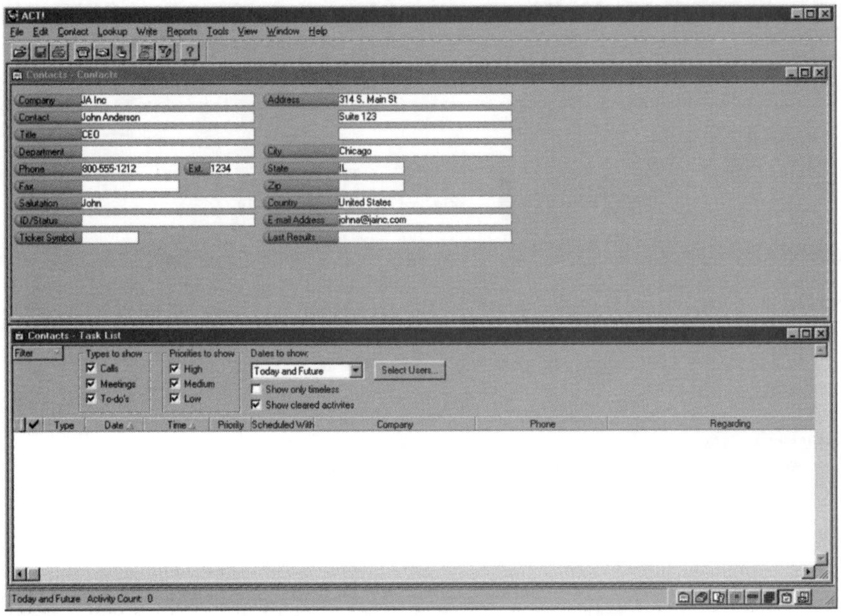

Figure 30.5 *Using Act! to leverage your sales team's performance.*

To learn more about Act!, or to download a demo version, visit the Symantic Web site at *www.symantic.com.*

BUSINESS WEB SITES YOU SHOULD VISIT

If you have a business, or if you are considering starting a new business, use your Web browser to visit the following Web sites shown in Figures 30.6 through 30.9. As you browse, you will find considerable information that will improve your existing business or will shape your business planning.

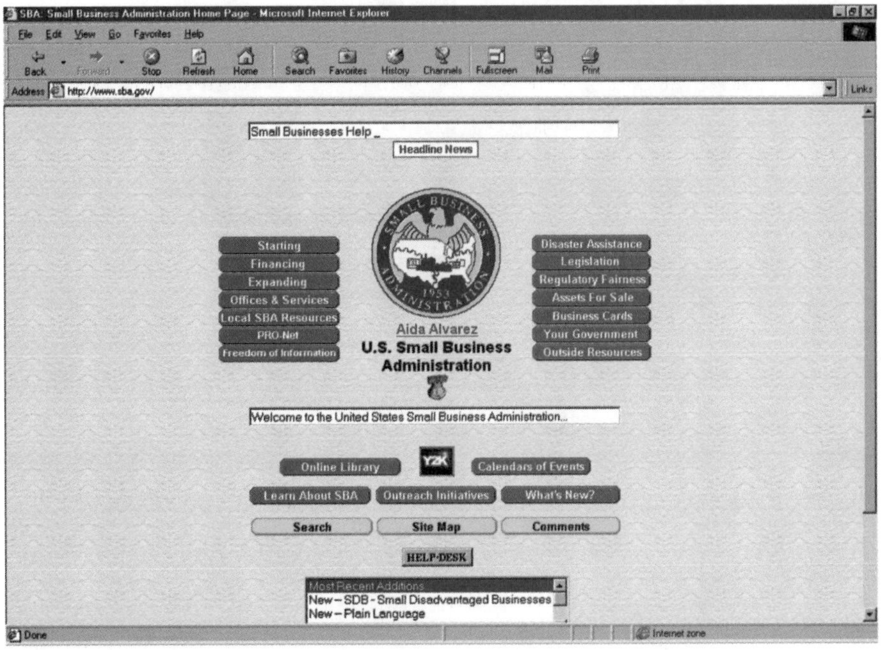

Figure 30.6 *Small business information at www.sba.gov.*

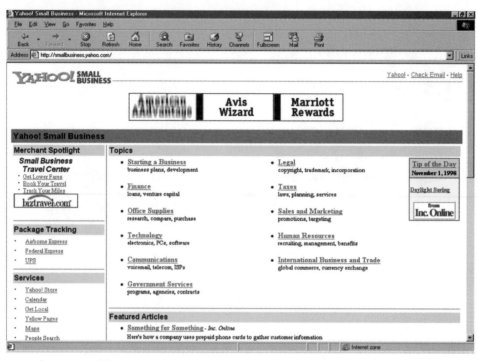

Figure 30.7 *Business facts at smallbusiness.yahoo.com.*

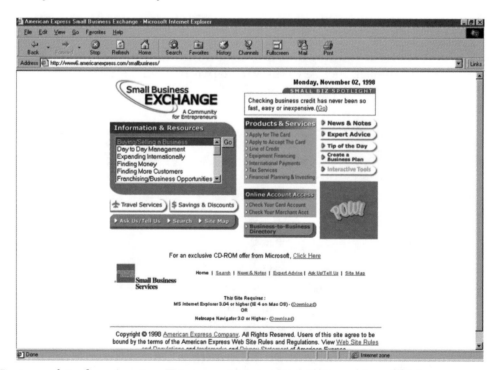

Figure 30.8 *Business advice from American Express at www.americanexpress.com\smallbusiness.*

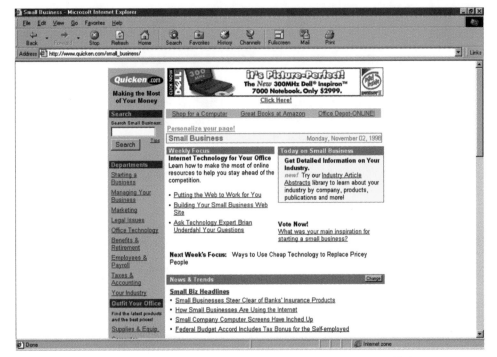

Figure 30.9 *Recommendations from the creators of Quicken at www.quicken.com/small_business.*

WHAT YOU MUST KNOW

If you own a business or are planning to start a business, you will need key software programs if you want to best leverage your time, money, and staff. This lesson introduced several essential business programs and Web sites that you should visit to increase your business knowledge. In Lesson 31, "Connecting Devices to Your PC Ports," you will learn ways you can connect a variety of devices to your PC. Before you continue with Lesson 31, however, make sure you understand the following key concepts:

- ✓ Having the right software is essential for businesses who want to best leverage their resources.

- ✓ In addition to accounting programs, businesses need software to manage projects, inventories, employee reviews, as well as sales and marketing.

- ✓ The Web is filled with sites that offer a wide range of business tips and solutions.

Lesson 31

Connecting Devices to Your Personal Computer

In Lesson 3, "Setting Up Your Personal Computer," you learned that you attach devices, such as a keyboard, monitor, and printer, to ports that you will find on the back of your PC's system unit. Although a notebook PC obviously has a keyboard and monitor built-in, you will normally find of same ports you would find on a desktop PC on the back of a notebook computer. In this lesson, you will learn that some devices, such as disk drives, scanners, and external CD-ROM drives, do not connect to the ports you will normally find on the back of a PC. Instead, such devices connect to either a SCSI (pronounced "scuzzy") port or to a universal serial bus (USB) port.

By the time you finish this lesson, you will understand the following key concepts:

- To use a hardware device, you must connect the device to your PC. Users connect standard devices such as a keyboard, monitor, and printer to ports located on the back of the PC's system unit.

- Many non-standard devices, such as scanners or external tape, disk, and CD-ROM drives, use a special SCSI connection.

- Before a user can connect a SCSI-based device to his or her system, the user must install a SCSI-adapter card within his or her PC. Notebook PC users can install a PCMCIA-based SCSI card.

- Using one SCSI-adapter card, a user can connect up to seven SCSI-based devices. The user connects the first device to the SCSI card, the second device to the first device, and so on, to create a SCSI device chain.

- The universal serial bus (USB) is new technology that makes it easier for users to connect devices to their PCs. Many new PCs have USB ports, to which users can connect a USB-based device (such as a scanner or Zip drive) or to which they can connect a USB hub, into which they can then plug in multiple USB devices.

UNDERSTANDING *SCSI* CONNECTIONS

As your PC use grows, you may install additional devices such as a scanner, external tape drive, or even a CD-ROM burner with which you can create your own CD-ROMs. To attach these devices to your PC, you will normally use a SCSI-based connection. The term SCSI is an acronym for Small Computer Systems Interface. In general, SCSI simply defines a standard that hardware designers use then they create cables and device ports, and that software developers follow when they write the programs that let the device communicate with your PC. Most PCs do not have a SCSI port. Instead, you must install a SCSI card within your system unit. After you install the card, you can connect a device to the card's port. SCSI devices are unique in that if you have two or more SCSI devices, you simply connect the first device to your SCSI adapter and then you connect the second SCSI device to the first, forming what users call a *SCSI device chain*, as shown in Figure 31.1.

Figure 31.1 *Connecting two SCSI devices to form a SCSI device chain.*

If you have a third SCSI device, you would connect that device to the second device. Within a SCSI device chain, you can attach up to seven devices. After you attach your last hardware device to the SCSI chain, you must terminate the chain by either using a terminator switch within the final device or by attaching a small terminator to the device, as shown in Figure 31.2. If you do not terminate the SCSI chain, you will experience errors when you try to use the SCSI-based devices. Should you later purchase another SCSI device, you unterminate the chain, attach the new device, and then terminate the new device.

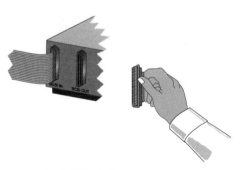

Figure 31.2 *Terminating the final device in the SCSI chain.*

When you connect a device to a SCSI chain, you must assign a unique identification number to the device that users refer to as the device's SCSI channel number. When your PC must communicate with a device, it will use the channel number to distinguish one device from the next. Unfortunately, depending on the device you are adding, the steps you must perform to set the device's SCSI address will differ. Some devices will provide a small switch that you can use to set the address, while other devices may require that you change electronic jumpers within the device. When devices in a SCSI chain do not work, it is normally because the chain is not terminated or two devices are using the same SCSI address. Using SCSI-based devices is quite convenient. Because you simply attach devices to the SCSI chain, you can, provided you have a PC with its own SCSI adapter, move devices from one system to another, as your needs require. In addition, you can use most SCSI devices on either a Mac or a PC. You might, for example, move a CD-ROM burner or scanner from a Mac to a PC (provided that you had software for both the Mac and the PC).

UNDERSTANDING USB CONNECTIONS

As you just learned, using SCSI-based devices, you create a device chain that can contain up to seven devices. And, although its seems relatively easy to connect devices to the chain, users must make sure that they terminate the device chain correctly and that they assign a unique device number (SCSI address) to each device. To make it easier for users to connect hardware devices to their PCs, hardware manufacturers have created a new device called the universal serial bus (USB). The USB's goal is to increase the user's ability to install and use a device without having to worry about configuring a device address or terminating the device. In other words, using the universal serial bus, users should be able to simply plug in a hardware device and use it instantly (even without having to power down the computer). Many newer notebook PCs support USB ports. You can connect a device directly to a USB port, or, you can connect a USB hub to the port and then connect multiple devices to the hub. Recently, scanners, joysticks, and even Zip drives that support USB connections have become available.

CONNECTING DEVICES TO A NOTEBOOK PC

In Lesson 34 "Mobile Computing Using a Notebook PC," you will examine notebook PCs in detail. As you will learn, on the back of most notebook PCs, you will find a series of ports to which you can connect various devices, such as a printer. Within an office, most PC users have a desktop PC. If you normally work with a desktop PC, but you travel with a notebook (and possibly use the notebook PC at home), you may find the notebook's keyboard and mouse a little awkward to use. Using the ports on the back of a notebook PC, you can often connect a standard keyboard and mouse. Earlier in this lesson, you learned that for a desktop PC to access a SCSI device, you have to install a SCSI card within the desktop. The same, is true for notebook PCs. To insert a SCSI card into a notebook PC, users insert a PCMCIA-based card into the notebook, as shown in 31.3. Then, the user simply connects the first device in the SCSI chain to the PCMCIA-based SCSI card.

Figure 31.3 *To connect a SCSI device to a notebook PC, users insert a PCMCIA-based SCSI card.*

Earlier in this lesson, you also learned that users are now starting to use a universal serial bus to connect devices to their PCs. Most newer notebook PCs have a built-in universal serial bus port.

USING INFRARED CONNECTIONS TO ELIMINATE CABLES

Depending on how you work, or possibly your desire to reduce the number of cables you have on your desk, you may find using infrared devices is convenient. In Lesson 34, you will find that you may have times when you will need to exchange documents between your notebook and desktop PCs. As you will learn, one way to exchange files between the two PCs is to run a cable between each computer's serial port, across which software on each PC will then send or receive files. Many new PCs, however, support infrared connections that allow a PC (or various PC devices) to send or receive signals much that are similar to those of a TV's remote control. Using infrared communications (provided you have a PC and devices that support infrared operations), two PCs can exchange files, a PC can send a file to a printer, or, as shown in Figure 31.4, you can eliminate the need for a mouse and keyboard cable on your desk.

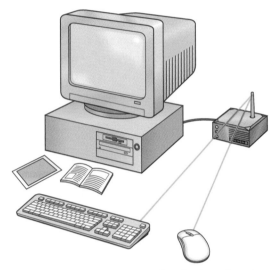

Figure 31.4 *Using infrared communications between a PC and its keyboard and mouse.*

What You Must Know

Before your PC can use a device, you must connect the device to the PC. For traditional devices, such as a keyboard, monitor, and printer, you will find ports on the back of the PC's system unit, to which you can connect the device. For other devices, such as a scanner or external tape or disk drive, you may need to connect the device to a SCSI chain or to your PC's universal serial bus. This lesson examined various techniques you can use to connect devices to your PC. In Lesson 32, "Creating Electronic Images Using Scanners and Digital Cameras," you will learn how to use a scanner or digital camera to create electronic images that you can use within your documents. Before you continue with Lesson 32, however, make sure that you have learned the following key concepts:

✓ Before your PC can use a hardware device, you must connect the device to the PC. Users connect standard devices such as a keyboard, monitor, and printer to ports located on the back of the PC's system unit.

✓ To connect high-speed devices, such as an external disk or CD-ROM drive, users normally connect the device to a SCSI adapter (a hardware card the user must install into his or her system).

✓ If a user has multiple SCSI-based devices, the user can connect together up to seven SCSI devices to form a SCSI device chain.

✓ Recently, hardware manufacturers have started creating devices for the universal serial bus (USB) that are easier to install and use than SCSI-based devices. Many new PCs have USB ports, to which users can connect a USB-based device (such as a scanner or Zip drive) or to which they can connect a USB hub, into which they can then plug in multiple USB devices.

✓ At the back of a notebook PC's system unit, you will find standard device ports. To attach SCSI-based devices to a notebook PC, users normally buy a PCMCIA-based SCSI-adapter card.

Lesson 32

Creating Electronic Images Using Scanners and Digital Cameras

In Lesson 53, "Surfing Your Way to Information on the World Wide Web," you will learn how to "surf" (view) sites on the Web. As you will learn, across the Web, sites make extensive use of images to present new products, news events, information about people, and much more. In Lesson 47, "Integrating Clipart and Photos into Your Documents," you will learn how to insert an illustration or photo into the memos and reports you create using a word processor. Finally, in Lesson 52, "Using E-Mail to Exchange Files with Other Users," you will learn how to attach files (such as reports or even photographs) that you send to another user across the Net.

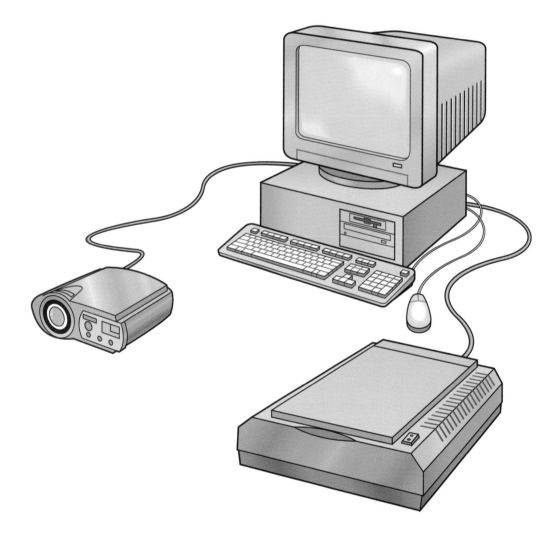

In this lesson, you will learn how you can create electronic photographs using scanners and digital cameras. You will also learn that many photo labs can convert your photos to electronic images for you and will store the images on a photo CD-ROM. By the time you finish this lesson, you will understand the following key concepts:

- An electronic image is simply a file that contains an image, such as photograph.

- To create an electronic image yourself, you can use a scanner or digital camera.

- There are several photographic labs across the country to which you can send your film or negatives that will send you a photo CD that contains your photos in an electronic format.

- A scanner is similar to a photocopy machine in that it copies a document or photo's contents. The scanner, however, stores its copy within an electronic file on disk.

- If you scan a text document, the scanner will store the text as a graphic image, not as text. To convert the scanner's graphic image to text, you must use optical-character recognition (OCR) software.

- A digital camera is a camera that stores the pictures you take in an electronic format. Using software that accompanies the digital camera, you can transfer the photos from the camera to your PC.

UNDERSTANDING THE SCANNING PROCESS

In general, a scanner is much like a photocopy machine (a copier) that copies the contents of one page to another. However, as shown in Figure 32.1, rather than printing a copy of your page (or photo), a scanner stores the copy as an electronic image within a file on disk. When you purchase a scanner, it will come with the software you need to scan and save images.

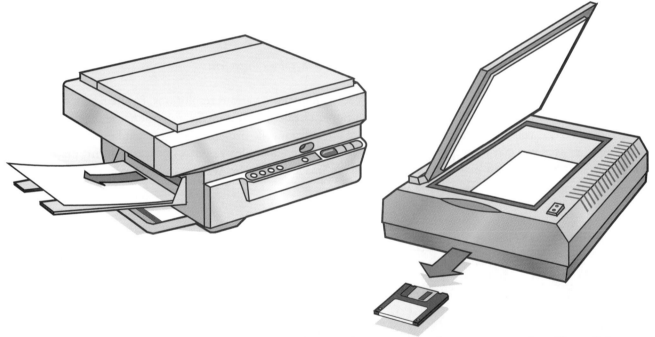

Figure 32.1 *A scanner copies a document or photograph to an electronic image that you can store in a file on disk.*

To display an image, a computer monitor represents the image colors using various shades (intensities) of the colors red, green, and blue. By combining different shades of these three colors, computer monitors can represent up to 16-million different colors. When you scan an image, your scanner determines the image's red, green, and blue color components, which it then saves to a file on disk. Although most new scanners determine an image's color components in one step, you can think of a scanner using three steps.

To determine the image's red color components, the scanner first reflects a red light off of the image. Then, the scanner determines the image's green components by reflecting a green light off of the image. Finally, the scanner determines the image's blue components by reflecting a blue light off of the image. By combining the image's red, green, and blue components, the scanner builds the composite image. Figure 32.2 illustrates this three-step process.

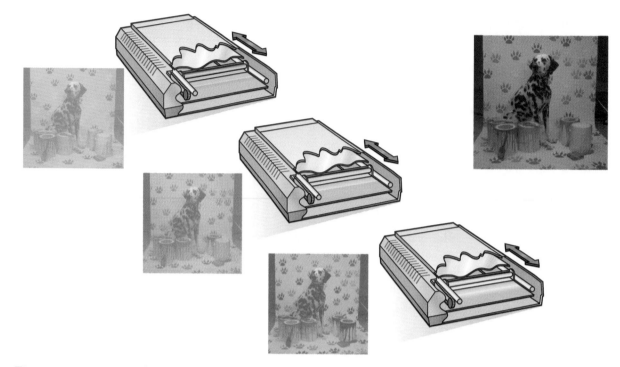

Figure 32.2 *A scanner determines an image's red, green, and blue color components.*

Depending on your scanner's type, you can normally scan an image at various resolutions. Figure 32.3, for example, shows the same image scanned at three different resolutions. The higher your image resolution, the sharper the image quality. However, as your image resolution increases, so too will your file size. If you want to send the image across the Net to another user, you may want to sacrifice a little quality for a smaller file size. Also, if you are sending images across the Net to another user, you may want to compress the images using the Winzip utility discussed in Lesson 56, "Compressing a File's Contents Using the Winzip Utility."

Figure 32.3 *Scanning an image at three different resolutions.*

USING A BUILT-IN SCANNER

With more and more users exchanging photographs across the Net using e-mail, several PC manufacturers are now including a small photographic scanner within their system unit, as shown in Figure 32.4. Using the built-in scanner, you simply insert the photo that you want to scan into the scanner's slot, much like you would insert an ATM card into an automated teller machine.

Figure 32.4 *Some PCs now include a built-in scanner.*

SEND YOUR PHOTOGRAPHS OUT FOR A PHOTO CD

If you have photographs that you want in an electronic format, but you do not have a scanner, you can send your film or negatives to one of several companies which, in turn, will return a photo CD that contains your images. Lesson 40, "Understanding CD-ROMs, CD-Rs, Audio CDs, Photo CDs, and DVDs," discusses photo CDs. To find a company near you that can produce a photo CD, use a Web-based search engine, as discussed in Lesson 54, "Using Search Engines to Find Information on the Web," to search for the words **Photo CD**. When you receive your photo CD, you will normally find files that contain your photos in two or three different resolutions (from high to low quality).

USING SCANNERS WITH TEXT

In Lesson 60, "Using Your PC to Send and Receive Faxes," you will learn that if your PC has a modem, you can use your PC to send and receive faxes. Although using your PC for faxing eliminates your need to buy a fax machine, it presents one problem. With a fax machine, you can easily fax documents you have in a paper format, such as a contract or even a hand-written note. With your PC, you can only fax items that you have in an electronic format. If you have a scanner, however, you can use your scanner to scan your paper documents and then use your fax software to fax your electronic images to another user. With the price of scanners becoming very affordable, many users may choose to purchase a scanner as opposed to a fax machine.

As you learned, when you scan a photo or document, your scanner creates an electronic image of the photo or document. In other words, regardless of whether you are scanning text or pictures, your scanner is going to create a graphic file. Your scanner will not place the text from a document within a text file that you can edit with your word processor.

If you need to create a text from a document that you have scanned, you will need to use special optical-character recognition (OCR) software. The OCR software will examine the scanner's graphic image and convert the image into text. Most scanners come with a simple OCR program. As a rule, if you have scanned a clean sheet of text, the OCR software should convert the scan into a document whose text is 90% accurate (meaning that the software will convert most of the words correctly). After the OCR software converts the scanned image into a text document, you must edit the document using your word processor to correct any errors.

Note: Many OCR software programs will advertise accuracy rates much higher than 90%. If your OCR software can convert images to text with accuracy greater than 90% on a regular basis, consider yourself lucky.

USING A DIGITAL CAMERA TO CREATE ELECTRONIC IMAGES

Over the past year, several high-quality, relatively inexpensive digital cameras have hit the market. Unlike traditional cameras that record pictures to film, a digital camera records images in an electronic format, storing the images either on a disk or on a special "flash memory."

Depending on how the camera stores its images, the steps you will perform to transfer the images from the camera to your PC will differ. If the camera stores the images on disk, you can simply insert the disk into your PC's floppy drive. If the camera stores the images in a flash memory, you will normally connect a special cable to the camera and to your PC's serial port.

When you take photographs using a digital camera, you can choose the image quality (resolution) the camera uses for each picture. As you increase image resolution, you improve the image quality, however, you also increase the image size—the larger your image size, the fewer images your camera will be able to hold. Just as you can add memory to a PC, you may be able to add memory to your digital camera. Many cameras, for example, ship from the manufacturer with 4 to 8Mb of memory. Depending on your camera's type, you may be able to replace your camera's existing memory with a 32Mb card. A 32Mb card, for example, can store about 50 high-resolution (1280 x 1024) images. As shown in Figure 32.5, a camera's flash memory is a small plastic device, a little thicker than a credit card.

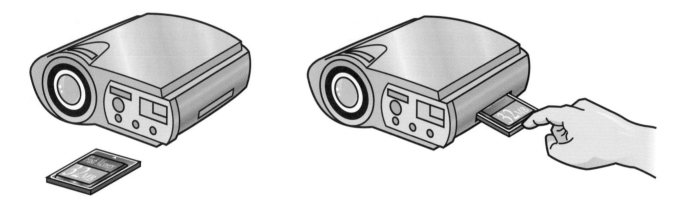

Figure 32.5 Depending on your camera's type, you may be able to increase the camera's memory.

Note: If you need very high resolution and price is not an issue, several cameras exist that can take images with a resolution of 3,060 x 2,036.

What You Must Know

Thanks to the visual nature of the World Wide Web, users are used to viewing documents that contain images. In this lesson, you learned that you can create your own electronic images using a scanner or digital camera. In addition, you can also send your film to photo processing labs that can provide you a photo CD. In Lesson 33, "Connecting PCs to a Network," you will learn how networks let users share resources (such as files and printers) as well as common network types. Before you continue with Lesson 33, however, make sure you understand the following key concepts:

✓ Electronic images are files that contain images in a graphics format. To create electronic images, users use scanners and digital cameras.

✓ If you do not have a scanner, you can send your film or negatives to a photographic lab that will send you a photo CD that contains your photos in an electronic format.

✓ To create an image, a scanner determines the image's color components by reflecting red, green, and blue lights off of the image.

✓ When you scan a text, the scanner will store the text much as it would a photo, using it as a graphic image, not as text. Using optical-character recognition software, you can convert the scanner's graphic image to text.

✓ Digital cameras let you create your own electronic photographs. Using software that accompanies the digital camera, you can transfer the photos from the camera to your PC.

Lesson 33

Connecting PCs within a Network

Over the past few years, the home computer market has continued to grow rapidly. During this same time period, the use of PCs within business kept pace with the fast-growing home PC market. The major difference between home and business PC use is that most businesses connect PCs to form a computer network. Within a network, users share resources, such as files, printers, disks, and even modems. In addition, using electronic-mail software, users can readily communicate across the network.

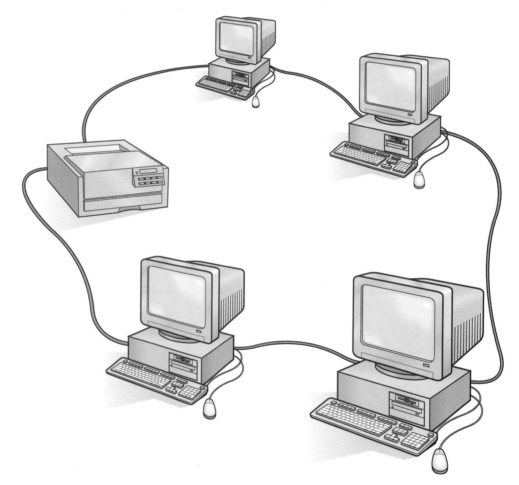

This lesson will introduce you to PC networks. By the time the time you finish this lesson, you will understand the following key concepts:

• Computer networks let users within a business or university share resources such as files or printers, and communicate using programs such as electronic-mail.

• Users classify networks as either a local-area network or wide-area network, based on the distance that separates computers within the network. A local-area network normally connects computers that reside within the same office building. A wide-area network connects computers that may reside across town, across the state, across the country, or even on the other side of the globe.

- Within a network, network administrators often select one or more computers to serve as a file or printer server. Users within the network (clients) can normally share such server's resources.

- Within a network, administrators must protect each user's files from other users. Network administrators combine hardware and software to implement various security policies.

- The Internet is a network of networks that connects computer networks around the globe.

COMPUTER NETWORKS LET USERS SHARE RESOURCES

Computer networks exist to help users share resources such as files, printers, disk space, CD-ROM drives, and even modems. The simplest computer network consists of only two computers, as shown in Figure 33.1. Users refer to simple networks, within which no computer plays the role of a server, as a peer-to-peer network—meaning, the computers within the network each have the same capabilities—they are peers.

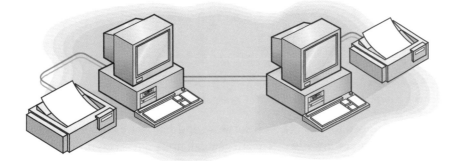

Figure 33.1 *Forming a simple network by connecting two computers.*

Within a network, companies often select one computer to which they attach disks or printers that other users within the network can share. Users refer to such computers as *servers*, because when the user needs disk space or to print a file, the computer can provide the services. The user, in this case, becomes the server's client. Figure 33.2, for example, shows a print server within a network to which the network administrator has connected multiple printers that users within the network can share. Likewise, Figure 33.3 shows a disk server that provides disk drives that users across the network can use to store and retrieve files.

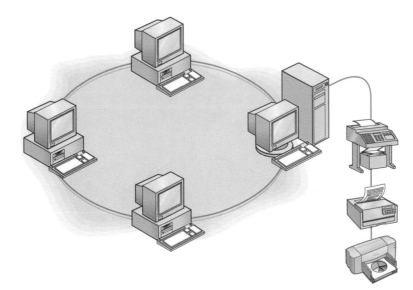

Figure 33.2 A *print server is a computer that provides one or more printers that other users within a network can share.*

199

Figure 33.3 *A disk server is a computer that provides one or more disk drives that users across the network can access.*

Within a network, network administrators use various software and hardware components to implement security policies that protect your files from access by other users. In general, users can access only files and devices within the network to which the network administrator has given the user access.

HOW USERS CONNECT COMPUTERS TO NETWORKS

To connect computers and other devices, such as printers, networks normally connect cables between each device. Depending on the network's design, the network may run a cable from one computer to the next, or the network may connect the devices to a central network hub, as shown in Figure 33.4.

Figure 33.4 *Connecting network devices to a central hub.*

Depending on the network software you are running, the steps you must perform to access network resources will differ. Normally, you will access network disk drives using a disk drive letter, just as you would access the hard drive and floppy-disk drives connected to your PC. For more information on how you access drives within your network, see your network administrator.

UNDERSTANDING LOCAL-AREA AND WIDE-AREA NETWORKS

Computer networks exist to help users share resources, such as files or printers, or to communicate, using electronic mail. Within a business, users categorize computer networks based upon the distance that separates the computers. Most businesses use a local-area network, within which the computers reside in the same office building, as shown in Figure 33.5. Users refer to a local-area network as a LAN.

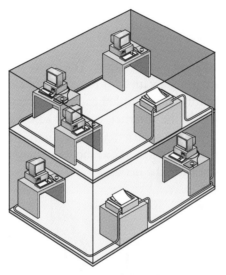

Figure 33.5 *PCs within a local-area network reside in reasonably close proximity, such as the same office building.*

In contrast, as shown in Figure 33.6, in a wide-area network (which users refer to as a WAN), the computers may reside across town, the state, or even across the globe. Depending on the distance that separates computers within a wide-area network, the network may use phone cables, fiber-optic connections, or even satellite communications to connect the network computers.

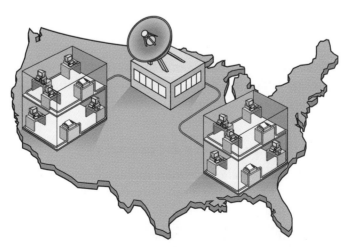

Figure 33.6 *Computers within a wide-area network may reside in different cities, states, or countries.*

THE INTERNET IS A NETWORK OF NETWORKS

A network consists of two or more computers, connected to share resources, such as files or printers or to communicate using electronic-mail. In Lesson 49, "Understanding the Internet and World Wide Web," you will learn that the Internet is a network of networks, as shown in Figure 33.7. In other words, the Internet connects computer networks around the world.

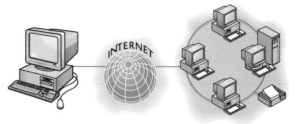

Figure 33.7 *The Internet is a network of networks.*

Networks exist to help users share resources and communicate. The Internet is no exception. Across the Internet, users share files and devices and communicate using a variety of programs, one of which is electronic-mail. As you have learned, within a network, network administrators implement various security policies to protect each user's files. When companies connect their networks to the Internet, network administrators must protect the network from hackers and computer viruses. Often, to increase security, network administrators will place a hardware and software firewall between the network and the Internet. In general, as shown in Figure 33.8, the firewall acts a security guard, controlling the messages that can enter or leave the network.

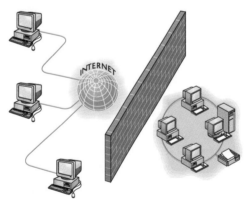

Figure 33.8 *Network administrators use firewalls to control incoming and outgoing messages.*

WHAT YOU MUST KNOW

Networks connect computers to help users share resources such as files and printers, and to help users communicate. This lesson introduced computer networks. In Lesson 34, "Mobile Computing Using a Notebook PC," you will examine notebook personal computers in detail. Before you continue with Lesson 34, however, make sure you have learned the following key concepts:

✓ Networks exist to help users share resources and communicate.

✓ Network administrators often select one or more specific computers within the network to act as file or printer servers. The computers can share resources that users across the network (clients) can access.

✓ Within a network, network administrators use hardware and software techniques to implement various security policies that protect each user's resources from other users (both users connected to the network and users outside of the network).

Lesson 34

Mobile Computing Using a Notebook PC

Over the past few years, the use of notebook PCs has grown as fast, and in some cases faster, than the desktop PC market. Today, many people carry a notebook PC with them everywhere they go. As notebook PCs are becoming smaller and lighter, they are also becoming more powerful and more affordable. In fact, in terms of RAM, processing speed, and even hard disk capacity, many notebook PCs can match most user's desktop PCs. Throughout this book's lessons, you have examined the notebook PC's keyboard, mouse, monitor, and ways you can connect devices to the PC's PCMCIA slots.

This lesson examines a few operations you can perform to fine-tune your notebook PC operations. By the time you finish this lesson, you will understand the following key concepts:

- If you travel with a PC or carry your PC between your home and office, you should create a document on your Desktop that offers a reward for your PC's safe return. Within the document, you should include your name, phone number, and e-mail address.

- Using the Control Panel Power Management icon, you can display the Power Management Properties dialog box, within which you can customize your PC's power use.

- If you often run your PC on a battery, consider buying a second battery that you keep charged and with you while you travel.

- If you travel with your notebook PC, you may want to buy a lightweight portable printer. Many newer portable printers will even print in color. Some will run on a battery, which lets you print documents during a plane flight!

- Using the Control Panel PC Card icon, you can display the PC Card (PCMCIA) Properties dialog box, within which you can view information about your current PCMCIA cards.

- Windows lets you hot swap PCMCIA cards while your system is running. Before you remove a PCMCIA card from your system, however, you should first stop Windows use of the device from within the PC Card (PCMCIA) Properties dialog box.

OFFER A REWARD FOR YOUR PC

If you travel with a notebook PC or carry your notebook PC with you to and from the office, you should create a file that you store your Desktop that offers a reward for your notebook PC's safe return. Using your word processor, create a document similar to that shown in Figure 34.1, which includes your name, phone number, e-mail address, and the fact that you will offer a reward for your PC's return.

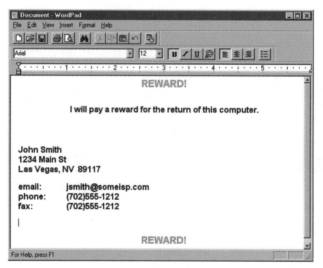

Figure 34.1 *Place a document on your Desktop that offers a reward for your PC's safe return.*

To store a document on your Desktop, use the Save As dialog box to select the Desktop folder, as discussed in Lesson 15, "Using Electronic Folders to Organize Your Files." Next, name your document REWARD! so that it stands out on your Desktop, as shown in Figure 34.2.

REWARD!
.doc

Figure 34.2 *A Desktop icon for the REWARD! document.*

UNDERSTANDING YOUR NOTEBOOK PC'S KEYBOARD, MONITOR, AND MOUSE

Several of this book's lessons focus on specific hardware devices, such as the keyboard, mouse, and monitor. Within each of those lessons, the book discusses device-specific issues for notebook PCs. In addition to reading the information this lesson presents, you should take time now to review the following lessons for notebook-related topics:

Lesson 22 Getting the Most from Your Keyboard and Mouse

Lesson 23 Getting the Most from Your Monitor

Lesson 31 Connecting Devices to Your Personal Computer

Lesson 48 Understand the "Ins and Outs" *of PC Modems*

COMPARING THE CAPABILITIES OF A NOTEBOOK AND DESKTOP PERSONAL COMPUTERS

If you compare the inner-workings (the electronics) of a notebook and desktop PC, you will find that, in general, both use the same processor and support the same amount of RAM. And, as shown in Figure 34.3, most notebook PCs support hard disks large enough to meet user needs. As such, both systems will run the same software.

Figure 34.3 *Notebook and desktop PCs essentially offer the same hardware capabilities.*

Where notebook and desktop PCs differ is in their keyboard and monitor size. Because the desktop PC is larger than the notebook, the desktop PC can offer larger devices. If you examine high-end PCs, you will find that notebook PCs generally lag desktop PCs by about six months. In other words, when the 450MHz Pentium becomes the standard processor for desktop PCs, it will take about six months for it to become the standard processor for notebook PCs. The reason notebook PCs take longer to release new products is that the hardware designers must often find ways to fit a newer, slightly larger chip into the notebook's cramped system unit as well as a way to better vent the heat the newer, faster chip generates.

MANAGING YOUR NOTEBOOK PC'S BATTERY LIFE

If you use your notebook PC while you commute, you are well aware of the importance of prolonging the notebook's battery life. Within the Windows Control Panel, discussed in Lesson 45, "Configuring Your PC's System Settings," you will find a Power Management icon. If you double-click your mouse on the icon, Windows will display the Power Management Properties dialog box, as shown in Figure 34.4. Within the dialog box, you can customize your PC's power-management settings and control how the PC notifies you when your battery power is getting low. (Your PC will notify you of a low battery so you can save your current documents to files on disk.)

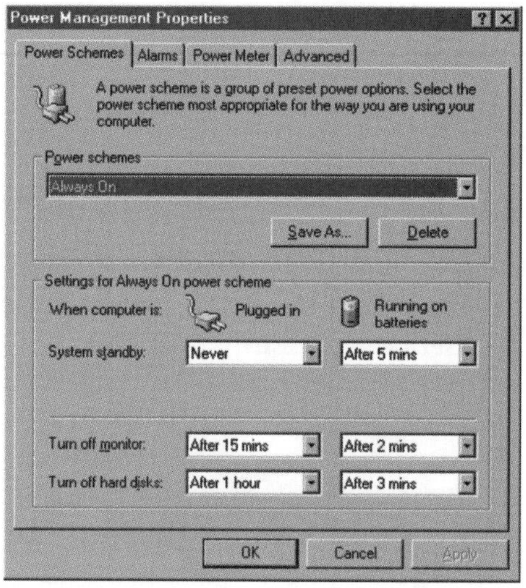

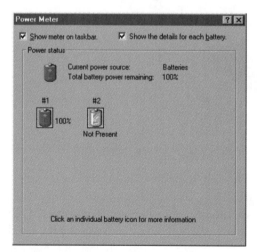

Figure 34.4 *The Power Management Properties dialog box.*

Within the Power Management Properties dialog box, direct Windows to display an icon for a power meter on the Windows Taskbar. If you click your mouse on the power meter icon, Windows will display a dialog box, similar to that shown in Figure 34.5, that shows the amount of power left in your battery.

Figure 34.5 *Using a battery meter to monitor your notebook PC's battery level.*

If you normally run your notebook PC from its battery for long periods of time, you should buy a second battery that you keep charged and with you.

IF YOU MUST PRINT DOCUMENTS ON THE ROAD, A PORTABLE PRINTER IS IDEAL

If you travel with a notebook PC, you may have made midnight runs to a Kinkos to print a document or have waited nervously for your hotel's business center to open so you could print some last-minute slides. If you find that you need to print documents while you are on the road, you should buy a portable printer, similar to that shown in Figure 34.6. If you shop for printers, you will find that they have become quite affordable (a few hundred dollars) and that they weigh only a few pounds. You can even purchase portable printers that print in color, as well as battery-powered printers, that let you do that last minute printing as you travel.

Figure 34.6 For most business travelers a portable printer is a great investment.

USING THE PC CARD (PCMCIA) PROPERTIES DIALOG BOX

Throughout this book's lessons, you have learned how to connect devices, such as a scanner or external CD-ROM drive, to a notebook computer. You will normally attach the device to a SCSI-adapter card that you insert into the notebook's PCMCIA slot. Likewise, many notebook PCs use PCMCIA-based modems. When you shop for PCMCIA-based devices, your salesperson may ask you what type of PCMCIA cards your PC supports. As it turns out, there are three different PCMCIA card types, to which manufacturers assign the meaningful names of Type I, Type II, and Type III cards. The difference between each card type is the card's thickness (Type I cards are 3.3mm thick, Type II are 5.0mm, and Type III are 10.5mm). Most notebook PCs provide PCMCIA slots that will hold either two Type I or Type II cards, or one Type III card. Within the Control Panel folder, you will find a PC Card icon. If you double-click your mouse on this icon, Windows will display the PC Card (PCMCIA) Properties dialog box, as shown in Figure 34.7.

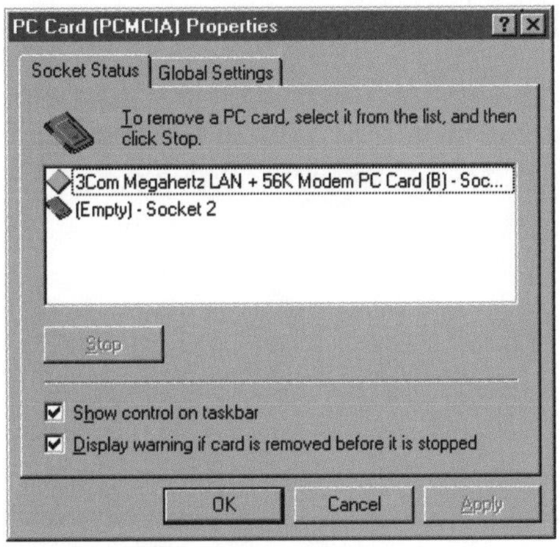

Figure 34.7 The PC Card (PCMCIA) Properties dialog box.

Within the dialog box, you can view which PCMCIA cards are currently in your PC's slot. In addition, you can use the dialog box to direct Windows to stop using a PCMCIA-based device before you remove the card. Assume, for example, that your PCMCIA slot currently has a SCSI card and a modem card, and you want to replace the modem card with a network card. Windows will let you swap the cards without shutting down your system (users refer to this process as *hot swapping* the cards). Before you remove the modem card, however, you should turn it off. To turn off a card's use, click your mouse on the card within the PC Card (PCMCIA) Properties dialog box and then click your mouse on the Stop button. Windows, in turn, will display a dialog box telling you that you can now remove the card.

EXCHANGING INFORMATION BETWEEN A NOTEBOOK AND DESKTOP PC

As you have learned, a notebook PC runs the same software as a desktop PC. If you use a notebook PC while you travel, and a desktop PC in your office, there may be times when you must exchange documents between your two computers. To start, you find that the easiest way to exchange documents is simply to e-mail document to your desktop or notebook PC (provided the two computers use separate e-mail accounts). Second, you can use a null-modem cable (or an infrared link) to connect your notebook and desktop PC serial ports and then use the Windows Direct Cable Connection utility to exchange documents between the two PCs. For more information on the Direct Cable Connection utility, refer to the book *1001 Windows 98 Tips*, Jamsa Press, 1998.

WHAT YOU MUST KNOW

Today, notebook PCs offer the same computing power as most desktop systems and they offer mobility. Throughout this book's lessons, you have examined specific notebook PC hardware considerations. In this lesson, you learned ways you can fine-tune your notebook PC's battery and PCMCIA-card use. In Lesson 35, "Putting Computing Power in the Palm of Your Hand," you will examine palmtop PCs, which normally weigh less than two pounds and that will fit within the palm of your hand. Before you continue with Lesson 35, however, make sure you have learned the following key concepts:

- ✓ To increase your chance of getting your notebook PC back, should your PC become lost or stolen, place document on your Desktop that offers a reward for your PC's safe return and that provides your name, phone number, and e-mail address.

- ✓ If you use your notebook PC on battery power on a regular basis, you can use the Control Panel Power Management icon to customize your PC's power use. In addition, you should consider buying a second battery that you keep charged and with you while you travel.

- ✓ If you travel with your notebook PC and you find that you must print documents while you are on the road, you should buy a portable printer. Most portable printers are lightweight, some let you print in color, and some will run on a battery.

- ✓ Windows lets you hot swap PCMCIA cards while your system is running. Before you remove a PCMCIA card from your system, however, you should first stop Windows use of the device from within the PC Card (PCMCIA) Properties dialog box.

Lesson 35

Putting Computing Power in the Palm of Your Hand

When PC manufacturers released the first portable computer in the 1980s, the system's near 30-pound weight made the PC anything but portable. In Lesson 34, "Mobile Computing Using a Notebook PC," you learned that today's notebook computers provide high-speed Pentium processors, fast modems, and even high-capacity hard disks—and the notebook PCs provide these features while weighing less than 7 pounds! As chip and circuit technology continues to improve, PCs are becoming faster and smaller at an amazing rate. In fact, you can now purchase a palmtop computer (so named because you can hold the computer in the palm of your hand, or at least almost, depending on the size of your hand) for less than $1,000 that contains a Pentium processor, hard disk, and into which you can even install a modem. In addition, many of the palmtop computers run Windows and Windows-based software (such as Word and Excel), with which you are already familiar. Using a palmtop computer, you can create memos, spreadsheets, send and receive electronic mail, and even surf the World Wide Web. This lesson examines palmtop PCs. By the time you finish this lesson, you will understand the following key concepts:

- Palmtop computers are so named because they are small enough and light enough to fit in the palm of your hand.

- Depending on your palmtop computer's size and weight, the palmtop may include a hard disk and modem.

- Many palmtop computers run Windows and Windows-based programs, such as Word and Excel.

- If you are willing to move up a few ounces in weight, up to 2 to 3 pounds, you can purchase a palmtop computer with a fast Pentium processor, 32Mb or RAM, and a 1Gb hard disk.

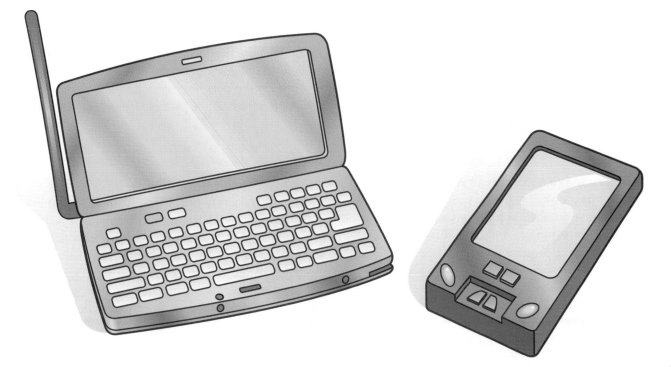

WHAT'S AVAILABLE IN THE PALMTOP WORLD

If you pick up a computer magazine, you will find that many companies offer small palmtop PCs. As you examine each palmtop's product description, you will find that some, such as the Palm Pilot, use a proprietary operating system (an operating system of their own design which only runs programs written specifically for that system), while other palmtops will run a special version of Windows (often called Windows CE for, depending who ask, stands for: Compact Edition, Connectable Edition, Compatible Edition, or Companion Edition) that lets you run such programs as Word, Excel, and even Internet Explorer.

LOOKING UNDER THE PALMTOP'S HOOD

If you look at the product specification, you will be surprised to find that palmtop computers conitain a high-speed processor and 8 to 16Mb of RAM. Depending on the palmtop's size, cost, and weight, the palmtop may or may not have a hard disk, as shown in Figure 35.1.

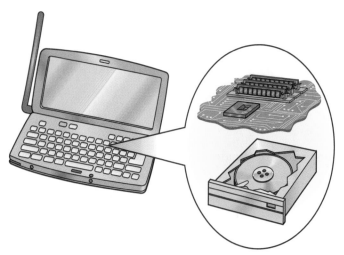

Figure 35.1 *Many palmtop PCs include the same hardware as a desktop or notebook PC.*

If your palmtop computer does not have a hard disk, the palmtop will store the documents that you create, or e-mail that you receive, within a battery-powered RAM. A palmtop with 8Mb of RAM, for example, will normally use 4Mb to store your programs and 4Mb to store your documents. If your palmtop does not have a hard drive, and you use your palmtop to store documents, make sure that you keep its batteries fresh. If the palmtop's batteries die, you will lose the information you have stored.

HOW PALMTOP COMPUTERS STORE YOUR PROGRAMS

If your palmtop computer has a hard disk, your palmtop will store your programs on the disk. If you palmtop does not have a hard disk, it will store your programs using a special chip, called a read-only memory (or ROM), that can store information, such as programs whose contents do not change. Before the palmtop's manufacturer ships the palmtop, it stores programs, such as Windows 98 and Word, within ROM. The read-only memory is special in that it does not require constant power (as does the information you store in RAM). Should your palmtop's batteries fail, you won't lose the information the read-only memory contains. Later, when you turn on your palmtop's power, the programs are available for your use. Because you cannot change the contents of read-only memory, the only way you can upgrade the palmtop's software (if the palmtop does not have a hard disk and stores its programs in ROM) is to replace the ROM chip itself. For most users, however, the software current palmtops provide should meet their needs for at least the next year, at which point, much faster and less expensive palmtop computers will be available.

CONNECTING YOUR PALMTOP TO THE INTERNET AND THE WORLD WIDE WEB

Depending on your palmtop's type, it may include a built-in modem or it may let you insert a PCMCIA-based modem, as shown in Figure 35.2. In addition, some palmtop computers offer built-in cellular-based modems that simplify your Internet connections.

Figure 35.2 *A palmtop with a built-in modem and a second palmtop that supports a PCMCIA-based modem.*

Using the modem, you can connect your palmtop to the Internet and then send and receive electronic mail. In addition, you may be able to use your palmtop to surf the Web.

EXCHANGING INFORMATION BETWEEN YOUR PALMTOP AND DESKTOP PC

If your palmtop PC and your desktop PC use the same software, such as Windows 98, Word, or Excel, you can exchange documents between your two computers. To start, you can use e-mail to exchange documents between your palmtop and desktop PCs. Likewise, most palmtop PCs provide software you can use to exchange documents with a desktop system. As shown in Figure 35.3, to exchange files between two pieces, you first must connect the PCs, either using a cable or an infrared connection.

Figure 35.3 *Connecting a palmtop and desktop PC to exchange files.*

To simplify the process of exchanging documents between your palmtop and desktop PC, most palmtops will provide the software and cable you require. If your palmtop does not, but your palmtop runs Windows, you can probably use the Windows Direct Cable Connection utility program and a null-modem cable to exchange documents between your two PCs. For more information on the Direct Cable Connection utility, refer to the book *1001 Windows 98 Tips*, Jamsa Press, 1998.

POWERFUL PALMTOPS FOR SLIGHTLY LARGER HANDS

Although having a small palmtop PC may win the "who has got the coolest toy in the office" contest, you may find that by moving up a little bit in weight and cost, you get a more powerful (and more useful) resource. For example, Figure 35.4 shows a 2-pound PC that runs Windows 98. It includes a Pentium processor, 32Mb of RAM, a PCMCIA slot for a modem or external CD-ROM, a detachable floppy disk drive, and an 800Mb hard disk! Although you may not be able to hold the PC in the palm of your hand, you can easily carry it in your briefcase or purse.

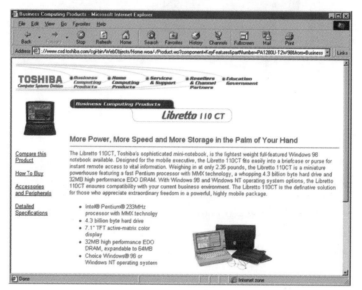

Figure 35.4 A slightly larger, yet much more useful PC.

In the near future, you will see these small PCs in many meetings, on airplanes, and even subway trains. Using one of these small PCs, you can connect a projector to one of the PCs ports and then use software, such as Microsoft PowerPoint, to display a presentation on a screen or blank wall, as shown in Figure 35.5.

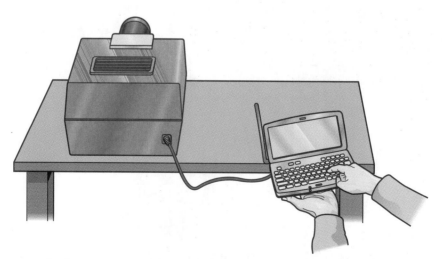

Figure 35.5 Connecting a display projector to a palmtop PC.

WINNING THE COOLEST TOY CONTEST

If you are out of the office on a regular basis, and you need to keep in touch by phone or e-mail, you can achieve your goals and win the "coolest toy" contest by purchasing a high-end Nokia cellular phone. As shown in Figure 35.6, the Nokia phone looks like a traditional cellular phone. However, when you open it, the phone provides a screen and keyboard that you can use to send and receive e-mail, faxes, and even to surf the Web. For more information on Nokia phones, visit the Nokia Web site at *www.nokia.com*.

Figure 35.6 *The future of communications, today.*

WHAT YOU MUST KNOW

This lesson examined palmtop PCs, which seem to become smaller, more powerful, and less expensive on a monthly basis. Using a palmtop PC, you can run software such as Windows, Word, and Excel, you can send and receive electronic mail, and some models will even let you surf the Web. In Lesson 36, "Protecting Your Data Using Backup Files," you will learn how to make backup copies of the files you create or change. Before you continue with Lesson 36, however, make sure you understand the following key concepts:

✓ Palmtop computers differ from notebook PCs in that the palmtop fits (or almost fits) into the palm of your hand.

✓ Palmtop computers are ideal for sending and receiving e-mail and tracking small documents, such as your weekly schedule.

✓ Some palmtops provide a built-in modem and provide a hard disk, while other palmtops support external devices.

✓ Most palmtop computers run a special version of Windows (called Windows CE) and Windows-based programs such as Word, Excel, and the Internet Explorer.

Lesson 36

Protecting Your Data Using Backup Files

Throughout this book's lessons, you have learned how to run numerous programs, many of which you will use in the future to create documents that you store on disk. Depending on the documents that you create, the files on your disk may store reports, memos, spreadsheets, presentations, and even multimedia content, such as audio or video.

Although hard disks have become very reliable, they do periodically fail. Depending on the disk error you experience, the information that you store on your disk may be lost. In Lesson 18, "Recovering a Deleted File from the Windows Recycle Bin," you learned that if you inadvertently delete a file, you may be able to recover the file's contents from a special folder on your disk called the Recycle Bin. As a rule, to protect yourself against the loss of key files, you must make backup copies of your files' contents that you store on another disk or tape, ideally in a location away from your original copy.

This lesson examines ways you can make backup copies of your key files. By the time you finish this lesson, you will understand the following key concepts:

- Because hard disks can fail, you must protect the information that you store on disk by creating backup copies of your files.

- You do not have to backup every file on your hard disk. You do not, for example, have to backup programs that you can reinstall from the program's CD-ROM, such as Microsoft Word. You do, however, need to backup the files that you create using the programs, such as a Word document.

- You can backup your files to floppy disks, to a Zip disk, to a network disk, to magnetic tape, or to a remote disk on a local-area network. If you purchase a magnetic-tape drive or CD-ROM burner to perform your backups, the device will come with the software you need to create your backups.

- To help you perform your backup operations, Microsoft bundles backup software, Microsoft Backup, with Windows.

- Many of your application programs, such as Word and Excel, let you create backup copies of your document's contents each time you save the document's contents to disk.

DETERMINING WHICH FILES YOU MUST BACKUP

As you have learned, hard disks are capable of storing several gigabytes (several billion bytes) of information. Most users have a unique way of consuming their available disk space. Fortunately, you do not have to backup every item on your disk. Instead, you must backup only items you cannot reinstall from another source, such as a program's CD-ROM. In other words, you would not backup the Microsoft Word software on your disk, but rather, the documents that you create within Word. If you ever experienced a disk error, you could reinstall the Word program from CD-ROM and then install your documents from your backup. If, for example, at the end of each day, you backup only the files you have created or changed that day, your backups will normally complete quickly and require only a little disk space.

DETERMINING TO WHICH DEVICE YOU ARE GOING TO WRITE YOUR BACKUPS

In the past, users would backup their hard disks to floppy disks. Because hard disks were quite small (10 to 30Mb), backing up a user's files to floppy disk made sense. As disk capacity grew, however, backing files up to floppy disk soon became an unreasonable task, simply because of the number of floppy disks required. Instead, users backed up their systems to a magnetic tape drive which, as shown in Figure 36.1, could be an internal or external drive. Today, magnetic tapes provide one of the most efficient ways to backup a large disk. In Lesson 39, "Exchanging Files Using a Zip Disk," you will learn that Zip disks, which look like large floppy disks, can store over 100Mb of data. For most users, Zip disks provide a very effective way of backing up their key files. In fact, many users use Zip disk to transfer files between their home and office PC.

Similarly, in Lesson 40, "Understanding CD-ROMs, CD-Rs, Audio CDs, Photo CDs, and DVDs," you will learn that for a few hundred dollars, you can buy a CD-ROM burner, a device that looks much like a CD-ROM drive, with which you can create your own CD-ROM discs. Using the CD-ROM burner, you can create a CD-ROM disc that contains over 650Mb and normally do so in less than one hour. If you work within an office that connects PCs using a local-area network, your network administrator may direct you to backup your files to a disk that resides across the network. In this way, should anything happen to your disk or to your PC, you have a copy of your key files accessible on the network. If you must backup more than one PC, and the PCs are not connected to a network, you should purchase an external tape drive, zip drive, or CD-ROM burner that you can move from one system to the next to perform your backups. Although using the external device to perform backups requires that you move the device from PC to PC, you can perform your backups using only one backup device, which is very cost-effective.

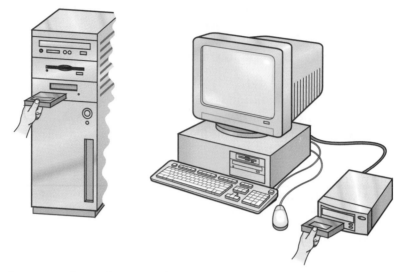

Figure 36.1 An internal or external tape drive provides a convenient way to perform hard disk backups.

UNDERSTANDING BACKUP SOFTWARE

If you buy a tape drive to perform your file backups, your tape drive will come with the software that you need to perform your file backups. Likewise, if you purchase a CD-ROM burner, as discussed in Lesson 40, the burner will come with the software you need. If, however, you are backing up your system to floppy disks or Zip disks, you can use the Microsoft Backup program that Microsoft bundles with Windows, as shown in Figure 36.2.

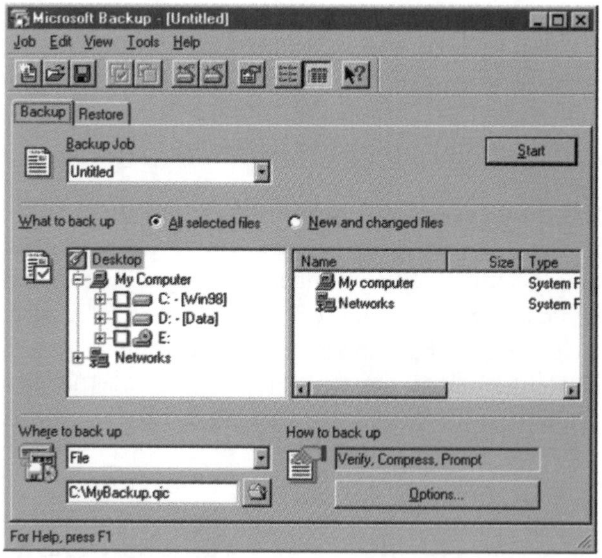

Figure 36.2 Using the Microsoft Backup program.

USING THE WINDOWS EXPLORER TO CREATE A BACKUP COPY OF YOUR KEY FILES

Backup files exist to help prevent you from losing information should you lose the original files' contents. How you create your backup files is much less important than the fact that you create the backups. Often, you can use the Windows Explorer, discussed in Lesson 17, "Using the Windows Explorer to Manage Your Files and Disks," to create copies of your key files on a floppy disk, Zip disk, or even a network disk. For more information on copying files within Windows using the Explorer, turn to Lesson 17.

As you have learned, you should create your backup file copies on a disk other than the one that stores your original file's contents. In so doing, should your original disk experience an error, you will not lose both your original files and backup files. If you are working with a notebook PC, however, there may be times when you cannot backup your files to another disk. At such times, you should create a second folder on your disk within which you place a backup copy of your files. Later, when you can access a different disk drive, you should create a backup copy of your files on a second disk.

DIRECTING YOUR PROGRAMS TO CREATE BACKUP COPIES OF YOUR FILES

To provide you with a way to revert to a file's previous contents, many software programs, such as Word and Excel, can save backup copies of your files for you as you work. Assume, for example, that you open your company's budget report within Word and that you edit the document's contents. Later, when you save the file's contents, you can direct Word to store both the file's new content and its previous contents on your disk. Word will store the document's current contents within a file with the DOC extension and the document's previous contents in a backup file that uses the BAK extension (for backup). By directing your software to keep backup copies of your files on your disk, you may reduce the amount of information you lose should your original file become damaged or should you decide that you want to revert to the file's previous contents. Depending on your software, the steps you must perform to direct your software to create a backup copy of your documents will differ. Within Word, for example, you can enable backup copies by selecting the File menu and choosing Options. Word, in turn, will display the Options dialog box, within which you will click your mouse on the Always Create Backup Copy checkbox.

WHAT YOU MUST KNOW

As you use your PC, you will store a variety of files on your disk. Depending on the programs you use, your files may contain word-processing documents, spreadsheets, presentations, graphics, and so on. Although hard disks are very reliable, you should protect your data by creating backup copies of your key files that you store on a disk other than the one that contains your original files. In this lesson, you learned that you can create your backup copies on floppy disks, Zip disks, magnetic tape, CD-ROMs that you create, and even network drives. In Lesson 37, "Experiencing Multimedia Sights and Sounds," you will learn that multimedia is the use of text, pictures, audio, and video to present information. You will also learn how to run simple multimedia programs that Microsoft bundles with Windows. Before you continue with Lesson 37, however, make sure that you have learned the following key concepts:

- ✓ Although hard disks are very reliable, they do fail. Likewise, even if you are careful, you may periodically erase the wrong file from your disk. To protect the information that you store on disk, you must create backup copies of your files.

- ✓ Your hard disk may store thousands of files that require hundreds of megabytes of storage. Fortunately, you don't have to backup every file on your disk. You do not, for example, have to backup programs that you can reinstall from the program's CD-ROM. You need only to backup the files that you create using the programs.

- ✓ Depending on the size and number of files that you must backup, you can backup your files to floppy disks, to a Zip disk, to a network disk, to magnetic tape, or to a remote disk on a local-area network.

- ✓ If you purchase a magnetic-tape drive or CD-ROM burner, you will receive software that you can use to backup your files.

- ✓ If you are backing up your files to floppy disks or to a Zip disk, you can use the Microsoft Backup program that Microsoft bundles with Windows.

- ✓ Many programs let you create backup copies of your document's contents each time you save the document's contents to disk.

Lesson 37

Experiencing Multimedia Sights and Sounds

Multimedia is the use of two or more media (such as text, pictures, sounds, and video) to present information. Today, programs make extensive use of multimedia. CD-ROM-based encyclopedias, such as Microsoft Encarta, provide thousands of pages of text, thousands of images, as well as audio and video clips. In Lesson 57, "Using RealAudio to Bring the Web's Sounds to Life," for example, you will learn how to add video and software capabilities to your browsing capabilities. Likewise, in Lesson 40, "Understanding CD-ROMs, CD-Rs, Audio CDs, Photo CDs, and DVDs," you will learn how to play full-length movies on your PC using a DVD-compatible CD-ROM drive.

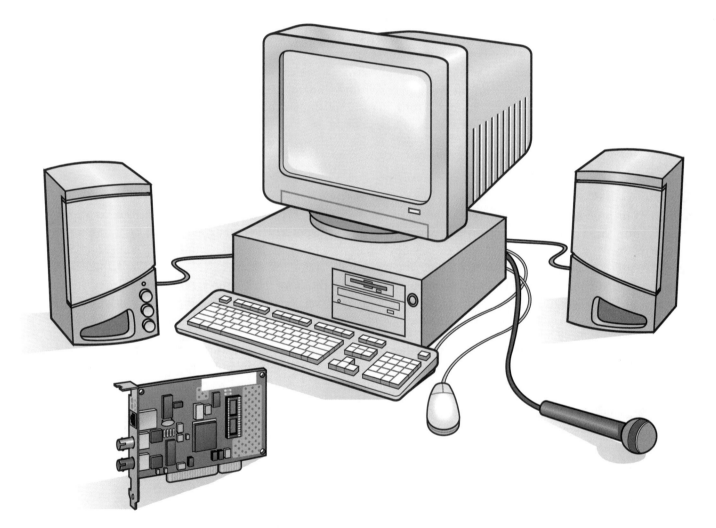

In this lesson, you will examine several multimedia programs that Microsoft bundles with Windows. By the time you finish this lesson, you will understand the following key concepts:

- Multimedia is the use of text, pictures, audio, and video to present information in a meaning way.

- Most PCs sold today provide the hardware you need to experience multimedia programs: a sound card, speakers, and a microphone.

- To get you started with multimedia, Windows bundles a few multimedia programs that you can use to record your own sounds, play audio CDs, and play MIDI music files.

- Depending on your sound card type, your PC may have a volume-control knob you can use to adjust your PC's volume.

- If you examine the Windows Taskbar, you will find a small speaker icon. If you click your mouse on the icon, Windows will display a volume-control slider that you can use to adjust your speaker volume.

UNDERSTANDING MULTIMEDIA HARDWARE

To experience multimedia, you need a sound card, speakers, and a CD-ROM, as shown in Figure 37.1. Also, depending on the programs you plan to use, you may also want to have a microphone with which you can record your own audio files. Fortunately, most PCs sold today come with these multimedia hardware devices. In fact, most notebook PCs support these multimedia devices.

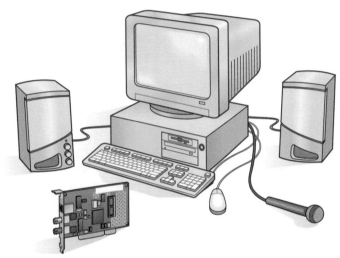

Figure 37.1 *Traditional multimedia hardware devices.*

TEST DRIVING A FEW MULTIMEDIA PROGRAMS

If your PC has a sound card, speakers, and a microphone, you can use them with a few simple multimedia programs that Microsoft bundles with Windows. To start, you will use a program called the Media Player to play some MIDI files. MIDI is an acronym for Musical Instrument Device Interface, a standard that defines how electronic instruments connect to a PC and other devices.

Your PC's sound card has a chip called a synthesizer that lets your sound card simulate various music devices. A MIDI file contains the notes various instruments would use to play a song. When you open a MIDI file within the Media Player accessory program, the Media Player will use your sound card's synthesizer to generate sounds for a set of instruments. The best way to understand how your sound card can generate such sounds is simply to open and play a MIDI file within the Media Player. To start the Media Player, perform these steps:

1. Click your mouse on the Start button. Windows will display the Start menu.

2. Within the Start menu, click your mouse on the Programs menu Accessories option. Windows, in turn, will cascade the Accessories menu.

3. Depending on your Windows version, you will either find the Media Player option within the Accessories menu, the Multimedia submenu, or the Entertainment submenu. When you click your mouse on the Media Player option, Windows will open the Media Player window, as shown in Figure 37.2.

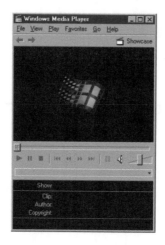

Figure 37.2 *The Media Player window.*

Next, within the Media Player, you can open the MIDI file *Canyon.MID*, that Microsoft includes with Windows. To open the file, perform these steps:

1. Within the Media Player window, click your mouse on the File menu and choose Open. Windows, in turn, will display the Open dialog box.

2. Within the Open dialog box, select the *\Windows\Media* folder and click your mouse on the *Canyon.MID* file and then click your mouse on OK. The Media Player, in turn, will load the MIDI file's contents.

3. Within the Media Player, click your mouse on the Play button. The Media Player, in turn, will start playing back the file's contents.

Note: *If your Accessories menu does list the Media Player or other multimedia programs or if the* **\Windows\Media** *folder does not contain the* **Canyon.MID** *file, you can install programs and files from the Windows CD-ROM using the Control Panel Add/Remove Programs icon. In Lesson 45, "Configuring Your PC's System Settings," you will learn how to use the Control Panel.*

RECORDING YOUR OWN SOUNDS

If your PC has a microphone, you can use the Windows Sound Recorder to record your own sounds. To start the Sound Recorder, perform these steps:

1. Click your mouse on the Start button. Windows, in turn, will display the Start menu.

2. Within the Start menu, click your mouse on the Programs menu Accessories option. Windows, in turn, will cascade the Accessories menu.

3. Depending on your Windows version, you will either find the Sound Recorder option within the Accessories menu or the Entertainment submenu. When you click your mouse on the Sound Recorder option, Windows will open the Sound Recorder window, as shown in Figure 37.3.

Next, to record a sound, turn on your microphone (providing your microphone has an on/off switch) and then click your mouse on the Sound Recorder's Record button. If you are using a notebook PC, your PC's microphone is normally on. As you record, the Sound Recorder will display sound analog waves that correspond to the sounds you are recording. After you are done recording, click your mouse on the Sound Recorder's Stop button.

Figure 37.3 *The Sound Recorder window.*

To play back your recording, click your mouse on the Play button. To save your recording to a file on disk, select the File menu Save As option. Windows, in turn, will display the Save As dialog box, within which you can specify the name of the file within which you will save the recording.

CHANGING YOUR PC'S SPEAKER VOLUME

Depending on your PC's hardware devices, you can adjust your PC's play back volume using one of several techniques. To start, if your speakers have a volume control knob, use the knob to increase or decrease your playback volume, as shown in Figure 37.4.

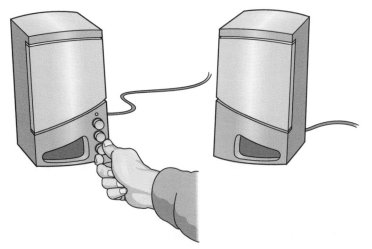

Figure 37.4 *Using a speaker's volume-control knob to increase or decrease your system's play back volume.*

Second, as shown in Figure 37.5, many sound cards and most Notebook PCs have a volume-control knob that you can use to change your system's play back volume.

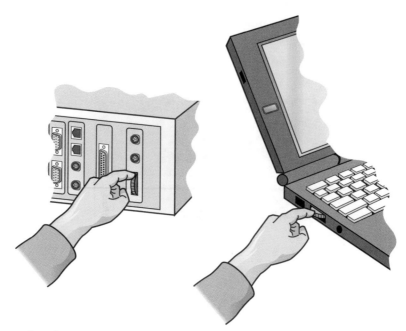

Figure 37.5 *Using a sound card or notebook PC volume control.*

Finally, if you examine the Windows Taskbar that normally appears at the bottom of your screen, you will find a small speaker icon. If you click your mouse on the icon, Windows will display a volume-control slider, as shown in Figure 37.6.

Figure 37.6 *Using the Windows volume-control slider to increase or decrease your system's play back volume.*

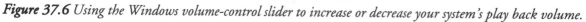

USING VOICE-RECOGNITION SOFTWARE

If your PC has multimedia capabilities, you can use your hardware to experience voice recognition, which may some day be how each of us interacts with our PC. Using your browser, you can visit the Command Corp., Inc. Web site at *www.commandcorp.com* and download the In3 Voice Command software. Using the demo version of the In Cube Voice Command software, you can start programs, maximize a window, and even cut-and-paste text by speaking into your PC's microphone!

From the Command Corp. Web site, you will download a Zip file that contains the installation program you must run to install the software. Before you install the program, however, you must unzip the file, using the Winzip utility program discussed in Lesson 56, "Using the Winzip Utility to Compress Files."

Using Your PC to Play Audio CDs

An audio CD is a music CD that you would normally play within a stereo or audio CD player. If your PC has a sound card and speakers, you can use the Windows CD Player accessory program to play an audio CD with your PC. Normally, to play an audio CD, you simply insert the audio CD into your PC's CD-ROM drive. Windows, in turn, will recognize the audio CD's format and will start playing back the songs the CD contains. If, for some reason, Windows does not automatically play an audio CD's contents, you can start the CD Player software yourself by performing these steps:

1. Click your mouse on the Start button. Windows, in turn, will display the Start menu.

2. Within the Start menu, click your mouse on the Programs menu Accessories option. Windows, in turn, will cascade the Accessories menu.

3. Depending on your Windows version, you will find the CD Player option within either the Accessories menu or the Entertainment submenu. When you click your mouse on the CD Player option, Windows will open the CD Player window, as shown in Figure 37.7.

Figure 37.7 *The CD Player window.*

4. Within the CD Player, click your mouse on the Play button to play the audio CD's contents.

Note: *The CD Player accessory lets you control the track order it uses to play back the audio CD's songs. In addition, the CD Player lets you assign information about the CD, such as the artist name, CD name, as well as the name of each song's tracks.*

What You Must Know

Multimedia is the use of text, sound, pictures, and video to present information. In this lesson, you learned how to use several multimedia programs that Microsoft bundles with Windows. You also learned how to download a demo version of the In Cube voice-recognition software. In Lesson 38, "Preventive Maintenance You Can Perform to Increase Your PC's Longevity," you will learn several simple steps you can take to clean and maintain your PC. Before you continue with Lesson 38, however, make sure you understand the following key concepts:

✓ Multimedia programs combine text, pictures, audio (voice, music, and sound), and video to present information in a meaning way.

✓ Most new PCs provide a multimedia sound card, speakers, and a microphone.

✓ Using the Windows Sound Recorder accessory, you can use your PC's microphone to record your own sounds.

✓ To play an audio CD using PC's CD-ROM drive and speakers, simply insert the CD into your drive. Windows, in turn, will start the CD Player accessory to play the audio CD's contents.

✓ The Windows Taskbar normally displays a small speaker icon upon which you can click your mouse to display a volume-control slider. Using the volume-control slider, you can adjust your speaker volume.

Lesson 38

Preventative Maintenance You Can Perform to Increase Your PC's Longevity

Although personal computers contain thousands of sensitive electronic components, PCs are amazingly durable. Many notebook PCs, for example, often get bounced about in a briefcase as the user jumps into a cab, places his or her bags into an airplane's overhead storage, or simply tosses the PC into the back seat of the car as he or she drives to work. Fortunately, PC manufacturers design PCs to sustain more than a user's typing.

As a general rule, if you keep your PC in a dust-free environment, you will not have to perform much maintenance. In fact, most users will never have a need to open their PC's system unit. This lesson examines several simple preventative maintenance steps you can perform on your PC. By the time you finish this lesson, you will understand the following key concepts:

- The most important steps you can take to preventing damage to your PC is to keep your system in a dust-free environment.

- To clean dust off your PC, monitor, printer, and keyboard, you should use a small aerosol can of air. As you use the air blower to clean an object, hold the can about one foot away from the object.

- If your PC is working and you are not installing a new hardware card, leave your system unit closed. Normally, you are more likely to damage your PC by trying to clean out dust than simply leaving the dust inside the system unit.

KEEP YOUR PC REASONABLY DUST FREE

PC manufacturers design PCs for use in homes, schools, business offices, and even on planes, buses, and subways. In general, there are not many places where you should not feel free to use your PC. If you keep your PC relatively dust free, your PC should last a long time. A good way to keep dust off of your PC is to use an aerosol blower (a can of compressed air) that you can purchase at a computer store for a few dollars.

To use the air blower, hold the sprayer about a foot or so from the object that you want to clean. For example, if you want to clean out your keyboard (which often seems to attract cookie and pizza crumbs), you would tilt your keyboard and use the blower. If you hold the air blower too close to the object that you want to clean, the air blower may damage the object by freezing a condensation (the air coming from the can is very cold) on the object.

CLEANING YOUR MONITOR

If you use an aerosol blower on a regular basis, your monitor will stay fairly dust free. However, if your monitor needs additional cleaning, you can use a little rubbing alcohol and a soft cloth, as shown in Figure 38.1.

Figure 38.1 *Use a soft cloth and if necessary, dampen the cloth with a little rubbing alcohol to clean your monitor.*

Before you clean your monitor, turn off the monitor's power and unplug the monitor from your wall socket. If you can clean your monitor using a soft cloth, do so. However, if the cloth alone cannot get the finger prints off your screen, dampen the cloth slightly with rubbing alcohol. Because the alcohol evaporates quickly, it will not streak your screen.

KEEPING YOUR PC'S FAN CLEAN

As your PC runs, its electronic components generate a considerable amount of heat. To help the heat escape from within the PC's system unit, PC manufacturers include a small fan that you will normally find at the back of the system unit, as shown in Figure 38.2. Over time, the PC's fan will accumulate dust, which you should blow out using the aerosol blower. Also, if you place your PC under your desk or close to a wall, make sure that you provide sufficient room for the fan to vent. If the fan is too close to your desk or bookshelf, the fan may not be able to vent the hot air and over time the heat that builds up within your system unit may damage the PC's sensitive electronic components.

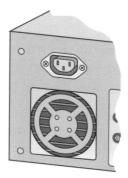

Figure 38.2 *The PC's fan vents warm air from within the system unit.*

CLEANING YOUR PRINTER

In Lesson 21, "Getting the Most from Your Printer," you examined several different printer types. Like your PC, if you keep your printer dust free, your printer will last a long time. Unfortunately, paper (particularly inexpensive paper) is dusty. When your printer prints, the paper that passes through your printer leaves dust inside. As a rule, when you change your printer's toner cartridge, you should use an aerosol blower to "dust out" your printer. As Lesson 21 discussed, always make sure you unplug your printer before you change your printer cartridge or clean inside your priter. If you find that your laser printer is starting to leave streaks of ink on the pages you print, your printer drum may be dirty. In some cases, you may be able to clean the drum using a very soft cloth that you dampen with a little rubbing alcohol. If you print color images, it is not uncommon for the ink jets to accumulate ink, which causes streaking. Many color printers actually provide a special sheet that you run through the printer to clean the ink jets. If your color printer is streaking images, refer to the manual that came with your printer. You may simply need to run the cleaning sheet through the printer.

LEAVE YOUR SYSTEM UNIT CLOSED

As discussed in several of this book's lessons, most users do not have a need to open their system unit. If your PC is working and you do not need to install a new hardware card, leave your system unit closed. Admittedly, over time, dust may accumulate within your system unit. In most cases, the dust within the system unit will not cause a problem. If you must install a hardware card into your PC and you open the system unit and find dust, try to ignore the dust. In most cases, you may cause more damage to your system by trying to brush or blow out dust than the dust itself would have caused. If, however, you install the card and it fails to work, you may need to blow dust out of the card's slot, as shown in Figure 38.3.

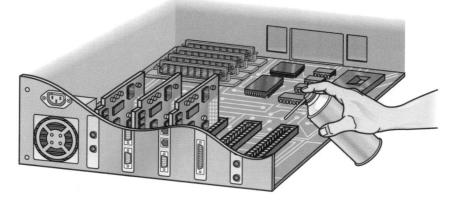

Figure 38.3 *Before you install a card into the slot of a dusty system unit, you may want to use an aerosol blower to blow dust out of the card's slot.*

CLEANING YOUR MOUSE

If, as you move your mouse, you find that your mouse pointer does not move or does not move smoothly across your screen, your mouse may be dirty. To clean your mouse, first unplug the mouse from your PC. Then, turn the mouse over, turn the unlock plastic lock that holds the ball in place, and remove the ball, as shown in Figure 38.4. Using your aerosol can of compressed air, blow air into the mouse to remove any dust it may contain. (Remember to hold the aerosol can a foot or so away from your mouse.) Next, using a cloth that you dampen with rubbing alcohol, clean the rubber ball. After the ball is dry, place it back in the mouse and secure the plastic lock. Finally, attach your mouse back to your PC.

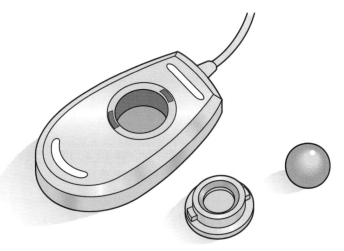

Figure 38.4 *Cleaning dust and dirt from within a mouse and off of the mouse ball.*

WHAT YOU MUST KNOW

In general, the best prevention you can take with respect to your PC is to keep your PC in a dust-free environment. In this lesson, you learned a few simple cleaning operations you can perform to keep your PC clean. In Lesson 39, "Exchanging Files Using Zip Drives," you will learn about Zip disks, which look similar to a floppy disk, but can store over 100Mb of data. Before you continue with Lesson 39, however, make sure you understand the following key concepts:

- ✓ If you keep your PC reasonably dust free, your PC should last for a long time.

- ✓ To keep your PC clean, all you need is an aerosol can of air, a soft cloth, and a little rubbing alcohol.

- ✓ Before you clean devices such as your monitor or printer, make sure you first unplug the device.

- ✓ On the back of your system unit, you will find a small fan that vents hot air from within the PC. Make sure you keep the fan dust free and that you provide space between the fan and your desk or wall.

Lesson 39

Exchanging Files Using a Zip Disk

In Lesson 13, "Storing Information on Disk," you examined floppy disks and how you can use floppies to exchange files with another user or to move files from your notebook PC to your desktop PC. As you learned, a floppy disk can store 1.44MB of data. Although floppy disks are well-suited for exchanging small files, such as a word-processing document, many documents today include graphics which make the documents too large to fit onto a floppy. If you often exchange a large number of files with other users or if you need to exchange one very large file, you will want to purchase a "Zip" drive, which you can think of as a very high-capacity floppy drive. Using your Zip drive, you will use a Zip disk that is capable of storing over 100MB! A Zip disk looks like a large floppy disk. The Zip disk only works in a Zip drive; you could not insert a Zip disk into a floppy drive. This lesson examines Zip disks in detail. By the time you finish this lesson, you will understand the following key concepts:

- A Zip disk, which looks like a large floppy disk, is a high-capacity removable disk, capable of storing over 100MB.

- To use a Zip disk, you must have a Zip drive. Depending on the type of Zip drive you buy, you will connect the Zip drive to a parallel or SCSI port.

- Although a floppy disk and Zip disk are similar in appearance, you cannot use a Zip disk within a floppy drive or a floppy disk within a Zip drive.

- Windows will treat your Zip drive just as it would any drive. You will see the Zip drive within Windows' list of available drives and you can use programs, such as the Windows Explorer, to copy, delete, rename, and move files on the Zip drive.

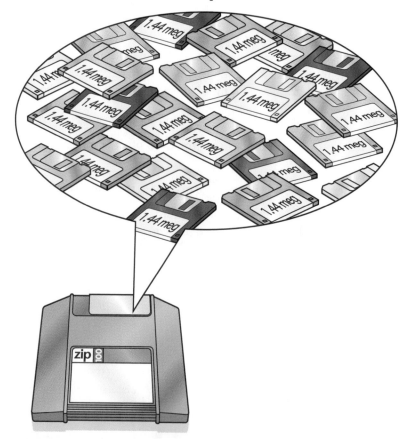

UNDERSTANDING ZIP DRIVES AND DISKS

A Zip disk is a high-capacity removable disk, capable of storing over 100Mb of data. Although Zip disks look similar to a floppy disk, a Zip disk is actually quite a bit bigger than a standard floppy. You cannot, therefore, use a Zip disk within a floppy drive, or a floppy disk within a Zip drive. To use a Zip disk to exchange files with another user, both users must either have a Zip drive or have access to a drive they can connect to their system. As shown in Figure 39.1, Zip drives are normally external drives, but many PC manufacturers are now including Zip drives within their system unit.

Figure 39.1 *Zip drives are normally external drives, however, some newer PCs now ship with a built-in Zip drive.*

CONNECTING A ZIP DRIVE TO YOUR PC

Normally, you connect a Zip drive to your PC in one of two ways, depending on your Zip drive's type. First, if your Zip drive is a "Parallel Zip Drive," you will attach your drive to your PC's parallel port—the port to which you normally attach your printer. As shown in Figure 39.2, you attach your Zip drive to the parallel port and then you attach your printer to the Zip drive. In this way, you will have access to both your Zip drive and your printer.

Figure 39.2 *You connect a Parallel Zip Drive to your PC's parallel port and then connect your printer to the Zip drive.*

If your Zip drive is a "SCSI Zip Drive," you must connect the drive to a SCSI port on your PC. Lesson 31, "Connecting Devices to Your PC," discusses SCSI ports. Figure 39.3, for example, shows a Zip drive connected to a SCSI port. In the first case, the user has simply connected the Zip drive within the SCSI device chain. In the second case, the user has connected the Zip drive to a PCMCIA-based SCSI card on a notebook PC.

Figure 39.3 Connecting a Zip drive within the SCSI device chain.

If you have an internal Zip drive, your drive probably connects to an IDE controller that may also control your hard disk. Recently, Zip disks that support the Universal Serial Bus (USB), discussed in Lesson 31, have become available.

What makes a Zip drive convenient is that the drive is very easy to connect to a PC. Assume, for example, that you need to share a large file with the user in the office next to you, who does not have a Zip drive or access to a local-area network. To start, you would simply copy the file from your system onto a Zip disk. Then, you would connect the Zip drive to the other user's system, run the Zip disk's software installation on the user's system, and then copy the file from the Zip drive onto the user's system.

Note: If you are shopping for a Zip drive, and your PC does not have a SCSI card, make sure you purchase Parallel Zip Drive.

USING YOUR ZIP DRIVE

After you connect your Zip drive to your PC, you will run a Setup program that installs the software Windows will use to access your Zip drive. After the Setup program completes, you will be able to use your Zip drive just as you would any drive on your system. Windows will list your Zip drive within the Explorer's drive list and within the File Open and Save As dialog boxes, as shown in Figure 39.4.

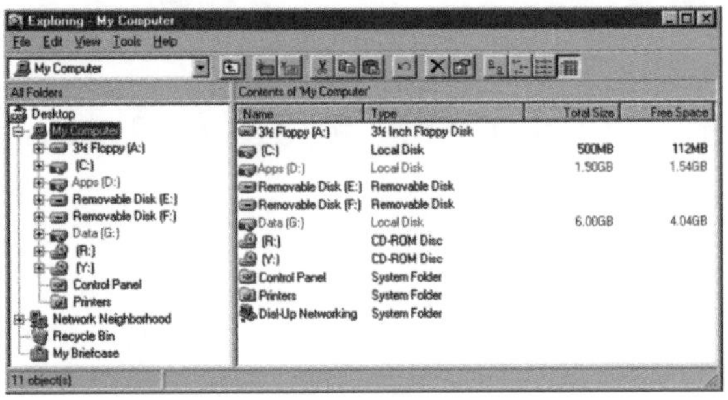

Figure 39.4 *Windows will display a drive letter for your Zip drive, just as it does for each of your drives.*

USING A ZIP DRIVE AT THE OFFICE

Today, many businesses backup user files to a central location on the company's local-area network. Should something happen to the files on your disk, you can recover your data from the company's backup. You may, however, want to use a Zip drive to make periodic (possibly daily) backups of your files that you keep yourself. That way, should something happen to the company's network, you have your own copies of your files. Note, however, that some companies do not allow the removal of files from their offices and may consider your files the company's intellectual property. Before you remove your files from the company's premises, make sure you fully understand your company's policies.

USING A ZIP DRIVE TO BACKUP YOUR SYSTEM

In Lesson 36, "Protecting Your Files by Making Backups," you learned that you should make backup copies of your files on a regular basis. If your PC has a Zip drive, you can use a Zip disk to hold your backup copies (which is easy and convenient). If you are working on key documents, you should consider copying your documents to a Zip disk at the end of each day. Then, keep the Zip disk that contains your backups in a safe location away from your PC.

WHAT YOU MUST KNOW

As users make extensive use of images within documents, the size of most documents has become too large to fit on a floppy disk. If you need to exchange large documents (or a large number of small documents) with another user, a Zip disk provides an ideal solution. In this lesson, you learned how to connect and use a Zip drive. In Lesson 40, "Understanding CD-ROMs, CD-Rs, Audio CDs, Photo CDs, and DVDs," you will examine the various CD-ROM-like discs your PC may support. Before you continue with Lesson 40, however, make sure you understand the following key concepts:

- ✓ A Zip disk is a high-capacity removable disk, capable of storing over 100MB.

- ✓ A Zip disk looks like a large floppy disk. To use a Zip disk, you must have a Zip drive. You cannot use a Zip disk within a floppy drive or a floppy disk within a Zip drive.

- ✓ Depending on your Zip-drive type, you will either connect your Zip drive to a parallel port or to a SCSI port.

- ✓ Windows will display a drive letter for your Zip drive, just as it would any drive. Using the Windows Explorer, you can copy files to or from a Zip drive, delete or rename files on the drive, or perform other file and disk-related operations, just as you would with a floppy or hard disk.

Lesson 40

Understanding CD-ROMs, CD-Rs, Audio CDs, Photo CDs, and DVDs

Today, most personal computers come with a CD-ROM drive. Most users, therefore, may have used a CD-ROM in the past to install new software on their system. Because of their tremendous storage capacity, CD-ROMs provide software manufacturers with a great way to distribute large programs. Without CD-ROMs, an operating system, such as Windows 98, would require hundreds of floppy disks! In addition, the CD-ROM's storage capacity is ideal for multimedia programs that use video and audio (which result in very large files).

This lesson examines CD-ROMs in detail. As you will learn, the speed of your CD-ROM drive has a dramatic effect on your system performance. This lesson also examines CD-Recordable (CD-R) drives that let you create your own CDs, as well as photo CDs that contain photographic images, audio CDs that contain music, and digital-video discs (DVDs) that can hold a movie. By the time you finish this lesson, you will understand the following key concepts:

- The term CD-ROM stands for Compact Disc Read-Only Memory. When you insert a CD-ROM into your CD-ROM drive, you can read the CD-ROM's content, but you cannot write to (store information on) the CD-ROM.

- A CD-ROM can store over 650MB of data, making the CD-ROM well-suited for distributing large programs and for storing multimedia applications that consist of large audio and video files.

- By purchasing a special hardware device, called a CD-ROM burner, you can use a special disc, called a CD-R, to create your own CDs.

- Most users are familiar with audio CDs (users sometimes call them music CDs) that contain tracks of music. Using the Windows CD Player program, you can play audio CDs within your PC.

- Photo CDs let you store photographic images on a CD-ROM. Across the country, you can find several photo-processing labs who can store your photos in an electronic format on a photo CD.

- DVD, which stands for Digital-Video Disc, is a high-capacity disc that can store nearly ten times as much information as a CD-ROM. Today, motion-picture companies use DVDs to store movies in a digital format.

UNDERSTANDING CD-ROMs

Although "CD-ROM" has become a household word, most users do not know that the term stands for Compact Disc Read-Only Memory. The Read-Only Memory, or ROM, part of CD-ROM refers to the fact that you cannot (write) store information on a CD-ROM. Instead, you can only read the information that the CD-ROM contains.

A CD-ROM stores information using billions of microscopic pits that reside on the disc's surface. A CD-ROM only stores information on one side (the side without the printed label). In Lesson 13, "Storing Information on Disk," you learned that a disk stores information by recording a series of ones and zeros (binary digits) on the disk's magnetic surface. If you were to look closely at the surface of a CD-ROM, you would find that the CD-ROM places a pit on its surface to represent a one and no pit to represent a zero, as shown in Figure 40.1.

00100110110

Figure 40.1 *CD-ROMs represent data through the presence or absence of pits on the disk's surface.*

To read a CD-ROM's contents, your CD-ROM drive spins the CD-ROM past a small laser. The laser, in turn, reflects a light off the CD-ROM's surface. If the surface area does not have a pit, the light will reflect faster (telling the drive that the current value is zero). If the surface has a pit, the light will not reflect (telling the drive that the current value is one). A CD-ROM can store over 650MB of data. If you consider the fact that a single-spaced typed page requires 4,000 bytes, a CD-ROM can hold over 150,000 pages of single-spaced typed text—more than the number of pages in an encyclopedia! Although most PCs ship with a CD-ROM drive, all drives are not created equal. Some CD-ROM drives are much faster than others. If you are using a multimedia CD-ROM, for example, a faster CD-ROM drive can display a larger video window with a higher-quality video display. Likewise, if you are installing software from a CD-ROM, a PC with a faster CD-ROM drive will finish the installation in faster time than a PC with a slower drive.

Users express CD-ROM drive speeds as double-speed (2x), quad-speed (4x), twelve-speed (12x), and so on. To understand what such drive speeds mean, you must know that a single-speed drive transfers data at a rate of 150,000 bits per second (150Kbs). A double-speed drive, therefore, transfers data at 300,000 bits per second. Likewise, a 36-speed drive transfers data at 5,400,000 bits per second (5.4Mbs). Assume, for example, that a CD-ROM contains a video that you want to display on your screen at 320x240 resolution (which is about ¼ of a screen). Assuming that the video uses 256 colors, so that each pixel requires only one byte of data, one video frame (one screen image) would require 76,800 bytes (320x240=76,800). To display full-motion video, you must display 30 frames per second, which would require a CD-ROM that can transfer 2,304,000 bytes of data per second, which most CD-ROM drives cannot do (you need a 16-speed drive). Fortunately, as is the case with most PC hardware, CD-ROM drives are becoming faster and less expensive every day.

UNDERSTANDING COMPACT DISC-RECORDABLE (CD-R) DISCS

As you just learned, you can only read information from a CD-ROM—you cannot store information on a CD-ROM. Likewise, most CD-ROM drives are only capable of reading as opposed to recording information. You can buy, however, a hardware device called a CD-ROM burner, that uses special discs, called Compact-Disk Recordable (CD-R) discs upon which you can record information. A CD-ROM burner records information on a CD-R disc (which looks just like a traditional CD-ROM disc) using a laser that burns the small bits into the disc's surface. A CD-ROM burner looks very much like a CD-ROM drive. As shown in Figure 40.2, you can purchase an internal (a burner that you install in your system unit) or an external CD-ROM burner.

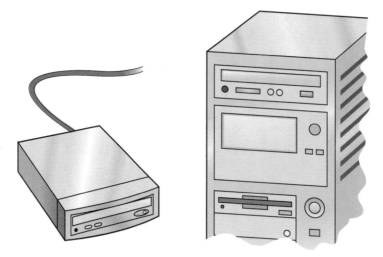

Figure 40.2 *Using a CD-ROM burner and CD-R discs, you can create your own CDs.*

Today, you can purchase a CD-ROM burner for a few hundred dollars. Likewise, the CD-R disks cost only a few dollars each. In the future, all PCs may include a CD-ROM burner, which can read and write CDs, in place of the traditional CD-ROM drive.

> ### USING A CD-ROM BURNER TO CREATE SYSTEM BACKUPS
>
> In Lesson 36, "Protecting Your Files by Making Backups," you will learn that many users backup the files on their disks to floppy disks, Zip disks, as well as magnetic tapes. If you have a CD-ROM burner, you should consider using the burner to create your backups. By storing your data on a CD-R disk, you protect the data from being destroyed by a magnetic source (such as telephone) and you make the data easy to restore. (Any CD-ROM drive can read a CD-R disc. If create a magnetic-tape backup, only a system with a tape drive can read your backup.)

UNDERSTANDING AUDIO CDs

An audio CD is a disc that you can play using a stereo or audio CD player. Users often refer to audio CDs as music CDs. If you are using Windows and your PC has a CD-ROM drive, sound card, and speakers, you can use your PC to play audio CDs. In most cases, to play an audio CD, you simply insert the audio CD into your CD-ROM drive. Windows, in turn, will recognize the audio CD's format and will start playing the music tracks that the audio CD contains. Actually, to play the audio CD, Windows will start a program called the CD Player. For more information on the CD Player, turn to Lesson 37, "Experiencing Multimedia Sights and Sounds."

UNDERSTANDING PHOTO CDs

A photo CD is a CD that stores photographs in an electronic format. In Lesson 32, "Creating Electronic Images Using Scanners and Digital Cameras," you learned that you can send your film to one of several photo processing labs across the country who in turn, will send you a photo CD that contains your photographs in an electronic format. Normally, a photo CD will provide several different resolutions of the same image. A high-resolution image (4,096 x 6,144) for example, might require an 72MB file. Likewise, a low-resolution image (256 x 384) might require 288KB.

UNDERSTANDING DIGITAL-VIDEO DISCS (DVDs)

Today, many PCs come with CD-ROM drives that support Digital-Video Discs (DVDs). A DVD is a high-capacity disc, capable of storing up to 4.7GB. Because of their tremendous storage capacity, a DVD can store an entire movie— much like a VHS tape. If your CD-ROM supports DVDs, you can play a movie within a window on your screen. Although some PCs can play DVDs, the discs are most primarily used today within home entertainment systems, replacing video cassette recorders.

WHAT YOU MUST KNOW

Today, most PCs come with a CD-ROM drive. Depending on the drive's type, its speed and capabilities will differ from other drives. This lesson examined various types of CDs. In Lesson 41, "Taking a Break with PC-Based Games," you will learn to play several common games that Microsoft installs with Windows, as well as a few demo games Microsoft includes on the Windows 98 CD-ROM. In addition, you will learn how to download games from specific sites on the Web. Before you continue with Lesson 41, however, make sure that you understand the following key concepts:

- ✓ CD-ROM is an acronym for Compact Disc Read-Only Memory.

- ✓ An audio CD is a music CD, that you normally play using a stereo or audio CD player. Windows provides a special program called the CD Player that lets you play audio CDs using your PC.

- ✓ A photo CD is a CD that contains photographic images. The easiest way to create a photo CD is to send your film to a photo processing lab that can store your images in an electronic format.

- ✓ DVD is an acronym for Digital-Video Disc. A DVD can store nearly ten times as much information as a CD-ROM. Today, motion-picture companies use DVDs to store movies in a digital format.

235

Lesson 41

Taking a Break with PC Games

In this book's later lessons, you will learn a variety of ways to use your PC to find information on Internet and the World Wide Web. You will find software to improve your business productivity, software that lets you send and receive faxes, and even software that you can install and run today that will provide you simple video-conferencing capabilities. If you have kids, or if you are a still a kid at heart, you will eventually use your PC to play the latest video games.

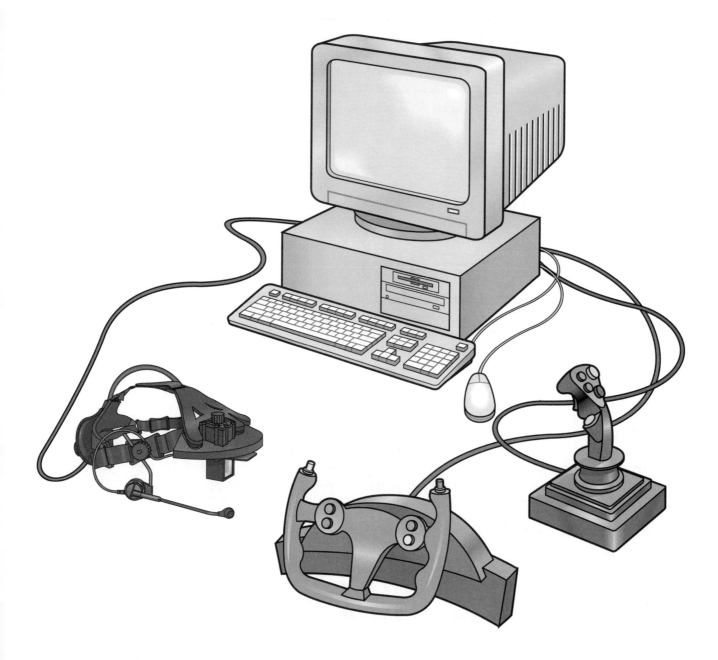

To get you started, this lesson examines several games that Microsoft bundles with Windows, as well as games that you can download and run from across the Web. By the time you finish this lesson, you will understand the following key concepts:

- Today's PCs, with fast processors, video cards, and CD-ROM drives are ideal for video games.

- Microsoft bundles several simple games with Windows that include Hearts, Minesweeper, and FreeCell. Depending on your Windows version, you may even find Solitaire.

- If you take precautions to avoid computer viruses, you can download hundreds of games from across the Web.

- To let you sample their latest video games, Microsoft has bundled several game demos on the Windows 98 CD-ROM.

GETTING STARTED WITH WINDOWS-BASED GAMES

Although the Justice Department ignored the Windows' games existence, Microsoft does bundle several simple games with Windows. Depending on which version of Windows that you are running, your system may contain one or more of the games shown in Figures 41.2 through 41.5. To start one of the Windows-based games, perform these steps:

1. Click your mouse on the Start button. Windows, in turn, will display the Start menu.

2. Within the Start menu, click your mouse on the Programs menu Accessories option. Then, click your mouse on the Games option. Windows, in turn, will display the Games submenu, as shown in Figure 41.1.

Figure 41.1 The Windows Games submenu.

3. Within the Games submenu, click your mouse on the game you desire.

Note: *Depending on your version of Windows, you may find the games within the Accessories submenu, as opposed to the Games submenu.*

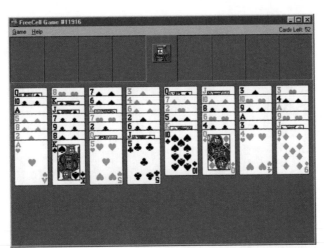

Figure 41.2 *In FreeCell, a derivative of Solitaire, your goal is to move cards from their location at the bottom of the window into the home cells that appear near the top of the window. As you order cards by face value and suit, you can take advantage of four free cells to temporarily hold cards.*

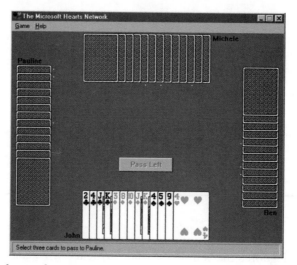

***Figure** 41.3 In Hearts, you can play cards against your PC or other users across your local-area nework. You do not want to be caught with the most hearts.*

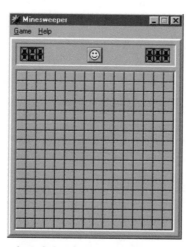

***Figure** 41.4 In Minesweeper, your job is to identify land mines within a minefield, without detonating one of the mines.*

***Figure** 41.5 In Solitaire, your goal is to stack cards, in order, by suit.*

INSTALLING THE WINDOWS GAMES ONTO YOUR SYSTEM

If the Windows Games do not appear within your Accessories submenu, someone has probably removed the games from your system. If, however, you have a Windows CD-ROM, you can install the games by performing these steps:

1. Click your mouse on the Start button. Windows, in turn, will display the Start menu.

2. Within the Start menu, click your mouse on the Settings menu and choose Control Panel. Windows, in turn, will display the Control Panel folder, discussed in Lesson 45, "Configuring Your PC's System Settings."

3. Within the Control Panel, double-click your mouse on the Add/Remove Programs icon. Windows, in turn, will display the Add/Remove Programs Properties dialog box.

4. Within the Add/Remove Programs Properties dialog box, click your mouse on the Windows Setup tab. Windows, in turn, will display the Windows Setup sheet, as shown in Figure 41.6.

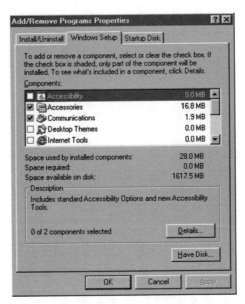

Figure 41.6 *The Windows Setup sheet.*

5. Within the Windows Setup sheet, click your mouse on the Accessories option and then click your mouse on the Detail buttons. Windows, in turn, will open the Accessories dialog box.

6. Within the Accessories dialog box, click your mouse on the checkbox that appears next to the Games option, placing a checkmark within the box. Then, click your mouse on the OK button.

7. Within the Windows Setup dialog box, click your mouse on the OK button. Windows, in turn, will prompt you to insert the Windows CD-ROM and will then install the games onto your system.

Note: *Depending on your version of Windows, the Windows Setup sheet may place the games into their own component group, as opposed to the Accessories group.*

REMOVE THE WINDOWS-BASED GAMES FROM PCS IN AN OFFICE

If you manage employees who have PCs in their office, eliminate employee temptations to play games on the company PCs by simply removing the games from their systems. In addition, if your company has an Employee Manual, you should include a directive within the manual that the employees will not play video games or use other "recreational" software programs on company PCs. To remove the Windows-based games from employee PCs, you will use the Control Panel Add/Remove Programs icon, as discussed in Lesson 45.

PLAYING FREECELL

FreeCell is a card game within which your goal is to place cards, organized by face value and suit, into the home cells that appear near the upper-right hand corner of the game's window. To start FreeCell, the first card you can place must be an ace. Then, you can place either a second ace (beside the first one) or a two (of the same suit) on top of the ace. After that, you can either place aces or you must place the next face card on top of an existing card. To win, you must create four stacks, one for each suit, from ace to king. If you cannot move a card, the game is over. To move a card, you simply drag the card using your mouse.

If you need a card that another card is covering, you can move the top card into one of the four available free cells. If a cell contains a card, however, you cannot use the cell until you place its card. In addition, you can move a card to a different stack, provided that the card you are moving is the opposite color and one face-value less than the card onto which you want to place it. Figure 41.7 shows a FreeCell game in progress.

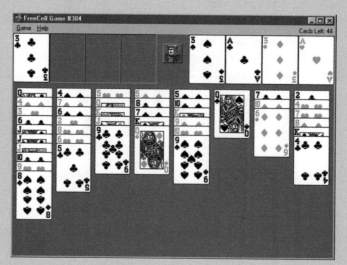

Figure 41.7 Moving and stacking cards within FreeCell.

PLAYING MINESWEEPER

Minesweeper is a board game within which your goal is to identify all the mines on a grid, without getting blown up. Within the Minesweeper grid, each square is either empty, contains a mine, or contains a number that represents the number of surrounding squares that contain mines. For example, if a box contains the number 1, you know that only one of the boxes surrounding the box contains a mine. If the box contains the number 2, you know two of the surrounding boxes contain mines, and so on. By examining the numbers that surround various boxes, you can determine which boxes contains mines. As you determine mine locations, you can mark each location with a red flag, so you know not to click on it. If you click your mouse on a box that contains a mine, the game ends. Figure 41.8 shows a Minesweeper game in progress.

Figure 41.8 *Marking mines within a Minesweeper mine field.*

PLAYING HEARTS

Hearts is an interactive card game that you can play either against your computer or other users within your local-area network. Within Hearts, your goal is to end the game with the fewest points. Each game consists of multiple hands. When one of the players accumulates 100 points, the game ends. To start a hand, the player with the two of clubs throws the card into the middle of the window. The other players must then play cards of the same suit. The person who plays the highest card must take the other cards. If a player does not have a card in the suit, he or she can play any card (ideally a heart or the Queen of Spades) and he or she will not have to take the cards. The person who takes the trick will start the next play (called the next trick) by throwing a card into the center of the window. After the users have played all the cards, each user will receive one point for each heart he or she holds and 13 points for the Queen of Spades. Figure 41.9 shows a Hearts game in progress.

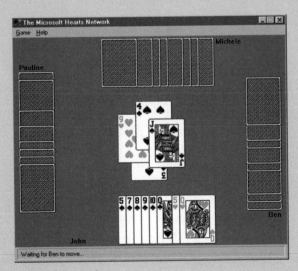

Figure 41.9 *Playing a trick during a hand of Hearts.*

PLAYING SOLITAIRE

Solitaire is a card game that you play against the computer, within which your goal is to stack cards, in order from ace to king, by suit. As you play, you will use two different stacks. At that top of the window, you will stack aces, followed by a 2, a 3, and so on of the same suit. At the bottom of the window, you will stack cards from highest to lowest, alternating colors. To move a card, you simply drag the card using your mouse. As you play, you can draw cards from the card pile. When you empty the card pile, simply click your mouse on the empty card holder to reshuffle the cards. The game ends when you successfully stack the cards or when you cannot place a card. Figure 41.10 shows a Solitaire game in progress.

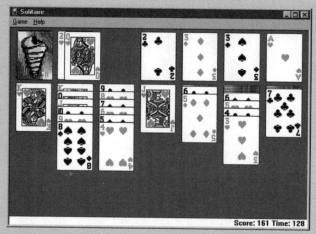

Figure 41.10 *Stacking cards within Solitaire.*

LOCATING GAMES YOU CAN DOWNLOAD FROM ACROSS THE WEB

In Lesson 59, "Protecting Your System from Computer Viruses," you learned that to avoid viruses, you should download only programs across the Net from reputable companies, and then, use a virus-detection program to test the program before you run it. If you take such precautions, you can find hundreds of games that you can download from reputable Web sites. You might start your game pursuit, for example, at the Yahoo game site, as shown in Figure 41.11. Then, you should check out games at ZDNet, as shown in Figure 41.12.

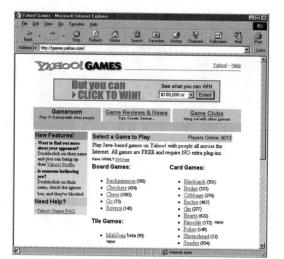

Figure 41.11 *Downloading games from **http://games.yahoo.com**.*

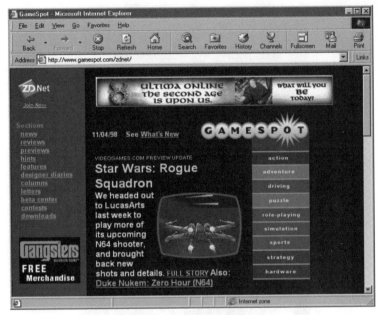

Figure 41.12 *You'll find many games at **http://www.gamespot.com/zdnet**.*

TEST DRIVING DEMOS OF MICROSOFT'S LATEST GAMES

If you are running Windows 98 and you have the Windows 98 CD-ROM, you can install demos of several new Microsoft and DreamWorks games from the CD-ROM. Figure 41.13, for example, shows the Microsoft Golf demo program. Likewise, Figure 41.14 shows PacMan, one of the industries first video games.

Figure 41.13 *Hitting the links with Microsoft Golf.*

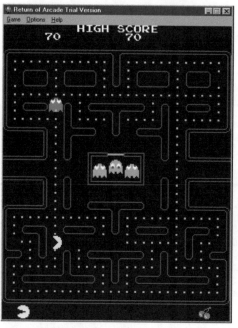

Figure 41.14 *PacMan, one of the games that created the video-game industry.*

To install the demo game software from the Windows 98 CD-ROM, perform these steps:

1. Insert the Windows 98 CD-ROM into your CD-ROM drive.

2. Click your mouse on the Start menu Run option. Windows, in turn, will display the Run dialog box.

3. Within the Run dialog box, use the Browse button to locate and run the *Sampler.exe* program file within the cdsample folder on the Windows 98 CD-ROM. Windows, in turn, will run a demo video and will then display a demo screen similar.

4. Within the demo screen, click your mouse on the Install Software icon. Windows, in turn, will start a setup program within which you can choose the games (and other sample software) you want to install.

WHAT YOU MUST KNOW

As PCs and their peripheral devices (such as CD-ROM drives and video displays) get faster and faster, the PC is well suited to play many high-end video games. This lesson introduced to you to several such games. In Lesson 42, "Exchanging Information within a Newsgroup," you will learn how to share information on specific topics with users who have interests that are similar to yours. Before you continue with Lesson 42, however, make sure you understand the following key concepts:

✓ Microsoft bundles several simple games within Windows. Depending on your version of Windows, you will start the games from either the Accessories or Games submenu.

✓ If you manage workers in an office, you should consider removing all games from their systems.

✓ If you take proper virus-protection precautions, you can download hundreds of games from reputable sites across the Web.

✓ Microsoft bundles several demos of its latest games on the Windows 98 CD-ROM.

Lesson 42

Exchanging Information within Internet Newsgroups

Across the Internet, there are many different ways you can exchange information with other users. You can, for example, browse Web sites to find specific information that you desire, or you can participate in interactive chat sessions, or you can exchange electronic-mail messages, just to name a few. In this lesson, you will learn how to read and post messages within Internet-based newsgroups.

Think of a newsgroup as a message board (an electronic bulletin board) to which users post messages. Across the Net, there are tens of thousands of newgroups at which users discuss an unlimited number of topics, ranging from archeology to zoology. In between these two topics, you will find newsgroups that discuss business, sports, finance, government, sex, travel, movies, and even Barney the Dinosaur. This lesson examines newsgroups in detail. By the time you finish this lesson, you will understand the following key concepts:

- Internet-based newsgroups let users exchange messages at electronic bulletin boards. Across the Internet, there are tens of thousands of newsgroups that discuss a variety topics.

245

- Most newsgroups focus on a specific topic, such as sports, business, or travel. Within a newsgroup, users post questions, statements, or answers or responses to other user postings.

- To view a newsgroup's postings, or to post your own messages to a newsgroup, you must have newsgroup software.

- Within your newsgroup software, you can view or print a posting, or, you can respond to the posting with a message of your own.

TO PARTICIPATE IN A NEWSGROUP, YOU MUST HAVE NEWSGROUP SOFTWARE

As you have learned, before you can surf the Web, you must have a Web browser—software that lets you connect to sites across the Web to download and view the site's content. Likewise, before you can send an electronic-mail message, you must have e-mail software. Using newsgroups is no different; before you can read or post messages at a newsgroup, you must have newsgroup software.

If you are using Microsoft Outlook or Outlook Express to send and receive e-mail, you can also use the software to read messages from and to post messages to a newsgroup. Likewise, if you are using Netscape Communicator, you can use its newsreader to access newsgroups. If you are not using these programs, you can download a newsreader software from sites across the Web, such as the Gravity newsreader from *www.microplanet.com*.

UNDERSTANDING NEWSGROUP NAMES

As discussed, you should think of a newsgroup as an electronic bulletin board at which users post messages. Depending on the board's topic (newsgroups normally focus on a specific topic), the messages that users post will vary. At a Windows 98 newsgroup, for example, some users may post questions while other users may post answers. Each newsgroup has a unique name and, before you can connect to a newsgroup, you must know the newsgroup's name. Because there are almost 100,000 newsgroups on the Net, finding the newsgroup that you desire may take a little time.

Fortunately, newsgroup names are fairly easy to understand. To begin, all newsgroup names begin with a general name, such as a *biz* (for business newsgroups), *K12* (for education newsgroups), *rec* (for recreational news groups), and so on. Within each general topic group, the newsgroup names become more specific. For example, if you were interested in basketball, you might first look for a newsgroup named *rec.basketball*. As newsgroup names become more specific, the names use periods to separate the topics. If you were interested in the Chicago Bulls or Michael Jordan, you might look for *rec.basketball.bulls* or *rec.basketball.bulls.jordan*. For a listing of newsgroups, visit the World Wide Web Consortium (W3C) Web site at *www.w3.org*.

VIEWING A LIST OF NEWSGROUPS

When you start your newsgroup software, your program may ask the name of the server to which you want to connect. Across the Net, you can find many servers that support newsgroup operations. Some servers, however, will provide you with a complete list of newsgroups, while other servers will restrict the list to the most common groups. After you connect to a newsgroup server, your software may ask you if you want to download the server's newsgroup list. The first few times you use newsgroups, you will want the server to give you its complete list, so you can determine which newsgroups you like.

After that, you can subscribe to specific newsgroups and each time you start your newsgroup software, your software will automatically download those newsgroups. Figure 42.1 shows a newsgroup list within the Outlook Express Newsgroups dialog box. Using your mouse or keyboard arrow keys, you can scroll through the list of newsgroups. To display the newsgroup list within Outlook Express, click your mouse on the Go menu News option.

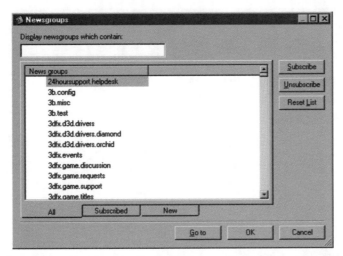

Figure 42.1 *Viewing a list of newsgroups within the Outlook Express Newsgroups dialog box.*

To view a newsgroup's postings, click your mouse on the newsgroup you desire from within the Newsgroup's list. For example, if you click your mouse on the *biz.marketplace* newsgroup, Outlook Express will display the newsgroup's postings, as shown in Figure 42.2.

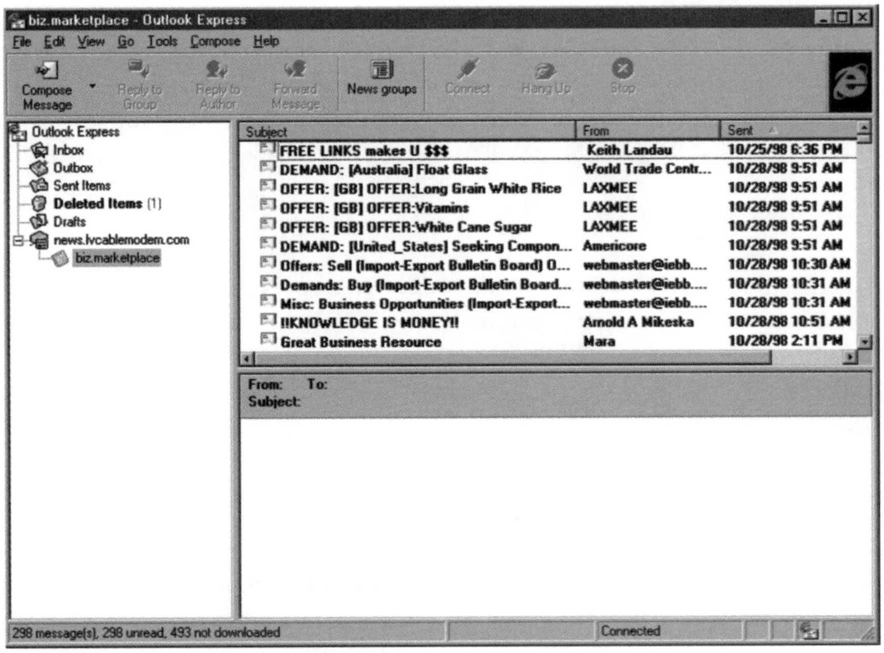

Figure 42.2 *Viewing a list of newsgroup postings.*

Using your mouse or keyboard arrow keys, you can scroll through the newsgroup's postings. To view a specific posting, simply click on the posting using your mouse and then click your mouse on the Go To button. Your newsgroup reader, in this case Outlook Express, will display the posting within a window frame, as shown in Figure 42.3. Within your newsgroup software, you can normally use the file menu to print the current posting's contents.

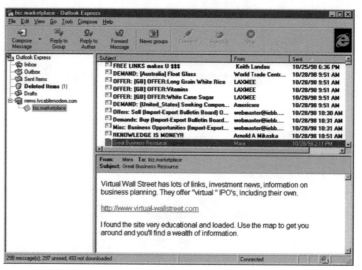

Figure 42.3 *Displaying a newsgroup posting.*

To view a different posting, simply click your mouse on a posting within the posting list. Depending on your newsreader software, the steps you must perform to change newsgroups will differ.

POSTING A MESSAGE TO A NEWSGROUP

As you view newsgroup postings, there will be times when you will want to post your own messages. In some cases, you may want to respond to another user's questions or you may want to debate a user's statements. Likewise, there may be times when you want to ask your own questions. Depending on your newsgroup software, the steps you must perform to post a message will differ. Within Outlook Express, you can click your mouse on the Reply to Group button.

A WORD OF WARNINGS TO PARENTS

As briefly discussed, across the Net, you can find newsgroups that discuss a variety of topics. Many newsgroups are adult-oriented and contain content (both textual and photographic) that is not well-suited for children. In Lesson 62, "Child Proofing the Internet and the World Wide Web," you will examine software that lets you restrict which sites on the Web your child can browse. When you consider purchasing such software, try to find a program that also restricts your child's access to newsgroups as well.

WHAT YOU MUST KNOW

Across the Internet, users communicate using a variety of programs, ranging from chat software, to e-mail, to Internet Phone software, and even Internet-based video conferencing. In this lesson, you learned to exchange messages with other users at newsgroups—which you can think of as an electronic bulletin board, at which you can read and post messages. In Lesson 43, "Chatting On-Line with Users Around the World," you will learn how to use chat software to communicate with a group of users, in real time, across the Net. Before you continue with Lesson 43, however, make sure you have learned the following key concepts:

✓ Across the Internet, users exchange messages at electronic bulletin boards, called newsgroups. In general, each newsgroup focuses on a specific topic.

✓ To view a newsgroup's postings, or to post your own messages to a newsgroup, you must have newsgroup software.

✓ Within your newsgroup software, you can view or print a posting, or, you can respond to the posting with a message of your own.

Lesson 43

Banking and Budgeting Online

For years, computers users would joke that they used their home PCs to track their recipes and to balance their check book. Today, however, with the capabilities of personal finance programs such as Intuit's Quicken and Microsoft Money, using a PC to manage personal finances is something that all users should consider. This lesson briefly examines personal finance software and online investing.

By the time you finish this lesson, you will understand the following key concepts:

- Using personal finance software, you can plan your budget, track your expenses, and track your cash flow.

- Most personal finance programs provide tools that can help you determine how much money you should set away for retirement as well as for short-term setbacks.

- Within a personal finance program, you can track the checks that you write by hand, use your printer to print your checks, pay your bills electronically, or you can use a combination of all three payment methods.

- Personal finance programs let you create a variety of reports. You can create reports to monitor your budget, to track specific expenses, or to help your tax advisor prepare your income tax forms.

- Most personal finance programs do not provide the tools you need to prepare complex income tax forms. You can, however, purchase additional software that you can use to assist you in preparing your tax forms.

- Across the Web, there are many sites where you can buy and sell securities on-line. If you want to buy and sell stocks on-line, make sure you deal only with reputable companies.

USING PERSONAL FINANCE SOFTWARE

Personal finance software consists of programs that you can use to pay your bills, create and monitor your budget, prepare tax forms, and track your investments. Across the United States, tens of millions of users rely on personal finance software to help them manage their finances. You can use personal finance software in several different ways. First, if you don't want to use the software's on-line banking capabilities, you can simply write your checks by hand. Later, you can record your checks within your personal finance software. When you receive your monthly bank statement, you can then use the personal finance software to help reconcile your account. The reason you would want to enter checks into your personal finance software in this way is that, using the software, you can assign categories to each check. Later, you can use the software to generate reports that show you how you are spending your money. You might also generate a report that lists your tax-deductible expenses.

Many users, who don't want to bank on-line, will use their personal finance software to print their checks. When you purchase your personal finance software, the documentation that accompanies your software will provide companies from which you can order checks that you can print on using a laser or ink-jet printer. You might print checks for your regular monthly expenses, such as your house payment, utilities, car payments, and so on. If you write checks by hand, you must simply enter the information about the check within your personal finance software. Figure 43.1 shows how you to write a check within a personal finance software program.

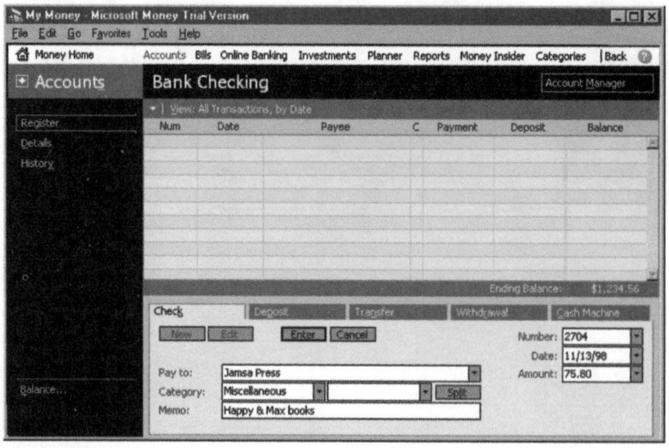

Figure 43.1 Using a personal finance program to create and print checks.

The ideal way to use personal finance software is to take advantage of on-line banking. Most larger banks now let you pay your bills on-line. Using your personal finance software, you prepare a check that, rather than printing, you direct your software to pay on-line. Your software, in turn, will use your modem to dial your bank's computer. Then, your software will tell your bank about the electronic payment. Your bank, in turn, will issue the check which it can send to the recipient either electronically (to the recipient's bank account) or by using the U.S. mail. As the bank clears both your electronic and hand-written checks, the bank will download information regarding the checks as well as your current account balance to your personal finance software. Using personal finance software to pay bills electronically is as easy as sending and receiving electronic-mail. Talk to your bank to get more information about their on-line banking services.

TAKING MICROSOFT MONEY FOR A TEST DRIVE

If you are using Windows 98, Microsoft bundles a trial version of Microsoft Money on the Windows 98 CD-ROM. To install the trial version of Microsoft Money, perform these steps:

1. Insert the Windows 98 CD-ROM into your CD-ROM drive.

2. Click your mouse on the Start menu Run option. Windows, in turn, will display the Run dialog box.

3. Within the Run dialog box, use the Browse button to locate and run the Sampler.exe program file within the *cdsample* folder on the Windows 98 CD-ROM. Windows, in turn, will run a demo video and will then display a demo screen within which you should click your mouse on the Install Software icon. Windows, in turn, will start a setup program within which you can choose to install Microsoft Money (as well as other programs).

4. After you install the software, you can run the trail version from the Start menu Programs option.

PREPARING YOUR INCOME TAX FORMS

Across the Web, you can find several software programs that can assist you in preparing your income tax forms. If you don't itemize your deductions, you can use the software to complete and print your return or to submit your return to the IRS electronically. If your income tax return is complex, you may want to use such software to prepare a draft return that you then give to a tax consultant for review. Figure 43.2, for example, shows the Tax Estimator software program that you can run from the Intuit Web site, at *www.intuit.com*.

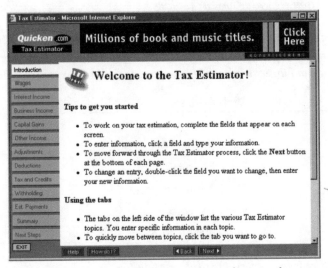

Figure 43.2 *Using the Tax Estimator software to estimate your taxes and quarterly payments.*

To help you locate tax programs, Table 43.1 lists several sites on the Web you may want to visit.

Software	Web Address
TurboTax	www.intuit.com/turbotax
Kiplingers TaxCut	www.kiplinger.com

Table 43.1 Sites across the Web featuring income tax software.

ON-LINE INVESTING

If you buy and sell stocks, participate in a 401(k) plan, or if you are interested in learning more about investing for your child's education or your retirement, you will find thousands of sites on the Web that discuss investing. Many of these sites will also let you buy and sell securities (such as stocks and bonds on-line). If you want to trade securities on-line, only do so through a reputable brokerage firm. Also, if you are just getting started, do not be in a rush to invest your money.

Instead, do some research first. You might start by interviewing brokers at local, yet reputable, investment companies. Get some advice. You may find that you simply want to track your investments on-line—while making your actual trades through your local broker. In so doing, you may benefit from your broker's recommendations and experience. That said, most large brokerage firms do let you buy and sell securities on-line.

To get started, you might want to visit the Web sites listed in Table 43.2. Even if you don't trade securities on-line, you may learn considerable information from the on-line trading Web sites. In addition, many of the sites will let you look up a stock's current pricing information.

Company	Web Address
Charles Scwabb	www.schwab.com
E*TRADE	www.etrade.com
Merrill Lynch	www.plan.ml.com
Saloman Smith Barney	www.smithbarney.com

Table 43.2 Sources for information regarding on-line trading.

If you are interested in researching your investments, the Web hosts thousands of sites that discuss various investment strategies. To get started, you can may want to visit the sites listed in Table 43.3. Figure 43.3, for example, shows the Business Week Web site, at *www.businessweek.com\quote.htm*, at which you can receive stock quotes on-line.

Site	Web Address
Barrons	www.barrons.com
Business Week	www.businessweek.com
Kiplinger	www.kiplinger.com
Red Herring	www.redherring.com
Wall Street Journal	www.wsj.com
Yahoo!	quote.yahoo.com

Table 43.3 Sites on the Web that feature investment information.

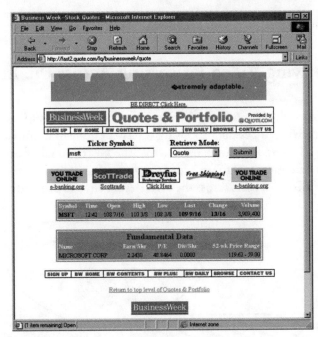

Figure 43.2 *Looking up stock quotes on-line at the Business Week Web site.*

WHAT YOU MUST KNOW

Every day, banks, securities firms, check clearing houses, and even users who do their checking on-line contribute to the billions of dollars that move around the world electronically. Soon, most bank transactions will occur electronically, either at ATM machines, at retailers that debit and credit bank cards as opposed to exchanging cash, or via users who pay their bills on-line. This lesson introduced you to several software programs you can use to today to help you manage your personal finances. In Lesson 44, "Using Your PC to Send and Receive Faxes," you will learn how to use encryption and digital signatures to protect your electronic mail. Before you continue with Lesson 44, however, make sure you have learned the following key concepts:

- ✓ In addition to helping you balance your checkbook, personal finance software, can help you plan your budget, track your expenses, and track your cash flow.

- ✓ Most personal finance programs let you pay your bills on-line. However, if you choose to write your checks by hand, or print your checks using your PC, personal finance programs can download statements from your bank and help you reconcile your account.

- ✓ Most larger banks support and encourage on-line banking. In fact, if you sign up for an on-line banking account, many will provide you with the software you need.

- ✓ Personal finance programs let you create a variety of reports. You can create reports to monitor your budget, to track specific expenses, or to help your tax advisor prepare your income tax forms.

- ✓ Most personal finance programs do not provide the tools you need to prepare complex income tax forms. You can, however, purchase additional software that you can use to assist you in preparing your tax forms.

- ✓ The Web has thousands of sites that discuss investing and investment opportunities. Do not use the Web as a source for hot tips on stocks you should buy. If you want to buy and sell stocks on-line, make sure you deal only with reputable companies.

Lesson 44

Test Driving Video Processing Across the Internet

In Lesson 43, "Chatting On-Line with Users Around the World," you learned how to use chat software to communicate with users around the globe. Likewise, in Lesson 55, "Using Internet Phone to Eliminate Long Distance Phone Bills," you will learn how to use your PC to talk with the users across the Net or to talk from your PC to a user over his or her phone. In this lesson, you will learn how to use video-conferencing programs to chat, talk, exchange files, share applications, and to exchange video with users across the Net. Best of all, you can perform these operations using your existing PC and modem.

By the time you finish this lesson, you will understand the following key concepts:

- Video conferencing is the use of video to achieve face-to-face communication from remote sites. Today, there are several programs that let you perform simple video conferencing across the Internet.

- If your PC has a video camera, you can use the camera and video-conferencing software to send video to other users across the Net. If your PC has a microphone and speakers, you can use them and video-conferencing software to talk with users around the globe, across the Net, for free.

- Using the CU-SeeMe software, you can chat, talk, or exchange video with multiple users from across the Web.

- If you are using Windows 98, you can use NetMeeting, virtual-meeting software that Microsoft bundles with Windows.

- Using NetMeeting, you can chat, talk, and exchange video with other users. In addition, NetMeeting makes it easy for you to exchange files with other users, share ideas on a whiteboard, and even share application programs.

TO SEND VIDEO YOU MUST HAVE A VIDEO CAMERA

The term "video conferencing" implies that users will exchange video with one another as they communicate. If you do not have a video camera, you can still receive and display video on your PC. You simply cannot send video. If you do not have a camera, you can purchase one for about $50 that you can connect to your PC's serial port, as shown in Figure 44.1.

Figure 44.1 Attaching a video camera to a PC's serial port.

Recently, as shown in Figure 44.2, many notebook PC's have started shipping with an attachable video camera that you can snap on and off, as your needs require.

Figure 44.2 *Attaching a video camera to a notebook PC.*

USING THE CU-SEEME VIDEO-CONFERENCING SOFTWARE

Across the Internet, you will find several programs that are capable of providing simple video conferencing. One of the best known Internet-based video-conferencing products is CU-SeeMe. As shown in Figure 44.3, within CU-SeeMe, you can display up to 12 video windows at one time. Depending on the speed of your Internet connection, the speed at which CU-SeeMe updates each window's video will differ.

In addition to letting you send and receive video, CU-SeeMe also lets you chat (via typed text) with other users and talk with other users, much like the Internet Phone software you will examine in Lesson 55. If you decide you want only to speak with a specific user, CU-SeeMe lets you turn off the audio or video to other users. When you send and receive video with only one user, the speed and quality of your video improve considerably. Remember, if you do not yet have a video camera, you can still use the CU-SeeMe software to view video and talk and chat with other users. You simply cannot send video.

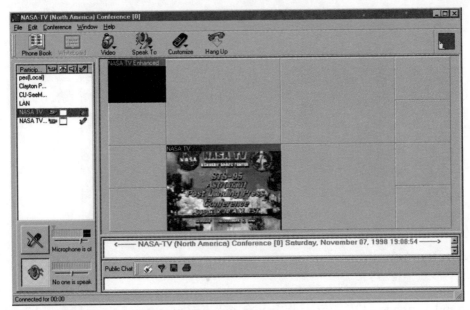

Figure 44.3 *Viewing multiple video windows within CU-SeeMe.*

DOWNLOADING AND INSTALLING THE *CU-SeeMe* SOFTWARE

Using your Web browser, you can download a trial copy of the CU-SeeMe software from the White Pine Web site, as shown in Figure 44.4.

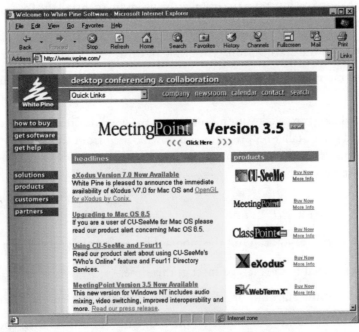

Figure 44.4 *You can download a trial version of CU-SeeMe from **www.wpine.com**.*

To download and install the CU-SeeMe software from the White Pine Web site, perform these steps:

1. Using your browser, connect to the White Pine Web site at *www.wpine.com.* The White Pine Web site will have instructions you can follow to initiate the software download. Your browser, in turn, will display the File Download dialog box, as shown in Figure 44.5.

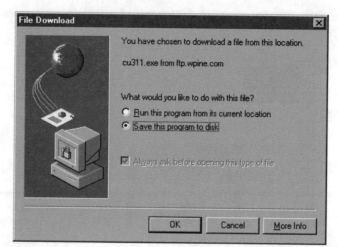

Figure 44.5 *The File Download dialog box.*

2. Within the File Download dialog box, click your mouse on the Save this program to disk button and then choose OK. Windows, in turn, will display a Save As dialog box, within which you can specify the folder within which you want to store the installation program.

3. Within the Save As dialog box, select the folder within which you want to save the file. Also, write down the file's name, so you can find the file later to run the installation program. Click your mouse on the Save button to initiate the file download.

After the file download completes, you must run the installation program to install the Internet Phone software on your system. To run the installation program, perform these steps:

1. Click your mouse on the Start button. Windows, in turn, will display the Start menu.

2. Within the Start menu, click your mouse on the Run option. Windows will display the Run dialog box.

3. Within the Run dialog box, click your mouse on the Browse button and locate the file within which you stored the installation program you downloaded from the White Pine Web site. Next, click your mouse on the installation program and then Click OK. Windows, in turn, will run the installation program.

RUNNING CU-SEEME SOFTWARE

After you install CU-SeeMe software, you can run the program by performing these steps:

1. If you are not connected to the Net, connect at this time.

2. Click your mouse on the Start button. Windows, in turn, will display the Start menu.

3. Within the Start menu, click your mouse on the Programs option and then choose the CU-SeeMe option. Windows, in turn, will cascade the CU-SeeMe submenu. Within the CU-SeeMe submenu, select the CU-SeeMe option. Windows, in turn, will open the CU-SeeMe window, as shown in Figure 44.6.

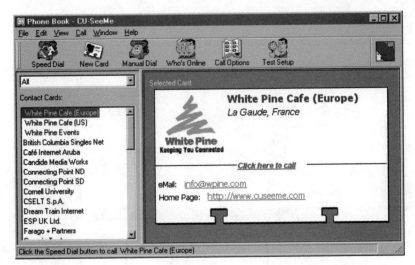

Figure 44.6 *The CU-SeeMe window.*

Within the CU-SeeMe program, you must first connect to a server. (CU-SeeMe refers to servers as "reflectors" because the computer "reflects" your video discussion to each member of the discussion group.) If you want to meet with a specific user within a CU-SeeMe conference, both of you must connect to the same reflector. To select a reflector, click your mouse on the reflector that you desire within the CU-SeeMe reflector list. After you connect to the reflector (in some cases, if the reflector is busy, you may not be able to connect), CU-SeeMe will display a list of discussion groups the reflector offers, as shown in Figure 44.7.

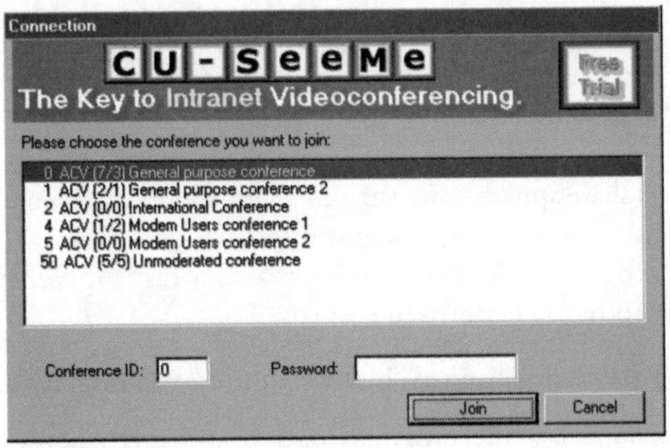

Figure 44.7 *Each CU-SeeMe reflector offers various discussion groups.*

From within the discussion group list, double-click your mouse on the discussion group you desire. CU-SeeMe, in turn, will open Windows within which you can display video and chat with group members.

Note: *For more information on CU-SeeMe, you can download additional documentation from the White Pine Web site.*

USING MICROSOFT NETMEETING

If you are using Windows 98, you can use NetMeeting, a video-conferencing program that Microsoft bundles with Windows. Like CU-SeeMe, NetMeeting lets you send and receive video, chat, and talk with other users. In addition, as shown in Figure 44.8, NetMeeting lets users exchange information using a shared whiteboard. As each user draws or writes on the whiteboard, all other users in the chat immediately see the user's edits.

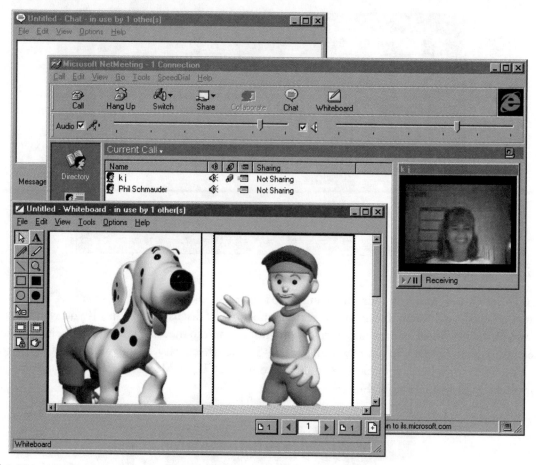

Figure 44.8 *Using a whiteboard to share information within Microsoft NetMeeting.*

In addition, NetMeeting lets users share applications, such as Word and Excel (even if the other users in the group do not have the programs you are sharing). By sharing an application in this way, users might, for example, share an Excel spreadsheet to collaborate on a budget. Finally, NetMeeting makes it easy for users to send and receive files to one another. To run the NetMeeting software, perform these steps:

1. Click your mouse on the Start button. Windows, in turn, will display the Start menu.

2. Within the Start menu, select the Programs option and then choose Internet Explorer. Windows, in turn, will cascade the Internet Explorer submenu.

3. Within the Internet Explorer submenu, click your mouse on the NetMeeting option. Windows will open the NetMeeting window.

If your Internet Explorer menu does not contain the NetMeeting option, you can install the software from the Windows 98 CD-ROM by performing these steps:

1. Click your mouse on the Start button. Windows, in turn, will display the Start menu.

2. Within the Start menu, click your mouse on the Settings menu Control Panel option. Windows will display the Control Panel folder, discussed in Lesson 45, "Configuring Your PC's System Settings."

3. Within the Control Panel folder, double-click your mouse on the Add/Remove Programs icon. Windows will display the Add/Remove Programs Properties dialog box.

4. Within the Add/Remove Programs Properties dialog box, click your mouse on the Windows Setup tab. Windows, in turn, will display the Windows Setup sheet.

5. Within the Windows Setup sheet, click your mouse on the Communications component and then click your mouse on the Details button. Windows will display the Communications dialog box.

6. Within the Communications dialog box, click your mouse on the NetMeeting check box, placing a check mark within the box. Next, click your mouse on the OK button. Windows will return you to the Windows Setup sheet.

7. Within the Windows Setup sheet, click your mouse on the OK button. Windows will install the NetMeeting software. To install the NetMeeting software, Windows may prompt you to insert the Windows CD-ROM into your CD-ROM drive.

Note: *For more information on the NetMeeting software, refer to the book* **1001 Windows 98 Tips**, *Jamsa Press, 1998.*

WHAT YOU MUST KNOW

In previous lessons, you learned how to communicate with users across the Net using chat software. When you chat with other users, you communicate by typing your messages. In this lesson, you learned how to use video-conferencing software to chat or talk with other users. In addition, you also learned how to send and receive video with other users. In Lesson 45, however, you will learn how to fine-tune Windows settings using the Control Panel. Before you continue with Lesson 45, make sure you understand the following key concepts:

✓ Today, several programs let you perform simple video conferencing across the Internet. If your PC has a video camera, you can use the camera and video-conferencing software to send video to other users across the Net.

✓ Using your PC's microphone and speakers, you can use video-conferencing software to talk with users across the Net, for free.

✓ CU-SeeMe is a program you can use to chat, talk, or exchange video with multiple users from across the Web.

✓ Windows 98 includes NetMeeting, software you can use for simple video conferencing across the Net.

✓ Within NetMeeting, you can chat, talk, and exchange video with other users across the Net. NetMeeting also lets you exchange files with other users, share ideas on a whiteboard, and even share application programs (even if the remote users do not have the shared programs).

Lesson 45

Configuring Your PC's System Settings

Although this book's lessons present a variety of hardware devices and software programs, the truth is that most users will probably run only two or three key programs, such as Word, Excel, and a Web browser, and that most will seldom install new hardware. Thus, if you are like most users, you normally will not have to configure many system settings. However, should you install a new modem or printer or if you want to remove software from your system, you will need to know how to perform a few basic operations.

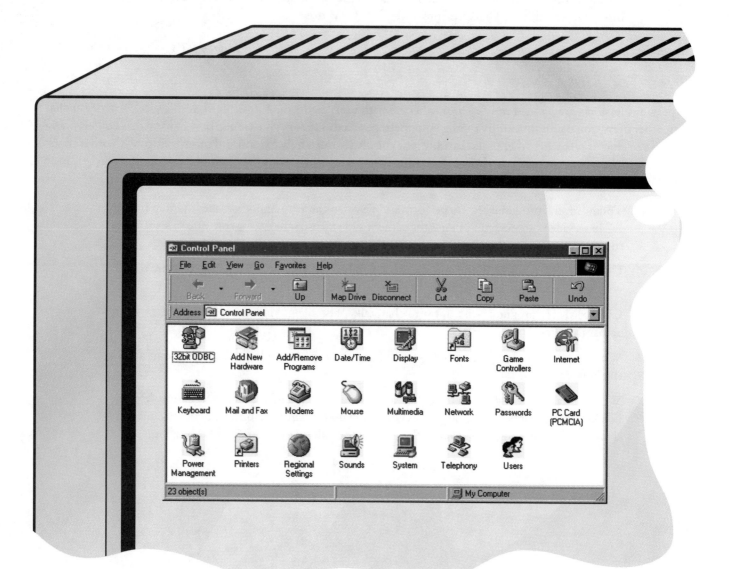

This lesson introduces you to the Windows Control Panel that you will use to configure your hardware and software settings. By the time you finish this lesson, you will understand the following key concepts:

- The Control Panel is a folder within which Windows places icons that correspond to your system devices.

- By double-clicking your mouse on a Control Panel icon, you can configure the corresponding device's settings.

- Using the Control Panel Add/Remove Programs icon, you can install (or remove) software that Microsoft bundles with Windows.

OPENING THE CONTROL PANEL FOLDER

In Lesson 15, "Using Electronic Folders to Organize Your Files," you learned to organize the files that you store on disk and that you should group related files into folders. In a similar way, to organize the programs you will use to configure your system settings, Windows provides a special folder called the Control Panel. As shown in Figure 45.1, the Control Panel contains icons that correspond to various hardware devices.

Figure 45.1 *To configure system settings, you will normally use a program you will find within the Control Panel folder.*

To display the Control Panel folder, perform these steps:

1. Click your mouse on the Start button. Windows, in turn, will display the Start menu.

2. Within the Start menu, click your mouse on the Settings options. Windows, in turn, will cascade the Settings menu, as shown in Figure 45.2.

3. Within the Settings submenu, click your mouse on the Control Panel option. Windows will open the Control Panel window, as previously shown in Figure 45.1.

In Lesson 21, "Getting the Most from Your Printer," you learned that if you install a new printer, you must also install software (a printer driver) that Windows will use to communicate with the printer. To install such printer software, you will double-click your mouse on the Control Panel Printers icon. Windows, in turn, will display the Printers folder, within which you will double-click your mouse on the Add Printers button to install your new printer's software.

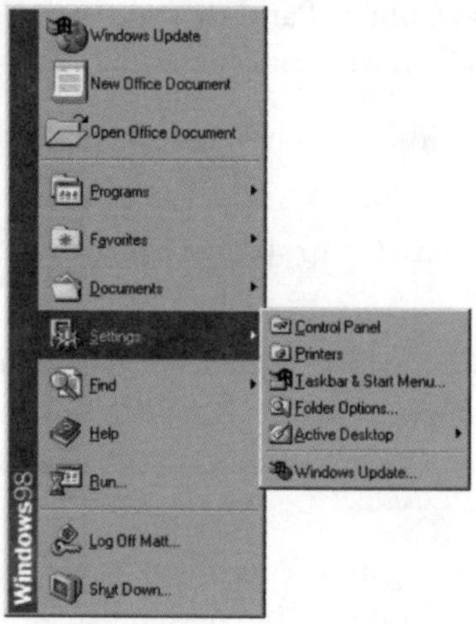

Figure 45.2 Cascading the Start menu Settings submenu.

Likewise, in Lesson 48, "Understanding the Ins and Outs of PC Modems," you will learn that if you install a new modem, you must also install software that Windows will use to communicate with the modem. As you might guess, to start the modem software installation, you can double-click your mouse on the Control Panel Modems icon.

In addition to using the Control Panel icons to install new software, there may also be times when you use them to configure hardware settings. For example, in Lesson 22, "Getting the Most from Your Keyboard and Mouse," you learned that to adjust your keyboard settings (perhaps to improve your keyboard's responsiveness), you first double-click your mouse on the Control Panel Keyboard icon. Windows, in turn, will display the Keyboard Properties dialog box, as shown in Figure 45.3, that you can use to configure your keyboard settings.

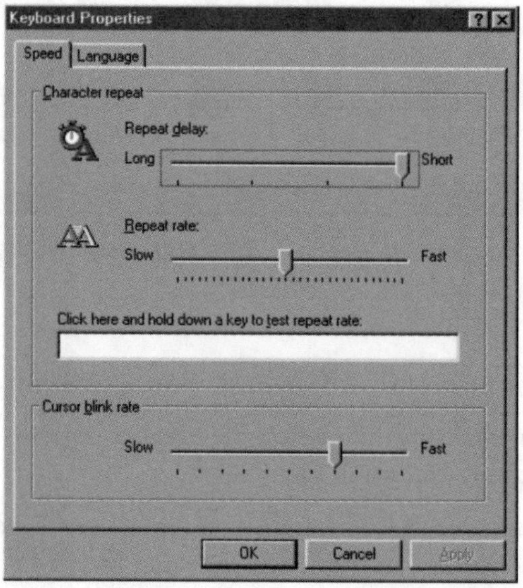

Figure 45.3 Using the Control Panel Keyboard icon to adjust your keyboard settings.

Likewise, to adjust your mouse settings, you must first double-click your mouse on the Control Panel Mouse icon. Windows, in turn, will display the Mouse Properties dialog box, as shown in Figure 45.4, within which you can configure your mouse settings.

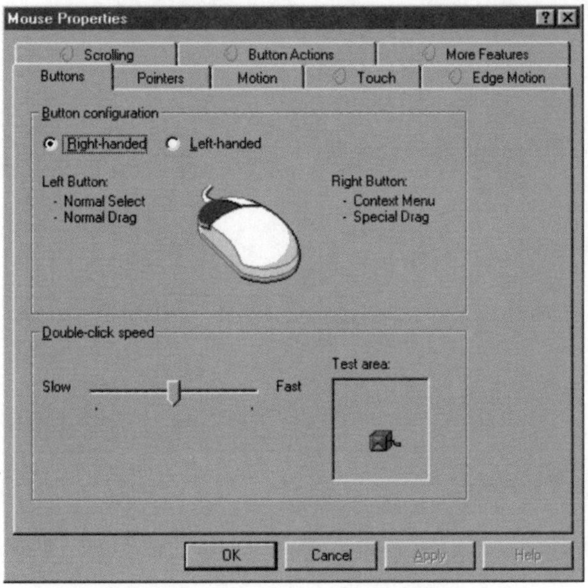

Figure 45.4 Using the Control Panel Mouse icon to adjust your mouse settings.

SETTING YOUR SYSTEM DATE AND TIME

In Lesson 9, "Running Programs within Windows," you learned that to switch from one program to another within Windows, you can click your mouse on the program's Taskbar icon. If you examine the Taskbar, you will find that in addition to icons, the Taskbar also contains a small clock that displays the current system time, as shown in Figure 45.5.

Figure 45.5 The Taskbar system clock.

If you aim your mouse pointer at the system clock for a few seconds (do not click your mouse on the clock, simply hold the mouse pointer over the clock), Windows will display the current system date, as shown in Figure 45.6.

Figure 45.6 Using the Taskbar to display the current system date.

If your system date or time is not correct, you can double-click your mouse on the Control Panel Date/Time icon and correct them by performing these steps:

1. Within the Control Panel folder, double-click your mouse on the Date/Time icon. Windows, in turn, will display the Date/Time Properties dialog box, as shown in Figure 45.7.

2. Within the Date/Time Properties dialog box, use the calendar fields to select the current month and day. Then, click your mouse on the hours, minutes, and seconds fields to set your system clock.

3. Click your mouse on the OK button to put your date and time settings into effect.

265

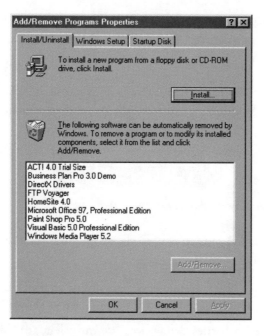

Figure 45.7 *The Date/Time Properties dialog box.*

USING THE CONTROL PANEL TO ADD OR REMOVE WINDOWS SOFTWARE

Several of this book's lessons discuss software programs that Microsoft bundles with Windows. If you cannot find a specific program on your system, it is probably because the software was never installed on your system. If you have the Windows CD-ROM, however, you can use the Control Panel Add/Remove Programs icon to install the software by performing these steps:

1. Within the Control Panel folder, double-click your mouse on the Add/Remove Programs icon. Windows will display the Add/Remove Programs Properties dialog box, as shown in Figure 45.8.

Figure 45.8 *The Add/Remove Programs Properties dialog box.*

2. Within the Add/Remove Programs Properties dialog box, click your mouse on the Windows Setup tab. Windows, in turn, will display the Windows Setup sheet, as shown in Figure 45.9.

Figure 45.9 *The Windows Setup sheet.*

3. Within the Windows Setup sheet, locate the component group that contains the program you desire. The Accessories group, for example, contains the games Lesson 41 discusses. To determine the programs a component group contains, click your mouse on the group's name and then click your mouse on the Details button. Windows, in turn, will display a dialog box that lists the component programs. Within the dialog box, place a checkmark next to each program you want to install and then click your mouse on the OK button.

4. Within the Windows Setup sheet, click your mouse on the OK button. Windows, in turn, will prompt you to insert the Windows CD-ROM and will then install the software.

REMOVE THE WINDOWS COMPONENTS YOU DO NOT USE

In the previous discussion, you learned how to use the Control Panel Add/Remove Programs icon to install software that Microsoft bundles with Windows. If you have Windows-based programs (installed on your system) that you do not use, such as the WordPad word processor or the Paint drawing program, you can use the Add/Remove Programs icon to remove the software from your disk. By removing the programs, you free up disk space you can use for other purposes. To remove Windows components from your system, perform these steps:

1. Within the Control Panel folder, double-click your mouse on the Add/Remove Programs icon. Windows, in turn, will display the Add/Remove Programs Properties dialog box.

2. Within the Add/Remove Programs Properties dialog box, click your mouse on the Windows Setup tab. Windows, in turn, will display the Windows Setup sheet.

3. Within the Windows Setup sheet, locate the component group that contains the program you want to remove. To determine the programs a component group contains, click your mouse on the group's name and then click your mouse on the Details button. Windows, in turn, will display a dialog box that lists the component programs. Within the dialog box, remove the checkmark from beside each program you want to remove and then click your mouse on the OK button.

4. Within the Windows Setup sheet, click your mouse on the OK button. Windows, in turn, will prompt you to insert the Windows CD-ROM and will then remove the software from your disk.

Note: *For more information on each of the Control Panel icons and how you use each icon to adjust your system settings, refer to the book* **1001 Windows 98 Tips**, *Jamsa Press, 1998.*

WHAT YOU MUST KNOW

In this lesson, you learned that you will use the Windows Control Panel whenever you need to add hardware or to change device settings. In general, the Control Panel groups your key system programs into one location. In Lesson 46, "Getting the Most from Your PC's Performance," you will learn several ways you can "tweak" your PC to help it perform better. Before you continue with Lesson 46, however, make sure that you understand the following key concepts:

✓ To configure your system settings, such as your keyboard's responsiveness, you will use the Windows Control Panel.

✓ In general, the Control Panel is simply a folder within which Windows groups key system software.

✓ To configure a device's settings, double-click your mouse on the device icon within the Control Panel. Windows, in turn, will display a dialog box that you can use to assign device settings.

✓ Using the Control Panel Add/Remove Programs icons, you can install or remove software that Microsoft bundles within Windows. If you are not using the programs, removing the program files from your disk will free up disk space you can use for other purposes.

Lesson 46

Getting the Most from Your PC's Performance

One of the most frustrating aspects of buying a personal computer is that the instant you take the PC home, your new high-speed, state-of-the-art computer is obsolete. Because technology is advancing so quickly, newer, less expensive, and faster systems will be readily available over the next six months. However, if you put off buying your PC today, the same will be true tomorrow. Fortunately, for most users, the PC that you buy today will more than meet your needs for the next three years. So, if the PC meets your needs, it really is not critical that a newer, slightly faster machine is now available. If you use your PC on a regular basis, there are a few simple things that you can do to improve your PC's performance, several of which will not cost you anything, while others, because the cost of PC products, such as memory and modems, is decreasing quickly, will not cost you much.

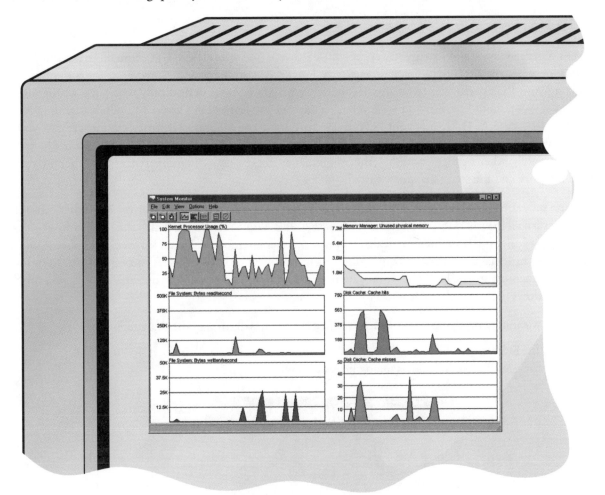

This lesson examines a few simple, yet effective ways that you can improve your PC's performance. By the time you finish this lesson, you will understand the following key concepts:

- A simple, but effective way to improve your system performance is to restart your PC once a day.
  By restarting your PC, you free up memory that a program may not have returned to Windows.

- Windows and Windows-based programs often create temporary files as they run. If your disk is low on space, such programs may run slowly or not at all. Take time once a month to remove files you no longer need from your disk.

- As you create, edit, and delete files, the locations on your disk (the sectors) Windows uses to store a file may eventually become fragmented (dispersed) about your disk. It takes Windows longer to access a fragmented file than one that resides in consecutive sector locations. As a rule, once a month, you should use the Windows Disk Defragmenter program to fix fragmented files.

- Most users use one or two key programs each day. To take advantage of performance improvements in upgrades to the software, users should install new software upgrades as the software becomes available.

- If you spend more than an hour a day on the Net, you should upgrade your modem to the fastest modem your phone lines will support.

RESTART YOUR SYSTEM EACH MORNING

With the advent of screen savers and EnergyStar compliant hardware (monitors, PCs, and printers) that reduce their power consumption when they are not in use, many users no longer turn off their PCs. However, if you are concerned about maximizing your PC's performance or, if you experience program errors periodically that cause a program to crash (stop working), you should restart your system once a day. As you learned in Lesson 11, "Understanding How Your PC Uses Its Memory (RAM)," before your PC can run a program, the program's instructions must reside within your PC's memory. When a program ends, the program should release its memory back to Windows, for use by other programs. Unfortunately, when a program crashes, the program may not release its memory. As a result, other programs cannot use the memory and the space becomes wasted.

In addition, some programs (ones that may not crash) have errors (programmers call such errors *bugs*) that cause the programs not to return all their memory to Windows when they end. Users refer to programs that end without giving back their memory as "suffering from memory leaks." Over time, such memory leaks can leave considerable amounts of memory unusable until, that is, you restart your system. By restarting your PC every day, you will provide Windows with a clean, unused memory space. To restart your system, you do not have to power off your PC. Instead, you simply need to restart Windows itself, which you can do by performing these steps:

1. Click your mouse on the Start button. Windows, in turn, will display the Start menu.

2. Within the Start menu, click your mouse on the Shut Down option. Windows, in turn, will display the Shut Down Windows dialog box, as shown in Figure 46.1.

Figure 46.1 *The Shut Down Windows dialog box.*

3. Within the Shut Down Windows dialog box, click your mouse on the Restart option and choose OK. Windows, in turn, will restart your system, giving Windows unused RAM with which to work.

CLEAN UP YOUR HARD DISK

In Lesson 19, "Cleaning Up Your Disk," you learned ways you can delete unnecessary files from your disk to free up disk space. As they run, many programs create temporary files on your disk. A drawing program, might apply your changes to a copy of your drawing, so you can later revert to the original image if you do not like the changes you have made. Likewise, a word processing program may keep a backup copy of your document in a temporary file on disk. If your hard disk is low on space, the programs may not be able to create the temporary files they need, or doing so may take them longer than normal (because Windows must search your disk for available storage locations). In some cases, if a program cannot create the temporary files it requires, the program will display an error message and stop its current operation. Other programs, however, may simply fail. Unfortunately, should a program fail, the program may not clean up the temporary files it has created on disk, which, in turn, will simply waste storage space.

Depending on how you use your PC, and how often, the frequency with which you should clean up your disk will vary. However, most users should (at a minimum) clean up their hard disk once a month. If you are using Windows 98, you can use the Disk Cleanup Wizard discussed in Lesson 19 to automatically clean up your disks at night. If you are not using Windows 98, follow the steps Lesson 19 presents to manually clean up your disk.

DEFRAGMENT YOUR DISK

As you have learned, your PC consists of very fast electronic components (chips and circuits). Your PC's two mechanical components (the pieces with moving parts) are your disks and printer. Compared to the speeds of your computer's electronic devices, mechanical devices are very slow (it simply takes longer to move mechanical parts than to send electrons down a wire). One way to improve your PC's performance is to reduce the number of operations a mechanical device must perform. Unfortunately, because you have to print your documents and you must store and later retrieve files from your disk, not using your mechanical devices is not an option. What you can do, however, is to fine-tune how Windows stores information on disk, so that when Windows must store or retrieve information, Windows does so efficiently. To fine-tune your disk, you must perform a process called *defragmenting your disk*. Fortunately, Windows provides software, called the *Disk Defragmenter*, that makes this process very easy.

UNDERSTANDING HOW DISKS BECOME FRAGMENTED

As you learned in Lesson 13, "Storing Information on Disk," when you store data within a file, Windows records the information in one or more storage locations on your disk called sectors. Depending on a file's size, the number of sectors Windows needs to store files will differ.

When you use a file's contents, Windows locates the file's sectors on disk and reads each sector into RAM, where your programs can access the data. To read the file's contents, the disk drive will spin the disk's surface past the disk's read/write head (the device that reads a sector's content or writes, magnetically records, the sector's contents on the disk's surface). Depending on the sector's location on your disk, the drive may have to move its read/write head in or out in order to locate the sector's track—another slow mechanical operation.

Over time, as you create, edit, and delete files, the sectors Windows uses to store a file may become dispersed across your disk. To read the file's contents, your disk drive must perform more mechanical movements than it would if the file's sectors were in consecutive locations on disk. When you defragment a disk, you move each file's data so that the file's contents reside in consecutive sector locations on your disk.

By ordering a file's disk sectors in this way, your disk drive can read a file's contents quickly, without having to perform any excess slow mechanical movements.

To defragment the files on your disk, perform these steps:

1. Click your mouse on the Start button. Windows, in turn, will display the Start menu.

2. Within the Start menu, select the Programs menu and choose Accessories. Windows will display the Accessories submenu. Within the Accessories submenu, select the System Tools option and then choose Disk Defragmenter. Windows, in turn, will start the Disk Defragmenter program that will display the Select a Drive dialog box.

3. Within the Select a Drive dialog box, click your mouse on the pull-down list and select the disk you want to defragment and then choose OK. The Disk Defragmenter program, in turn, will start defragmenting your disk.

RECOGNIZING THE SYMPTOMS OF A FRAGMENTED DISK

As a general rule, if you defragment your disk once a month, most of the files on your disk will not be fragmented. However, if you find that programs or data files seem to be taking longer to load or that you can actually hear your disk as it reads files (what you are hearing is the disk's read/write head moving in and out), the files on your disk may have become fragmented. In such cases, you should defragment your disk. After you defragment your disk, you should find that your symptoms have gone away.

ADD MORE RANDOM ACCESS MEMORY (RAM)

As you learned in Lesson 11, "Understanding How Your PC Uses Its Memory (RAM)," before your PC can run a program, the program's instructions and data must reside within your computer's memory. When you run two or more programs at the same time, each program's data and instructions must reside in memory before each can run. Depending on how many programs you run, Windows may eventually run out of RAM. When that occurs, Windows will swap one or more programs out of memory to disk (into a special swap file).

Ideally, when Windows must choose a program to swap from RAM to disk, Windows will swap an inactive program. For example, assume that you have three programs running: Microsoft Word, Excel, and the Internet Explorer. Further, assume that you are currently typing a memo within Word (which means that Excel and Internet Explorer may be inactive). If you later start a fourth program, such as PowerPoint, Windows may have to swap a program out of RAM to disk. Hopefully, Windows will select Excel or Internet Explorer, since you are using Word. Should you later click your mouse on the Excel window (making Excel active), Windows would need to swap a different program out of RAM so it can make room for Excel.

By continually swapping programs between RAM and the swap file on disk, Windows lets you run more programs than will actually fit in RAM at any one time. Unfortunately, because your disk drive is a mechanical device, such swapping operations are slow. One way to improve your system performance is to reduce swapping. The only two ways to reduce swapping are to run fewer programs at the same time or to install more RAM. Fortunately, the price of RAM has dropped dramatically over the past few years, making it very affordable. Although it is possible for you to purchase and install RAM yourself, most users should let a hardware technician (the store where you purchase the RAM should have a hardware specialist) install the RAM for you. If, however, you are determined to install the RAM yourself, refer to the book *Rescued by Upgrading Your PC, Third Edition*, Jamsa Press, 1998.

UPGRADE YOUR SOFTWARE TO THE MOST RECENT VERSIONS

Most users have a small set of key software programs, such as Word, Excel, and the Internet Explorer that they use on a regular basis. As a rule, you should keep the programs that you use on a regular basis. In other words, if a new version of your key software becomes available, you should upgrade your software to the new version. When software manufacturers release new software, the software not only offers new features, it often includes fixes to bugs as well as performance improvements. Most Windows 95 users, for example, will see a 30% performance increase by upgrading to Windows 98. Some users will tell you that you should not upgrade to a software program within the first six months following the program's release, because the program "is likely to contain errors." In general, most users will never experience such errors. Today, before a software company releases a product to the public, the company lets thousands of users (and, in some cases, hundreds of thousands of users) test the software. Because 90% of users only use 10% of a program's capabilities, most users would never encounter an error in the program's first release. However, early program adopters will benefit from the software's new capabilities.

Note: *If you are responsible for computers within an office, make sure you test a new software upgrade with all of your existing programs before you install the upgrade on each computer within the office.*

BUY AND INSTALL A FASTER MODEM

Most users make extensive use of the Internet (for e-mail) and the World Wide Web. When you use the Web, the item that influences your performance the most is not your PC or your browser, but rather, your modem. Lesson 48, "Understanding the Ins and Outs of Modems," discusses modems in detail. In that lesson, you will learn that if you spend more than an hour a day connected to the Net, you should consider an ISDN connection (which requires a more expensive modem and a higher monthly fee from your Internet Service Provider), or you should consider installing a second phone line and running two modems at the same time (which requires that your Internet Service Provider support multilink connections).

WHAT YOU MUST KNOW

No matter how fast PCs become, it seems that users always want better performance. In this lesson, you learned several simple steps you can take to improve your PC's performance. In Lesson 47, "Integrating Clipart and Photos into Your Documents," you will learn how to insert photos or illustrations into the documents that you create using such programs as Microsoft Word. Before you continue with Lesson 47, however, make sure that you understand the following key concepts:

- ✓ A simple step you can take to improve your system performance is simply to restart your PC once a day.

- ✓ When you run multiple programs, Windows and Windows-based programs make extensive use of space on your disk. If your disk is full, such programs may run slower or the programs may fail, because they cannot create temporary files on your disk. If your disk is low on space, perform the steps Lesson 19 presents to remove unnecessary files from your disk.

- ✓ Before a program can run, the program's instructions and data must reside within RAM. If you run multiple programs at the same time, you will improve your system performance by installing more RAM.

- ✓ If you use one or two key programs each day, make sure you upgrade those programs whenever a new version becomes available.

- ✓ If you spend more than an hour connected to the Net each day, you should upgrade to the fastest modem your phone lines will support.

Lesson 47

Integrating Clipart and Photos Into Your Documents

Most people are familiar with the expression that "a picture is worth a thousand words." Assuming that the expression is true, you will want to include photos and illustrations (such as clipart images) within the documents that you create. In this lesson, you will learn how to insert images into the documents that you create using Microsoft Word. If you are using software other than Word, you will find that the steps you must perform to insert a image within other programs are quite similar to the steps this lesson will present.

By the time you finish this lesson, you will understand the following key concepts:

- Clipart images are illustrations that you can use within your documents that an artist has created in an electronic format.

- Software programs, such as Word and PowerPoint, normally provide several clipart images you can use to get started. You can also purchase, from most computer stores, clipart CD-ROMs that will contain thousands of images.

- When an artist creates a clipart image, the artist can store the image using a variety of file formats. Before your can insert a clipart image into a document, you must ensure that your software supports the image file format.

- After you insert a clipart image into your document, you can use your mouse to size the image, as your needs require.

WHERE TO FIND CLIPART IMAGES

Clipart images are illustrations that an artist has created that you can use within your documents, such as a fax, report, or even a book. Because most users are either not great artists or have not yet mastered drawing software, such as Adobe Illustrator, clipart images provide users with a great source of electronic artwork.

To help you get started, many programs, such as Microsoft Word, provide several clipart illustrations that you can insert into your documents. As your clipart needs grow, you can purchase clipart packages that offer thousands of clipart illustrations for pennies a piece, at most computer stores. Figure 47.1, for example, shows a variety of clipart images.

Figure 47.1 Samples of clipart images.

If, in addition to clipart images, you want to include photos within your presentations, you will find that most computer stores also sell photo CDs that contain hundreds of photos. Figure 47.2, for example, shows three sample photos that are comparable to photos you can find on a photo CD.

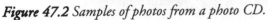

Figure 47.2 Samples of photos from a photo CD.

If you want to place your own photos within a document, you must first convert your photo into an electronic format. Lesson 32, "Creating Electronic Images Using Scanners and Digital Cameras," discusses ways you can convert your photos to files that contain electronic images.

You Must Understand File Formats

In Lesson 14, "Storing Information in Files," you learned that programs (and users) use a file's extension to determine the type of information the file contains. For example, files with the DOC extension normally contain a Word document, whereas a file with the XLS extension contains an Excel spreadsheet. When you work with clipart images and electronic photos, you must pay close attention to file extensions because your programs will not support all graphics file formats. Table 47 briefly describes the common graphics file formats.

File Extension	File Contents
BMP	A bitmap graphic file, such as photograph or computer-screen image. Bitmap images are very common. The computer screen images shown in this book are bitmap images.
TIF	Another form of a bitmap graphic image.
EPS	An encapsulated Postscript file. Postscript images are well-suited for printing (but you need a printer that supports Postscript). The illustrations that appear in this book are EPS files.
WMF	A Windows metafile. Microsoft often uses WMF files to store clipart images for use in programs such as Word and PowerPoint.
JPEG	Normally a photographic image stored in a compressed format. Many images you will find on the Web are JPEG images. When a program opens a JPEG image, the program decompresses the image. JPEG images store high-quality images in relatively small files.
GIF	A graphics image format which may contain a picture or illustration. GIF images are low quality images well-suited for use on the Web because of their small file size.

Table 47 *Common graphics file extensions.*

To insert an image within a document, the program you are using must support the image-file format. Normally, if you stick with BMP and TIF images, you will find that most software programs will support the formats. To determine the image types that your software supports, you must turn to the documentation that accompanied your software. If you are not sure whether or not your software will support the image format, simply try to insert the image (save your document's contents first or use a new document for your test).

Understanding Image Filters

As you have learned, before you can insert an image into a document, your software must support the image file format. As you can imagine, if software developers included support within your programs for every possible file type, your programs would become very large. Worse yet, if a new file format was introduced, your program would have no easy way to support the format. As a solution, software developers created special software, called filters, that you can install into your program. By installing a JPEG filter, for example, you let your program support JPEG images. Likewise, by installing a GIF filter, you let your program support GIF images. If a new file format is introduced, software developers can also introduce a filter that you can install within your program.

If you find that your program does not support a specific image type, your problem may actually be that you have not installed the correct filter. In some cases, you may have the filter you need on your program's CD-ROM. In other cases, you may be able to download a filter from across the Web. To learn more about filters, turn to the documentation that accompanied your program, or call your program's technical support.

INSERTING AN IMAGE INTO A WORD DOCUMENT

As discussed, the steps you must perform to insert an image into most programs (such as Word, Excel, or PowerPoint) are quite similar. To insert an image into a Word document, perform these steps:

1. Within your Word document, use the keyboard arrow keys or your mouse to position the cursor at the location at which you want to place the image.

2. Next, select the Insert menu Picture option and choose From File. Word, in turn, will display the Insert Picture dialog box, as shown in Figure 47.3.

Figure 47.3 The Insert Picture dialog box.

3. Within the Insert Picture dialog box, locate the folder that contains the image that you want to insert. Within the folder, click your mouse on the image file and then choose Insert. Word, in turn, will insert the image into your document.

When you insert an image into a document, your software may place the image into your document as a selected image, meaning, that your software will place sizing handles at each corner and on the sides of your image. If your image is not selected, simply click your mouse on the image to select it. By dragging one of the sizing handles using your mouse, you can increase or decrease the image size, as shown in Figure 47.4.

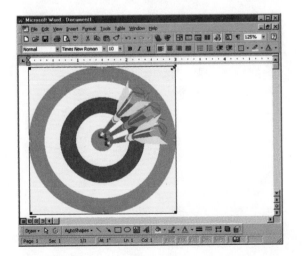 

Figure 47.4 Dragging sizing handles to change an image's size.

Note: *To help you get started, Microsoft bundles several clipart images with Office. You will find the images within the Clipart subfolder within the MSOffice or Microsoft Office folder.*

WHAT YOU MUST KNOW

As you create word processing documents, or presentations using software such as PowerPoint, you can improve your document's appearance and content by inserting illustrations and photos into the document. This lesson examined clipart, illustrations an artist has created in an electronic format, that you can insert into your documents. As you learned, the steps you will perform in most programs to insert a clipart image are quite similar (normally, you use an Insert menu option). In Lesson 48, "Understanding the Ins and Outs of PC Modems," you will learn how modems work, how to fine-tune your modem settings, and how to install software to support your new modem. Before you continue with Lesson 48, however, make sure you understand the following key concepts:

✓ Clipart images are illustrations that an artist has created in an electronic format that you can insert within your documents.

✓ Many software packages include a few sample clipart images that you can use as you create images using the software. In addition, most computer stores sell CD-ROMs that may contain thousands of images.

✓ Before you can insert a clipart image into a document, you must ensure that your program supports the file's format.

✓ When you insert an image into a document, your software may automatically select the image, placing sizing handles on each corner and on the sides of the image. If your software does not select the image, click your mouse on the image to select it. Then, by dragging one of the handles using your mouse, you can increase or decrease the image size.

Lesson 48

Understanding the "Ins and Outs" of PC Modems

Today, most PC users make extensive use of the Internet to send and receive electronic-mail and the World Wide Web to "surf" for information. Several of the lessons that follow introduce new Internet-based programs, such as RealAudio technologies, that let you receive audio and video from across the Web, or Internet Phone, a program that lets you talk with other users across the Internet using your PC microphone and speakers. A key to your success and enjoyment with these new technologies is a fast modem.

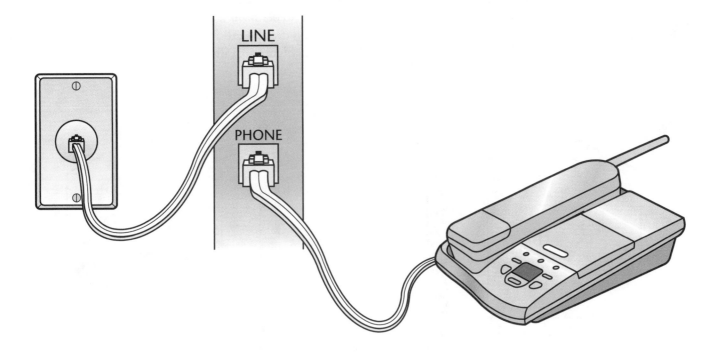

 In this lesson, you will examine different modem types. By the time you finish this lesson, you will understand the following key concepts:

- Using a modem, you can connect your PC to a remote computer over standard telephone lines.

- A modem is named after the modulation and demodulation process the modem performs to convert signals from the digital format that the PC understands into an analog wave format it can transmit over phone lines, and then back again at the receiving end to covert the analog signal to digital.

- If you spend more than an hour a day connected to the Net, you want to make sure you have the fastest modem your phone line and Internet connection can support.

- ISDN offers users a high-speed but high-cost connection to the Net.

- Many cable TV companies now offer cable-modem connections to the Net which offer a high-speed, low-cost connection.

- If you travel with a notebook PC and a cellular phone, you should consider buying a cellular modem that you can connect to a standard phone line or your cellular phone.

- Although most users think of modems as a means of connecting to the Net, you can also use a modem to send and receive faxes, to dial into a remote network other than the Net, and even to provide voice and telephone processing.

- To view or change your modem settings, double-click your mouse on the Control Panel modem icon. Windows, in turn, will display the Modem Properties dialog box.

UNDERSTANDING WHY WE CALL THEM MODEMS

As you know, a modem lets you connect your PC to a remote PC using phone lines. The term modem is an acronym for MOdulator-DEModulator, which describes the process the modem performs to convert the digital signals the PC uses (signals based on ones and zeros) into the wave-like analog signals the phone lines carry (that's the modulate part) and back to digital signals at the receiving end (the demodulate part). Figure 48.1 illustrates the modem's modulation and demodulation process.

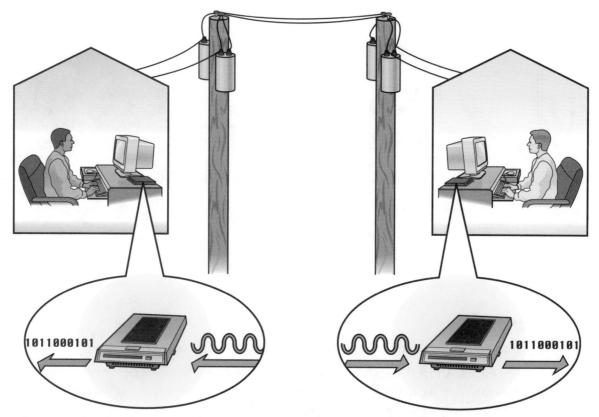

Figure 48.1 *A modem converts the PCs digital signals into analog signals that can travel across the phone lines. Upon receiving an analog signal, the modem converts the signal back into the digital format the PC understands.*

UNDERSTANDING MODEM TYPES

To start, as shown in Figure 48.2, modems are either internal or external devices. If you have an external modem, you will connect the modem to either a serial port or parallel ports depending on your modem type. If you have a notebook PC, your PC may have a built-in modem, or you may use a PCMCIA-based modem card. In addition, you can also connect an external modem to a notebook PC.

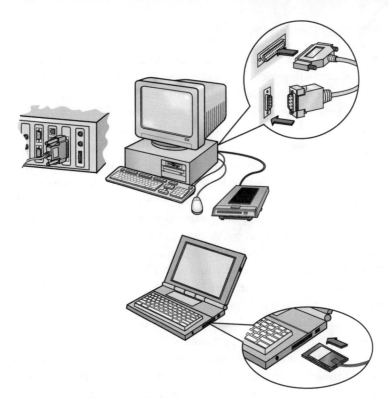

Figure 48.2 *Modems are either internal or external devices.*

Users categorize modems based on the modem's speed. Today, most users have 28.8Kbs or 56Kbs modems. As discussed in Lesson 12, "Understanding the Myriad of PC Speeds and Sizes," a 28.8Kbs modem can send and receive about 3,000 bytes a second. Likewise, a 56Kbs modem can send and receive twice that (6,000 bytes per second). To download a 1MB file using a 28.8Kbs modem would require roughly five and a half minutes.

As you shop for modems, you may encounter modems that advertise 2X speeds. Such modems use hardware and software compression techniques to let the modems transmit and receive more information using to fewer bytes. Before a modem can take advantage of the 2X technology, the modem must be connected to a modem that also supports 2X compression. Lastly, if you are a notebook PC user who travels on a regular basis, you may want to consider buying a cellular modem that you can connect to a standard phone line or to your cellular phone, as shown in Figure 48.3.

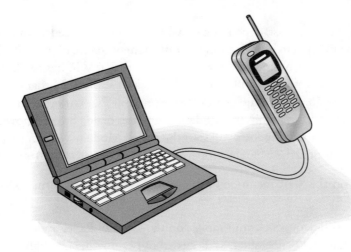

Figure 48.3 *A cellular modem lets you connect your PC to either a standard phone or a cellular phone.*

LOOKING FOR BETTER PERFORMANCE

If you spend considerable time on the Web, you should shop for the fastest modem your phone connection will support. In addition, you should consider upgrading your connection to an ISDN line or to a cable modem. ISDN, which stands for Integrated Services Digital Network, combines multiple telephone lines and high-speed digital signal transmissions (that don't require the digital to analogy conversion) to achieve data rates of 64Kbs to 128Kbs. To use ISDN, you must first establish an ISDN connection with your phone company. Then, you must find an Internet Service Provider or on-line services that supports ISDN. Allthough your ISDN connection is much faster than a standard connection, it is also much more expensive. You must pay a higher monthly phone bill for the ISDN lines and service and you must pay a higher monthly fee with your Internet Service Provider. In addition, you must purchase an ISDN modem. As an alternative to ISDN, you should contact your cable TV company and ask them if they offer cable-modem connections, that let you receive high-speed digital signals using a special cable modem (which you may have to purchase or lease from your cable company). Currently, most cable modems can send and receive data at 512Kbs (for download operations) and 64Kbs for uploads (many cable companies offer upload and download speeds greater than 1Mbs). If an ISDN connection is too expensive, and your cable TV company does not yet offer cable modems, you might consider installing a second modem within your PC and establishing a multilink connection to your on-line service or Internet Service Provider, as shown in Figure 48.4. When you use a multilink connection, your PC can send and receive data over two modems, which almost doubles your performance (your modem software must manage the incoming and outgoing data which consumes some performance). In fact, if you have more than two modems and you have a phone line for each modem, you may be able to use each of your modems within a multilink connection. For many users, establishing a multilink connection is a very cost-effective way to improve the speed of their Internet connection. Before you can use a multilink connection, your Internet Service Provider must enable multilink operations for your account.

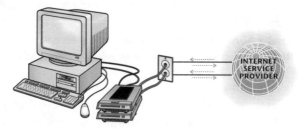
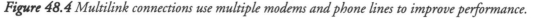

Figure 48.4 *Multilink connections use multiple modems and phone lines to improve performance.*

INSTALLING A NEW MODEM

When you purchase a new modem, you must, depending on whether you purchased an internal or external modem, install your modem within your PC system unit or connect your modem to one of your PC ports. Then, you must connect your modem to your phone line. Next, you must install software that Windows will use to communicate with your new modem. In some cases, your modem will come with a disk or CD-ROM that contains a Setup program, similar to those discussed in Lesson 20, "Installing New Software on Your PC." At other times, you must install your software by selecting the Add button from within the Modem Properties dialog box, as shown in Figure 48.5. When you click your mouse on the Add button, Windows will start the Install Modem Wizard, that walks you through the software installation process. To display the Modem Properties dialog box, perform these steps:

1. Click your mouse on the Start menu Settings option. Windows, in turn, will display the Settings submenu.

2. Within the Settings submenu, click your mouse on the Control Panel option. Windows, in turn, will open the Control Panel folder, as discussed in Lesson 45, "Configuring Your PC's System Settings."

3. Within the Control Panel folder, double-click your mouse on the Modems icon.

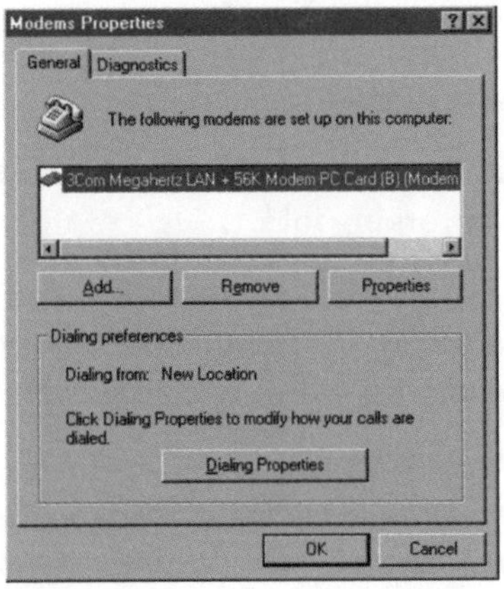

Figure 48.5 *The Modem Properties dialog box.*

CONFIGURING YOUR MODEM SETTINGS

In addition to using the Control Panel's Modems icon to install software for a new modem, you can also use it to configure your modem settings. If you experience errors when you try to dial into a remote computer, a technial support specialist who is helping you troubleshoot the error may ask you for your modem settings, which you can display by clicking your mouse on your modem within the Modem Properties dialog box and then clicking your mouse on the Properties button. Figure 48.6, for example, shows the Modem Properties dialog box General sheet and Connection sheet, which you can use to display or change your modem settings.

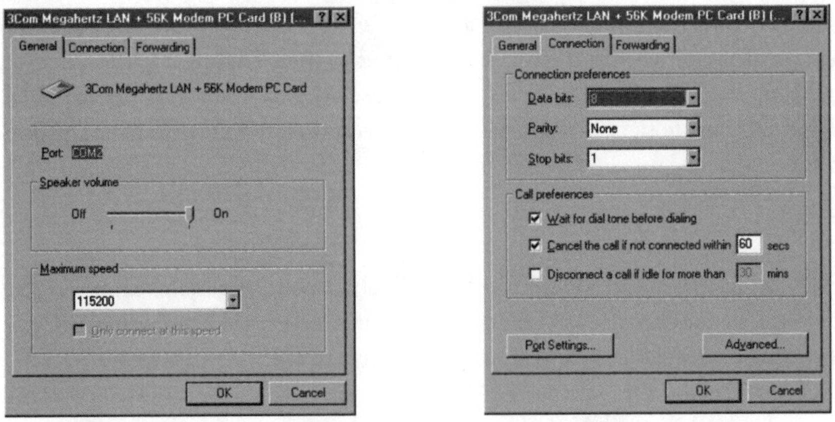

Figure 48.6 *Viewing modem settings within the Modem Properties dialog box.*

Note: *For more information on configuring your modem properties, refer to the book 1001 Windows 98 Tips, Jamsa Press, 1998.*

CONNECTING TO AN INTERNET SERVICE PROVIDER

In Lesson 50, "Getting Connected to the Internet," you will learn that most on-line services will provide you with the software you need (either on a CD-ROM that you receive from the service, or using software, such as that for America Online and the Microsoft Network, that Microsoft bundles with Windows). If you are joining an Internet Service Provider, however, the provider may simply give you a phone number that your modem can dial to connect to the service. Fortunately, Windows actually provides the software you need to connect to an Internet Service Provider. To configure Windows to use your Internet Service Provider, you must use the Make New Connection Wizard, that you will run from within the Dial-Up Networking folder. To start the Make New Connection Wizard, perform these steps:

1. Click your mouse on the Start menu Programs option and choose Accessories. Windows, in turn, will display the Accessories submenu.

2. Within the Accessories submenu, click your mouse on the Communications option. Windows will display the Communications submenu.

3. Within the Communications submenu, select the Dial-Up Networking option. Windows, in turn, will open the Dial-Up Networking folder.

4. Within the Dial-Up Networking folder, double-click your mouse on the Make New Connection icon. Windows, in turn, will start the Make New Connection Wizard that will walk you through the steps you must perform to configure your Internet connection.

Note: For more information on Dial-Up Networking, refer to the book 1001 Windows 98 Tips, Jamsa Press, 1998. Also, if your Accessories submenu does not contain a Communications submenu, or the Communications submenu does not contain a Dial-Up Networking option, you must install the Dial-Up Networking software from the Windows CD-ROM using the Control Panel Add/Remove Programs option.

OTHER WAYS YOU CAN USE YOUR MODEM

When most users think about modems, they immediately think about connecting to the Internet or the World Wide Web. A modem, however, lets you do much more than simply connect your PC to the Net. In Lesson 60, "Using Your PC to Send and Receive Faxes," you will download software from the Net that you can use to send and receive faxes using your modem. In addition to letting your PC answer incoming fax calls, you can let your PC answer all incoming calls using a program such as Symantec's Talkworks Pro (of which you can download a trial version from the Symantec Web site at *www.symantec.com/talkworks*) that lets your PC record voice messages or provide users with recorded product information. If you travel on a regular basis and you must access programs or data that reside on your office's local-area network, you can use your modem to dial into a server PC at your office and then access network resources over your modem connection, as if you were in the office connected to the network. Further, if you want to eliminate your need to place a long-distance call to a dial-up server, you can use your modem to connect your PC to the Internet and you can then create a virtual-private network connection with a server at your office that again provides you with access to your network resources.

WHAT YOU MUST KNOW

Because of the popularity of the Internet and the World Wide Web, most users make extensive use of their modem. This lesson took a detailed look at modems, ways you can use your modem that go beyond electronic-mail and the surfing the Web, and options you can consider for a faster connection to the Internet. Lesson 49, "Understanding the Internet and World Wide Web," introduces you to the "Net" and the "Web." Before you continue with Lesson 49, however, make sure you have learned the following key concepts:

✓ A modem lets you connect your PC to a remote computer over standard telephone lines. Modems convert your PCs digital signals into an analog format for transmission across phone lines.

✓ ISDN offers users a high-speed but high-cost connection to the Net.

✓ Many cable TV companies now offer cable-modem connections to the Net, which although they are not as fast as an ISDN connection, they are also not as expensive.

✓ If you travel with a notebook PC and a cellular phone, you should consider buying a cellular modem that you can connect to a standard phone line or your cellular phone.

✓ Many users find a multilink connection, that takes advantage of two (or more) modems and phone lines, gives the user reasonable performance at an acceptable price.

Lesson 49

Understanding the Internet and World Wide Web

Each day, tens of millions of users connect to the Internet (users often refer to the Internet as simply the Net) and World Wide Web to exchange electronic-mail messages, to view research information and Web sites, or to pursue recreational activities such as on-line shopping, on-line chats with other users, or even to use their PC speakers and microphone to talk with other users across the Net for free. Several of the lessons that follow will present a wide variety of Internet software.

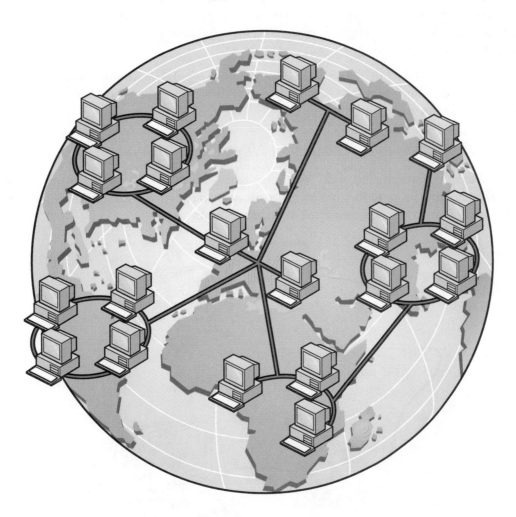

This lesson will introduce you to the Internet and World Wide Web. In Lesson 50, "Getting Connected to the Internet," you will learn how to use an on-line service, such as America Online (AOL), or an Internet Service Provider, to connect to the Net. By the time you finish this lesson, you will understand the following key concepts:

- A network consists of two or more PCs, connected to let users share resources or to communicate via electronic-mail.

- The Internet (which stands for Internetwork) is a network that connects other computer networks worldwide.

285

- Every day, millions of users connect to the Internet to exchange electronic-mail messages, share files, or browse documents on the World Wide Web.

- To connect a network to the Internet, a company simply pays the cost to connect their network to a nearby network that is already connected to the Net. No one company owns the Internet.

- To connect your PC to the Net, you must join an on-line service, such as America Online, or an Internet Service Provider. For a monthly fee you can use your modem to dial into the service which will then provide you with access to the Net.

- Across the Internet, there are millions of documents that cover a wide range of topics. To help users locate the documents they need, programmers created a way to link related documents. Using a program called a browser, users can view a document's contents, and if the document has a link to a related document, the user can click his or her mouse on the link to display the related document's contents.

- After you connect to the Internet, you can run your browser program to view documents on the World Wide Web. You do not need a separate connection to access the Web. The Web is part of the Internet.

THE INTERNET IS A NETWORK OF COMPUTER NETWORKS

In Lesson 33, "Connecting PCs within a Network," you learned that users connect PCs to a network so they can share resources, such as files and printers, or so they can exchange messages via electronic mail. As shown in Figure 49.1, a network is simply two or more computers connected to exchange information.

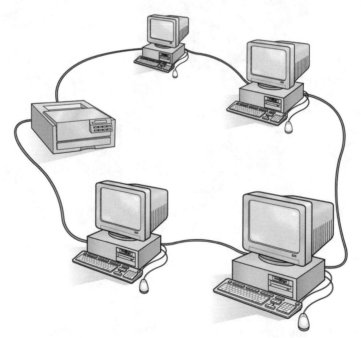

Figure 49.1 *Users connect PCs to networks so they can share resources and communicate electronically.*

The term Internet is an abbreviation for Internetwork—which means between networks. The Internet is simply a network of computer networks. As shown in Figure 49.2, the Internet connects millions of networks worldwide. Because the Internet connects the networks, users in one network can share resources (again, such as files) with users on a different network. Likewise, users can send and receive electronic-mail messages across the Net.

Figure 49.2 *The Internet is a network of networks that connects millions of networks around the globe.*

NO ONE PERSON OR COMPANY OWNS THE INTERNET

The Internet was originally created over 20 years ago to provide users at universities, government facilities, and other research institutions with a way to exchange files and ideas. Initially, the Internet connected only a few networks. At that time, it was easy to think of the Internet as the cables that connected each of the networks. Over time, other universities wanted to connect their networks to the Internet so they too could share resources and communicate with other users across the Net. To connect their network to the Internet, a university would simply pay to install the cables necessary to connect them to another network that was connected to the Net. Over time, the Internet began to grow as facilities would connect their networks to the Net. Depending on the facility's needs and location, the facility might use a fiber-optic connection, a satellite connection, or even a less expensive phone connection. The key point, however, is that the Internet was growing on its own, without ownership by a particular company or country. To maintain organization and to set standards, there are several key organizations that coordinate software design, the issuance of Web-address names, and so on. Many of these organizations are non-profit.

HOW USERS USE THE INTERNET

As you will learn in the lessons that follow, users make extensive use of the Net to send and receive electronic-mail messages and to browse sites on the World Wide Web for content. In addition, users use the Internet to chat with other users. (As you will learn, users chat with one or more other users by exchanging typed text; as one person in the chat types a sentence, the other members in the chat immediately see the user's text.), to exchange files, to talk with other users using a microphone and PC speakers, to play interactive games with one or more users across the Net, and even to exchange video within a Net-based video conference. As you will learn in the lessons that follow, you can participate in most of these Net-based activities using your existing PC and modem.

CONNECTING A NETWORK TO THE INTERNET

For years, the only way to access the Internet was to be fortunate enough to have access to a computer at an organization that was connected to the Net. Public use of the Net did not become widespread until around 1994, when companies, called Internet Service Providers, gave home users a way to connect to the Net. As shown in Figure 49.3, an Internet Service Provider is a company that connects their network to the Net. Then, for a monthly fee, users can gain access to the Internet by dialing into the Internet Service Provider's network using their PC modem. After a user connects his or her PC to an Internet Service Provider, or to an on-line service, such as America Online, the user can send and receive electronic mail across the Net, browse the Web, and use a variety of programs to chat, talk, or fax other users. The user's only cost for connecting to the Net is his or her monthly fee to the Internet Service Provider or on-line service. There are no charges for browsing sites on the Web or for sending and receiving e-mail. After you are connected to the Net, the operations you perform are free.

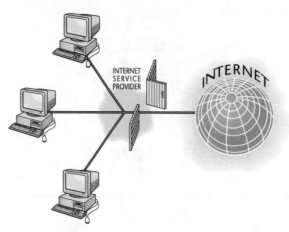

Figure 49.3 *Internet Service Providers and on-line services provide users with access to the Internet.*

UNDERSTANDING THE WORLD WIDE WEB

As the Internet started to grow, so too did the number of documents users would place on the Net. In the early 1990s, there were over a million documents on the Web and users were adding several thousand documents to the Net each day. Unfortunately, it was very difficult for users to determine what information was available on the Net and how to find the information. To organize the Net's content, programmers devised a way to connect related documents. Using a program called a browser, a user could locate a document and view the document's contents (browse the document). If there were other related documents, authors could include *links* to those documents within their text. By clicking his or her mouse on such a link, a user could quickly display the related document's contents. By tying together related documents in this way, authors created a web of related documents that connected documents that resided at computer sites around the globe. In other words, they created a World Wide Web, as shown in Figure 49.4.

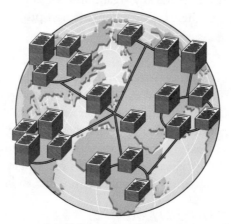

Figure 49.4 *The World Wide Web connects related documents dispersed about the globe.*

Using a Web browser (a software program), you can view the contents of a document that resides at a university on the east coast, and within that document, you may click your mouse on a link that directs your browser to display a document that resides on a computer on the other side of the world. As you move from one document to the next, which users refer to as "surfing the Web" for information, you do so for free. In other words, it does not matter if the document you are viewing resides within your city, state, or even another country, your cost to view the document's contents is the same: free. Figure 49.5 shows a document within a Web browser. Today, the World Wide Web consists of hundreds of millions of documents, whose topics cover just about every imaginable topic.

Figure 49.5 *Viewing a Web document within a browser.*

UNDERSTANDING WHAT YOU WILL NEED TO USE THE NET

Before you can send and receive electronic-mail messages across the Net, or search the Web for content, you must first have an Internet account, that you get through either an Internet Service Provider or an on-line service, such as America Online. Your Internet Service Provider or on-line service will give you the software you need to connect to the Net. In addition, they will likely give you software you can use to send and receive electronic mail and to browse the Web. You will then use your PC's modem to dial into your on-line service or Internet Service Provider. If you are using Windows 98, you can also take advantage of the Internet Explorer (a Web browser) and Outlook Express (an e-mail program) that Microsoft bundles with Windows. In addition, several of the lessons that follow will present software that you can download and install across the Net for free.

WHAT YOU MUST KNOW

Users connect computers to a network to share resources and to communicate on-line. The Internet is simply a network of networks that connects computers around the globe. This lesson introduced you to the Internet and World Wide Web. In Lesson 50, "Getting Connected to the Internet," you will learn how to connect your PC to the Internet using an on-line service or Internet Service Provider. Before you continue with Lesson 50, however, make sure you have learned the following key concepts:

- ✓ The Internet (or Net, as users call it) is a network that connects other networks worldwide.

- ✓ Using the Internet, users can exchange electronic-mail messages, share files, or browse documents on the World Wide Web.

- ✓ No one company or individual owns the Internet. To connect a network to the Internet, a company simply pays the cost to connect their network to a nearby network that is already connected to the Net.

- ✓ Users can connect their PCs to the Net by joining an on-line service, such as America Online, or an Internet Service Provider. For a monthly fee, the user can use his or her modem to dial into the service, which will then provide the user with access to the Net.

- ✓ Across the Internet, there are millions of documents that cover a wide range of topics. To help users locate the documents they need, programmers created the World Wide Web.

Lesson 50

Getting Connected to the Internet

In Lesson 49, "Understanding the Internet and World Wide Web," you learned that the Internet is a network of computer networks that connects computers around the globe. If you are using a PC within a computer network, such as your office or school, you may have access to the Internet through your local-area network. If you do not have such Internet access, you must join an on-line service, such as America Online (AOL) or the Microsoft Network (MSN), or you must subscribe to an Internet Service Provider before you can connect to the Net. After you get an account with a service or provider, you can use your PC's modem and standard telephone lines to connect your PC to the service or provider's network which, in turn, will give you access to the Net.

This lesson examines the steps you must perform to join an on-line service or to subscribe to an Internet Service Provider. By the time you finish this lesson, you will understand the following key concepts:

- If you work in an office that has a local-area network, you may have access to the Net through your network.

- To access the Internet from your personal computer, you must join an on-line service, such as America Online (AOL) or the Microsoft Network (MSN), or you must subscribe to an Internet Service Provider. The on-line service or Internet Service Provider will charge you a monthly fee that will normally give you unlimited access time on the Net.

- In addition to providing you with access to the Internet, most on-line services offer you additional services. You might, for example, shop at your on-line service, use your service to read the daily news or look up stock prices, or make reservations for your next vacation.

- In contrast to an on-line service, most Internet Service Provider's primary function is to provide you with access to the Net.

- When you subscribe to an on-line service or Internet Service Provider, you will receive a username and password that you must specify to access your account, as well as an e-mail address that other users will use to send you electronic mail.

- To connect to your on-line service or Internet Service Provider, you will start your connection software and then type in your username and password. After you are connected, you start other programs to send and receive e-mail, to browse the Web, and so on.

USING AN ON-LINE SERVICE

Even if you did not have a computer in the past, you quite likely, at some point in time, received a CD-ROM from America Online along with an offer to join the on-line service for free. America Online is currently the largest on-line service. Years ago, users would join an on-line service so they could exchange files, send and receive e-mail messages, and even chat with other members of the service. Today, with the popularity of the Internet and World Wide Web, on-line services also provide their users with access to the Internet and Web. In other words, when you join an on-line service, you can use the service itself, to chat, or shop, or even to look up information, or, as shown in Figure 50.1, you can use the service as your entry point to the Internet and the World Wide Web.

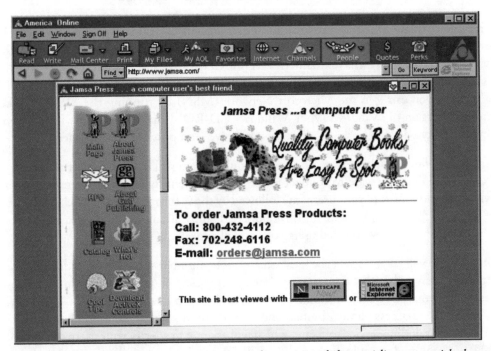

Figure 50.1 *Most on-line services host their own activities and resources while providing users with the option of traveling out on the Internet or World Wide Web.*

When you join an on-line service, you will pay a monthly fee that will normally grant you unlimited access to the service as well as the Internet. Depending on the service you join, the price of your monthly fee may vary slightly. To help you get started, most on-line services will let you try out their service for a month or so for free. The advantage of using an on-line service to access the Internet is that the service is relatively easy to use. Figure 50.2, for example, shows the America Online service. As you can see, within America Online, you can access your electronic-mail, view weather or stock-market reports, chat with other users, or even shop, with one click of your mouse.

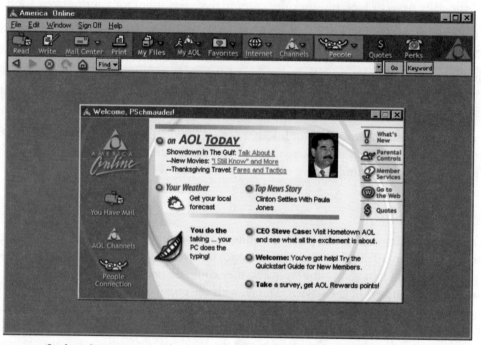

Figure 50.2 *New users find on-line services such as America Online very easy to use.*

Joining an on-line service is easy, you simply run the on-line service's installation program on your PC. The installation program, in turn, will load the on-line service software onto your hard disk and will talk you through the process of joining the service. For example, if you have an America Online CD-ROM, simply insert the CD-ROM into your drive and run the installation program, as discussed in Lesson 20, "Installing New Software on Your PC." Likewise, if you are running Windows, you can join the Microsoft Network (MSN) by running the MSN installation program. (Depending on your version of Windows, your Windows CD-ROM may contain the installation programs for America Online, the Microsoft Network, Prodigy, CompuServe, and possibly other services.)

When you install the on-line service software, the installation program will have you select a username and password that you must enter each time you want to connect to the service. The installation program will also tell you your e-mail address, which should consist of your username followed by the @ (pronounced "at") character, followed by your on-line service name, such as Happy@aol.com (pronounced Happy at aol dot com). Do not tell other users your password. You can and should, however, tell users your e-mail address.

The installation program will let you select the local-access phone number you will use to dial into the service. Write down your username, password (rather than writing down your password, you may want to write down a few words that will remind you of your password, so should someone find your paper, they cannot use its contents to log into your account), and the local-access phone number, and store them in a secure location. To connect to your on-line service, you will start your on-line service software, which will ask you to specify your username and password. Then, your software will use your modem and telephone line to dial the on-line service. Figure 50.3, for example, shows the America Online prompt for a username and password.

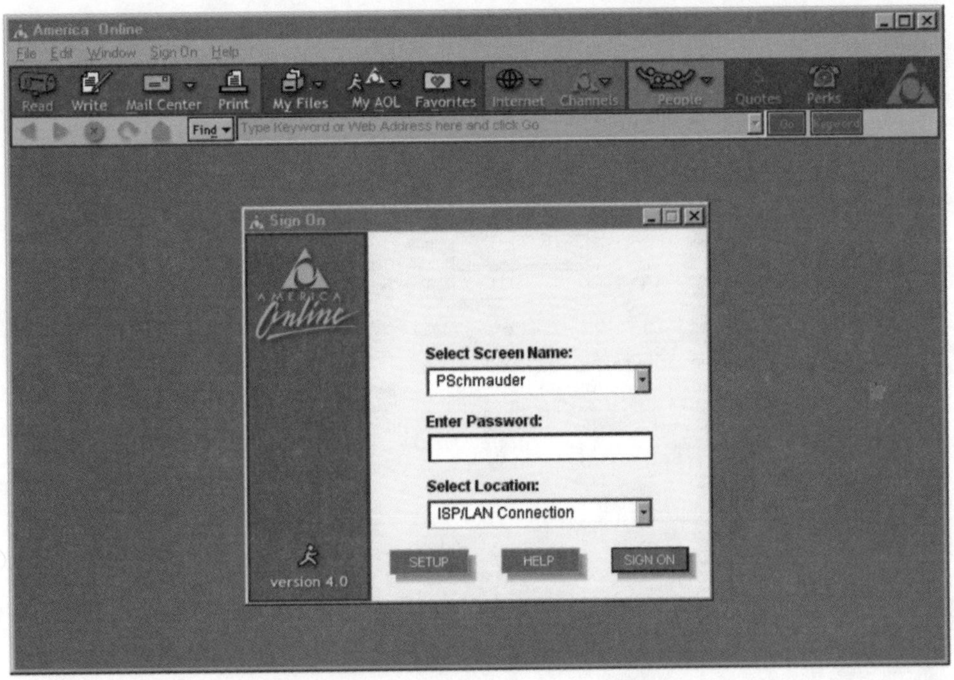

Figure 50.3 *To access your on-line service, you must specify a username and password.*

After you connect to the service, you can use the service's menu-driven interface to run programs or you can simply start your programs, such as the Internet Explorer or Outlook Express, from the Start menu Programs submenu. Figures 50.4 through 50.6 show various activities you can perform within America Online.

Figure 50.4 *Reading the latest world news.*

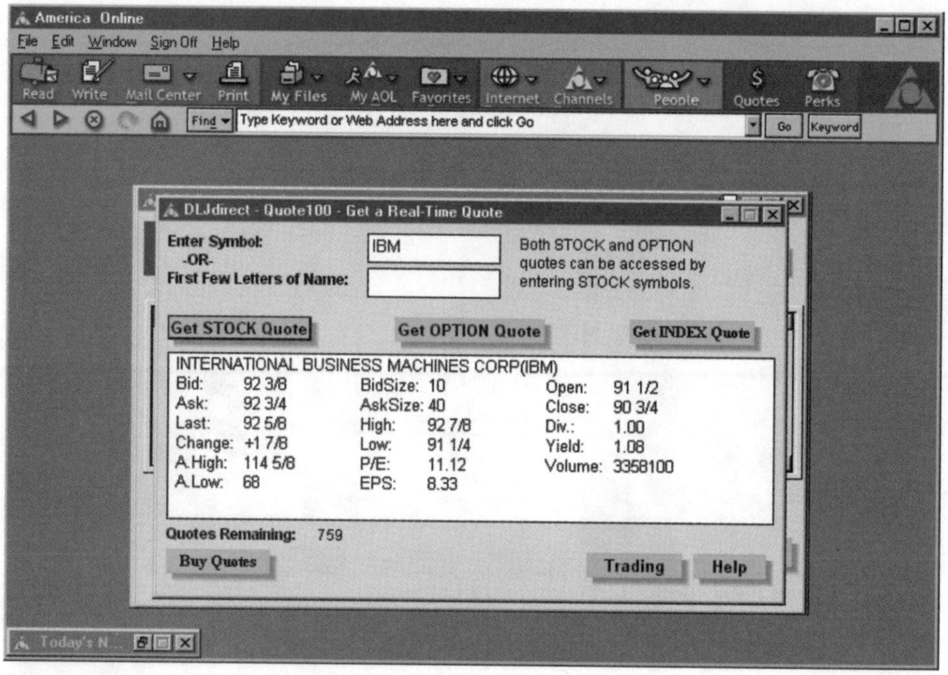

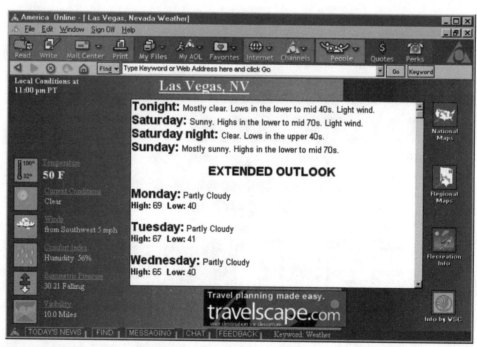

Figure 50.5 *Following your favorite stocks.*

Figure 50.6 *Checking the latest weather reports.*

After you are done using your service, you simply direct your software to disconnect (hang up). Should you later decide that you no longer want to be a member of the service, you can normally terminate your membership on-line or by calling the service on the phone.

USING AN INTERNET SERVICE PROVIDER

An Internet Service Provider differs from an on-line service in that most providers offer few services other than providing you with access to the Internet. You would not, for example, shop at your Internet Service Provider or receive the latest news and weather information. In the past, Internet Service Providers offered users faster access than did an on-line service. However, today, the on-line services, in most cases, have caught up. If you are just getting started, using an on-line service to connect to the Net is probably your best route. To help you get connected, some of the larger on-line services offer free (or very inexpensive) CD-ROMs, that you can get at most computer stores, which you can use to install the provider's software. If your Provider does not provide such software, you can use the Windows Dial-Up Networking Wizard to load the Windows software you need to connect to your Provider. To connect to your Internet Service Provider, you will start your connection software and then type in your username and password. After you are connected to the Net, you can run Internet-based programs, such as your e-mail software or Web browser.

Note: *Recently, cable-TV companies in many larger cities have started to offer high-speed cable-modem connections to the Net. Before you sign up with an Internet Service Provider, you may want to check what capabilities your cable company offers. Using a cable modem connection, you can send and receive e-mail, browse the Web, and run the Internet-based software this book presents. The advantage of the cable-modem connection is speed. The disadvantage is that you will pay a higher monthly fee for the cable-modem service.*

GET YOUR PROVIDER OR SERVICE'S LIST OF LOCAL-ACCESS NUMBERS

If you travel with a notebook PC and you use an on-line service to access the Internet, you can save money on phone charges by learning to use your service's local-access numbers. For example, assume that you live in Texas, but you have traveled to California for a meeting. To access your on-line service from California, you can use your Texas-based phone number to access your account, but in so doing, you must place a long-distance phone call for which you will be charged. Most on-line services provide local-access numbers within all major cities (even outside of the United States) that you can use to access your service as you travel. By using a local-access phone number to access your service, you eliminate long-distance phone charges. For more information on your service's local-access numbers, visit your service's Web site or use the service's on-line help.

WHAT YOU MUST KNOW

If you work in an office that uses a local-area network, you may have access to the Internet through your office network. To connect your home PC to the Internet, however, you must join an on-line service, such as America Online or the Microsoft Network or subscribe to an Internet Service Provider. This lesson briefly introduced you to the steps you must perform to connect your PC to the Net. In Lesson 51, "Exchanging Electronic-Mail (E-Mail) Messages with Users across the Net," you will learn how to send and receive e-mail messages across the Internet. Before you continue with Lesson 51, however, make sure you have learned the following key concepts:

✓ To access the Internet from your personal computer, you must join an on-line service or you must subscribe to an Internet Service Provider. An on-line service or Internet Service Provider will charge you a monthly fee that will normally give you unlimited access time on the Net.

✓ Beyond connecting you to the Net, most on-line services provide a variety of other activities, such as news and information, on-line shopping, on-line reservations and ticketing, and much more.

✓ When you subscribe to an on-line service or Internet Service Provider, you will receive a username and password that you must specify to access your account, as well as an e-mail address that other users will use to send you electronic mail.

✓ After you are connected, you start other programs to send and receive e-mail, to browse the Web, or run other Internet-based programs this book presents.

Lesson 51

Exchanging Electronic-Mail (E-Mail) Messages with Users across the Net

In Lesson 49, "Understanding the Internet and the World Wide Web," you learned how to connect your PC to the Internet. Today, tens of millions of users connect to the Internet each day, simply to send and receive electronic mail. Across the Net, the number of users exchanging e-mail messages each day far exceeds the number of users surfing the World Wide Web—making electronic mail the most widely used Internet-based program.

This lesson examines the steps you must perform to send and receive e-mail messages. The examples this lesson presents use Outlook Express, an electronic-mail program that Microsoft bundles with Windows 98. If you are using a different program for electronic mail, such as Netscape Communicator, or if you are using your on-line service to send and receive e-mail, the steps you perform to send and receive e-mail messages within other programs will be virtually identical to the steps you will perform within Outlook Express. By the time you finish this lesson, you will understand the following key concepts:

- Before a user can send you an electronic-mail message, the user must know your e-mail address. Your on-line service or Internet Service Provider will give you your e-mail name when you subscribe to their service.

- Your e-mail address will normally consist of the username you type to sign onto your Internet account followed by your service's name, such as kjamsa@msn.com. When you tell another user your e-mail address, you pronounce that @ symbol as "at" and the period as "dot," such as "kjamsa at msn dot com."

- Across the Web, there are several Web sites you can use to locate a user's e-mail address.

- To send an e-mail message, you will perform these steps: direct your software to create a new message, type in your recipient's e-mail address, type in a one-line description of your message's subject, type the message text itself, and then direct your e-mail software to send your message.

- To receive an e-mail message, you simply connect to the Net and start your e-mail software. Your e-mail software, in turn, will place an entry for each message you receive within your Inbox folder. To view a message's contents, you simply click your mouse on the message entry within the Inbox list.

- After you read a message, you can print, file, or delete the message. In addition, you can also reply to the user that sent you the message or forward the message to someone else.

- Many Web sites offer free Web-based e-mail accounts that you can use to send and receive e-mail using a Web browser. Such Web-based accounts provide a very convenient way to access your e-mail when you travel.

GETTING STARTED WITH ELECTRONIC-MAIL

To send and receive e-mail across the Internet, you must first have an Internet account or an account with an on-line service. As you learned in Lesson 50, when you get an Internet account, your service will provide you with a username that you will use to log into the service and an e-mail address that others will use to send you electronic-mail messages. Normally, your e-mail address will contain your username, followed by the @ character (pronounced "at"), followed by your service name. For example, if your username is Buddy and your on-line service is America Online (AOL), your e-mail address would be Buddy@aol.com (which you would pronounce as "Buddy at aol dot com). For example, if you wanted to send an e-mail message to the President of the United States, you would use the address president@whitehouse.gov.

Note: If you have business cards, make sure have your e-mail address printed on your cards.

USING E-MAIL, YOU CAN EXCHANGE MESSAGES WITH USERS AROUND THE WORLD FOR FREE

As you learned in Lesson 49, after you connect to the Net, you can view content from Web sites around the world or chat with other users in other cities, states, or countries for free. Likewise, when you send an electronic-mail message to another user across the Net, your message travels the Net for free! Because e-mail is fast and inexpensive, more and more users rely on e-mail each day as their primary means of communication.

Note: Many users will use electronic-mail to correspond with their customers. And, many customers will prefer receiving an e-mail message to a phone call. Although electronic-mail lets you reach customers for free, keep in mind that your customer may receive hundreds of such e-mail messages each day. To get your customer's attention, you may want to use a mix of e-mail, fax, and printed messages.

UNDERSTANDING HOW ELECTRONIC-MAIL WORKS

To send an electronic-mail message, you must first know your recipient's e-mail address. If you do not know an individual's e-mail address, you may be able to use your Web-browser software to look up the individual on the Web, using an e-mail search engine at *www.bigfoot.com* or *www.four11.com*. Lesson 54, "Using Search Engines to Find

Information on the World Wide Web," discusses search engines in detail. Figure 51.1, for example, shows an e-mail search engine at the Yahoo! Web site within which you can type in information about the user you desire. The search engine, in turn, will display a list of e-mail addresses for user's with matching names. If the user has registered with the directory, the user's name will appear within the list.

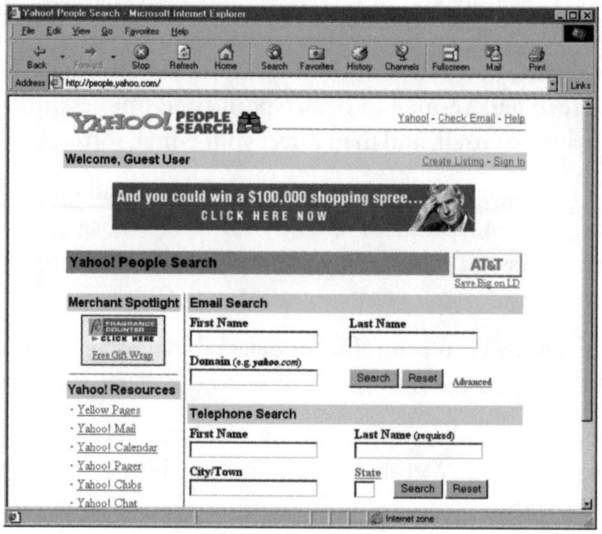

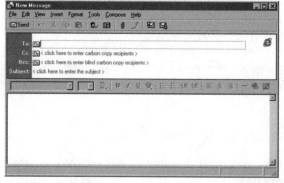

Figure 51.1 *Using a search engine to lo ok up a user's e-mail address.*

Note: *To make it easier for other users to locate your e-mail address, you should use your browser to visit the Bigfoot and Four11 Web sites and register your e-mail address.*

After you address, type, and then send your e-mail message, your message will travel across the Net to its recipient. If the user is currently connected to the Net, he or she will shortly receive your message. If the user is not on-line, your message will wait at the user's e-mail server (either at his or her on-line service or at his or her company) until the user connects to the Net and starts his or her e-mail software. If the user is traveling, he or she may forward his or her e-mail to a different e-mail account so that he or she can receive his or her messages while on the road.

SENDING AN E-MAIL MESSAGE

Before you can send or receive electronic -mail messages, you must first start your e-mail software. Depending on the e-mail program you are using, the steps you must perform to start the program will differ. Before you can send an e-mail message, you must first type and then address your message. To create a message within Outlook Express, for example, you click your mouse on the Compose button. Outlook Express, in turn, will display the New Message dialog box, as shown in Figure 51.2.

Figure 51.2 *The New Message dialog box.*

To address your e-mail message, click your mouse within the New Message dialog box To field and then type in your recipient's e-mail address. Next, click your mouse within the New Message dialog box Subject field and type in a brief one-line description of your message's contents. When your recipient receives your e-mail message, his or her e-mail software will list your message with the others he or she has received, displaying your name, your message topic, and the date and time his or her mail server recieved the message. Make sure, therefore, that you type in a descriptive message topic. Next, click your mouse within the message-text field that appears at the bottom of the New Message dialog box. Within the message-text field, type your message. Your message can be a few words long, a few sentences long, or it may contain as many pages as you need. Figure 51.3, for example, shows a brief e-mail message.

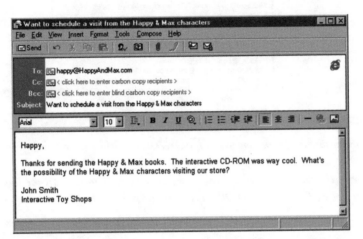

Figure 51.3 *An addressed and typed e-mail message.*

After you type your message, you simply click your mouse on the Send button to send your message across the Net. If, for some reason, the message does not reach its recipient (perhaps the user has changed e-mail addresses or you mistyped his or her address), you will normally receive an e-mail message within a few hours of sending your message that tells you that your message did not reach its recipient. If you do not receive an error message, you can feel confident that your message arrived. You cannot tell, however, whether or not the recipient has read your message. If you examine the New Message dialog box closely, you will find that in addition to the To field, the dialog box provides a Cc field and a Bcc field. The Cc field lets you send a courtesy copy of your message to other users. When your primary recipient receives your message, he or she will also see the names of any users to whom you have sent a courtesy copy. In contrast, the Bcc field lets you send a blind courtesy copy of your message to another user, of which your other recipients will be unaware.

Note: *To send an e-mail message to two or more users, you must type each user's e-mail addresses. Normally, you will separate one user's e-mail address from another using a semicolon, such as happy@jamsa.com; president@whitehouse.gov.*

RECEIVING AN E-MAIL MESSAGE

To receive e-mail messages, you simply need to connect to the Net and then start your e-mail software. As you receive messages, your e-mail software will place your messages within a special folder called your Inbox. Figure 51.4 shows a list of messages within a user's Inbox. Note that the software lists who sent each message, the message's topic, as well as the date and time the your mail server received the message. To read a message, you simply click your mouse on the message entry within the Inbox list. After you read the message, most e-mail programs will let you print, file, or delete the message. In addition, you can also reply to the message, which directs your e-mail software to send the original message, plus any new text that you type, back to the user who originally sent you the message. Likewise, you can forward the message to another user.

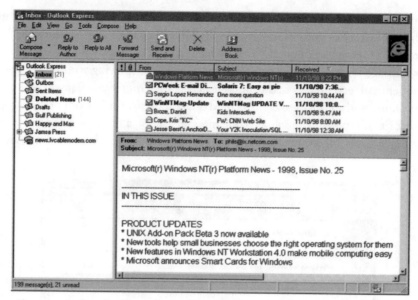

Figure 51.4 *Most e-mail programs list the messages you have received within your Inbox folder.*

Note: *This lesson only presents the very basics of sending and receiving electronic-mail messages. For more information on Outlook Express, refer to the book 1001 Windows 98 Tips, Jamsa Press, 1998.*

GET A FREE HOTMAIL ACCOUNT

As you have learned, when you use an on-line service or Internet Service Provider to access the Internet, you will receive an e-mail address which other users can use to send you electronic messages. To receive your messages, you must connect to your account and then start your e-mail software. If you travel, there may be times when you have trouble connecting to your account, either because your hotel does not offer a phone connection you can use to access the Net or possibly because your modem does not work with European dial tones.

To prevent problems accessing your e-mail, you should sign up with a free e-mail service, such as Hotmail, that lets you access your e-mail using a Web browser. When you sign up for a free Web-based e-mail account, you will get another e-mail address and a password.

If, for some reason, you have trouble accessing your e-mail account, you can have users send your mail to your free Web-based account. Then, from any computer that can access the Web, you can get access to your mail. If you are in Europe, for example, you could access your mail from an Internet café (a coffee bar that provides on-line access). Likewise, if you are at a hotel, you may be able to access your e-mail from a computer in the hotel's business center.

You can use your Web browser to sign up for a free Web-based e-mail account at Web sites such as *www.hotmail.com*. Figure 51.5, for example, shows an e-mail message being read within a browser from a Web-based e-mail account. In addition to letting you receive messages at a Web-based account, you can send messages.

Note: *If your family shares the same on-line service or provider-based Internet account, each member of your family can sign up for his or her own Web-based e-mail account, which lets everyone send and receive messages privately.*

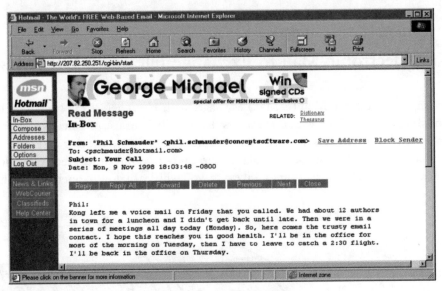

Figure 51.5 *Reading an e-mail message at a Web-based e-mail account.*

What You Must Know

Across the Internet, electronic-mail is, by far, the most widely-used application. Each day, hundreds of millions of e-mail messages make their way across the Net. In this lesson, you learned the basics of sending and receiving e-mail messages. In Lesson 52, "Using Electronic-Mail to Exchange Files with Other Users," you will learn how to exchange files, such as word-processing or spreadsheet documents, with other users by attaching the files to e-mail messages. Before you continue with Lesson 52, however, make sure you have learned the following key concepts:

✓ When you sign up with an on-line service or Internet Service Provider, your service will give you an e-mail address that other users will use to send you electronic messages.

✓ Before you can send an e-mail message to another user, you must know the other user's e-mail address.

✓ Within most e-mail programs, the steps you must perform to send an e-mail message are quite similar: direct your software to create a new message, type in your recipient's e-mail address, type in a one-line description of your message's subject, type the message text itself, and then direct your e-mail software to send your message.

✓ To receive an e-mail message, you simply connect to the Net and start your e-mail software. Your e-mail software, in turn, will place an entry for each message you receive within your Inbox folder. To view a message's contents, you simply click your mouse on the message entry within the Inbox list.

✓ After you read a message, you can print, file, or delete the message. In addition, you can also reply to the user that sent you the message or forward the message to someone else.

✓ Across the Web, many sites offer free Web-based e-mail accounts. By subscribing to a Web-based account, you can send and receive e-mail using a Web browser—from any computer that is connected the Web.

Lesson 52

Using Electronic-Mail to Exchange Files with Other Users

In Lesson 51, "Exchanging Electronic-Mail (E-Mail) Messages with Users across the Net," you learned how to use electronic-mail (e-mail) to communicate with users across the Net. As your use of e-mail grows, it will not take long before you will want to send word-processing documents or spreadsheet files to another user via e-mail. In this lesson, you will learn how to "attach" such files to your e-mail messages. When your recipient receives your message, he or she can open or save the document on his or her system. Likewise, you will learn how to open or save the files that another user sends to you via e-mail.

By the time you finish this lesson, you will understand the follow key concepts:

- Using electronic mail, you can send document files to another user. To send a user a file via e-mail, you must attach the file to an e-mail message that you send to the user.

- Just as you can send files via e-mail, you may also receive files that another user is sending to you. When an e-mail message contains an attached file, most e-mail programs will display an icon, such as a paper-clip next to the message title.

- Within your e-mail program, you can save your attached files to disk or you can open the files.

- To reduce your risk of encountering a computer virus, you should never open a document given to you by another user until you first scan the document for viruses using a virus-detection program.

ATTACHING A DOCUMENT FILE TO AN E-MAIL MESSAGE

As you have learned, using e-mail, you can send a message to another user anywhere in the world. When you send messages, you can direct your e-mail software to attach a file to the message you are going to send. For example, assume that you have spent the weekend using your home PC to create a report for your boss. After you complete the report, you can use your e-mail software to attach the document file to an e-mail message that you send to your boss, as shown in Figure 52.1.

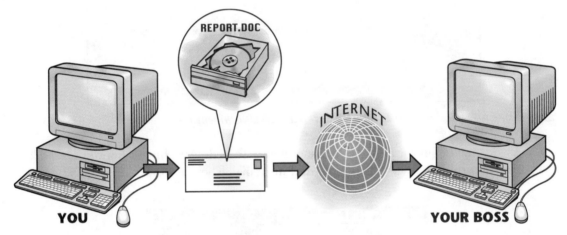

Figure 52.1 *Attaching a document file to an e-mail message.*

Later, when your boss receives your e-mail message, he or she can save the "attached" document to a file on his or her disk, as shown in Figure 52.2.

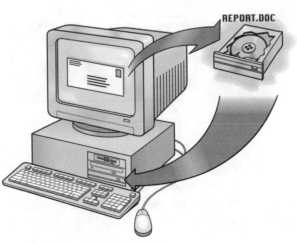

Figure 52.2 *Saving an attached document to a file on disk.*

Regardless of the e-mail software you are using, the steps you must perform to attach a document to an e-mail message are similar: you will create and address an e-mail message and then, normally, you will use an Insert menu option to attach the file to the message. For example, to attach a document to an e-mail message within Outlook Express, perform these steps:

1. Create and address your e-mail message. Within the message-text area, include a brief note explaining that you have attached a document file, as shown in Figure 52.3.

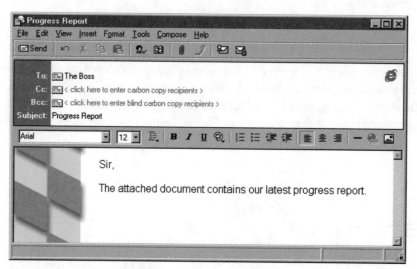

Figure 52.3 *Creating an e-mail message to which you can attach a document file.*

2. Click your mouse on the Insert menu and choose the File Attachment option. Outlook Express, in turn, will display the Insert Attachment dialog box, as shown in Figure 52.4.

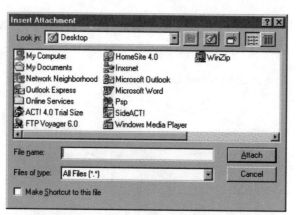

Figure 52.4 *The Insert Attachment dialog box.*

3. The Insert Attachment dialog box is similar to an Open dialog box, within which you first locate the folder that contains the document you want to insert and then you click on the document itself. After you select the file you want to attach, click your mouse on the Attach button. Outlook Express, in turn, will display an icon for your attachd file near the bottom of your message, as shown in Figure 52.5.

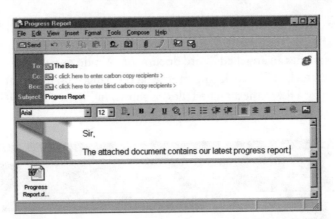

Figure 52.5 *Outlook Express displays icons for attached documents beneath your message.*

4.   To send your message and the attached file, click your mouse on the Send button.

Note: *Most e-mail programs let you attach multiple files to an e-mail message. However, as the number of files you attach to a message grows, so too will the message's size, which will increase the amount of time you need to transmit and that your recipient needs to receive the message. If you must send a user multiple files, you should consider compressing the files using the WinZip utility discussed in Lesson 56, "Compressing a File's Contents Using the WinZip Utility."*

Saving or Opening an Attached Message

When another user sends you a message that contains an attached file, your e-mail software will normally display a paper-clip icon on your message to inform you of the attachment. Figure 52.6, for example, shows a paper-clip icon within the current message's title bar.

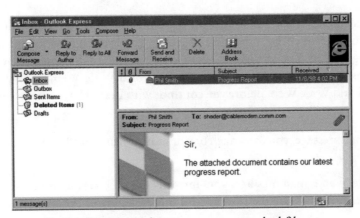

Figure 52.6 *The paper-clip icon tells you the message has one or more attached files.*

Again, depending on the e-mail software you are using, the steps you must perform to save or open an attached file will differ. Within Outlook Express, for example, you can save an attached file to a file on your disk by selecting the File menu Save Attachments option. Outlook Express, in turn, will display a Save Attachments As dialog box, within which you can select the folder within which you want to save the file.

If your message has multiple files attached, again select the File menu Save Attachments option. Outlook Express, in turn, will display the name of each attached file. Within the file list, you can select a specific file that you want to save, or you can select the All option to save all the files in one step. In either case, Outlook Express will display the Save Attachments As dialog box, within which you can select the folder within which you want to store the files.

In addition to letting you save an attached file to disk, you can also open the attached file from within your e-mail program (without first saving the file's contents). Windows, in turn, will start the program that corresponds to the file's type. For example, if the message has an attached Word document, Windows would start Microsoft Word to display the file's contents. To open an attached file, click your mouse on the paper-clip icon that appears in the message's title bar. Outlook Express will display a list of the attached files, as shown in Figure 52.7. To open a file, click your mouse on the corresponding filename within the list of attached files.

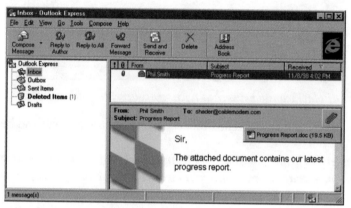

Figure 52.7 *Displaying a list of the attached filenames.*

Note: *Lesson 59, "Protecting Your PC from Computer Viruses," discusses how opening a document that you receive from another user via e-mail can infect your system with a virus. As discussed in Lesson 59, you should not open document files that you receive from another user until you scan the file using a virus-detection program.*

WHAT YOU MUST KNOW

As your use of electronic-mail grows, you will eventually use e-mail to send and receive documents, such as reports, memos, or spreadsheets, to and from other users. In this lesson, you learned how to attach a document file to an e-mail message you are going to send. You also learned how to save or open a document that you receive from another user. In Lesson 53, "Surfing Your Way to Information on the World Wide Web," you will learn how to locate and view information on the World Wide Web. Before you continue with Lesson 53, however, make sure you have learned the following key concepts:

✓ Within an e-mail message, you can attach one or more document files that you can then send to another user.

✓ To attach a file to an e-mail message, you normally use an Insert menu option. In Outlook Express, for example, you use the Insert menu File Attachment option.

✓ When you receive an e-mail message that has an attached file, your e-mail software will normally display an icon, such as a paper-clip, next to the message title to inform you of the attached files.

✓ To save attached files to your disk, you will normally use a File menu option. In Outlook Express, for example, you will use the File menu Save Attachments option.

✓ Most e-mail programs will also let you open an attached file's contents. To display the attached file's contents, Windows will start the program used to create the file, such as Word or Excel.

✓ To reduce your risk of encountering a computer virus, never open a document given to you by another user until you first scan the document for viruses using a virus-detection program.

Lesson 53

Surfing Your Way to Information on the World Wide Web

These days, it's hard to pick up a magazine whose advertisements don't include a company or product's address on the Web, or watch a TV show or motion picture that does not have its own Web site. In a few short years, the World Wide Web has become a very powerful vehicle for the dissemination of information. In Lesson 50, "Getting Connected to the Internet," you learned that after you connect to the Internet, you can use Web-browsing software to view sites on the World Wide Web.

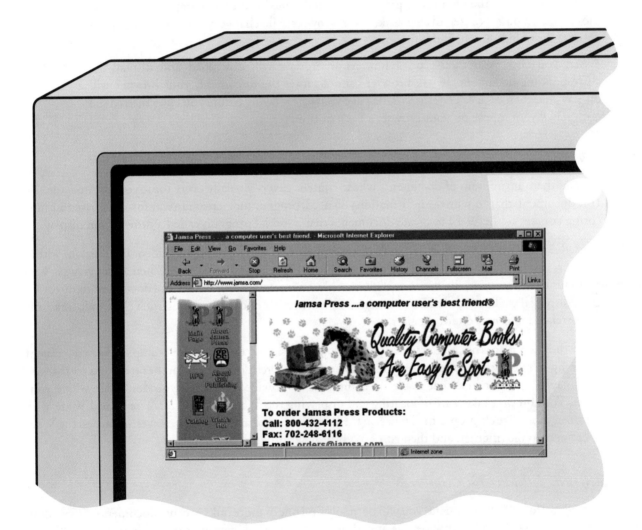

This lesson examines the steps you must perform to view Web documents and to move from one Web site to another (a process users refer to as *surfing the Web*). By the time you finish this lesson, you will understand the following key concepts:

- The World Wide Web, like electronic-mail, relies on the Internet. If you have access to the Internet, you can access the Web, much like you can send and receive e-mail. To view documents on the Web, you must have a Web-browsing program.

- The World Wide Web is so named because, conceptually, the documents that make up the Web contain links to other related documents. When you "surf" the Web, you really just use your browser to move from one document's contents to the next.

- The Web consists of millions of sites, each of which must have a unique name, such as *www.microsoft.com*. Users often refer to a Web site's name as the site's URL (Uniform Resource Locator).

- Within your browser, you view a Web site's content by typing in the site's address within your browser's Address field.

- Documents on the Web may contain text, graphics, and links to other documents. Depending on the site's design, the site may display a link as underlined text or as a graphic. When you move your mouse pointer over a link, your browser will change your mouse pointer's appearance to indicate the link's presence.

- When you click your mouse on a link, your browser will download and display the corresponding document. If you browser cannot locate the document, your browser will display an error message. To return to the page you were viewing before you encountered the error, click your mouse on your browser's Back button.

Understanding Why the Web Exists

Across the Internet, there are millions of documents whose content covers virtually every topic you can imagine. To help you find the documents that contain the information you need, programmers created a way for Web-based authors (people who bring content to the Web) to create documents that a special program called a browser can display.

Within Web-based documents, the authors can include text, photos, as well as audio and video. In addition, within a document, authors can include electronic references (links) to other related documents. When a user views a Web document within his or her browser, the user can click his or her mouse on a link within the document to direct his or her browser to display the related document's contents. By connecting documents using such electronic links, the Web ties together related information for the user.

When you browse the Web, it does not matter where your document resides. You might, for example, view a document that resides on a computer in Seattle that contains links to documents that reside in Europe or the far east. As you browse documents, you may view documents that reside on computers worldwide. As a user, you don't care where your document resides. Your browser takes care of locating and displaying the document for you. The World Wide Web relies on the Internet, much like electronic-mail relies on the Internet to send and receive messages. To access the Web, you must first connect to the Internet, and then run a Web-browser program.

Understanding Linked Documents

As you have learned, within a Web document, you will normally find one or more links to other documents. Depending on the page you are viewing, the link may appear as underlined text, or the link may appear as a photo or icon. Within a Web document, you can determine which items are links and which aren't by watching your mouse pointer. Normally, as shown in Figure 53.1, when you move your mouse pointer over a link, your browser will change your mouse pointer's appearance, normally to a pointing hand.

Figure 53.1 Your browser will change your mouse pointer's appearance when you move the pointer over a link.

When you click your mouse on a link, the browser will display the link's corresponding document. Depending on the Web designer who created your current page, the browser may display the new document within its current window, replacing its current contents, or the browser may open a new window within which it displays the new document's contents.

UNDERSTANDING HOW YOUR BROWSER RETRIEVES A WEB SITE'S FILES

As you have learned, to display a Web site's contents, you type in the site's Web address within your browser's Address field or, you click your mouse on a link that corresponds to the site. In either case, when you direct your browser to display a site, your browser will (behind the scenes) contact the site's Web server and ask the server to start downloading the text and graphics that make up the site's content. Depending on the number and size of the site's graphics files, and depending on the speed of your modem connection, the length of time you must wait for a site to download its contents will vary. As your browser downloads files from the site, you browser may display a small status bar at the bottom of its windows that you can use to determine the percentage of the site's files the browser has downloaded.

You won't have to visit very many sites on the Web before you start will thinking about buying a faster modem. Depending on a sites contents and your modem speed, you may have to wait a minute, or even several minutes, for a site to download its files.

If, as you browse, you return to a site whose contents you have previously viewed, you will find that your browser displays the site's contents almost instantly on your screen. That's because your browser stores the files for your recently viewed sites temporarily on your disk. In this way, if you revisit a site, your browser can contact the site to find out if any of the files it previously downloaded have changed, and, if not, your browser can quickly display the files it has stored on your disk.

Over time, your browser will replace one site's files with those of a site you visited more recently. After your browser discards a site's files, your browser will later need to download the site's files again should you revisit the site. Also, in Lesson 19, "Cleaning Up Your Disk," you learned that when your disk becomes low on space, you should delete your temporary Internet files—which are the files that correspond to the sites your browser has previously downloaded.

MOVING BACK A PAGE

As you browse, there will be times when you follow a link to either a site that no longer exists, in which case your browser will display a message telling you that it could not find the site, or to a site whose content is not what you desire. To return to your previous site, simply click your mouse on your browser's Back button, which appears similar to that shown in Figure 53.2. Your browser, in turn, will reload your previous page.

Figure 53.2 *To return to the previous page, click your mouse on your browser's Back button.*

WHAT YOU NEED TO BROWSE THE WEB

Just as you need e-mail software to send and receive electronic mail, to view documents on the Web, you must have Web-browsing software (which users refer to as a *browser*). Today, the two most widely used browsers are the Netscape Navigator and Microsoft Internet Explorer. When you subscribe to an on-line service, your service may provide you with one of these two browsers for free. If you are using Windows 98, Microsoft includes (bundles for free) the Internet Explorer software. Both the Internet Explorer and Netscape Navigator are excellent programs and both offer almost identical features. Figure 53.3 shows the Internet Explorer and Netscape Navigator each displaying the contents of the Happy & Max Web site, at *www.happyandmax.com*. As you can see, both browsers will display a site's content in much the same way.

Figure 53.3 *Viewing a Web site's contents within the Internet Explorer and Netscape Navigator.*

UNDERSTANDING WEB ADDRESSES

Across the Web, there are millions of sites that contain a variety of documents. Each site on the Web must have a unique name, such as *www.microsoft.com* or *www.jamsa.com*. Users will refer to a site's name as the site's Web address or the site's URL (Uniform Resource Locator). If you know a site's Web address, you simply need to type the address within your browser's address bar, as shown in Figure 53.4.

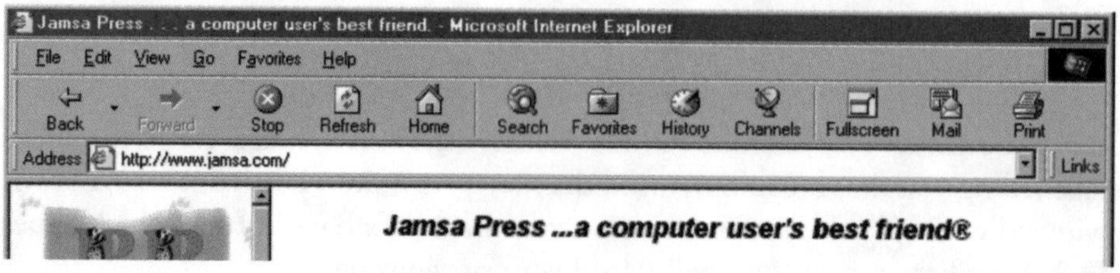

Figure 53.4 *To view a site's contents, simply type the site's Web address within your browser's address bar.*

To get you started, Table 53 lists the addresses for several sites you should visit. As you might guess, as you surf the Web, one of your first challenges is to find the sites that contain the information you need. In Lesson 54, "Using Search Engines to Find Information on the World Wide Web," you will learn that there are special sites on the Web, called *search engines*, that you can visit using your browser. Within the search-engine site, you type your topic of interest, such as computer, or sports, or wine, and the search-engine software will display a list of sites across the Web that discuss your topic.

Site	Web Address
NASA	www.nasa.gov
Whitehouse	www.whitehouse.gov
New York Times	www.nytimes.com
Jamsa Press	www.jamsa.com
Yahoo!	www.yahoo.com
CNN	www.cnn.com
Weather Channel	www.weather.com
MedicineNet	www.medicine.net

Table 53 *Sites you should visit as you surf the World Wide Web.*

As you type in a Web address, there may be times when you mistype one or more characters within the site's address. To edit the address, simply click your mouse within the Address field and then use your keyboard arrow keys to edit the address.

USING BOOK MARKS TO MARK THE CURRENT PAGE

As you browse, there will be times when you come across a site whose content you know you will want to view again. In such cases, you can assign a book mark to the site that you can later use within your browser to return to the site without having to type in the site's name. If you are using Netscape Navigator, you can create a book mark, by performing these steps:

1. Within Netscape Navigator, display the site you desire.

2. Select the Netscape Navigator Communicator menu Bookmarks option and then choose Add Bookmark. Netscape, in turn, will add the sites to its Bookmarks menu.

If you are using the Internet Explorer, rather than assigning a book mark to the site, you will assign the site to your list of Favorite sites, which you can access from the Favorites menu, as shown in Figure 53.5.

Figure 53.5 *Accessing a site from the Internet Explorer Favorites menu.*

To add a site to the Internet Explorer Favorites menu, perform these steps:

1. Within the Internet Explorer, display the site you desire.

2. Select the Internet Explorer Favorites menu Add to Favorites option. The Internet Explorer, in turn, will display the Add Favorite dialog box.

3. Within the Add Favorite dialog box, click your mouse on OK.

USING YOUR BROWSER'S HISTORY LIST TO RETURN TO A SITE YOU'VE PREVIOUSLY VISITED

As you surf for information on the Web, you will often return to a site that you have previously visited. To help reduce your typing, your browser maintains a list of the sites whose contents you have viewed—a history. If you want to return to a site you previously viewed, you simply open the history list and click your mouse on the site you desire. To open the history list within the Internet Explorer, click your mouse on the pull-down arrow that appears at the right end of the address bar. Internet Explorer, in turn, will display the pull-down list, as shown in Figure 53.6.

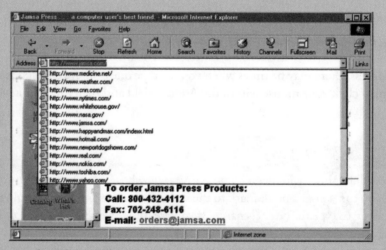

Figure 53.6 *Displaying a list of the Web sites you have recently visited within the Internet Explorer.*

To add the current site to the Netscape Navigator Bookmarks menu, select the Communicator menu Bookmarks option and choose Add Bookmark. The Netscape Navigator, in turn, will add the site to the Bookmarks menu.

UNDERSTANDING WEB PAGES THAT USE FRAMES

As you have learned, a window is a framed rectangular region on your screen, within which a program displays its output. Depending on the various types of information a site must present, some sites will direct the browser to display a series of window frames, similar to those shown in Figure 53.7.

Within the browser window, you can use the scroll bars the browser displays next to a frame to scroll through the frame's contents. In addition, you can normally size each frame to meet your needs. When you click your mouse on a link that appears within a frame, your browser will display the new page within only that frame, as opposed to overwriting the browser window's contents.

Figure 53.7 Some sights use frames to display different content within the same window.

SENDING A PAGE TO ANOTHER USER

As you surf the Web, there will be times when you find an informative or cool site whose contents you want to share with other users. An easy way to tell users about a site is simply to send them an e-mail message that contains the site's Web address—which you could do by creating a new e-mail message and typing in the address.

If you are using the Internet Explorer to surf the Web, the process becomes even easier. Simply select the Internet Explorer's File menu Send option. The Internet Explorer, in turn, will cascade the Send menu. Within the Send menu, click your mouse on either the Page by Email or Link by Email option, depending on whether you want to send the user the page's contents or simply a link to the page (most users will prefer to receive the link). Next, the Internet Explorer will open an e-mail dialog box within which you can type the addresses of each individual to whom you want to send the message and possibly a brief message explaining the link's contents. To send your message, click your mouse on the Send button.

If you are using Netscape, you can select the File menu Send Page option to send the page (and a link to the page) to your recipient.

PRINTING THE CURRENT PAGE

As you view a site's contents within your browser, there will be times when you will want to print the page's current contents. Normally, to print the current page, you can simply click your mouse on your browser's Print button. If, however, the page contains one or more frames, the Print button will direct your browser to only print the current frame. If you want to print each frame's contents, you should select the File menu Print option. Your browser, in turn, will display the Print dialog box, within which you can specify how you want the browser to print each frame's contents. If you are using Netscape, you can use the File menu to print the current frame.

WHAT YOU MUST KNOW

Each day, millions of users browse the World Wide Web in pursuit of a wide range of content. In this lesson, you learned that to view a Web site's content, you simply type in the Web site's address within the browser's Address field. As you view a site's content within your browser, you may find a link that corresponds to a related document. When you click your mouse on the link, your browser will display the new document's contents. At that point, you have officially "surfed" the Web. In Lesson 54, "Using Search Engines to Find Information on the World Wide Web," you will learn how to use search-engine sites, such as Yahoo!, to locate information on the Web. Before you continue with Lesson 54, however, make sure you have learned the following key concepts:

✓ The World Wide Web is part of the Internet. If you have access to the Internet, you can access the Web.

✓ Across the Web, there are millions of sites, each of which that will present information on a specific topic. Each site on the Web must have a unique name, such as *www.microsoft.com*. Users often refer to a Web site's name as the site's URL (Uniform Resource Locator).

✓ To view a Web site's content, you simply type in the Web site's address within your browser's Address field.

✓ As you view a site's content within your browser, you may encounter links to related documents. Depending on the site's design, the site may display a link as underlined text or as a graphic. When you move your mouse pointer over a link, your browser will change your mouse pointer's appearance to indicate the link's presence.

✓ When you click your mouse on a link, your browser will download and display the corresponding document. If your browser cannot locate the document, your browser will display an error message. To return to the page you were viewing before you encountered the error, click your mouse on your browser's Back button.

Lesson 54

Using Search Engines to Find Information on the World Wide Web

In Lesson 53, "Surfing Your Way to Information on the World Wide Web," you learned that the Web consists of millions of sites with hundreds of millions of documents. Across the Web, there are documents that discuss virtually every topic you can imagine. The challenging part of surfing the Web is locating the documents that contain the information that you need. In this lesson, you will learn how to use special software called a search engine to locate sites that discuss topics you desire. As you will learn, across the Web there are several sites, such as Yahoo! at *www.yahoo.com*, that feature search engines that you can use to locate information.

In general, to locate information on the Web, you will use your browser to connect to a search-engine site, such as Yahoo!. At that site, you will type in your topic of interest and then direct the site to perform a search. The search engine, in turn, will display a list of documents across the Web that discuss your topic. In some cases, the search engine will find thousands of sites that discuss your topic. At other times, the search engine will find only a few sites or possibly none at all.

This lesson examines how you can use search engines to find the information you desire, and then how you can fine-tune your searches to produce a higher quality list of topic sites. By the time you finish this lesson, you will understand the following key concepts:

- Across the Web, there are millions of sites and hundreds of millions of documents. To find information on the Web, you must use a search engine.

- A search engine is software that examines a topic you specify and then returns a listing of sites that discuss your topic.

- Across the Web, several companies offer search engines, the best known being the Yahoo! Web site at *www.yahoo.com*.

- When you search for information on the Web, you should type in several words that relate closely to your topic. If, for example, you are interested in children's books, you might direct the search engine to search for **children's books**. However, if you are interested in the Happy & Max books, you might direct the search engine to search for **Happy & Max children's books**.

- Normally, a search engine will return a list of several hundred sites (sometimes hundreds of thousands of sites) that discuss your topic. If, for some reason, the search engine cannot find sites that discuss your topic, try searching for a more general topic or try searching at a different search engine.

WEB SITES THAT FEATURE SEARCH ENGINES

As briefly discussed, a search engine is special software you can use to search a Web site or several Web sites for a specific topic. Across the Web, there are several Web sites that feature search engines. Table 54 lists several of the most popular search-engine sites. To locate information on the Web, use your browser to connect to one of the sites listed in Table 54. Your browser, in turn, will display the site's home page. For example, if you connect to the Yahoo! search engine, your browser will display the Yahoo! home page, as shown in Figure 54.1.

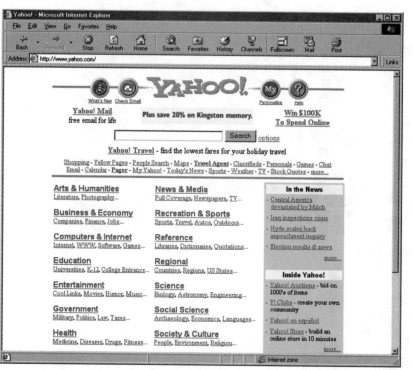

Figure 54.1 Using your browser to connect to the Yahoo! search engine.

Site	Address
AltaVista	www.altavista.com
Excite	www.excite.com
InfoSeek	www.infoseek.com
Lycos	www.lycos.com
Yahoo!	www.yahoo.com

Table 54 *The Web addresses of popular search-engine sites.*

Within the Yahoo! Web page, you will find a small text box, within which you will type the topic you desire. For example, if you are interested in computer books, you would type **Computer Books** within the text box and then click your mouse on the Search button. The Yahoo! search engine, in turn, will display a list of sites that discuss computer books, as shown in Figure 54.2.

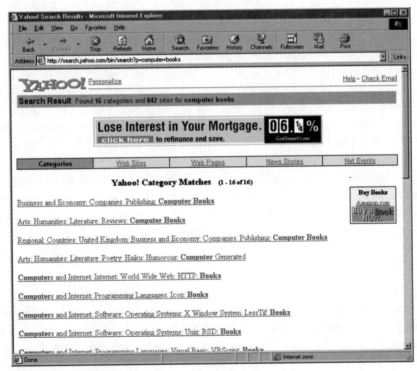

Figure 54.2 *The search engine's list of sites that discuss computer books.*

If you examine the search engine's results page, you should see text that describes the number of sites the search engine located that discussed your topic. Within the search engine's site list, you simply click your mouse on an entry's link to display the site's contents. If the site does not have the content you desire, you can click your mouse on your browser's Back button to return to the search engine's site list, within which you can click your mouse on a different link to view another site's contents.

Depending on your topic, the search engine may locate thousands, if not hundreds of thousands, of sites that discuss your topic. Normally, the search engine will sort its topic list beginning with the site the search engine considers most likely to contain the information that you desire. As you scroll down through the search engine's results page, you may find a link to the next page of matching sites. To view the next page, simply click your mouse on the link.

How Search Engines Work

As you have learned, across the Web there are millions of Web sites and hundreds of millions of documents. It is the job of companies that run Web sites to locate and index these documents. To learn about documents, these companies write programs that scour the Web for content (programmers refer to programs that move from one Web site to another in pursuit of topics as *Web crawlers* or *robots*). Also, to ensure that sites such as Yahoo! know about their products, many companies will send the search engine companies specifics about their Web sites and documents they contain. Each search engine simply maintains huge databases that store topic indexes and related sites. The companies that run search engines earn their revenues through advertisements. If you examine the search engine's home page, you will encounter numerous advertisements. Then, after you perform a search operation, you will find that the advertisements often relate, in some way, to your search topic.

REFINING YOUR SEARCH

As you search for topics on the Web, there will be many times when a search engine returns more sites than you can ever possibly search. In such cases, you must refine your search criteria, which you can do by simply typing in a more descriptive topic. For example, if, rather than viewing sites on computer books in general, you want to view sites that discuss Jamsa Press computer books, you could type in **Jamsa Press computer books** as your search criteria. If you are interested in Jamsa Press computer books that discuss programming, you might type **Jamsa Press computer books programming**. As you make your topic more specific, the search engine can better identify sites that will contain the information that you desire. In addition, some Web sites will let you use the words AND and OR within your within your search criteria. For example, assume that you are interested in sites that discuss computer programming and the Internet. Within your search topic, you might type **Computer programming AND Internet**. Likewise, if you are looking for sites that discuss either Bill Gates or Janet Reno, you would use the word OR within your search topic: **Bill Gates OR Janet Reno**. If, for some reason, the search engine does not find sites that discuss your topic, try your search again using a more general topic. For example, if you are interested in dinosaur footprints, you may have to search first for dinosaur. In addition, try your search at other search engines. Remember, Table 54 lists several popular search engines, of which will list different documents for various topics.

WHAT YOU MUST KNOW

To make effective use of the Web, you must be able to find the information you need. To find information on the Web, you should take advantage of search engines. In this lesson, you learned how use a search engine to find sites on the Web that discuss a specific topic. Often, you will start your travels across the Web at a site, such as Yahoo!, that offers a search engine. In Lesson 55, "Using Internet Phone to Eliminate Long Distance Phone Bills," you will learn how to use Net-based software and your PC microphone and speakers to talk with other users across the Net for free. Before you continue with Lesson 55, however, make sure that you understand the following key concepts:

✓ The World Wide Web consists of hundreds of millions of documents. To find information on the Web, you must use a search engine, which is software that lists sites on the Web that discuss your topic of interest.

✓ There are several well-known search engines on the Web, the best known being the Yahoo! Web site at *www.yahoo.com*.

✓ As you search the Web for information, you should use a search engine to search for words that relate closely to your topic. The more precise your search topic, the better your chances that the search engine will find the information that you desire.

✓ Should a search engine not find sites that discuss your topic, try searching on a more general topic and then try searching at a different search engine.

Lesson 55

Using Internet Phone to Eliminate Long Distance Phone Bills

As you learned in Lesson 49, "Connecting to the Internet and World Wide Web," the Internet is a vast network of computer networks that span the globe. Today, the Internet connects computers from every country in the world. After you connect to the Internet, you can send and receive messages or files from users near or far, and you can use a browser to view content from Web sites worldwide. Best of all, as you send and receive information across the Internet, you do so for free.

In this lesson, you will learn how to use a software program called Internet Phone to talk with other users across the Internet for free. To communicate with another user using Internet Phone, you both must be running the Internet Phone software and your PCs must have a sound card, speakers, and a microphone. As you speak, the other user will hear your voice through his or her speakers, much as if the two of you were talking on the phone. This lesson presents the steps you must perform to download and install a demo version of Internet Phone. By the time you finish this lesson, you will understand the following key concepts:

- If your PC has a microphone and speakers, you can use the Internet Phone software to talk with other users across the Net for free.

- When you talk with another user via Internet Phone, the user to whom you are speaking will hear you through his or her PC speakers.

- In addition to using Internet Phone to talk with users across the Net for free, you can use Internet Phone to call a telephone from your PC. Before you can place a call to a telephone from your PC, you must subscribe to an Internet Telephony Service Provider.

- Using Internet Phone, you will connect to the Internet Telephony Service Provider who, in turn, will place a local phone call on your behalf. Placing a PC-to-phone call is not free; you must pay a fee to the Internet Telephony Service Provider which, in most cases, will be less than what you would have to pay for a standard long-distance phone call.

- In addition to talking to a user across the Net, you can use Internet Phone to chat (send typed messages to other users), exchange video, send and receive files, and share data using a whiteboard.

DOWNLOADING AND INSTALLING THE INTERNET PHONE SOFTWARE

Across the Net, you may find several programs that are similar to Internet Phone that let you talk with other users across the Net. This lesson presents the Internet Phone software because it is widely available on the Web as well as within most computer stores. In addition, by connecting to the VocalTec Web site, at *www.vocaltec.com*, you can download a trial version of Internet Phone for free.

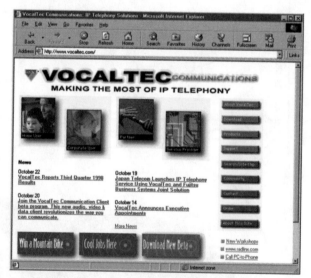

Figure 55.1 Downloading a trial version of Internet Phone from the VocalTec Web site.

The installation program for the Internet Phone demo program is a fairly large file. If, after reading this lesson, you do not feel like sitting through a long file-download operation, you can purchase Internet Phone at most computer stores. Should you decide to download the demo program, the download operation will place an installation program on your disk that you must later run to install the Internet Phone demo. To download the Internet Phone software, perform these steps:

1. Using your browser, connect to the VocalTec Web site at *www.vocaltec.com*. The VocalTec Web site will have instructions you can follow to initiate the software download. Your browser, in turn, will display the File Download dialog box, as shown in Figure 55.2.

2. Within the File Download dialog box, click your mouse on the Save this program to disk button and then choose OK. Windows, in turn, will display a Save As dialog box, within which you can specify the folder within which you want to store the installation program.

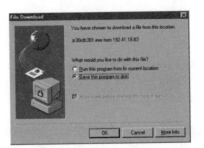

Figure 55.2 *The File Download dialog box.*

3. Within the Save As dialog box, select the folder within which you want to save the file. Also, write down the file's name, so you can find the file later to run the installation program. Click your mouse on the Save button to initiate the file download.

After the file download completes, you must run the installation program to install the Internet Phone software on your system. To run the installation program, perform these steps:

1. Click your mouse on the Start button. Windows, in turn, will display the Start menu.

2. Within the Start menu, click your mouse on the Run option. Windows will display the Run dialog box.

3. Within the Run dialog box, click your mouse on the Browse button and locate the file within which you stored the installation program you downloaded from the VocalTec Web site. Next, click your mouse on the installation program and then Click OK. Windows, in turn, will run the installation program.

RUNNING INTERNET PHONE

After you install Internet Phone, you can run the program by performing these steps:

1. If you are not connected to the Net, connect at this time.

2. Click your mouse on the Start button. Windows, in turn, will display the Start menu.

3. Within the Start menu, click your mouse on the Programs option and then choose Internet Phone. Windows, in turn, will open the Internet Phone window, as shown in Figure 55.3.

Figure 55.3 *The Internet Phone window.*

Note: *The first time that you run Internet Phone, your screen will display a dialog box within which you can test your microphone to verify that it is working. After you perform the test, click your mouse on the OK button to close the dialog box.*

If you do not have anyone in particular that you want to chat with, you can open the Internet Phone Community Browser that, as shown in Figure 55.4, lists topic groups you can select and then discussion groups within each topic. Within a discussion group, you can double-click your mouse on a user's entry to place a call to the user.

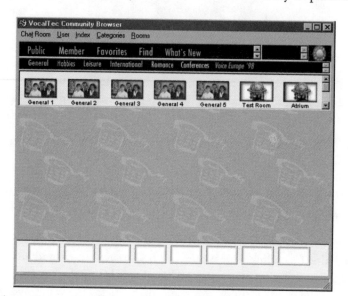

Figure 55.4 *The Internet Phone Community Browser provides a variety of discussion groups within which you can find individuals to call.*

If a user answers your call, you can use the Internet Phone software to talk, chat, or exchange video, as shown in Figure 55.5. To place a call to a specific user using Internet Phone, you simply need to type in the user's nickname or e-mail address.

Figure 55.5 *Using Internet Phone to communicate within another user.*

USING INTERNET PHONE TO CALL A TELEPHONE

Internet Phone was originally designed to let two users communicate for free across the Internet using PCs. Using Internet Phone, you can also call a telephone from your PC. When you place a PC-to-telephone call, your call is not free. Instead, you must pay a small fee to a service provider, who will actually place the phone call on your behalf. Depending on the provider you use, the cost of placing your call will differ. In general, if you are placing calls within the same country, you will not save much money by using Internet Phone. If, however, you are calling another country, you may save money using Internet Phone. Keep in mind that if the other user has Internet Phone, the two of you can talk across the Net for free, regardless of where the other user resides. If you want to call telephones using Internet Phone, you must first register with an Internet Telephony Service Provider, which you can do from the VocalTec Web site. Then, from within the Internet Phone dialer view, you simply click your mouse on the number that you want to dial.

WHAT YOU MUST KNOW

Throughout this book, you have learned numerous ways to communicate with other users across the Net. In this lesson, you learned how to use the Internet Phone software, your PC's speakers, and your microphone to talk with another user across the Net for free. Internet Phone differs from the video-conferencing software you examined in Lesson 44, "Test Driving Video Processing Across the Internet," in that using Internet Phone, you can place a call from your PC to a telephone. In Lesson 56, "Compressing a File's Contents Using the Winzip Utility," you will learn how to use the Winzip utility to compress files that you send across the Net. Before you continue with Lesson 56, however, make sure that you understand the following key concepts:

✓ Internet Phone is a software program that lets you talk with other users across the Net for free.

✓ Using Internet Phone, you talk into your PC microphone. The user with whom you are speaking will hear you through his or her PC speakers.

✓ Although Internet Phone was originally designed to let users talk across the Net for free, using Internet Phone, you can call a telephone from your PC.

✓ In addition to talk across the Web, the Internet Phone also lets you chat, exchange video, send and receive files, and share data using a whiteboard.

Lesson 56

Compressing a File's Contents Using the WinZip Utility

In Lesson 52, "Using E-Mail to Exchange Files with Other Users," you learned how to attach files to the electronic-mail messages you send to other users. Although exchanging documents via e-mail can be very convenient, messages with large documents attached can be quite frustrating to users who must wait for the messages to download across a slow modem connection. If you send and receive documents via e-mail, you can save transmit and receive time by compressing the documents that you attach to your messages.

In a similar way, assume that you must give a file that does not quite fit on a floppy disk to another user and the user is not connected to a network that supports e-mail. By using file-compression software such as WinZip, you may be able to compress the file's contents so that the file fits on a floppy. Later, the user who receives the compressed file can use the file-compression software to restore the file to its original state.

This lesson examines the WinZip file-compression program. In general, WinZip falls into the category of programs that you should have and use, much like a virus-protection program. In this lesson, you will learn how to download and install a trial version of WinZip from across the Web. By the time you finish this lesson, you will understand the following key concepts:

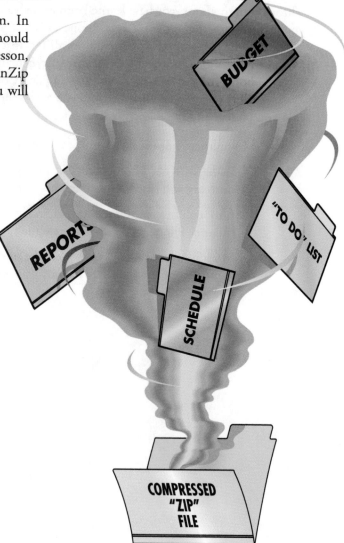

- If you exchange documents with other users via electronic mail or another program, such as *ftp*, you should first compress the file's contents to reduce the file's size and, thus, the amount of time required to transmit the file's contents across the Net.

- Using file-compression software, you can often compress a file that is too large to fit on a floppy to a size that will fit.

- WinZip is a Windows-based file-compression program. When you compress a file using the WinZip program, WinZip will create a compressed file with the Zip extension.

- When you later uncompress a Zip file using the WinZip program, WinZip will place the original file's contents (or the contents of multiple files if your Zip file contains more than one compressed file) on your disk.

- The WinZip utility lets you compress several files into one compressed Zip file.

DOWNLOADING AND INSTALLING THE WINZIP UTILITY

WinZip is a Windows-based program that you can buy in most computer stores or from the WinZip Web site at *www.WinZip.com*, shown in Figure 56.1. In addition, from the WinZip Web site, you can download a trial version of WinZip.

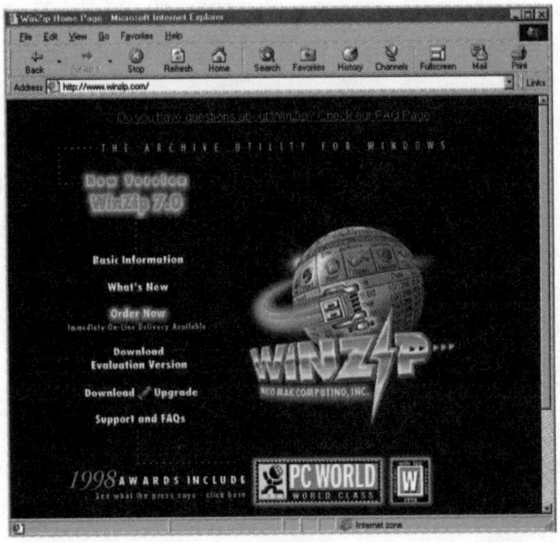

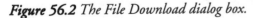

Figure 56.1 *The WinZip Web site.*

Within the WinZip Web site, you will find instructions that will walk you through the steps you must perform to download the WinZip installation program. To download the WinZip program, perform these steps:

1. Within the WinZip Web site, initiate the file download. Your browser, in turn, will display the File Download dialog box, as shown in Figure 56.2.

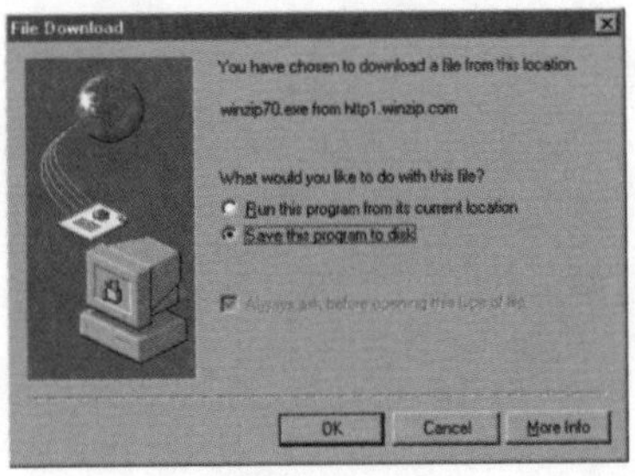

Figure 56.2 *The File Download dialog box.*

2. Within the File Download dialog box, click your mouse on the Save this program to disk button and then choose OK. Windows, in turn, will display a Save As dialog box, within which you can specify the folder within which you want to store the installation program.

3. Within the Save As dialog box, select the folder within which you want to save the file. Also, write down the file's name, so you can find the file later to run the installation program. Click your mouse on the Save button to initiate the file download.

After the file download completes, you must run the installation program to install the WinZip software on your system. To run the installation program, perform these steps:

1. Click your mouse on the Start button. Windows, in turn, will display the Start menu.

2. Within the Start menu, click your mouse on the Run option. Windows will display the Run dialog box.

3. Within the Run dialog box, click your mouse on the Browse button and locate the file within which you stored the installation program you downloaded from the WinZip Web site. Next, click your mouse on the installation program and then click OK. Windows, in turn, will run the installation program.

UNDERSTANDING FILE COMPRESSION SOFTWARE

When you compress a file using the WinZip utility, WinZip will create a Zip file (a file with the Zip extension) on your disk that contains your original file's contents in a compressed format. For example, assume that you have a very big Excel spreadsheet file named *Budget.XLS*, that is 5Mb in size. Using WinZip, you will create a file that you might name *Budget.ZIP* that contains the file's compressed contents. In this case, the Zip file, *Budget.ZIP*, may only require 1Mb of disk space, or less.

When you give the Budget.ZIP file to another user, that user can run the WinZip software on his or her system to uncompress the Zip file. In this case, when the WinZip software uncompresses (users refer to uncompressing a file as unzipping the file) the file, WinZip will create the file *Budget.XLS* on the user's system, as shown in Figure 56.3.

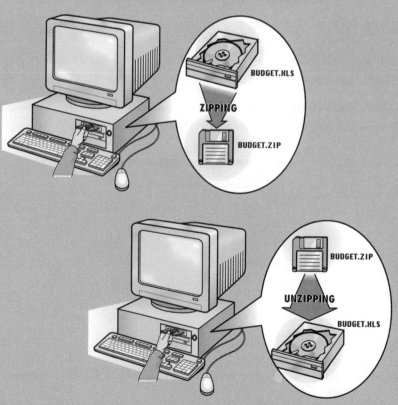

Figure 56.3 *Compressing a file into a Zip file and later uncompressing the Zip file to produce the original file.*

If you must send several files to another user, you can use WinZip to compress all of the files in one step, to create a single Zip file. Later, when the user uncompresses the file, WinZip will place each of the original files on the user's disk.

CREATING A ZIP FILE

To create a Zip file within WinZip, perform these steps:

1. Within the WinZip program, click your mouse on the New button. WinZip, in turn, will display the New Archive dialog box, as shown in Figure 56.4.

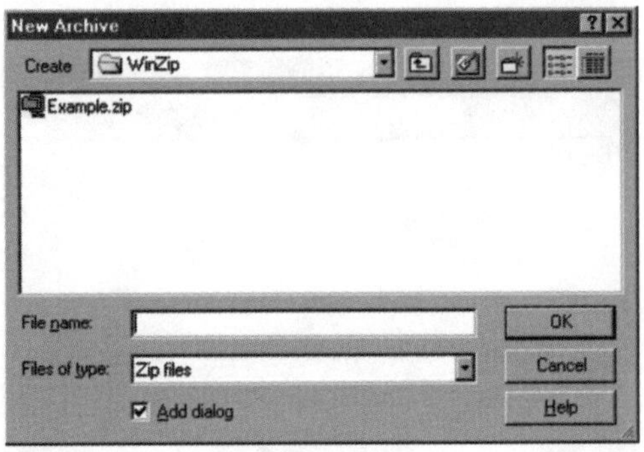

Figure 56.4 *The New Archive dialog box.*

2. Within the New Archive dialog box, type in the filename you want to use for your Zip file, such as Sample.Zip. Also, select the folder within which you want to store your Zip file and then click your mouse on the OK button. WinZip, in turn, will display the Add dialog box, as shown in Figure 56.5.

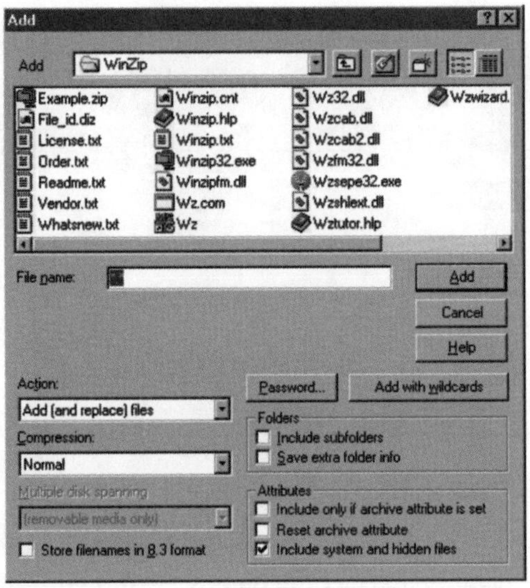

Figure 56.5 *The Add dialog box.*

3. Within the Add dialog box, locate the folder that contains the files whose contents you want to compress. Within the folder, click your mouse on the file you want to compress and then click your mouse on the Add button. If you want to compress multiple files, hold down the CTRL key as you click your mouse on each file and then click your mouse on the Add button.

4. To close your Zip file, select the File menu Close Archive option. You can now give your Zip file to another user.

UNCOMPRESSING A ZIP FILE

When you receive a Zip file from another user, you must use the WinZip program to uncompress the Zip file's contents. To uncompress a Zip file, perform these steps:

1. Within the WinZip program, click your mouse on the Open button. WinZip, in turn, will display the Open dialog box, as shown in Figure 56.6.

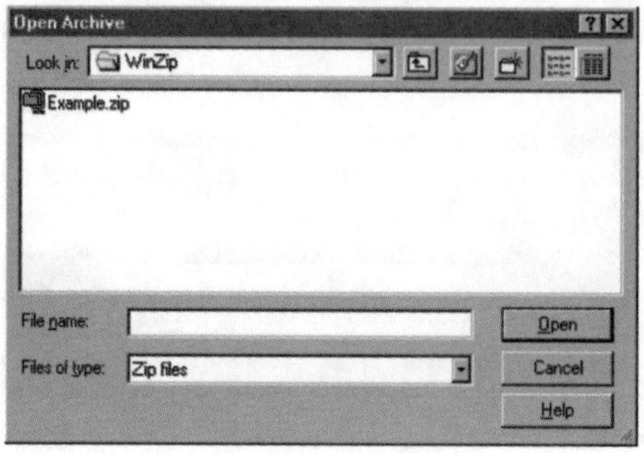

Figure 56.6 *The Open dialog box.*

2. Within the Open dialog box, locate the folder that contains the Zip file. Within the folder, click your mouse on the Zip file and then select OK. WinZip, in turn, will display a list of the files the Zip file contains, as shown in Figure 56.7.

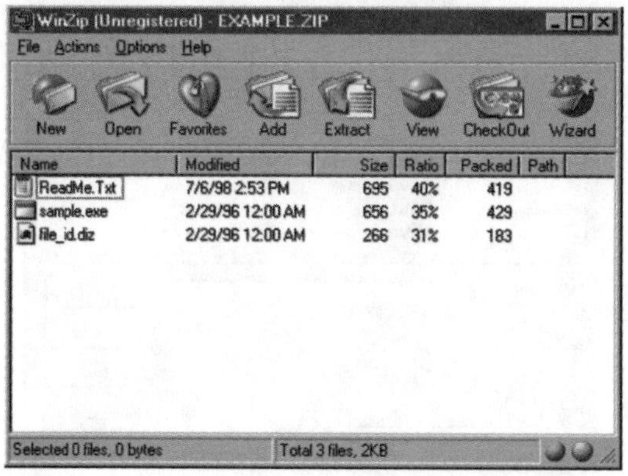

Figure 56.7 *Listing the files in a Zip file.*

3. To extract the compressed files onto your disk, click your mouse on the Extract button. WinZip, in turn, will display the Extract dialog box, as shown in Figure 56.8.

Figure 56.8 *The Extract dialog box.*

4. Within the Extract dialog box, select the folder into which you want WinZip to place the uncompressed files and then click your mouse on the OK button.

5. To close WinZip, click your mouse on the Close button.

USING ZIP FILES TO BACKUP YOUR FILES

As you have learned, when you no longer need a file's contents, you should delete the file to free up space on your disk. If you are not sure if you will need a file's contents in the future, you can use WinZip to compress the file. Then, you can delete the original file from your disk, leaving the Zip file which will consume less space. Should you need the file in the future, you can uncompress the Zip file's contents.

WHAT YOU MUST KNOW

If you attach documents to e-mail messages, you can save transmit and receive time by compressing files before you attach them. Likewise, if you need to exchange a large file or several files with another user using floppy disks, you may want to first compress the files to reduce the amount of disk space they consume. This lesson examined the WinZip utility that you can use to compress and uncompress files. In Lesson 57, "Using RealAudio to Bring the Web's Sounds to Life," you will learn how to download and install RealPlayer software that lets you receive and play back audio and video from sites across the Web. Before you continue with Lesson 57, however, make sure you understand the following key concepts:

- ✓ WinZip is a file-compression program that you can use to compress a file's contents to reduce the amount of disk space the file consumes.

- ✓ When you use WinZip to compress a file, WinZip creates a file with the Zip extension. Using WinZip, you or another user can later uncompress the Zip file to restore the original file's contents.

- ✓ Using WinZip, you can compress multiple files within the same Zip file.

- ✓ If you attach documents to e-mail messages that you send other users, you can reduce e-mail message's transmit and receive time by first compressing the document.

Lesson 57

Using RealAudio to Bring the Web's Sites and Sounds to Life

In Lesson 53, "Surfing Your Way to Information on the World Wide Web," you learned how to use your Web-browser program to traverse sites on the Web. In this lesson, you will get a chance to experience the future of the Web: audio and video. Using RealAudio software that you can download for free from the RealAudio site on the Web, you can use your PC to listen to live radio broadcasts, hear the latest news, or follow sporting events. Then, using RealPlayer software, you can use your PC to play back music videos and to preview upcoming movies. This lesson examines the steps you must perform to download and install the RealPlayer software. By the time you finish this lesson, you will understand the following key concepts:

- The RealPlayer software lets you receive audio data from a site (such as a radio interview or music) in pieces at a time, as opposed to waiting for an entire file to download.

- Across the Web, there are many sites that broadcast audio using RealAudio.

- Using the RealPlayer software, you can download and play video clips from across the Web.

Note: *Using your Web browser, you can download the software this lesson presents from the RealAudio Web site. Over time, the Web site may change, which may change slightly the steps you must perform to download the software. Fortunately, the RealAudio Web site normally provides detailed instructions you can perform to get the software up and running.*

WHY REALAUDIO IS UNIQUE

When you browse the Web, your browser will request the server at the sites you visit to download various files. When you download a large graphics file, you may, depending on the speed of your connection, experience a delay while you wait for the file to download. When a site broadcasts audio, such as a three-minute song or a 15-minute talk show, a file holding the audio data would become very large. In fact, for most users who connect to the Net using a modem, the file could take 15 minutes to an hour to download. As you might guess, few users would wait for such a download.

RealAudio software, in contrast, sends audio across the Net in pieces. When the RealAudio software on your system receives audio data, it starts playing it. By the time your software finishes playing the audio data, it has hopefully received more, so the process can continue. Users sometimes refer to RealAudio and RealVideo as streaming audio or streaming video because, rather than downloading and playing back an entire file at one time, the RealAudio software receives and plays the audio data as the data arrives. In other words, you can think of a stream of audio or video flowing from the server to the software running on your system.

INSTALLING THE REALAUDIO AND REALVIDEO SOFTWARE ON YOUR PC

Before you can use your PC to play back audio and video from across the Web, you must first download and install special software that you will find at the RealAudio Web site (*www.RealAudio.com*). To start, use your browser to connect to the RealAudio Web site, which is shown in Figure 57.1

Figure 57.1 *The RealAudio Web site.*

The RealAudio Web site will walk you though the steps you must perform to download a free version of the RealPlayer software. To download and install the RealPlayer software, perform these steps:

1. Within the RealAudio Web site, initiate the file download. Your browser, in turn, will display the File Download dialog.

2. Within the File Download dialog box, click your mouse on the Save this program to disk button and then choose OK. Windows, in turn, will display a Save As dialog box, within which you can specify the folder into which you want to store the installation program.

3. Within the Save As dialog box, select the folder within which you want to save the file. Also, write down the file's name, so you can find the file later to run the installation program. Click your mouse on the Save button to initiate the file download.

After the file download completes, you must run the installation program to install the RealPlayer software on your system. To run the installation program, perform these steps:

1. Click your mouse on the Start button. Windows, in turn, will display the Start menu.

2. Within the Start menu, click your mouse on the Run option. Windows will display the Run dialog box.

3. Within the Run dialog box, click your mouse on the Browse button and locate the file within which you stored the installation program you downloaded from the RealAudio Web site. Next, click your mouse on the installation program and then click OK. Windows, in turn, will run the installation program.

LISTENING TO REALAUDIO BROADCASTS

After you install the RealPlayer software, you can use your Web browser to play back broadcasts from across the Web. To experience RealAudio broadcasts, use your browser to connect to one or more of the sites Table 57.1 lists.

Web Address	RealAudio Content Broadcast
www.broadcast.com	A wide range of video and audio offerings
www.kbnp.com	Business radio
www.musicnet.com	Samples from music CDs
www.radionet.com	Technology radio
www.sportsworld.com	Sport radio

Table 57.1 *Sites that broadcast audio across the Web.*

When you connect to a site that is broadcasting audio, your browser will display the RealAudio controls, as shown in Figure 57.2, and you should start to hear the broadcast through your PC's speaker.

Figure 57.2 *The RealAudio controls.*

EXPERIENCING REALVIDEO BROADCASTS

In addition to letting your PC play broadcast audio, the RealPlayer software also lets your PC display broadcast video within a window on your screen, as shown in Figure 57.3.

Figure 57.3 *Using RealPlayer software to play broadcast video within a window.*

Depending on the speed of your modem connection, the size and quality of the video window will differ. To get started with broadcast video, visit one or more of the Web sites that Table 57.2 lists.

Web Address	RealVideo Content Broadcast
www.broadcast.com	A wide range of video and audio content
www.real.com	Sample videos from the RealAudio Web site
www.msnbc.com	World news
www.espn.com	Sports
www.cnn.com	World news

Table 57.2 *Sites that broadcast video across the Web.*

WHAT YOU MUST KNOW

In this lesson, you got to test drive video and audio technologies whose use will soon be commonplace across the Web. In Lesson 58, "Creating Your Own Web Site," you will learn how you can create your own Web site. Before you continue with Lesson 58, however, make sure that you understand the following key concepts:

✓ Using RealPlayer software, you can receive audio data from across the Web in small pieces, but at a fast enough rate that your PC can broadcast the audio smoothly.

✓ As you browse the Web, you will find Net-based radio stations that use RealAudio to broadcast music, sports, business, and more.

✓ Using RealPlayer software, you can receive video data from across the Web in small pieces, but at a fast enough rate that your PC can display the video smoothly.

✓ Across the Web, you will find many sites that broadcast video that you can play on your PC using the RealPlayer software.

333

Lesson 58

Creating Your Own Web Site

In Lesson 53, "Surfing Your Way to Information on the World Wide Web," you learned how to browse sites across the Web. If you have a business, or if you provide services you want to advertise, or if you just want to let other users know more information about you, you may want to create your own Web site.

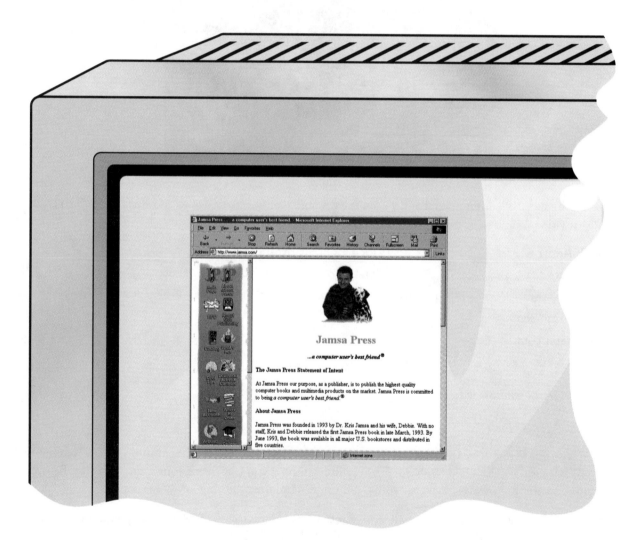

This lesson examines ways you can create your own Web site. By the time you finish this lesson, you will understand the following key concepts:

- If you require only a simple one-page Web site, many on-line services and Internet Service Providers will let you create a Web page that they will host on their system for free.

- As the complexity of your Web site increases, so too will your site's costs. To start, you must determine where you want to host your Web site. Then, you must hire a graphics artist to help you create your site.

- Many large companies use their own computers to host their Web site. For a small company, however, hosting a Web site on their own PC can be very expensive.

- As you design your Web site, you must pick a domain name, such as *www.jamsa.com*, that users will use to browse your site. After you select your name, you can visit the InterNIC Web site to determine if your name is in use by another company and, if not, you can pay a small fee to register the name.

- To create a Web site, designers create a set of files that contain HTML tags that format the site's text and graphics. A complex Web site requires complex HTML coding—a task most users will not want to undertake.

CREATING A SIMPLE WEB SITE USING YOUR INTERNET SERVICE PROVIDER

If you use an on-line service, such as America Online (AOL) or if you use an Internet Service Provider (ISP) to connect to the Net, you may be able to create a simple Web page, whose files will reside at the service itself. Often, your on-line service or provider may let you host a simple Web site at their site for free. In fact, some services will even let you create your Web page across the Net from your PC. Normally, the service will restrict your Web page to one page of information. Such a simple Web page might, for example, include a picture of yourself or your family as well as information about you, such as where you live, your e-mail address, and so on. By creating a simple Web site, you can keep your family and friends who have access to the Net fully informed about the things that are happening in your life. Figure 58.1 shows a simple one-page Web site.

Figure 58.1 A simple Web page containing information about a user.

If you are interested in creating a simple one-page Web site, contact your on-line service or Internet Service Provider and ask them if they provide Web-site hosting for simple Web sites. If you use your service to host your Web site, your site's Web address will contain the address of your service, followed by your name, such as *www.service.com\yourname*.

CREATING MORE THAN A SIMPLE WEB SITE

If you need more than a simple Web site, your task will start to become more complex. Assume, for example, that you have a small pizza business, Phil's Pizzeria, and you want your customers to be able to order pizzas on-line. If you are better at making pizzas than working with computers, you will need to find someone who can help you create your Web site. If you look in the phone book under computer services, you may find several Web-page designers who can create your site. But, be prepared, designing and implementing a Web site can be an expensive project.

YOU WILL NEED A LOCATION TO HOST YOUR WEB SITE

For users to have access to your Web site, you must place your site's files on a computer that is connected to the Internet 24 hours a day, seven days a week. One option you can consider is to buy a PC that you dedicate to serving as your Web site. To start, you must purchase Web-server software that will respond each time a user connects to your site. Then, you will need to get a fast connection to the Net which, unfortunately, will require more than a simple modem and telephone line. Most large businesses that maintain their own Web sites use an ISDN connection to the Net and possibly a "T1" connection. Such connections will cost you several hundred dollars to several thousand dollars a month! In addition, you will have to hire someone who can maintain your Web site's software—which, again, is expensive. Put simply, you probably do not want to use your own PC and connection for your Web site. A better option for hosting your Web site is, again, to have your Internet Service Provider host your site. Your provider will place your Web site files on their computers (which have a fast connection to the Net). Your provider will also be responsible for making sure that your Web site is available and is secure. Depending on the size and number of files you want your provider to host, the monthly fee to host your Web site on the provider's system will vary. Whether you choose to host your Web site on your own PC or on one of your provider's PCs, you can assign a meaningful address to your site, such as *www.phils_pizzeria.com*.

YOU MUST CHOOSE A WEB ADDRESS (A DOMAIN NAME)

As you design your Web site, you will need to determine your site's Web address, such as *www.phils_pizzaria.com*. Users refer to Web addresses as domain names. To get a domain name, you must first choose a name that is not currently in use on the Web. Then, you must register the name with an organization named InterNIC. To register your Web address, you will need to pay a small fee (less than $100 for two years). To learn more about domain names, or to register your domain name, visit the InterNIC Web site at *www.internic.net*, as shown in Figure 58.2.

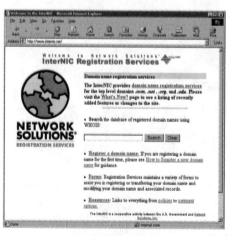

***Figure 58.2** Learning about or registering domain names at InterNIC.*

UNDERSTANDING HTML

A Web site is simply a collection of files that contain information and images that you want your Web site to display. To create a Web page, designers use a special text-markup language called HTML (which stands for Hypertext Markup Language). In general, to create a Web page using HTML, a designer creates a file that contains the text they want the site to display. Within the file, designers place special HTML symbols (designers call the symbols tags) to format the text. For example, to display specific text using **boldface**, the designer would place the tag <*B*> at the start of the text to turn on bolding, and the tag </*B*> following the text to turn off bolding. For example, consider this example that uses bold and normal text:

> This word is **bold** and these are not.

To bold the text within the HTML file, the designer would use the following tags:

> This word is <B>bold</B> and these are not.

Likewise, to turn *italics* on and off, the designer would use the <*I*> and </*I*> tags. For example, consider the following text that uses italics and normal text:

> This word is *italic* and these are not.

To italicize the text within the HTML file, the designer would use the following tags:

> This word is <I>italic</I> and these are not.

HTML provides a myriad of tags that designers use to format Web pages. Many tags deal specifically with text while others control the size and placement of graphics on the Web page. As you might guess, to create a complete Web page, the HTML file can become quite complex.

VIEWING A SITE'S HTML

As you use you browser to view sites across the Web, you can direct the browser to display the site's HTML file. Within Internet Explorer, you can view the current site's HMTL by selecting the View menu Source option. Likewise, within the Netscape Navigator, you can view a site's HTML source file by selecting the View menu Page Source option. Figure 58.3, for example, shows a page from the Jamsa Press Web site and the corresponding HTML file.

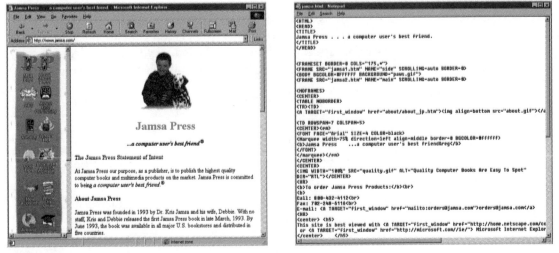

Figure 58.3 *Using a browser to display a site's HTML.*

Fortunately, unless you want to learn HTML, you can leave your site's HTML to your Web-site designer. If, however, you want to learn more about HTML, visit the W3C Web site at *www.w3c.org*, as shown in Figure 58.4.

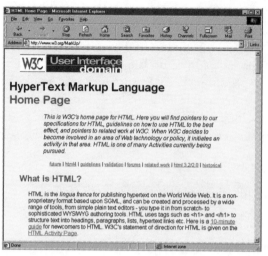

Figure 58.4 *Learning about HTML at the W3C Web site.*

WINDOWS 98 INCLUDES FRONTPAGE EXPRESS AND THE PERSONAL WEB SERVER

If you are interested in learning more about Web-site design and you are using Windows 98, you can take advantage of two programs that Microsoft bundles with Windows: FrontPage Express the Personal Web Server. To start, you can use FrontPage Express to create your Web site files. In general, FrontPage Express is a Web-site editor, with which you can format your site's text and place your site's graphics. Using FrontPage Express, you do not have to know or understand HTML. If you are interested in learning about FrontPage Express, you will find that most Windows 98 books will discuss FrontPage Express.

As you have learned, a Web site must run server software that downloads the site's files to a browser when a user views the site's contents. If you are hosting your Web page on your own PC, you will need your own Web-server software. To help you get started, Windows 98 includes the Personal Web Server software. For more information using the Personal Web Server software, turn to the book *1001 Windows 98 Tips*, Jamsa Press, 1998.

WHAT YOU MUST KNOW

Each day, thousands of companies and individuals create their own sites on the World Wide Web. In this lesson, you learned ways you can create your own Web site. In Lesson 59, "Protecting Your System from Computer Viruses," you will learn what a computer virus is, how viruses infect your system, and ways you can reduce your PC's risk of infection. Before you continue with Lesson 59, however, make sure that you understand the following key concepts:

✓ Many on-line services and Internet Service Providers will let you create a simple one-page Web site that they will host on their system for you for free.

✓ If you require more than a simple Web page, you will need to determine where you want to host your Web site. In other words, you must determine at which computer (and it must a computer that is connected to the Net) you will store your site's files.

✓ Although you can use your own computer to host your Web site, doing so will require that you purchase Web-server software, acquire a fast connection to the Net, and that you can maintain your Web site and related programs. Hosting a Web site on your own PC is often your most expensive option.

✓ To create your Web site, you should hire a graphics artist who is familiar not only with HTML, but also the steps you must perform to register your site's domain name.

Lesson 59

Protecting Your PC from Computer Viruses

A computer virus is a software program that a programmer has intentionally written to perform mischief or possibly to raise havoc on your system. Depending on the programmer's intentions, the virus may simply display a message, such as "You've been infected!" and then shut down your system. Other, more serious viruses, however, may delete all the files on your disk before rendering your PC inoperable. If you exchange disks with other users, download and run programs from across the Web, or even exchange documents with other users via e-mail, your system is susceptible to a computer virus.

This lesson examines steps that you can perform to reduce your PC's risk of catching a virus. By the time you finish this lesson, you will understand the following key concepts:

- Computer viruses are programs that a programmer has written intentionally to damage the information you store on your PC.

- A computer virus travels from one PC to another by attaching itself to files (the virus infects the files) that users unknowingly exchange.

339

- A virus is a program, which means the virus must reside in your PC's RAM before it can run. Virus programs normally attach themselves to other programs. When you later run the program, you unknowingly load the virus into your PC's RAM.

- To reduce your risk of computer viruses, do not run programs that you receive from other users on disk or via e-mail or programs that you download from across the Net.

- Should you download programs from across the Net, only download such programs from reputable companies. Then, use a virus-detection program to scan the program file for viruses before you run the program.

- Computer viruses can also attach themselves to documents, such as a Word or Excel document. When you later open the document, the virus will load itself into memory. Your only protection against such viruses is to use virus-detection software. Never open a document that you receive from another user on disk or via e-mail without first scanning the document for viruses.

A VIRUS IS A COMPUTER PROGRAM

As briefly discussed, a virus is a computer program, software that a programmer has written with the intent to damage a computer or the information on the computer's disk. In Lesson 11, "Understanding How Your PC Uses Its Memory (RAM)," you learned that before a program can run, the program must reside within your PC's memory. A virus is no exception. Before a virus can infect your system, the virus must reside within your PC's memory. Before a virus can reside within your PC's memory, you must run the virus program. Unfortunately, the programmers who create viruses often disguise the virus as a computer game, shareware business software, or some other innocent-looking program.

Most users infect their PC by running a program that they receive from another user on a floppy disk or that they download from across the Internet. Again, depending on the programmer's intention, some viruses will not immediately harm your system. Instead, when the user runs the program that contains the virus, the virus, as shown in Figure 59.1, will often copy itself to other programs that reside on the user's hard disk. By infecting other files, the virus increases the likelihood that you will run the virus program again in the future and that you may (without your knowledge) infect another user's PC by sending the user an infected file.

Figure 59.1 *Virus programs often attach themselves to other files on a user's disk.*

VIRUSES MUST ATTACH THEMSELVES TO A PROGRAM

The programmers who write viruses are normally pretty clever. Rather than simply place the virus onto your disk, the programmer will normally have the virus attach itself to one of your commonly used programs, such as Microsoft Word (in other words, the virus will infect one of your programs). In this way, each time you run Word, for example, you load the computer virus into your PC's memory (RAM). The only time a virus can damage your system is when the PC executes the instructions the virus program contains. As you learned in Lesson 11, a program must reside in RAM before the CPU can execute the program's instructions. Therefore, a virus that resides on a disk is relatively harmless until you (normally unknowingly) load the virus program into your PC's memory. Some viruses will immediately harm your system the first time they run. Other viruses, however, may wait for a specific date to occur, such as Halloween or April fools day, before they "come alive" and damage your system. By waiting to damage your system, viruses make it more difficult for users to trace their origin.

DOCUMENT-BASED VIRUSES—A NEW BREED OF TROUBLE

In the past, if you did not download and run programs from across the Internet, or run programs given to you by another user, your chance of encountering a computer virus was low. Because viruses could only attach themselves to programs (as opposed to documents, such as a word-processing file or spreadsheet), users could exchange document files without the risk of contracting a virus.

Today, unfortunately, viruses can attach themselves to documents, and later, when you open the document, the virus can "come alive" and harm your system. As a result, as shown in Figure 59.2, if another user gives you a Microsoft Word document, the document file may have an attached virus!

Figure 59.2 *Today, viruses can attach themselves to document files as well as programs.*

As you have learned, a virus is a computer program. It seems impossible, therefore, that a word-processing document could contain a virus—and a few years ago it was impossible. As programs such as Word and Excel have become more powerful, Microsoft has provided users with the ability to create macros, which are simple programs that perform a specific operation. You might, for example, create a macro within Microsoft Word that performs spell checks, saves, and then prints your document in one step. Likewise, you might create a macro in Microsoft Excel that automatically updates the totals for each row and column before you print your spreadsheet.

Macros are simple programs. As Word and Excel have become more powerful, so too have the macros that users can create within each program. Unfortunately, some users now use macros to create computer viruses. When you open a document that contains such a macro, Word or Excel automatically loads the macro into RAM and executes the instructions it contains.

Fortunately, most virus-protection software can identify such document-based macros. As a rule, you should never open a document file that you have not first scanned using your virus-protection software. In addition, within programs that support macros, such as Word and Excel, you can disable the program's automatic macro execution. In this way, when you first open a document, Word or Excel will not run a potentially damaging macro.

HOW TO PROTECT YOUR PC AGAINST COMPUTER VIRUSES

Across the Net, there are thousands, if not tens of thousands, of different computer viruses. Your first tool for protecting your system from computer viruses is to install and use anti-virus software. Across the Web, you will find many companies selling anti-virus software. Two of the best known and most commonly used anti-virus programs are Norton AntiVirus and McAfee VirusScan.

To learn more about Norton AntiVirus, or to download a trial version of the software, visit the Symantec Web site at *www.symantec.com*. Likewise, to learn about McAfee VirusScan, or to download a trial version, visit the McAfee Web site at *www.mcafee.com*.

You can use virus-protection software in one of two ways. First, when another user gives you a disk or file, you can run your virus-protection software and direct it to scan the file for viruses. If the virus-detection software detects a virus, it will ask you how you want it to proceed. Most virus-protection software, for example, can delete the file or possibly remove the virus from the program. Figure 59.3, for example, shows the McAfee VirusScan software window, within which the software asks the user which location (such as a disk, folder, or file) the user wants the software to scan. Assuming the user has just received a floppy disk from another user, the user could direct the VirusScan software to scan the floppy drive. Likewise, if the user had just received an e-mail message that contained an attached file, the user can direct the software to scan only that file.

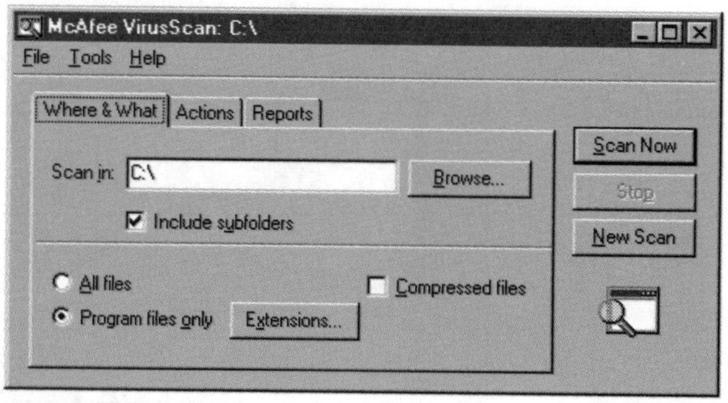

Figure 59.3 The McAfee VirusScan software.

You can also direct most virus-protection programs to run continuously, so that the software scans each file you plan to open, run, save, and so on. By running the virus-protection software continuously, you increase your chances of detecting a virus in files that you download from across the Net.

STEPS YOU SHOULD TAKE TO PROTECT YOUR SYSTEM FROM VIRUSES

To reduce your chance of infecting your PC with a virus, perform these steps:

1. Install virus-protection software and use the software to examine every file you receive from other users, regardless of whether the file came on disk or via e-mail.

2. Before you open or copy files from a floppy disk or zip disk, use your virus-protection software to examine the disk for viruses.

3. Do not run programs sent to you by users across the Net or given to you on floppy disk. Many users will send greeting cards via e-mail that run as small programs. Such programs provide an ideal way for viruses to infect your system. Delete such programs, do not run them.

4. If you download programs from across the Net, only download programs from reputable companies, such as McAfee, Microsoft, Netscape, and Symantec—in other words, from companies that are well known. Then, before you run the programs you download, use your virus-protection software to scan the program files for viruses.

5. Do not open documents that you receive as files attached to e-mail messages without first scanning the document's files for viruses.

UNDERSTANDING DIGITAL SIGNATURES

As you have learned, if you download programs from across the Net, you should only download from reputable companies. When programmers create programs that they place on the Web, programmers can attach a special *digital signature* to their program file that you can use to authenticate that the programmer actually created the program (as opposed to a hacker who is impersonating the programmer or the programmer's company) and to authenticate that no one has changed the program since the programmer created it. (If, for example, a virus has infected the program, the digital signature will no longer be valid because the file's contents have changed.) When you download a file that contains a digital signature, your browser will verify that the signature is correct. Should your browser detect that the signature is not valid, delete the file immediately and do not run or open the file's contents.

WHAT YOU MUST KNOW

In this lesson, you learned that a virus is a computer program that a programmer has written to maliciously damage your PC or the files your disk contains. As a rule, to avoid viruses, you should not download programs from across the net (unless the program comes from a reputable Web site and the program file contains a digital signature) and you should not run programs given to you by another user on disk. In addition, you should immediately purchase and install virus-protection software and then use the virus-protection software to examine every file that you receive from another user (regardless of whether the user sent you the document file via e-mail or on a floppy disk). By taking proper precaution, you can reduce your chance of a virus infection. In Lesson 60, "Using Your PC to Send and Receive Faxes," you will learn how to use your PC to send and receive faxes. Before you continue with Lesson 60, however, make sure that you understand the following key concepts:

✓ A virus is a software program that a programmer has written to intentionally cause mischief or to damage the information you store on your PC.

✓ Viruses normally attach themselves to files (infect the files). As users unknowingly exchange the infected files, the virus can move from one system to another.

✓ Because a virus is a program, the virus must reside in your PC's RAM before it can run. Normally, virus programs will attach themselves to other programs, such as games. When a user loads the program, he or she unknowingly loads the virus into his or her PC's RAM.

✓ The best way to reduce your risk of computer viruses is to not run programs that you receive from other users on disk or via e-mail or programs that you download from across the Net.

✓ If you must run programs that you download from across the Net, only download such programs from reputable companies and then use a virus-detection program to scan the program file for viruses before you run the program.

343

Lesson 60

Using Your PC to Send and Receive Faxes

Throughout this book, you have used your PC and modem to connect to the Internet and the World Wide Web. As it turns out, most modems are capable and can connect not only to remote computers, but also to remote fax machines. As a result, if your PC has fax software installed, you can use your PC to send or receive faxes. This lesson examines the steps you must perform to send and receive faxes using your PC.

By the time you finish this lesson, you will understand the following key concepts:

- If your PC has a fax modem (and most modems are fax modems), you can use your PC to send and receive faxes.

- Most PC-based fax programs normally let you send faxes in one of two ways. First, you can use a fax Wizard that will take you step-by-step through sending a fax. Second, you can print your document to a special fax printer which, in turn, will fax the document's contents.

- By installing fax software on your notebook PC, you can send and receive faxes using your notebook PC, even when you are on the road traveling.

- After you start your fax software, the software will wait for an incoming fax. After your software receives the fax, you can view the fax's contents on screen, print the fax or, in some cases, use optical-character recognition software to convert the fax image to text.

- Using a fax program, you may be able to direct the software to send a custom fax to each of your key customers (using your existing databases, such as a customer database). You can even direct your software to send the faxes at night when the phone rates are the lowest.

WHAT YOU NEED TO SEND AND RECEIVE FAXES

To send and receive faxes using your PC, you need a modem, phone, connection, and fax software. Across the Web, you will find many programs that can send and receive faxes. The examples that this lesson presents, use WinFax PRO, one of the best-known and most used fax programs. You can learn more about WinFax Pro and download a trial version of the software from the Symantec Web site at *www.symantec.com*. To download the trial version of WinFax PRO, perform these steps:

1. Using your browser, connect to the Symantec Web site at *www.symantec.com*. The Symantec Web site will have instructions you can follow to initiate the software download. Your browser, in turn, will display the File Download dialog box, as shown in Figure 60.1.

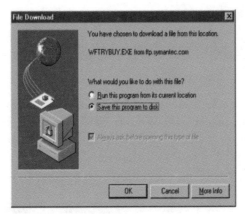

Figure 60.1 *The File Download dialog box.*

2. Within the File Download dialog box, click your mouse on the Save this program to disk button and then choose OK. Windows, in turn, will display a Save As dialog box, within which you can specify the folder within which you want to store the installation program.

3. Within the Save As dialog box, select the folder within which you want to save the file. Also, write down the file's name, so you can find the file later to run the installation program. Click your mouse on the Save button to initiate the file download.

After the file download completes, you must run the installation program to install the WinFax PRO software on your system. To run the installation program, perform these steps:

1. Click your mouse on the Start button. Windows, in turn, will display the Start menu.

2. Within the Start menu, click your mouse on the Run option. Windows will display the Run dialog box.

3. Within the Run dialog box, click your mouse on the Browse button and locate the file within which you stored the installation program you downloaded from the Symantec Web site. Next, click your mouse on the installation program and then Click OK. Windows, in turn, will run the installation program.

SENDING A FAX USING WINFAX PRO

After you download and install the WinFax PRO software, you can use the software to send and receive faxes. WinFax PRO provides you with two primary ways of sending a fax. First, you can use the Send Fax Wizard, shown in Figure 60.2 to send a simple fax.

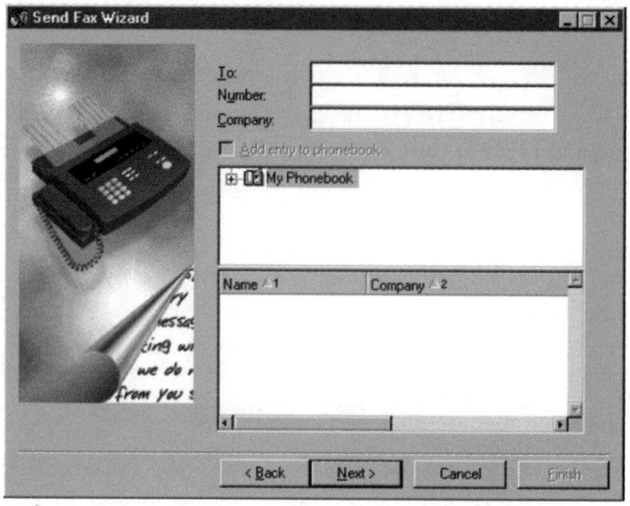

Figure 60.2 *The Send Fax Wizard.*

To start the Send Fax Wizard, select the Start menu Programs option. Windows, in turn, will display the Programs submenu. Within the Programs submenu, select the WinFax PRO option and choose Send Fax Now. Within the Send Fax Wizard, you will first type in information about your fax recipient, such as the person's name and fax number. After you type in the recipient information, you will click your mouse on the Next button. The Send Fax Wizard, in turn, will display a dialog box similar to that shown in Figure 60.3, within which you can type in your fax message.

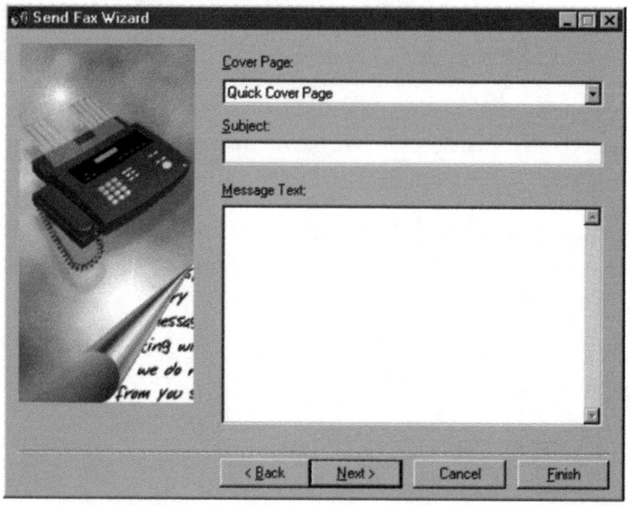

Figure 60.3 *Typing a fax message within the Send Fax Wizard.*

After you type your message, you can click your mouse on the Finish button to direct the Send Fax Wizard to send your fax, or you can click through an additional dialog box that lets you attach documents to your fax. When you attach a document to your fax, WinFax PRO will do one of two things. First, if you are calling a fax machine, WinFax PRO will send the document's contents as printed text. If, instead, you are calling a PC that is running fax software, WinFax PRO will attach the document file to a fax much like an attached document within an e-mail message.

In addition to typing a fax message within the Send Fax Wizard, WinFax PRO lets you send a fax from within your applications by printing your documents to the WinFax PRO printer. For example, assume that you create a document in Word that you want to fax to another user. To fax the document from within Word, you would perform these steps:

1. Within Word, select the File menu Print option. Word, in turn, will display the Print dialog box.

2. Within the Print dialog box, click your mouse on the Printer pull-down list and select WinFax.

3. Within the Print dialog box, click your mouse on the OK button. Windows, will start the Send Fax Now Wizard, which will send your document to a remote fax.

As you can see, sending a fax using WinFax PRO is almost as easy as printing the document's contents.

RECEIVING A FAX USING WINFAX PRO

When you install the WinFax PRO software on your system, the installation program will direct Windows 98 to start a program named Controller that waits for incoming fax calls. When a fax arrives, the Controller software places the fax into a message folder, as shown in Figure 60.4.

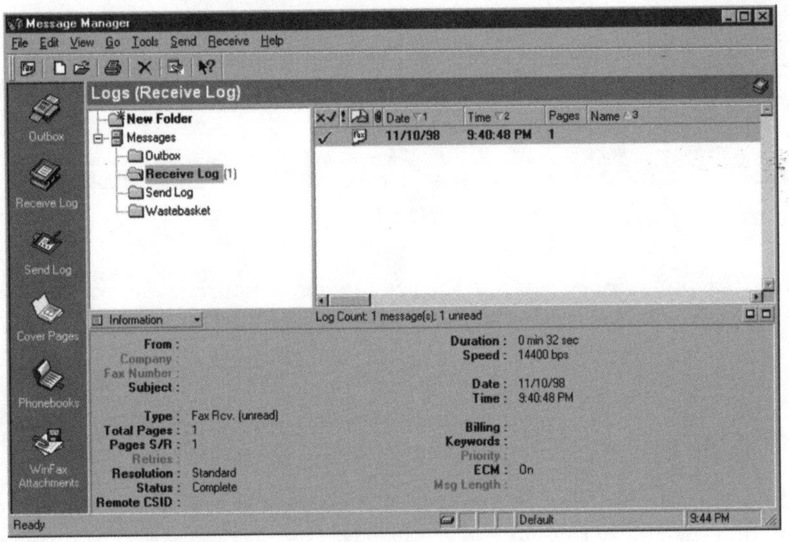

Figure 60.4 WinFax PRO places incoming faxes into a message folder.

If you double-click your mouse on a file within the file list, WinFax PRO will display a window within which it will display the fax's contents, as shown in Figure 60.5. You can then view the fax's contents on-line or print a hardcopy.

ADVANTAGES OF PC-BASED FAXING

If you do not have a fax machine, using your PC to send and receive faxes will provide a good alternative. If you have a fax machine, however, you may wonder why you would want to use fax software on a PC. As it turns out, PC-based fax software has many features that you may find quite convenient. To start, using fax software, you can schedule your PC to send faxes at a specific time, such as at night, when the phone rates are the lowest. Second, if you need to send faxes to a large group of people, many fax programs let you perform merge operations from your customer databases which automatically send the faxes you desire to each customer, eliminating much of the time you would have spent at the fax machine in the past.

In addition, if you are traveling, you can configure your fax machine so that it automatically forwards the faxes you receive to your current location. Some fax programs will even send you a page on your pager when a you receive an incoming fax. Finally, some fax programs come with optical-character recognition software that you can use to convert a faxed image into character text that you can edit using a word processor.

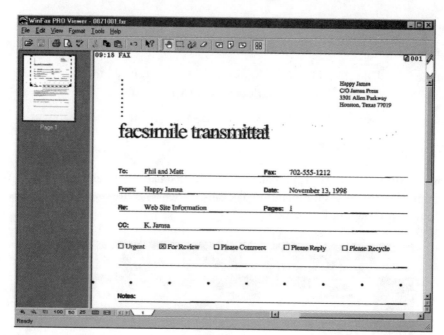

Figure 60.5 *Viewing a received fax within WinFax PRO.*

Note: *Several of this book's lessons examine ways that you can communicate across the Net for free. Just as programmers are creating ways for users to chat and talk across the Net, they are also creating ways for users to send and receive faxes across the Net. For more information on Internet faxing, you can visit* www.faxpower.com *or* www.savetz.com\fax-faq.html.

WHAT YOU MUST KNOW

If your PC has a modem, you can use your PC to send and receive faxes. If, for example, you are traveling with a notebook PC, you may find the ability to send and receive faxes quite convenient. In this lesson, you examined the steps you must perform to send and receive faxes using PC-based fax software. In Lesson 61, "Shopping Online across the World Wide Web," you will learn that across the Web, you can find "virtual shops" that sell just about every product you can imagine. You will also learn that if you shop at reputable companies, shopping on the Web is efficient and secure. Before you continue with Lesson 61, however, make sure you have learned the following key concepts:

✓ If your PC has a modem, you can use your PC to send and receive faxes.

✓ Most PC-based fax programs provide a fax Wizard that will take you step-by-step through sending a fax.

✓ If you travel with a notebook PC, you can eliminate many trips to your hotel's front desk or to a business services store by using your notebook PC to send and receive faxes.

✓ To receive a fax using your PC, you simply start your fax software and direct it to wait for an incoming fax. After your software receives the fax, you can view the fax's contents on screen, print the fax or, in some cases, use optical-character recognition software to convert the fax image to text.

✓ Many fax programs can use your existing databases, such as a customer database, to let you send custom faxes to each of your accounts, automatically. You can even direct your software to send the faxes at night when the phone rates are the lowest.

Lesson 61

Shopping Online Across the World Wide Web

In Lesson 53, "Surfing Your Way to Information on the World Wide Web," you learned how to browse sites across the Web. As you surf, you will find a variety of sites, from bookstores to florists, at which you can purchase products online. If you are shopping online, or thinking about shopping online, you are not alone. In the first half of 1998, over 20-million people purchased products online (with books being the most widely purchased item). Consumers are also using the Net to purchase airline tickets, purchase audio CDs, buy computers and software, purchase and sell securities, and even buy and sell cars. As a general rule, if you are browsing a reputable site and you establish a secure connection, you can feel reasonably comfortable using a credit card to purchase products online. This lesson examines online shopping. By the time you finish this lesson, you will understand the following key concepts:

- If you shop at reputable companies and ensure that the site uses a secure transaction to receive your credit-card information, shopping on the Web is quite safe.

- Across the Web, you will find companies and online malls that are selling virtually every product you can imagine, from PCs to pizzas.

- Should another user (a hacker) steal your credit-card information during a Web transaction, your credit-card company may require that you only pay a small portion of the fraudulent bill (if any), which is normally $50 or less.

SAMPLE OF ONLINE STORES

In Lesson 54, "Searching for Information on the World Wide Web," you learned how to use search engines, such as Yahoo! or Excite, to locate information on the Web. If you are looking for products or services, follow the steps Lesson 54 presents to find locations on the Web that can meet your needs. To give you a feel for the products you will find on the Web, this lesson presents a random sample of several sites at which you may want to shop in sites 61.1 thrrough 61.5.

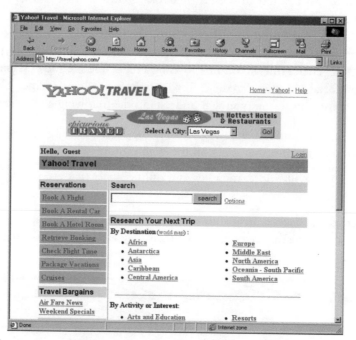

Figure 61.1 Making travel arrangements online at travel.yahoo.com.

Figure 61.2 Ordering flowers for last-minute occasions at www.1800flowers.com.

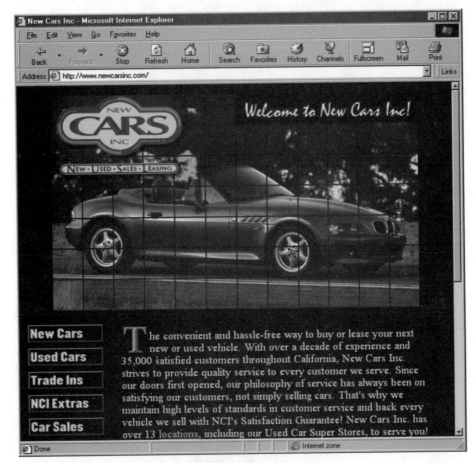

Figure 61.3 Shopping for new cars at www.newcarsinc.com.

Figure 61.4 Finding hard-to-find refrigerator magnets at www.fridgedoor.com.

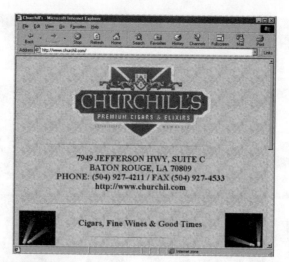

Figure 61.5 *Ordering the best wines or cigars at www.churchil.com.*

UNDERSTANDING SECURE TRANSACTIONS

When you send credit-card information to a site across the Net, the site's server will normally initiate a secure transaction with your browser. During the secure transaction, your browser and the site's server will encrypt the information they exchange. Should a hacker try to intercept your messages, the hacker will be unable to access your credit-card information due to the encryption. Depending on your browser configuration, your browser may display a dialog box, similar to that shown in Figure 61.7, each time you start or end a secure transaction.

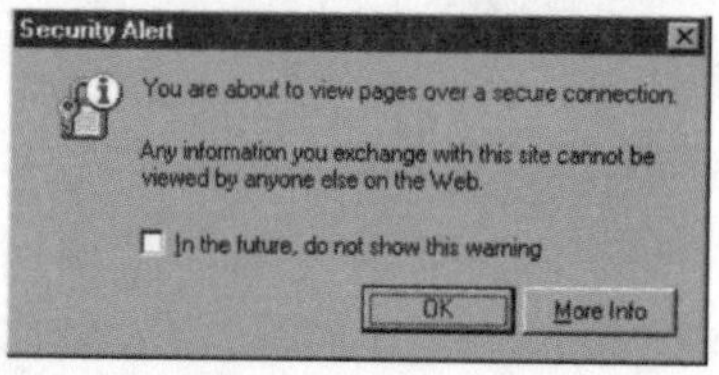

Figure 61.7 *A browser's notification of a secure transaction.*

Also, while the secure transaction is taking place, your browser may display a small lock icon within its status bar, as shown in Figure 61.8, to let you know a secure transaction is taking place.

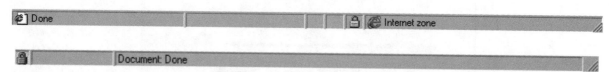

Figure 61.8 *The *** icon within the browser's status bar indicates a secure transaction.*

YOUR RESPONSIBILITY REGARDING CREDIT CARD LOSS

If you deal with reputable companies (whose names and products you recognize) and if you use secure transactions to transmit your credit-card information (as opposed to sending your credit-card number within an e-mail message), it is very unlikely that you will ever experience problems such as a stolen credit-card number or bills for items you did not purchase.

If, however, a hacker manages to steal you credit-card number from an Internet transaction, your liability is no more than if someone were to steal and use your credit card. In most cases, you will be responsible (at most) for $50 of the fraudulent purchases. For specifics, contact your credit-card company's customer service.

UNDERSTANDING MICROSOFT WALLET

If you shop online on a regular basis, you have undoubtedly filled out numerous forms that require you to type in your credit card number and shipping information. If you are using Windows 98, some sites may let you take advantage of the Microsoft Wallet. As shown in Figures 61.9 and 61.10, the Microsoft Wallet lets you record your credit-card number and shipping information. In the future, when you make a purchase from a Web site, your browser may use the Wallet's information to specify your shipping and payment information for you automatically.

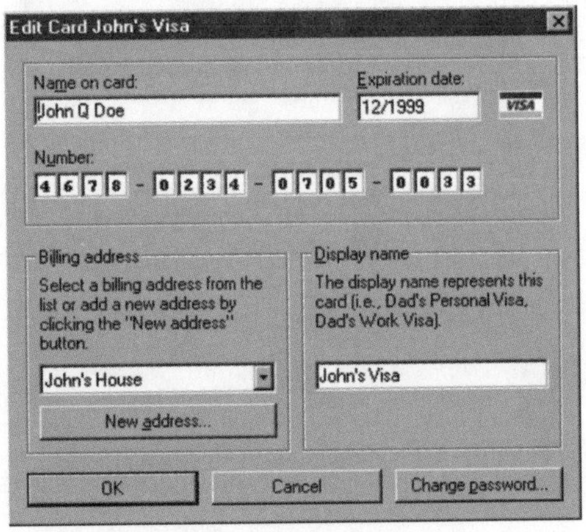

Figure 61.9 Using Microsoft Wallet to store credit-card information.

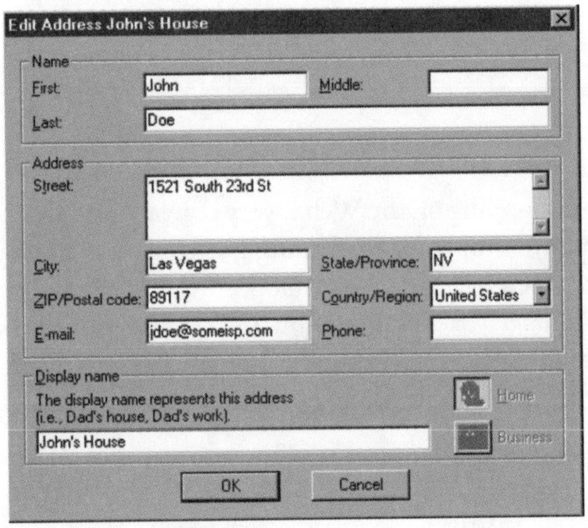

Figure 61.10 Using Microsoft Wallet to record shipping information.

Looking for Something Hard to Find or Have Something to Sell— Try Internet Classifieds

Across the Web, you will find thousands of Web sites that sell millions of different products. You do not, however, have to have your own Web site if you have something to sell. Just as newspapers offer classified advertising, so too do many online services. In fact, most of the sites will let you post your advertisement for free. Figure 61.11, for example, shows the Yahoo classifieds.

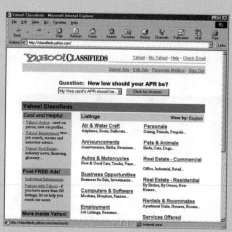

Figure 61.11 Posting and viewing classified ads at http://classifieds.yahoo.com.

Your Recourse If You Encounter Problems

Should you experience problems with an online order, you may need to pick up the phone and call the company's customer support line. If you restrict your online purchases to reputable companies, the customer-service staff should work hard to resolve your problem. You can always contact the Better Business Bureau for additional help and if you made your purchase through a company that your online service advertised, you should by all means contact your online service.

What You Must Know

Each day, more and more users find shopping on the Web is very convenient. Today, the most widely purchased item on the Web is books. However, many companies are finding great success selling expensive items, such as Personal Computers. This lesson previewed a few places you can shop on the Web. If you use a search engine and look up "Shopping," you will find thousands of related sites. In Lesson 62, "Child Proofing the Internet and World Wide Web," you will learn steps you can perform to restrict the Web sites your children can access. Before you continue with Lesson 62, however, make sure you understand the following key concepts:

✓ By using secure transactions and shopping at reputable companies, you will find shopping on the Web safe and convenient.

✓ The easiest way to find Web sites that are selling the product you need is to use a search engine, as discussed in Lesson 54.

✓ Should your credit-card information get stolen as you shop on the Web, most credit-card companies will limit your liability for fraudulent purchases.

Lesson 62

Child Proofing the Internet and the World Wide Web

As you have learned, the World Wide Web consists of millions of Web sites, each of which may contain hundreds, if not thousands, of documents. Across the Web, you can find articles on just about any topic you can imagine. Unfortunately, so too can your children. This lesson examines ways you can child proof your Internet connection. As you will learn, child proofing the Web is much easier than child proofing programs, such an Internet Relay Chat, which may pose a greater threat to your child. By the time you finish this lesson, you will learn the following key concepts:

- The Web consists of hundreds of millons of documents, many of which are well-suited for children to explore. Unfortunately, there are many sights on the Web that contain content that is inappropriate for children.

- The best way to prevent your child from visiting adult-oriented sites is to monitor your child's Web use. Ideally, you should participate with your child as he or she browses the Web.

- There are several software packages you can purchase that will restrict the sites your child can visit. As you shop for such programs, try to find a program that also restricts access to adult-oriented newsgroups and chats.

- If your child is spending too much time on the Web, consider installing a program that monitors and restricts his or her Web use.

PARENT SUPERVISION IS YOUR BEST TOOL

As is often the case with many of your kid's activities, the way to monitor your child is to be involved. As a rule, if your child is surfing the Web, try to be there with him or her. Not only can you then monitor the sites your child visits, you can participate in a variety of discussions that relate to topics you encounter.

If you cannot monitor your child's Internet use all day long, consider putting time limits on when your child can connect to the Net, much as you might limit the times when your child can watch TV. Later in this lesson, you will learn how to use the Time's Up! program to set such time limits automatically. Lastly, take time to sit down with your child and discuss which content is acceptable to you and which is not. Define the rules to your child. Also, let your child be aware of the dangers of chatting with adults online.

USE YOUR BROWSER'S HISTORY LIST TO LEARN WHAT SITES YOUR KIDS ARE VISITING

To make it easier for you to revisit a site whose contents you recently browsed, most Web browsers maintain a list (a history) of the sites they have recently viewed. If you are interested in the sites your child is visiting, you can view the contents of the history list. To display the history list within Microsoft Internet Explorer, for example, you simply click your mouse on the down arrow that appears at the right end of the browser's address bar. Internet Explorer, in turn, will display the pull-down history list, as shown in Figure 62.1.

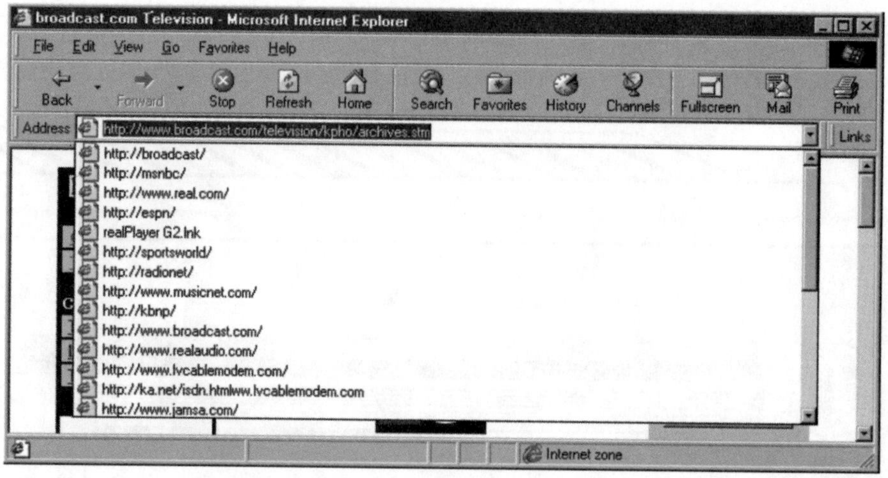

Figure 62.1 *Using the history list to display the addresses of recently viewed sites.*

After your child gets off the Web for the night, you can view the history list's contents to determine at which sites your child is spending his or her time. If you d onot want your child being able to view the sites you have been viewing, you can clear the browser's list. If you are using Windows 98, you can clear the history list by performing these steps:

1. Click your mouse on the Start button. Windows, in turn, will display the Start menu.

2. Within the Start menu, click your mouse on the Settings menu and choose Control Panel. Windows, will open the Control Panel folder, discussed in Lesson 45, "Configuring Your PC's System Settings."

3. Within the Control Panel, double-click your mouse on the Internet icon. Windows, in turn, will display the Internet Properties dialog box, as shown in Figure 62.2.

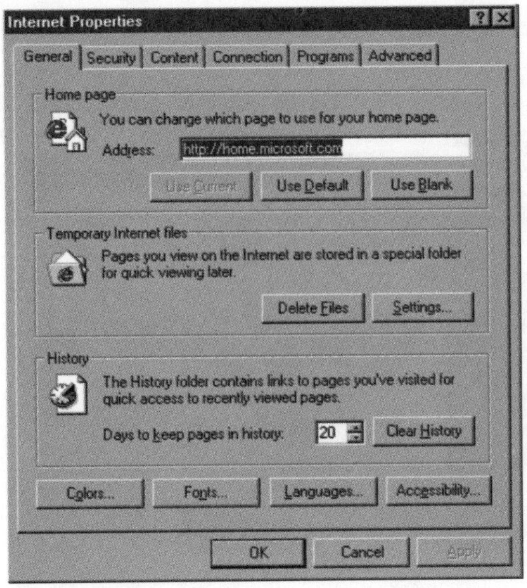

Figure 62.2 The Internet Properties dialog box.

4. Within the Internet Properties dialog box, click your mouse on the Clear History button. Windows, in turn, will display a dialog box asking you to confirm that you want to discard the list. Select Yes.

5. Within the Internet Properties dialog box, click your mouse on OK. Windows will close the dialog box.

6. Click your mouse on the Control Panel's Close button to close the Control Panel window.

INSTALLING PARENTAL CONTROLS ON YOUR BROWSER

Across the Web, you can find several programs that offer parental controls for Web browsers and other Internet-based programs. In general, these programs restrict the Web sites to which your child can connect. Although many of these software programs provide an effective way to prevent your child from viewing specific Web sites, many of the programs do not provide adequate controls to prevent your child from participating in adult chats, receiving adult-oriented e-mail messages, or from viewing adult-oriented content within a newsgroup. To truly restrict your child's access to Internet-based content outside the Web, your best choice may be to remove chat and video-conferencing software from your system.

USING SURFWATCH TO RESTRICT WEB SITES

Across the Internet, about 10-million parents, schools, and businesses restrict access to Web sites using SurfWatch, a software program that restricts the sites a user can browse. Each time a user types in a Web address, or clicks his or her mouse on a hyperlink, the SurfWatch software compares the address to a database of restricted sites (a list to which, you, as well as members of the Surf community-based Advisory Committee, can add). If a user tries to access a restricted site, the SurfWatch software will prevent the user's access, displaying a dialog box that tells the user that the site is restricted.

The SurfWatch developers are working on software that will provide greater controls within such programs as *ftp* (that users use to transfer files), newsgroups, and chat programs. To learn more about the SurfWatch program, or to download a demo version of the product, visit the SurfWatch Web site at *www.surfwatch.com*, as shown in Figure 62.3.

Figure 62.3 *The SurfWatch Web site.*

CONTROLLING WHEN YOUR CHILD CAN ACCESS THE WEB AND FOR HOW LONG

Although there is a lot of content for a child to experience on the Web, you may want to control when your child browses the Web and for how long. To monitor your child's Web use, you can take advantage of a product called Time's Up!. Using the Time's Up! software, you can set controls that restrict your child's Web access to specific days and hours of the week. To learn more about the Time's Up! program, or to download a demo version, visit the Time's Up! Web site at *www.timesup.com*, as shown in Figure 62.4.

Figure 62.4 *The Time's Up! Web site.*

USING WINDOWS 98 TO ENABLE BROWSER SUPPORT FOR WEB SITE RATINGS

To reduce the possibility of children browsing a site that contains nudity, sex, violence, or inappropriate language, many browsers support the Web-site ratings policies from the Recreational Software Agency Council rating service for the Internet (RSACi). If you enable your browser's ratings support, your browser will password protect sites that exceed the RSACi ratings they specify. Unfortunately, not all sites comply with the RSACi ratings. If a site does not specify its rating, and you have enabled RSACi support, your browser will not display the site's contents until you or your child types in a password. So, today, if you enable RSACi support on your system, you may spend considerable time typing in a password before you can access any Web site. In the future, however, as more sites start to support the RSACi ratings systems, configuring your browser to support RSCAi will help you control which sites your child can and cannot access. If you are using Windows 98, you will use the Content Advisor dialog box, shown in Figure 62.5, to configure your browser's RSACi support. However, today, you will find that software programs such as Surf-Watch are more effective. For more information on using Content Advisor, refer to the book *1001 Windows 98 Tips*, Jamsa Press, 1998.

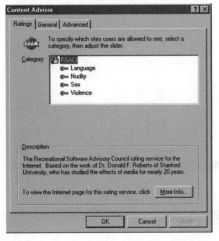

Figure 62.5 The Content Advisor dialog box.

WHAT YOU MUST KNOW

The Web is filled with thousands of sites that offer wonderful educational and entertainment experiences for kids. Unfortunately, the Web is also the home to sites whose content is not appropriate for children. In this lesson, you examined software programs you can use to restrict the Web sites your child can access. If you have children who surf the Web on a regular basis, you may want to install such software soon. In addition, you should sit and talk to your child about what content is and is not acceptable to you and why. In Lesson 63, "Chatting On-Line with Users Around the World," you will learn how to use chat software to send typed (one-line) messages to a group of users across the Net in real time. Before you continue with Lesson 63, however, make sure you understand the following concepts:

✓ The Web offers sites that provide your child with wonderful learning opportunities. Your child should have an opportunity to view sites on the Web. Ideally, you will have time to spend with your child as he or she surfs the Web.

✓ Across the Web, there are may sites that contain content that is inappropriate for children. To prevent your child from browsing such sites, you can install software, such as SurfWatch, that prevents your child from viewing specific sites. You can also purchase software that restricts the days and hours your child can connect to the Net.

✓ In addition to restricting the Web sites your child can visit, you should also monitor your child's use of on-line chat and newsgroup software.

359

Lesson 63

Chatting On-Line with Users Around the World

As you learned in Lesson 51, "Using E-Mail to Communicate Worldwide," across the Internet, users normally communicate using electronic-mail (e-mail). If you are a reasonable typist, you may want to use a chat program to communicate with other users. In general, a chat program lets you communicate with other users by sending and receiving typed messages. To chat with other users using chat software, you must first enter a chat room. Then, you simply start typing your messages. As you type, the other users in the chat room will see the messages you type. Likewise, you will see every message other users in the chat room type. Across the Internet, you can find chat rooms within which users discuss every topic you can imagine, from PCs to politics, and much more. Using chat software, you can chat with other users across the world for free.

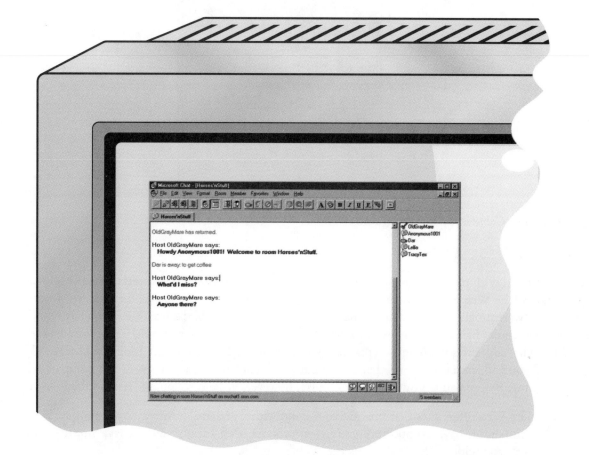

This lesson examines ways you can chat on-line. By the time the time you finish this lesson, you will understand the following key concepts:

- Chat software is a program that lets you communicate with other users across the Net by typing your messages.

- If you use an on-line service, such as America Online or the Microsoft Network, you can normally start chat software within your on-line service using a menu option or screen icon your service provides.

- To communicate with other users using chat software, you must first select a chat server and then you choose a chat room. Within the chat room, you will see a list of the room's members as well as a window within which each user's typed messages appear.

- To send a message within the chat room, simply type your message and press ENTER. Each member within the chat room will instantly see your text appear within the chat window on their screen.

- If you are using Windows 98, you can use either Microsoft Chat or NetMeeting to chat with other users. Microsoft bundles both of these programs with Windows.

- If you are not running Windows 98, you can download and install the Internet Relay Chat (IRC) program from across the Web. In addition, you can also use your browser to chat at sites such as Yahoo!.

CHATTING WITHIN YOUR ON-LINE SERVICE

If you use an on-line service, such as America Online (AOL) or the Microsoft Network (MSN), your on-line service will often provide you with the software you need to chat with other users who are connected to your service. If you are willing to chat with just about anyone who comes along, you will normally find thousands of users connected to your on-line service who want to do the same. Normally, your on-line service will let you run its chat software from a menu option.

If, however, you want to chat with a user who does not use your on-line service, you may need to use different software to chat with the user, such as the Internet Relay Chat (IRC) software that you can download from sites across the Web or the NetMeeting software that Microsoft bundles with Windows 98 (Lesson 44, "Test Driving Video Processing Across the Internet," discusses the NetMeeting software). Or, as you will learn in this lesson, you can connect to a site such as Yahoo! that supports on-line chats using your browser.

Regardless of which chat software you choose to use, or where you choose to chat, the steps you will perform to chat are quite similar: you will first start your software, use your software to join a chat room, and then start typing to chat.

LOOKING AT A TYPICAL CHAT SESSION

The best way to understand how a chat session works is simply to view a sample session. The following discussion will use Microsoft Chat, which Microsoft bundles with Windows 98. If you are using different chat software, the steps you will perform to chat will be similar.

To start, you must connect to your Internet Service Provider or on-line service. When you start Microsoft Chat (which you can do from the Start menu Programs submenu Internet Explorer option), Microsoft Chat will display the Chat Connection dialog box, similar to that shown in Figure 63.1.

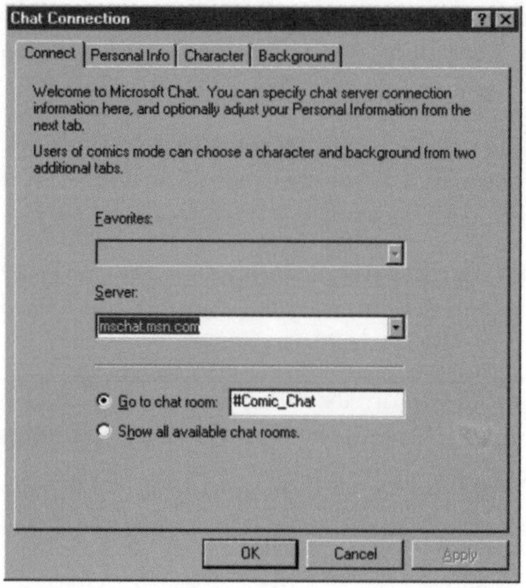

Figure 63.1 *The Chat Connection dialog box.*

Note: If your Internet Explorer submenu does not contain an option for Microsoft Chat, you can install the software using the Control Panel Add/Remove Programs icon, as discussed in Lesson 45, "Configuring Your PC's System Settings."

When you chat on the Web, you can use your name or you can choose a nickname (which makes you somewhat anonymous). To assign your nickname and other personal information that other users in the chat can view about you, click your mouse on the Chat Connection dialog box Personal Info tab. Microsoft Chat, in turn, will display the Personal Info sheet, as shown in Figure 63.2.

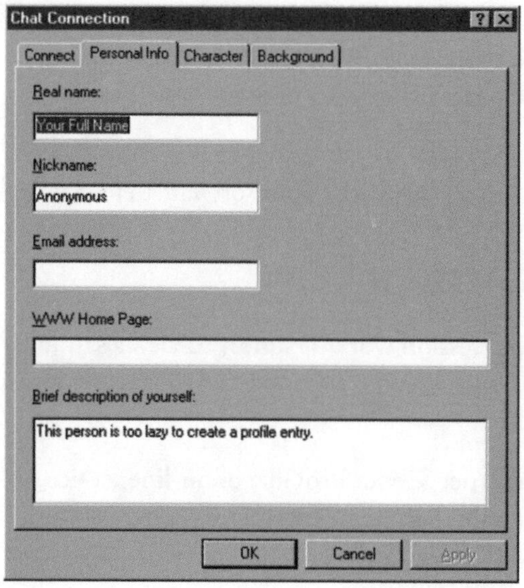

Figure 63.2 *The Personal Info sheet.*

Within the Personal Info sheet, much of the information is optional. If you want other users to be able to reach you, you may want to include an e-mail address to which the users can send you mail. Also, you may want to include a brief description of yourself. As you chat, other users can view your personal information.

Next, you must connect to a chat server—a computer that is running special chat software that you can use to select the room (some chat programs call chat rooms *channels* or *discussion groups*) that you desire. To connect to a server within Microsoft Chat, click your mouse on the pull-down server list and choose the server you desire, or simply type in the name of the server to which you want to connect. Normally, if you are not meeting anyone in particular, you can simply pick any chat server. However, if you are planning to chat with a specific user, each of you must pick the same chat server and chat room. If you know the name of the chat room you desire, you can type the room's name within the Go to chat room text field. Otherwise, click your mouse on the Show all available chat rooms button and then click OK. Microsoft Chat, in turn, will display the Chat Room List dialog box, as shown in Figure 63.3, within which it lists the various chat rooms you can enter.

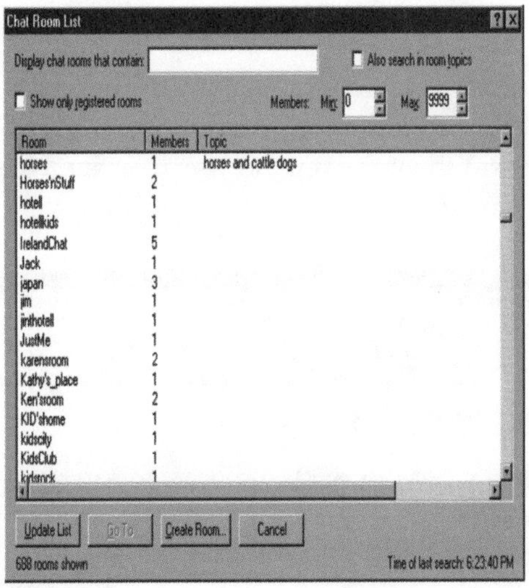

Figure 63.3 *The Chat Room List dialog box.*

Within the Chat Room List dialog box, you can read each chat room's name, view the number of people who are currently chatting within the room, and possibly the room's topic (normally, you can figure out the room's topic from the chat room name itself). To enter a chat room, simply double-click your mouse on the room's name. Microsoft Chat, in turn, will display a chat window, within which you can view each message the room's members type, view a list of members, and type your own messages, as shown in Figure 63.4.

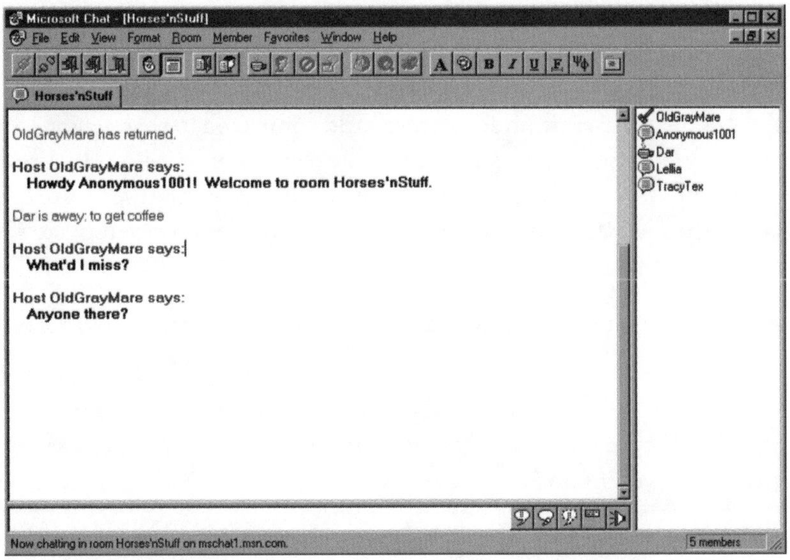

Figure 63.4 *Chatting within a chat window.*

To send a message to the group, click your mouse within the small message text box that appears at the bottom of the menu, type your message, and press ENTER. You will then see your message appear within the chat window, as will the rest of the group's members. If the current room's chat is not what you are looking for, simply click your mouse on the Room menu Leave Room to leave the room and then use the Room menu Room List option to display the list of available rooms. As you chat, there may be times when you want to send a message to a specific user in the group so that other members in the room cannot see. To chat with only one user, you can either whisper to the user or you can create your own chat room within which you and the other user can chat in private. To end your chat session within Microsoft Chat, simply click your mouse on the Close button or select the File menu Exit option. For more information on Microsoft Chat, refer to the book *1001 Windows 98 Tips*, Jamsa Press, 1998.

CHATTING WITH USERS AT YAHOO!

If you do not have chat software on your system, you can either download software from across the Net or you can use your browser to chat at Yahoo!. As it turns out, in addition to providing a search engine, Yahoo! also provides chat software that you can run within your browser. To chat at Yahoo!, use your browser to connect to *chat.yahoo.com*, as shown in Figure 63.5. After you download the chat software, you can view a list of chat rooms and then enter the chat you desire.

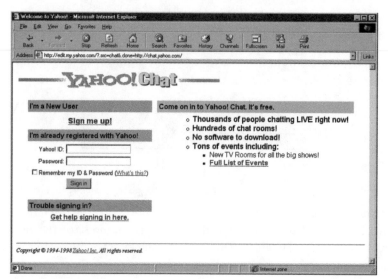

Figure 63.5 *Chatting at Yahoo! using a browser.*

WHAT YOU MUST KNOW

At any time, you can find thousands of users from across the world connected to chat sessions on the Net. In this lesson, you learned the basics of using chat software to communicate with users on-line. In Lesson 64, "Protecting the Information You Send across the Internet," you will learn how to use encryption software to protect electronic-mail messages that you send across the Net. Before you continue with Lesson 64, however, make sure you have learned the following key concepts:

- ✓ Chat software is a program that lets you communicate with other users across the Net by typing your messages.

- ✓ Using chat software, you first select a chat server and then you choose a chat room. Within the chat room, you simply type messages. After you press ENTER to send a message, each member within the chat room will instantly see your text.

- ✓ If you are using Windows 98, you can use either Microsoft Chat or NetMeeting to chat with other users. Microsoft bundles both of these programs with Windows.

Lesson 64

Protecting the Information You Send across the Internet

As you have learned, the Internet is a vast collection of computer networks. When you send electronic-mail to another user across the Internet, your message may actually travel past many PCs before it arrives at the destination computer. Although the Internet's ability to send a message from one computer to the next provides the message-passing background that lets computers on the Net communicate, it also means that at any point, as your message travels across the Net, someone (a hacker) can intercept and read (or even change) your message's contents. The only way to protect the messages that you send across the Net is to encrypt the messages.

This lesson examines the steps you must perform to encrypt e-mail messages. By the time you finish this lesson, you will understand the following key concepts:

- To protect the electronic-mail messages you send to other users across the Net, you should encrypt your messages.

- To encrypt your messages, you must have two encryption keys: a public key that you give to your friends, family, and associates, and a private key that only you can access. You can buy your encryption keys at the Verisign Web site.

- To send you an encrypted message, another user will encrypt the message using your public key. To decrypt the message, you will use your private key.

- When you purchase encryption keys from Verisign, the installation process will place a digital signature on your system that contains your public key. To give another user your public key (which he or she will need to send you encrypted messages), you can send your digital signature to the user within an e-mail message.

- You should digitally sign (attach your digital signature to) each message you send. Your digital signature authenticates to the recipient that you (as opposed to an electronic impostor) sent the message and that the message contents did not change as the message made its way across the Net.

UNDERSTANDING ENCRYPTION

When you encrypt a message, your e-mail software uses an electronic key (that is specific to the user to whom you are sending the message) to scramble the message's contents into meaningless content, as shown in Figure 64.1. When the recipient receives your message, he or she uses his or her key to unlock the message.

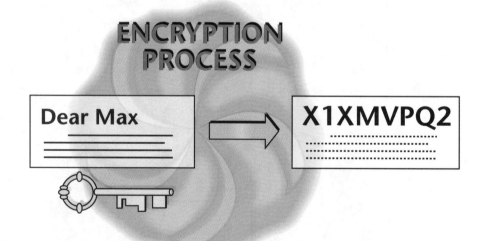

Figure 64.1 *Encryption uses an electronic key to scramble a message's contents.*

Assume, as shown in Figure 64.2, that as your encrypted message travels the Net, a hacker intercepts the message. Because the hacker does not have the key to unscramble to the message, he or she will not be able to understand the meaningless content.

Figure 64.2 *By encrypting your messages, you protect their contents from being read as the message travels across the Net.*

WHAT IT TAKES TO UNSCRAMBLE AN ENCRYPTED MESSAGE

When you encrypt the messages that you send across the Net, you can feel quite secure in the fact that another user will not intercept and unscramble your message's content. Computer programmers describe the encryption process in terms of the size of the encryption key, such as a 48-bit key or a 512-bit key. In Lesson 12, "Understanding the Myriad of PC Speeds and Sizes," you learned that most PCs are capable of executing several million instructions per second. Programmers have estimated that to unscramble a message that uses a 428-bit key would require a Pentium computer over 100 years of processing!

UNDERSTANDING PUBLIC-KEY ENCRYPTION

Today, the most commonly-used encryption technique is public-key encryption. If you want other users to send encrypted messages to you, you must first purchase your encryption keys (which this lesson will show you how to do). When you purchase your keys, you will receive two keys: a private key, that you will safeguard, and a public key, that you will send to all your friends, relatives, and associates who may send you e-mail. As shown in Figure 64.3, to send you an encrypted message, another user will encrypt the message using your public key. Later, to decrypt the message, you will use your private key.

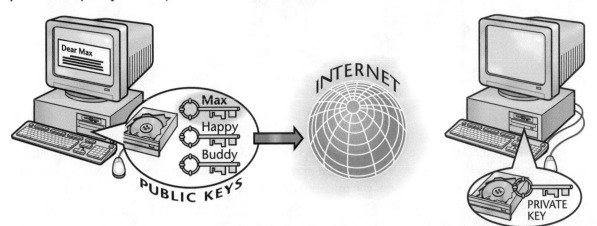

Figure 64.3 *When other users send you encrypted messages, they will use your public key to encrypt the message. You, in turn, will decrypt the message using your private key.*

367

You can send your public key to any user anywhere in the world. As shown in Figure 64.3, another user can send only you an encrypted message using your public key. Only your private key can decrypt the message. If you want to send an encrypted message to another user, you must use that user's public key to encrypt the message. Later, the user would use his or her private key to decrypt the message.

UNDERSTANDING DIGITAL SIGNATURES

When you purchase encryption keys, you will normally receive a digital signature that you can use to send your public key to other users. In addition to providing you with a way to disseminate your public key, your digital signature also lets you authenticate that the message is actually from you. As it turns out, it is quite easy for hacker to send messages that appear to have come from a specific user. By digitally signing the messages you send (or at least the very important messages), users can feel confident that the message did indeed come from you. In addition, should a hacker intercept and change a message you have digitally signed (a digitally signed message does not have to be encrypted), your recipient's e-mail software will use the digital signature to detect the fact that your message was changed in transit.

How to Purchase Encryption Keys

Across the Net, several companies sell encryption keys. The most widely-used of those companies is Verisign. To purchase your encryption keys, use your browser to visit the Verisign Web site at *www.verisign.com*, as shown in Figure 64.4. Versign also offers trial keys that you can use for a 60-day period for free. The Verisign software will refer to your encryption keys as your digital signature.

Figure 64.4 *You can purchase your encryption keys at the Verisign Web site.*

To download your encryption keys from the Verisign Web site, click your mouse on a button that corresponds to Individual Certificates. The Web site, in turn, will display a series of pages that walk you through the download and installation process. To perform the download and installation, you will provide Verisign information about you that you type at the Verisign Web page. Next, Verisign will send you an access code to your e-mail address that you will need before you can complete the installation process. Within your e-mail program, you can print the message that contains the access code. Then, you can type the code into the corresponding field on the Verisign installation Web page. Verisign, in turn, will finish the installation, updating your browser and e-mail software to use your digital signature.

After your digital signature is in place, you should send a message containing your signature to each of your friends and associates. Remember, they will need your signature in order to send you encrypted messages. To send a signed message (a message containing your digital signature) within Outlook Express, for example, create and address an e-mail message. Then, select the Tools menu Digitally Sign option. Outlook Express will attach your signature to your message. Later, when your recipient receives your message, his or her e-mail software should update his or her address book, storing your digital signature within your address book entry. That user can then send you encrypted messages. If another user has sent you his or her digital signature, you can use the signature to encrypt messages that you send to that user. To encrypt a message within Outlook Express, for example, you simply select the Tools menu Encrypt option before you send the message. It is that easy. When your recipient receives your message, his or her software will automatically decrypt it. Figure 64.5, for example, shows a digitally signed message explaining to users that the message has a digital signature they can use to send encrypted messages.

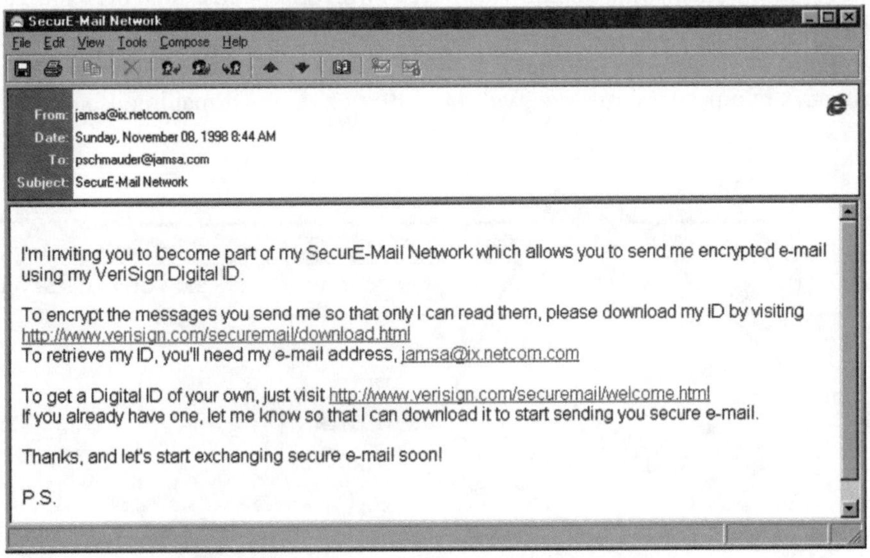

Figure 64.5 *Sending a message to users notifying them of your new digital signature.*

WHAT YOU MUST KNOW

When you send an electronic-mail message across the Net, your message may travel over many different computer networks. As your message makes its way to its destination, it is possible for a hacker to intercept, read, and possibly change your message. To protect your message contents, you should encrypt your messages. This lesson examined the steps you must perform so that other users can send you encrypted messages. In Lesson 65, "Using Mailing Lists to Stay Informed," you will learn how you can use e-mail to keep current on a variety of topics. Before you continue with Lesson 65, however, make sure that you understand the following key concepts:

✓ To protect messages that you send across the Net, you should encrypt your messages.

✓ To encrypt your messages, you must have two encryption keys: a public key that you give to your friends, family, and associates, and a private key that only you have access to.

✓ When another user sends you an encrypted message, that user will encrypt the message using your public key. To decrypt the message, you will use your private key.

✓ When you purchase encryption keys, you will receive a digital signature that you can attach to your messages that contains your public key. After users receive your public key, they can use the key to encrypt the messages they send you.

Lesson 65

Using Mailing Lists to Stay Informed

In Lesson 51 "Using Electronic Mail (E-Mail) to Communicate Worldwide," you learned how to use e-mail software to send and receive messages to and from other users. Likewise, in Lesson 53, "Surfing Your Way to Information on the World Wide Web," you learned how to locate and view vast amounts of content from sites on the Web. In this lesson, you will learn to use mailing lists, which combine the use of e-mail messages with the Web's volumes of content to provide you with a way to get the information you desire, delivered to your desktop. In general, a mailing list is somewhat like a newspaper or magazine subscription that delivers specific content to you on a daily, weekly, or monthly basis.

When you subscribe to a mailing list, your content will arrive in the form of an e-mail message. Across the Net, there are thousands of mailing lists to which you can subscribe. You can find mailing lists that discuss specific topics, such as business, sports, or world news, and you will find lists that focus on very specific topics. Depending on the specific mailing list, the frequency of your e-mail messages will vary. Best of all, most mailing lists are free.

This lesson examines the steps you must perform to subscribe to a mailing list (as well as how to unsubscribe should you later decide the list's content is not for you). By the time you finish this lesson, you will understand the following key concepts:

- A mailing list is an electronic subscription that you can join which will send you e-mail messages regarding a specific topic. Most mailing lists are free to join.

- To subscribe to a mailing list, you simply send an e-mail message to the list that contains the message SUBSCRIBE, followed by name of the list you want to join (SUBSCRIBE ListName).

- Depending on the mailing list you join, the frequency of the messages you receive will vary.

- To terminate your subscription to a mailing list, you simply send an e-mail message to the list that contains the message text UNSUBSCRIBE, followed by the list name.

- You can find a listing of over 90,000 mailing lists at *www.liszt.com.*

SUBSCRIBING TO A MAILING LIST

The best way to understand an Internet mailing list is to think of a magazine subscription. To receive a magazine, you must first subscribe by giving the magazine your mailing address. In a similar way, to subscribe to an Internet mailing list, you must provide the list with your e-mail address. To do so, you will send an e-mail message to the list that contains the message text **SUBSCRIBE,** followed by the name of the list to which you want to subscribe, as shown in Figure 65.1.

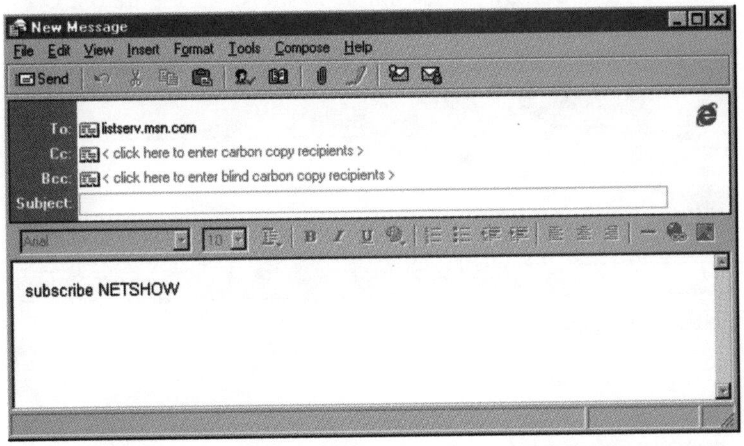

Figure 65.1 Subscribing to an e-mail list.

After you subscribe to a mailing list, the list's messages will simply start appearing with your other e-mail. Depending on the list to which you subscribe, the frequency of your messages will vary. Some lists send messages several times a day while others may only send one or two messages a week.

FINDING THE MAILING LISTS THAT ARE AVAILABLE ON THE NET

Before you can subscribe to a mailing list, you must know which list (or lists) you want to join, as well as the list's address to which you will e-mail your subscription request. Across the Net, you will find a variety of mailing lists whose topics range from anthropology to zoology. For a complete list of mailing lists (over 90,000 lists, in fact), visit the Liszt Web site at *www.liszt.com,* as shown in Figure 65.2.

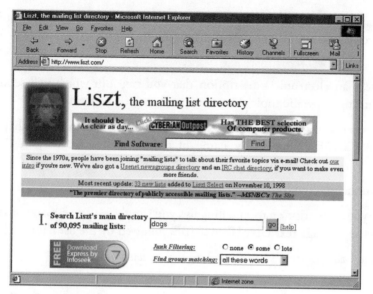

Figure 65.2 *You can get a list of mailing lists at www.liszt.com.*

CANCELING YOUR MAILING LIST SUBSCRIPTION

Should you subscribe to a mailing list and later decide that you no longer want to receive the list's contents, you simply need to unsubscribe from the list. To unsubscribe from a list, you simply send an e-mail message to the list that contains the message text UNSUBSCRIBE, followed by the list name, as shown in Figure 65.3.

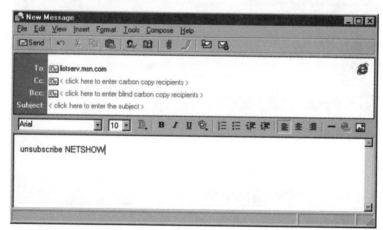

Figure 65.3 *Unsubscribing from a mailing list.*

MOST MAILING LISTS ARE AUTOMATED

Across the Net, most mailing lists are automated, which means a software program receives your subscription requests and adds you to the list. When you unsubscribe from a list, the software will automatically remove you from the list. Normally, therefore, if you send a message other than SUBSCRIBE or UNSUBSCRIBE to a mailing list, you will not get a response because the software may simply ignore your message. Depending on the mailing list, the messages you receive may include an e-mail address that you can use to send correspondence to the list (to a person, as opposed to the list's management software). Users often refer to mailing lists that are managed by software as *listserv mailing lists.*

USING A WEB SITE TO SUBSCRIBE TO A MAILING LIST

Across the Web, you may find several sites that let you subscribe to specific mailing lists right from the site itself. For example, Figure 65.4 shows the InfoBeat site at *www.infobeat.com* at which you can subscribe to specific news-related mailing lists and even request that the mailing list remind you of specific birthdays and anniversaries.

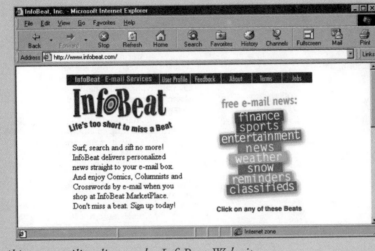

Figure 65.4 *Subscribing to mailing lists at the InfoBeat Web site.*

WHAT YOU MUST KNOW

Across the Internet and World Wide Web, you can find millions of documents that discuss a wide variety of topics. If you have specific interests, you may find that subscribing to a mailing list provides you with a very good way to keep abreast of the topic matter. In this lesson, you learned how to locate, subscribe to, and unsubscribe from Internet mailing lists. Congratulations! By completing this book's lessons, you are well on your way to mastering your PC. Before you continue on your way, however, make sure you understand the following key concepts:

✓ By subscribing to a mailing list, you can receive e-mail messages that provide information about a specific topic.

✓ To join a mailing list, send an e-mail message to the list that contains the word **SUBSCRIBE**, followed by the name of the list to which you want to subscribe.

✓ To end your subscription to a mailing list, send an e-mail message to the list that contains the word **UNSUBSCRIBE**, followed by the list name.

✓ Mailing lists provide a very convenient and inexpensive way to receive information about specific topics.

About the Author

Worldwide, millions of computer users regard Dr. Kris Jamsa as one of the leading experts in the industry. He is the author of over 80 books (mostly computer books), covering a wide range of topics, including MS-DOS, Windows, computer networks, programming languages, computer security, graphics, the Internet and the Web. He is known through his books for his ability to make the difficult concepts simple and understandable. On many occasions, he has been asked to speak regarding the most current topics of the computer industry.

In 1983, he earned a bachelor's degree in computer science from the United States Air Force Academy. After graduation, he worked in Las Vegas, Nevada as a VAX/VMS system manager for the Air Force, overseeing computer hardware, software, and network security. At the same time, Dr. Jamsa was earning his master's degree in computer science from the University of Nevada, Las Vegas. In August of 1993, the same year that he and his wife Debbie founded Jamsa Press, Dr. Jamsa received his doctorate in computer science with an emphasis on operating systems from Arizona State University. Continuing to broaden his education, he commuted from Las Vegas every week to San Diego State University, which awarded him an MBA in 1997. Dr. Jamsa is currently pursuing a Masters of Science in Financial Planning from the College for Financial Planning in Denver, Colorado.

In July of 1997, Jamsa Press was acquired by Gulf Publishing Company of Houston, Texas. In July of 1998, Dr. Jamsa, his wife Debbie, and their youngest daughter Stephanie, relocated to Houston, Texas. Today, Dr. Jamsa continues to author many Jamsa Press best-sellers, including his new line of children's books, which feature the adventures of Happy & Max™.